The Israeli Nation-State

Political, Constitutional, and
Cultural Challenges

ISRAEL: SOCIETY, CULTURE, AND HISTORY

ACADEMIC
STUDIES
PRESS

The Israeli Nation-State
Political, Constitutional, and Cultural Challenges

EDITED BY
Fania Oz-Salzberger and
Yedidia Z. Stern

Boston 2014

Library of Congress Cataloging-in-Publication Data:
A catalog record for this title is available
from the Library of Congress.

ISBN 978-1-618113-89-4 (hardback)
ISBN 978-1-618113-92-4 (paperback)
ISBN 978-1-618113-90-0 (electronic)

Book design by Ivan Grave

Published by Academic Studies Press in 2014
28 Montfern Avenue
Brighton, MA 02135, USA
press@academicstudiespress.com
www.academicstudiespress.com

This volume of essays follows a series of international conferences convened in 2010–2012 under the auspices of the Leon Liberman Chair in Modern Israel Studies at the Australian Centre for Jewish Civilisation, Monash University. The editors are grateful to Monash University, to the Posen Research Forum at the Faculty of Law, University of Haifa, and above all to Lee Liberman, for their generous support of this project at various stages.

Contents

Contributors

Fania Oz-Salzberger is professor of history at the University of Haifa Center for German and European Studies and Faculty of Law, where she directs the Posen Research Forum for Political Thought. She was Professor and Leon Liberman Chair of Modern Israel Studies at Monash University (2007–2012), and Laurance S. Rockefeller Visiting Professor for Distinguished Teaching at Princeton University (2009–10). Among her books are *Translating the Enlightenment* (1995), *Israelis in Berlin* (2001), and *Jews and Words*, co-authored with Amos Oz (2012). She recently edited, with Thomas Maissen, *The Liberal-Republican Quandary in Israel, Europe, and the United States* (2012).

Yedidia Z. Stern is the Vice President of Research at Israel Democracy Institute, where he heads the projects on "Religion and State" and "Human Rights and Judaism." He is a full professor at Bar-Ilan University Law School, and served as its Dean. His areas of professional interest are religion and state, Jewish law, public law, and corporate law. His awards include the Zeltner Prize for excellence in Legal Research in Israel (2009) and the Gorni Prize for special contribution in public law (2012).

Ayman K. Agbaria is a lecturer in the Department of Leadership and Policy in Education, University of Haifa. He studies citizenship education and religious education with a special interest in minority and identity politics. Recently, he co-edited with Hanan Alexander the volume *Commitment, Character, and Citizenship* (2012).

Aviad Bakshi is Director of Legal Affairs at the Kohelet Policy Forum and a lecturer at Ono Academic College and at Bar-Ilan University. His research interests include immigration law, linguistic rights, cultural and national rights, and separation of powers.

Ariel L. Bendor is Frank Church Professor of Legal Research at Bar-Ilan University Faculty of Law. Before joining Bar-Ilan, he served as the Dean of the Faculty of Law and the Dean of Students at the University of Haifa. His primary research area is constitutional law. He has published three books and numerous scholarly articles.

Ruth Gavison is the Haim H. Cohn professor emerita of human rights at the Faculty of Law in the Hebrew University, the founding president of Metzilah, a center for Zionist, Jewish, liberal and humanist thought, and a winner of the Israel Prize for Legal Research. She has published extensively on legal philosophy, human rights and Israel as a Jewish and democratic state.

Michael M. Karayanni is the Bruce W. Wayne professor of law, Faculty of Law, Hebrew University of Jerusalem. He held visiting positions at Stanford University (Law School and Ford Dorsey Program in International Policy Studies) and University of Melbourne Law School. His research interests include private international law and inter-religious law, multiculturalism, and civil procedure. He is the author of *Conflicts in a Conflict* (forthcoming, 2014).

David Passig is the director of the graduate program in communication technology and the director of the Virtual Reality Lab at the School of Education, Bar-Ilan University, Israel. He has been the consultant of the Commissionaire for Future Generations at the Israeli Parliament (Knesset) since 2002. Currently, he is serving as a member in the Israeli National Council for Research and Development.

Avi Sagi is professor of philosophy, founder of the interdisciplinary graduate program in hermeneutics and cultural studies at Bar-Ilan University, and a faculty member at the Shalom Hartman Institute, Israel. He has written and edited numerous books and articles in Jewish and general philosophy, among them *Kierkegaard, Religion and Existence: The Voyage of the Self* (2000); *Albert Camus and the Philosophy of the Absurd* (2002); *Tradition vs. Traditionalism* (2008), and *To Be A Jew* (2011).

Gideon Sapir is professor at the Faculty of Law, Bar-Ilan University, the author of *Constitutional Revolution in Israel—Past, Present and Future* (2010 [Hebrew]) and co-author (with Daniel Statman) of *Religion and State in Israel—Legal-Philosophical Inquiry* (forthcoming, 2014 [Hebrew]).

Anita Shapira is founder of the Yitzhak Rabin Centre for Israel Studies and was head of the Weizmann Institute for the Study of Zionism at Tel Aviv University until 2012. Since 2008, she has been a senior fellow at the Israel Democracy Institute. Professor Shapira specializes in modern and contemporary Jewish history, particularly social and cultural history and questions of identity. In 2008 she received the Israel Prize.

Daniel Statman is professor of philosophy at Haifa University. His primary interests are in moral and legal philosophy, moral psychology, and modern Jewish philosophy. He is the author of *Moral Dilemmas* (1995), co-author of *Religion and Morality* (1995) and *Religion and State in Israel—Legal-Philosophical Inquiry* (forthcoming, 2014 [Hebrew]), and editor of *Moral Luck* (1993) and *Virtue Ethics* (1997).

Gadi Taub is a senior lecturer at the Federman School of Public Policy and Government, and the department of communications at the Hebrew University of Jerusalem. His book *The Settlers and the Struggle over the Meaning of Zionism* (2010) was published with Yale University Press.

He writes an op-ed column for *Yedioth Ahronoth*, Israel's largest daily newspaper.

Shira Wolosky received her PhD from Princeton, was an associate professor of English at Yale University before moving to the Hebrew University, where she is Professor of English and American Studies. Her books include *Emily Dickinson: A Voice of War* (1984); *Language Mysticism* (1995); *The Art of Poetry* (2001); *Defending Identity* with Natan Sharansky (2008); *Poetry and Public Discourse in Nineteenth-Century America* (2010); *Feminist Theories across Disciplines: Feminist Community* (2013), as well as other writings on literature, religion, and literary theory. Her awards include a Guggenheim Fellowship, a fellowship at the Princeton Institute of Advanced Studies, and the Drue Heinz Visiting Professorship at Oxford University. She is currently a Tikvah Fellow at NYU, working on a critique of cosmopolitanism.

Alexander Yakobson is associate professor in the history department at the Hebrew University of Jerusalem. He is the co-author (with Amnon Rubinstein) of *Israel and the Family of Nations: The Jewish Nation-State and Human Rights* (2009) and an op-ed columnist in the *Haaretz* newspaper.

Yaffa Zilbershats is professor of law and, since 2010, Deputy President of Bar-Ilan University. From 2004–2007 she held the position of the Dean of the Faculty of Law in the University. She specializes in international, human rights and constitutional law and has published extensively on these topics.

Acknowledgments

Ruth Gavison's chapter is a shortened adaptation of an article that was published in Hebrew in Aviezer Ravitzky and Yedidia Stern, eds., *The Jewishness of Israel* (Jerusalem: The Israel Democracy Institute, 2007), 107–78, and submitted for publication in 2004. It does not fully reflect present-day realities or authorial views. The author thanks Alon Kol for diligent work in preparing the essay for publication in English and Gadi Weber for the translation.

Fania Oz-Salzberger gratefully acknowledges the Liberman family of Melbourne, as well as her colleagues at the Australian Centre for Jewish Civilisation, directed by Professor Mark Baker. Thanks are also due to Alon Kol for his research assistance, to Keren Hakim for editorial help, and to participants in the International Association of Jewish Lawyers Congress, Dead Sea, 2011, for their helpful comments.

Avi Sagi thanks Batya Stein, who translated his chapter from Hebrew.

Part of Yaffa Zilbershats's chapter is expanded upon in the position paper of the Metzilah Center: *The Return of Palestinian Refugees to the State of Israel*, available at http://www.metzilah.org.il. The author thanks Nimra Goren-Amitai for her significant part in her work.

Alexander Yakobson's chapter is an updated version of a paper originally published in Hebrew in *Kivunim Hadashim* 18 (2008).

Aviad Bakshi thanks the Institute for Zionist Strategies for its support during his work on this study.

Introductory Remarks

FANIA OZ-SALZBERGER AND
YEDIDIA Z. STERN

T he scope of global fascination with Israel's unique political situation
is astounding. Israel has attracted the world's attention and captured its
imagination from the very moment of its birth, but present-day interest—
both friendly and hostile—is constantly rising. Today, more than ever
before, media consumers worldwide are tuned to Israel, the Palestinians,
and the Middle East at large. While the whole region is transforming
quickly and unpredictably, Israel's society and political culture change
as well, albeit in a less violent manner. This volume of original essays, by
some of Israel's most remarkable public and academic voices, offers a series
of state-of-the art, accessible analyses of Israel's ever-evolving theater of
statecraft, public debates, and legal and cultural dramas, its deep divisions
and—more surprisingly, perhaps—its internal affinities and common
denominators.

In the introductory chapters, Yedidia Z. Stern and Gadi Taub revisit
the basics—Israel's foundation as a democracy and a Jewish state—from
the interlocking perspectives of polity, identity, and Zionist thought. The
State of Israel was created and sanctioned by a United Nations resolution
in 1947, becoming part of the international community and a full member

of its major juridical institutions. At the same time, it retains the unique title of the world's only Jewish state. In what sense is Israel a nation-state? While ostensibly simple to answer—it is the state of the Jewish nation— this moniker has become, in recent years, increasingly controversial. Are the Jews a nation? Israel's founding fathers, most prominently Theodor Herzl, certainly thought so, as do most Israelis today. But Judaism is also a religion. What is the relationship between Jews as co-religionists and Israeli Jews as fellow-countrymen in a state comprising also a non-Jewish citizenry? Do the Jewish faith and nation overlap fully or partially, perhaps comparably to Greek Orthodoxy and nationhood, or to Thai Buddhism and nationhood? If so, what is the status of Jews living outside of Israel, and of Israelis who are not Jews? Some of the interfaces of state, nation, and religion, each furnishing the adjective "Jewish" with a different set of meanings, are explored in the chapters authored by Avi Sagi and Daniel Statman, and crop up in many of this book's other chapters too.

Even if we take Jewish nationhood for granted, Israel's demographic history differs from most other modern countries. It is an immigrant state as well as a nation-state, but does not easily fit into either category. In Europe, as well as in much of Asia, most modern nation-states grew from native ethnic majority groups; Israel's Jewish majority hails from a modern movement of mass immigration. To be sure, some modern nations, notably in the Americas and in the South Pacific, have risen from a plethora of immigrant communities. But Israel does not easily fit this model, either: Jews have formed the vast majority of its immigrants since 1948. They indeed hailed from many different countries and cultures, but their eligibility to Israeli nationality rested on their Jewish origin. Israel's Law of Return (1950) grants universal and unconditional entry and citizenship—regardless of age, education, or economic status—to all Jews and their immediate relatives. By contrast, Israel's Arab minority does not have a say in the country's immigration policy, and the Palestinians fleeing or evicted during their failed war against the Jews in 1947–48 are not eligible for repatriation. This policy is not dramatically different from the demographic realignments of European countries in the aftermath of the great human displacement caused by World War II. Arguably not *more* selective than other immigration policies, the Law of Return is *differently* selective: confined to Jews and their families, it pertains to each and every one of them, notwithstanding their personal status. Controversy pertaining to this particular immigration policy is nevertheless rife. In this volume, justifications for the Law of Return are freshly analyzed by Yaffa Zilbershats, and its repercussions echo in other chapters as well.

Does Israel's Jewish character trump its democratic regime, either necessarily or fortuitously? Can the two dovetail, or do they belong on different planes? What are the constitutional and practical significances of the Jewish adjective in Israel's self-definition? In the present book, this core issue is discussed by Fania Oz-Salzberger, Ruth Gavison, Ariel L. Bendor, Aviad Bakshi and Gideon Sapir. From a broader philosophical vantage point, Shira Wolosky explores the cosmopolitan–differential axis that runs across the tension fields of Jewish, not only Israeli, identity.

The complexity does not stop there. It is enhanced by three unique factors: the nature of the Jewish claim to the Land of Israel, the singular monstrosity of the Holocaust, and the Palestinians' ongoing historical plight and evolving national consciousness.

The Jews rested their claim to their ancient territory, as Israel's Declaration of Independence eloquently states, on a great bookshelf of written evidence: well over two millennia of testimony, beginning with the Hebrew Bible. This is buttressed by the documented longings of multitudes of Jews, over many centuries, to their lost homeland from which they considered themselves forcibly evicted. This is an unusual set of justifications for modern statehood. However, when the Zionist movement presented its claim to the global powers in the early twentieth century, and again in 1947, it gained gradual, and eventually overwhelming, official approval. The United Nations Resolution 181 on the Partition Plan for Palestine, creating two sovereign states for the Arabs and for the Jews, passed by a majority of thirty-three votes in favor versus thirteen against, with ten abstaining. Israel's international legitimacy, albeit vocally questioned ever since, is a fact of world history.

Nevertheless, the intricate questions surrounding Jewish nationhood continue to fascinate. The present volume hinges on this fascination, a persistent source of debate and creativity in Israeli public discourse and beyond. One line of debate revolves around the alleged antiquity of national consciousness: is the nation a modern construct, or can it claim ancient lineage? Theorists who ascribe all modern nations to modern ideology are prone to argue that the Jews were never a nation, but merely a religion, until Zionism "invented" Jewish nationhood. Other schools of political thought allow longer timeframes for the construction of national self-awareness. Jewish peoplehood, from such a perspective, overlapped with a religion that survived during two millennia without territory or sovereignty, until rising to reclaim it. The dispute goes on. It is, however, fairly safe to point out that Zionism is a modern ideology, drawing inspiration, lexicon, and intellectual sustenance from other national movements of the late nineteenth century, yet claiming a historical and textual lineage longer than most of them. Its singularity lies with its extraterritorial beginnings and its demand for mass migration of Jews—not to a new colony, but to an ancestral land.

The genocide of Europe's Jews by Nazi Germany did not trigger the demand for a Jewish state—which preceded it by half a century—but brought it to a new pitch of tragic urgency. Zionism does not stem from the Holocaust. Rather, the Holocaust has been understood by many Zionists as a horrible verification of the movement's historical analysis and a fulfillment of its warnings, albeit in a way far worse than its darkest predictions. This is only part of the story: the destruction of six million Jewish lives nearly destroyed the Jewish national ideal, and evidently curbed its human potential, far more effectively than any support it may have lent the Zionist cause. In her chapter, Anita Shapira reflects on some aspects of the complex relationships between the Holocaust and Zionist, as well as anti-Zionist, interpretations of Israel's existence and *raison d'être*.

The concept of an Israeli nation-state has been tested by an increasingly entangled reality, primarily because its creation deeply affected another budding nation, the Palestinians. This volume does not deal in depth with the issues of Palestinian nationhood, which are fraught by problems at times comparable to Jewish nationhood. It is important to note that a Palestinian sovereign state was granted by UN Resolution 181 but declined by the Palestinian leadership at the time; in our context, this point is not an axe to grind against the prospect of future Palestinian independence, but indeed the opposite: it is clear proof that a Jewish nation-state was never, in mainstream international or Zionist interpretation, formulated to exclude a Palestinian nation-state.

Despite the *de jure* viability of two neighboring nation-states, the unresolved status of Palestinians in the territories occupied by Israel in 1967, further confounded by the rise of the Jewish settler movement in Judea and Samaria (the West Bank), and by the escalating violence on both sides, projects deeply into every aspect of Israeli society, from jurisprudence to the arts. This volume engages with impacts of the Israeli–Palestinian conflicts on the inner cores of Israeli state and society, and several chapters dwell on the legal, political, and cultural concerns of Israel's one-fifth minority of Arab citizens. Michael M. Karayanni's contribution is informative on the legal status of various religious minorities in Israel, and at the same time usefully demonstrates that the Arab citizenry is not made of one skin, either religious or cultural. Interestingly, the legal rights and limitations affecting the Arab groups stem directly from the religious compromises reached within the Jewish majority, in Israel's early years, touching on disagreements about the very meaning of a Jewish state.

It is important, however, to note that neither the Arab minority, nor for that matter any other segment of Israeli society, passively accepts its constitutional and cultural destiny. Today, more than ever before, individuals and groups have grown vocal and assertive. It is too early to offer a scholarly reflection on the social protest movements of recent years, which often cut across traditional social, economic, and ethnic barriers. Looking at the Palestinian citizens of Israel, Ayman K. Agbaria's chapter suggests a new and proactive course taken in the field of education. This may well signal a future of enhanced civic activism, moderate or radicalizing, not only for the Arabs but also for other subgroups of Israeli society.

However, the rise of civil alertness and assertiveness need not spell doom for Israel's state and society. Two future-oriented chapters at the close of the volume, by Alexander Yakobson and David Passig, offer cautiously optimistic horizons for the future of Israel, both as a pluralist democracy and as a Jewish state. Optimism is a fairly rare commodity in mainstream Israel Studies of the past decade. However, the editors of the present volume, both of whom are no strangers to public activity and debate as well as scholarly analysis, support the claim that Israel's nation-state may surmount moral and political hurdles and evolve into a full-fledged democracy without losing its unique identity as a Jewish state, while enhancing its commitment to justice for each individual citizen and minority group, as envisaged by its Declaration of Independence.

Between them, the fifteen chapters in this book tackle a large portion of the theoretical spectrum underlying Israeli current affairs and public debates, although we do not pretend to run the full gamut of this intense, ever-evolving arena. Between them, the contributors offer historical, philosophical, social, and legal analyses of Israel's Jewish and democratic aspirations and the major tension fields on which these aspirations play out. No two authors are in full agreement with each other: we take this to reflect not only the sheer complexity of our subject matter, but also the fruitful diversity of Israel's public sphere.

PART I

REVISITING
THE BASICS

1 The State of Israel and National Identity

YEDIDIA Z. STERN

INTRODUCTION

Throughout the millennia during which Jews lived in the Diaspora, the public aspects of Judaism were silenced and it functioned as a way of life for individuals, families, and communities. This changed upon the establishment of the State of Israel. Once they acquired control of a territory, the Jews' perpetual existence as a controlled minority was replaced by a new status as a self-reliant majority. The founding of the state enabled the existence of Jewish politics, a Jewish military, a Jewish judicial system, and an array of institutions, activities, and experiences comprising a uniquely Jewish public sphere. All these constituted an exciting cultural, national, and religious renewal. The public potential of Jewish civilization, which had been hidden in the darkness of exile, was now tenable. The pupa had become a colorful butterfly, free to take flight. It is no wonder that the State of Israel was perceived as a miracle fulfilling the dreams of generations of Jews.

The establishment of the Jewish state was intended, ostensibly, to clarify the question of Jewish national identity. Concentrating a dispersed group in one place, shouldering it with full political responsibility, and creating cultural hegemony in the public sphere were supposed to serve as the nation's foundation. Yet sixty-four years later, it transpires that, instead of consolidating a national identity, the Jewish state has become the central arena for disagreements over its nature. Political Zionism's success awakened questions that demanded ideological and practical answers regarding the nature and meaning of collective Jewish existence. The practicalities of the Jewish state breathed new life into competing visions of the meaning, intent, and orientation of "Judaism" itself.

In this chapter I shall review the main disagreements about Israeli Jewish identity:

- Is the State of Israel a natural evolution of Diasporic Jewish existence or does it signify a new, revolutionary beginning?
- If this is a revolution, what kind? Does it center around a "new Jew" or around a Messiah bringing religious redemption to a stiff-necked people?
- What is the appropriate position of religion in a state in which most citizens are secular, but for whom large parts of their cultural heritage are of a religious nature?
- The State of Israel defines itself, in its laws, as both a "Jewish state" and a "democratic state"—can these two definitions coexist?
- Life in Israel is characterized by cultural duality: a traditional Jewish value system on the one hand, and a liberal-Western value system on the other. Is it possible to develop existential strategies that conduct a dialogue between the two cultural systems or enable them to exist dialectically?
- The dispute over national identity has prompted Israel's various factions to translate the cultural tension into a legal issue. They seek resolution through, on the one hand, secular Israeli law as interpreted by the courts and, on the other hand, religious Jewish law (halakha) as interpreted by Orthodox rabbis. What are the repercussions?

In closing, I shall offer a few introductory guidelines that might serve to soften Israel's crisis of national identity.

It is important to underscore the scope of this discussion. Nearly twenty percent of Israel's population belong to non-Jewish national minorities—Muslims, Christians, Druze, and Circassians. It goes without saying that their status and identity aspirations are key to any debate about the State of Israel as the Jewish national state. However, this essay is limited to depicting the country's internal Jewish discourse. Of course, the positions voiced in this dialogue are not unrelated to the identity discourse among Israel's minorities. We shall examine this relationship parenthetically, in the course of the chapter, but shall focus on describing the internal Jewish disagreement regarding the identity of the State of Israel.

BETWEEN DIASPORA AND STATEHOOD

The first years of the State of Israel saw a historic encounter between two extremely impressive personas: the legendary Prime Minister David Ben-Gurion, architect and builder of the state, and the charismatic leader of the ultra-Orthodox community, Rabbi Avrohom Yeshaya Karelitz, known as the "Chazon Ish" (after the title of his first publication). The meeting of these two short, weak-looking Jews was, in fact, a squabble between the two foundation cultures of burgeoning Jewish society in Israel: on the one hand, a civic-minded organization of Jews with a secular outlook and a modern, future-looking orientation; and on the other, an organization of community-driven Jews whose worldview was religious and whose orientation was towards the past.

One might have expected that this highly symbolic meeting would generate a merging of horizons between past and present, to benefit the future. Ben-Gurion would embrace the Chazon Ish as the representative of a religious worldview that had dominated the spiritual and practical Jewish worlds for generations, and that had helped to preserve Judaism as a unique way of life into the twentieth century. Indeed, the Zionist project could not have existed had religion not sustained the Jews' existence as a people with a distinct identity throughout its years in exile. One might also have assumed that the Chazon Ish would warmly embrace Ben-Gurion for having managed to elevate the post-Holocaust Jewish people to an independent sovereign state in the wake of their continued Diasporic deterioration, thereby fulfilling the ancient prophets' vision.

In reality, the meeting was quite different. Instead of embrace, there was struggle; there was no collaboration, but rather competition and extremity; no dialogue between narratives, but rather two monologues. The two were so at odds that, ultra-Orthodox legend has it, the elderly rabbi made a point of removing his spectacles for the entire meeting so as not to even catch sight of the secular leader. Why did this occur? Was it unavoidable?

Ben-Gurion wished to strengthen and fortify political Zionism. He believed this required the formation of a new Jewish identity that would be Israeli in nature. In his opinion, the Jewish identity that had emerged in the Diaspora was an obstacle to creating the brave, pioneering, independent, sovereign Jew. He rebelled against traditional Jewish identity and sought severance from Diasporic Judaism. Since practically almost all Jewish creation after the Bible had been produced in the Diaspora, Ben-Gurion knowingly relinquished it. The Talmud, halakha, philosophy, poetry, and all that filled the pages of the Jewish library—all were erased. He was attempting to found Jewish Israeli identity on the historical narrative of the Old Testament. The launching point for Ben-Gurion's Jewish culture was the Bible; its end point was the establishment of the State of Israel. He wished to skip from King David to David Ben-Gurion, and everything in the middle—two thousand years of formative experience—was irrelevant.[1]

The Chazon Ish, conversely, attributed little importance to political Zionism. It was not renewal he wanted, but continuity. He objected to the "new Jew" and turned the "old Jew" into a sacred ideal. His life's work was not political but spiritual. He wanted to rebuild the glorious European Jewish world of study that been destroyed in the Holocaust. He did not want to re-envision King David of Jerusalem, but rather the heads of *yeshivas* from the Eastern European *shtetls* and towns that had been active in the early twentieth century, prime among them in Vilnius, which was known in the religious world as "the Jerusalem of Lithuania." The Chazon Ish did not believe in cultural revolution but only in spiritual evolution. For him, the State of Israel was not a goal but merely an instrument meant to enable the renewal of the religious-scholarly civilization that the war had ruined. The state, in and of itself, had no value.[2]

It is no wonder that the front door of the private home of Ben-Gurion, the founding father of the Jewish state, bore no *mezuzah*. It is also not surprising that the rooftops of practically all the *yeshivas* that venerated the Chazon Ish, the founding father of ultra-Orthodox Judaism in Israel, waved no Israeli flag, not even on Independence Day. Yet it seems that the enormous chasm between the worldviews of these two impressive men enabled them to reach agreement on the practicalities of daily existence in Israel. Ben-Gurion, alongside his desire to act out of civic considerations, believed that it would not be long before the religious version of Judaism vanished from the world.[3] Progress and enlightenment were on Ben-Gurion's side, while religion had been in constant retreat since Enlightenment and Emancipation. As for the Chazon Ish, he was convinced that time would work in favor of ultra-Orthodox Judaism and that secular Judaism was doomed to atrophy and disappear. Jewish history, the divine promise, and the holy books were on his side. From his point of view, secular Judaism was merely a historical error that would surely end soon.

It is fascinating to discover that, despite each man's certainty that the other's position would be defeated, they managed to overcome their immediate priorities and reach an agreement on Jewish aspects of the state's practicalities. As early as 1947, Ben-Gurion signed what became known as "the status quo arrangement," which determined that the Jewish character of the Israeli public sphere would be maintained thus: marriage and divorce law for Jews in Israel would be based on halakha and implemented by rabbinical courts; businesses and public transportation would shut down on the Sabbath and on Jewish holidays; laws of *kashrut* (Jewish dietary laws) would be observed in all state institutions (including the Israel Defense Force); autonomy would be guaranteed for the various religious streams to manage their own state-funded education systems.[4]

Ben-Gurion yielded on these topics because he thought it was a temporary concession until religious Jews were gone and the battle was decided. The religious representatives, meanwhile, agreed to compromise on other issues—for example the implementation of halakha in civilian areas of law (such as contract, property and torts, which are at the basis

of Jewish law) and in all other areas of life in Israel. Here too, the concession was perceived as temporary, until all Jews returned to their father in
heaven.

Did the two men succeed in realizing their conflicting objectives?
The answer is complicated. On the one hand, the life work of each was
wondrously fulfilled: Ben-Gurion's political Zionism created a state that
became strong, independent, modern, technological, and eventually, after
his death, secular and liberal. There is no doubt that the State of Israel
is akin to Western countries. It seems highly fitting that the gateway to
Israel from the rest of the world—Israel's international airport—is named
after him. On the other hand, the Chazon Ish was incredibly successful in
rebuilding, within and by means of the state, the lost world of Torah. The
number of men engaged in full-time Torah study as their primary occupation in Israel today is probably greater than it ever was in the history
of the Jewish people. It is no wonder that a central street in Bnei Brak, an
ultra-Orthodox city not unlike prewar Jewish towns in Europe in many
ways, is named after him.

Yet both Ben-Gurion and Chazon Ish also suffered crushing failures.
Each operated out of his own "truth." Each was positive that history was
on his side. They made no effort, therefore, to bridge the two truths by
creating a common national identity. Instead of mediation, they chose
alienated coexistence. The ultra-Orthodox feared modernity, secularization, and nationality; the secular rejected the Diasporic past, religion,
and classical Jewish culture. And so each retreated into his own camp
and developed an independent and contradicting ethos. This was how a
profound identity rift emerged between the different sectors of the Jewish
people in Israel. The parallel monologues continue, with no real dialogue.
The sides are prepared, at best, to tolerate one another, but are unwilling
to adopt a national pluralistic way of life.

One sector did offer a third way, connecting the age-old Jewish
dream with the new reality of political Zionism and sovereign statehood.
This was religious Zionism, whose clear ideological leader was Rabbi
Avraham Yitzhak HaCohen Kook (known as "HaRaAYaH") (1865–
1935). Had Rabbi Kook been present at that historic meeting, could he
have led Ben-Gurion and the Chazon Ish on a path that might have

prevented the rift? Does the classical worldview of religious Zionism offer a prescription that would have enabled comfortable coexistence? I believe the answer is no.

At first glance, it would appear that religious Zionism bears an affinity with both hawkish camps. It views itself as a full partner to the Zionist endeavor and contributed to the Zionist revolution as much as it could. Like Ben-Gurion, it seeks a new beginning—a nation-state for the Jewish people—and its pursuit was translated by several prominent leaders into Messianic language. Yet it also sees itself as utterly connected with the Jewish religion, and its language is primarily religious, guided by theological thought. The two character traits of this group—which gave it its name, "religious Zionism"—created the expectation that it would serve as a meaningful bridge. Its adherence to Zionism closely connects it with Ben-Gurion the heretic and his secular camp: together they left the ghetto and set up an exemplary, independent Jewish society in Palestine; together they experienced the plethora of options offered by modernity; together they would be a light unto the nations; together they would work from a sense of national activism that comprehended the magnitude of the historical moment. At the same time, faith ties religious Zionism to the Chazon Ish and his ultra-Orthodox camp. It too perceives the supreme value of continuity between previous generations and the present, and asserts that the present cannot exist without spiritual sustenance from the past. Nor does it accept secular Zionism's aspiration for normalization or wish to live "as all the nations."

A golden mean between revolutionary secular Zionism and conservative ultra-Orthodoxy is not easily forged. For the ultra-Orthodox, religious Zionists shared the sin of Hellenization,[5] while for the secular they were guilty of preserving the primitive aspects of the old Jew. Both saw the midway as a contemptible compromise.

How did religious Zionism view itself? How did it explain the central role of secular Zionism in the religious act of "return to Zion"? How did it justify the continued partnership with a Ben-Gurion-style secular Zionist leadership, which regarded Zionism as a substitute for religion and believed the role of religion in contemporary Jewish life should be minimized? Rabbi Kook and others offered a dialectic that assigned Zionism mythic proportions and inscribed its secular agenda with hidden theological meaning. In this view, Jewish history is led not by the hand of man but by the hand of God. The state was intended to fulfill the purposes—Messianic or otherwise—of Divine Providence, and within that framework secular Zionism plays an important role. Ben-Gurion and his cohort are a pawn on the divine chess table, and their actions serve the historical course as viewed from a religious perspective. Their consciousness is secular, heretic even, but it is a false consciousness. The entire course of political Zionism—which boasts of acting within the confines of realistic history—is interpreted as part of a redemptive, meta-historical plan that hastens the coming of the Messiah.[6]

This dialectic served to magically self-justify religious Zionism's way, and so the broad consent it achieved among the group's religious and political leaders is not surprising. Indeed, in retrospect it could be argued that Rabbi Kook, like Ben-Gurion and the Chazon Ish, was extraordinarily successful at fulfilling his goals. Religious Zionism developed over the years into an extremely significant movement in Israel, far beyond its proportional numbers. Its members are involved in national life as a trend-setting ideological and revolutionary force. The internal consciousness of the religious Zionist community has grown unrecognizably: from a calm, humble group that sought consensus, it has become a force of fermentation in Israeli society in recent years. A significant portion of this dramatic change derives from the Messianic energy breathed into it by Rabbi Kook.

The core of religious Zionism's dialectical course, however, contains a powerful timebomb that negates its ability to bridge Israeli camps or offer a shared national agenda. Had Rabbi Kook proposed his framework to Ben-Gurion, it would certainly have been rejected. Secular Zionism, then and today, is unwilling to accept a patronizing exegesis of its great enterprise. No ideological group would, and certainly not a successful majority vibrantly leading a historic revolution. Indeed, the theological stance that negates the essence of secular Zionism is shared by both religious Zionism and the ultra-Orthodox. The religious and the ultra-Orthodox disagree about the interpretation of reality: are we at the beginning of redemption or "only" at the end of exile? Consequently, they differ over the meaning of the state, the role of the secular, and the intent of God, but both the religious and the ultra-Orthodox agree on one thing: they possess the secret code to decipher Jewish history, and it clearly reveals that secularism is a grave mistake.[7]

The overall picture that arises from this analysis is that beneath the surface of Jewish society in Israel, there is a fundamental disagreement about the state's ultimate purpose and the appropriate interpretation of the entire Zionist endeavor. Daily challenges (such as external security threats) often silence the disagreement, pushing it beyond active consciousness, and sometimes they fan it and then it bubbles to the surface with full force (as in the argument over issues of church and state). However, the ebb and flow of national consensus among Jews in Israel, as dictated by current events, cannot disguise the clear existence of ideological camps with contradictory versions of the Israeli narrative. Each has a unique and mutually exclusive view of the relationship between the Diasporic past and the statehood present.

The differing perceptions of the historical developments that culminated in the founding of the state take on fascinating manifestations in Israelis' complex relationship with religion and its role in the state.

BETWEEN RELIGION AND STATE

Studies have shown repeatedly that some eighty percent of the Jewish population in Israel maintains a favorable view of the traditional Jewish way of life. Thus, for example, although only a fifth of Israeli Jews define themselves as religious, whether Orthodox or ultra-Orthodox, more than three-quarters (seventy-seven percent) believe in God. Traditional Jewish practices are acceptable to a predominant portion of the public: Israelis fast on Yom Kippur (seventy-three percent), hang *mezuzahs* on their front doors (ninety-six percent), circumcise their sons (ninety-seven percent), and so forth. Of course, observing these practices is not necessarily an expression of religious intent, but it indicates an awareness of the significance of these actions from the perspective of the continuity of Jewish tradition. Interestingly, a growing number of Israeli Jews self-identify as religious or traditional. Moreover, more than half the population who do not observe any traditions would like their children to be somewhat observant. In short, the collective portrait of Jews in Israel is not only unestranged from tradition, it is influenced by it.[8]

Furthermore, in the past two decades Israel has absorbed roughly one million immigrants from the former Soviet Union. Although most of them grew up in an environment hostile to Jewish identity and lacked exposure to tradition, their integration within the fabric of Israeli society included an embrace of the Israeli preference for observing Jewish traditions. Nor did the rise of global forces and their affect on Israeli society at the turn of the twenty-first century alter the continuing connection of Jews in Israel with their traditions. Moreover, in the past decade we have seen that significant non-religious groups—mostly elites, such as artists, cultural figures, and intellectuals—are showing a renewed interest in Jewish texts. A Jewish renaissance is occurring right before our eyes. And so the desire for affinity with Jewish tradition is manifested not only practically, but also in a spiritual-cultural search. "The classical Zionist vision of a revolutionary, ideologically principled secular Israeli culture, which rejects tradition except as a source for transvalued national symbols, is in full retreat."[9]

It is worth considering, in this context, the words of prominent Israeli sociologist Baruch Kimmerling: "In Israel there are secular individuals and groups and even subcultures. Their daily conduct and self-identification is secular. There are even those who conduct a culture (or religious) war against this or the other use of the state to enforce this or the other religious custom, or even halakhic law, on the general public or part of it. But when most of the Jewish public in Israel relates to its national collective identity, this identity is largely defined by terms, values, symbols and a collective memory that are mostly anchored in Jewish religion. In other words, there are secular Jews in Israel and in the world, but it is highly doubtful whether secular Judaism exists."[10]

There is, however, a completely opposing aspect of Israeli Jews' approach to tradition and religion. It is an accepted truism that more than half of Israeli Jews estimate that the rift between religious and secular Israelis will eventually lead to civil war. Many believe that we are already in the throes of a culture war. Three-quarters of Jews in Israel think relations between religious and non-religious people are poor. The religious–secular rift might be the sharpest and most dangerous one in Israel. These are not merely pessimistic statements: in the 2003 elections, more than a third of the Knesset members were elected primarily because of their positions on the issue of state and religion. This is an astonishing fact: in a country where the daily agenda comprises existential problems of security, society, economy, immigration, and so forth, one out of three citizens believed they should use their vote to take a stand on state and religion.[11]

How might these contradictory data be reconciled? How is it possible that Israeli Jews are probably the most traditional population in the West in terms of their customs, yet the relationship between state and religion in Israel is among the worst in Western countries? If Israeli society is so connected to tradition and to the historical memory anchored in religion, why does the sharp conflict between religion and state not abate? The answer stems, I believe, from the enormous gap between practical life—the way people live—and ideological life—the way people perceive their lives.

The unsolved issue of Israelis' identity has weakened their common ideological foundation. In fact, it is difficult to identify a formulation or even an attempted formulation of shared ideology that penetrates the depth of Jewish existence in Israel. What is the common denominator of all Jewish citizens of Israel? Answers that might occur to an outsider—such as a commitment to "Zionism," to "Jewish culture," to "statehood," or to "the forefathers' heritage"—are not acceptable in Israel. It is for this reason that, as a matter of course, Israelis find themselves needing to belong to unique identity circles, thereby declaring their affiliation with a particular side in local identity politics. This affinity encompasses ideological, cultural, and social aspects. Moreover, after Ben-Gurion, the Chazon Ish and Rabbi Kook, the various camps' identity declarations do not suffice with self-definition and a commitment toward fellow members, but establish themselves by means of rigidly rejecting the other identities and delegitimizing alternative Jewish ways of life.

There was one point of convergence between the doctrines of Ben-Gurion and the Chazon Ish: decisive and principled objection to the

Jewish cultural "other." Ben-Gurion went down in Jewish history as the glorified architect of national life in Israel. However, his point of origin was a rebellion against tradition. He sought a Hebrew culture to replace Jewish culture. He believed religion was an obstacle for the state, and so rejected any affinity with it. He created a melting pot that aimed to castrate the unique traditions of various communities, even if they were centuries old, in favor of a civic uniformity whose core was a new national bond—an Israeli one.[12]

The Chazon Ish was even more extreme. He fashioned religious life in Israel on the basis of utterly delegitimizing the secular lifestyle and the national framework. Religious seclusion, in his teachings, comprised all aspects of existence: living in separate towns and neighborhoods; maintaining a separate education system; removing any trace of general studies from the ultra-Orthodox education system; idealizing non-participation in the military; harsh and continued condemnation of the state; lack of recognition for its main institutions (primarily the courts); avoiding all press and electronic media; and toughening the halakhic stance against those who are not religious.

As for the students of Rabbi Kook, the religious Zionists? It was precisely the importance they attributed to the state that drove their fervent desire to "repair" it in a religious-spiritual sense. In the spirit of the slogan coined by Rabbi Kook, religious Zionism believed that not only should "the old be renewed" (unlike the ultra-Orthodox position, which holds that "new is forbidden by the Torah"), but that "the new be sanctified" (in contrast to the secular position, which wanted anything new to be profane). It was the religious Zionists, then, more than the ultra-Orthodox, who were the prime motivators of religious legislation and the religious coercion that accompanied it into the beginning of the twenty-first century.[13]

From the outset, religious Zionism explicitly reached out to the "other." In recent decades, however, a dramatic change has been occurring, whereby significant portions of the group are choosing an isolationist lifestyle. There are voices calling to step away from the partnership with secular Zionism, despite its long and successful history. A large group known as "*Hardalim*" (from the Hebrew acronym for "national ultra-Orthodox") is renouncing its affinity with Western culture and modernity, becoming increasingly suspicious of democratic culture, tending to accept rabbinical authority even on non-halakhic matters, secluding itself in separate towns and education systems (starting in early childhood), and generally emulating the ultra-Orthodox by building "walls of holiness" between itself and the public at large.

What brought about this change? It seems that religious Zionists' deteriorating relationship with secular Zionism and the state must be viewed against the backdrop of their increasingly acute disappointment with the failure of history—the State of Israel as it is—to embody the spiritual-political model they had hoped would emerge under Jewish sovereignty. Until the 1970s, the religious Zionist utopia was significantly bolstered by facts. The establishment of the state against all odds by Ben-Gurion and Israel's decisive victory in the Six-Day War under Yitzhak Rabin and Moshe Dayan—all, of course, exemplary secular leaders—served as irrefutable evidence that secular Zionism was fulfilling, albeit unconsciously, its religious destiny by effecting the return to Zion.[14] The Messiah's footsteps were in the background of the encounter with new homeland territories in Judea and Samaria and the return to the Western Wall and the Temple Mount. Yet the close partnership with secular Zionism depended on fulfilling the vision— on making progress in redeeming the land. With no agreement on the purpose of the Zionist endeavor or a shared identity platform, the foundation of religious and secular Zionists' cooperation focused greatly on matters of their shared physical existence—Eretz Yisrael as territory. As long as the secular leadership advanced the agenda of liberating the land, it was a worthy partner and even (for the time being) anointed as legitimate national leadership. However, when Israel negotiated peace deals with some Arab countries and was subsequently required to give up Sinai and the Yamit area, a bitterly painful process of sobering began. As the notion of "land for peace" took hold among the Israeli public, religious Zionism increasingly distanced itself from secular Zionism. The Oslo Accords and other agreements with the Palestinians were perceived by some as criminal. Leading voices in the ongoing debate within religious Zionism viewed the surrender of their forefathers' lands as a betrayal by the state and by secular Zionism.

Disappointment with secular Zionism and criticism of the state grew deeper after the disengagement from Gush Katif in the Gaza Strip and the forced removal of some 2,000 settler families (the overwhelming majority of whom were religious Zionists) in 2005. The national inquiry committee set up to investigate how the authorities handled the evacuated settlers stated in its final report:

The great majority of religious Zionists feel that the state and its leaders turned their back on them. The sector's leaders—politicians, rabbis and educators—stood against the disengagement plan with tens of thousands of citizens behind them, with stormy spirits and rent souls. The fact that the disengagement was carried out by the security forces, who are entrusted with protecting the state against outside enemies, added insult to injury. This must be understood: the IDF is a "holy vessel" for religious Zionists, and here it was being used to perform an act that was, to them, sacrilegious. All these, as well as the controversial way in which the disengagement decision was reached in the state's democratic institutions, sent ideological shockwaves through some parts of religious Zionism.[15]

There have even been calls from ideological extremists in the national-religious camp to completely disconnect from the Zionist revolution and enlist Israeli society, led by the religious-national public, to perform a "faith-based revolution": "Zionist ideology—the only ideology of its time that had the power to bring about the modern 'return to Zion'—has finished its historical role." Instead, they present "the religious alternative as the only path that can extricate the Jewish people from the crisis and lead it to new expanses of creation and meaning."[16] In these approaches, the relationship between the would-be new society established by religious Zionism and the existing, decaying Israeli society is much like the relationship between a fresh seedling and the rotting seedcase from which it emerged.

BETWEEN JUDAISM AND DEMOCRACY

The argument over national identity manifests not only in the discord between state and religion, but also in a broader question concerning Israel's character. There are those who believe that identity is a matter for individuals and communities. The state is a framework that should ensure people's welfare and happiness, and enable different identities to flourish without preferring one over the other. For them, the State of Israel is an "ordinary" democratic state with a universal nature, in which the vast majority of citizens are Jewish. Others believe the public political sphere is the arena for developing a group identity, including a Jewish one. In this view, the establishment of Israel enabled a revival of the public characteristics of the Jewish people that had been silenced and suppressed during the long years of exile. They want a democratic state that is identifiably Jewish. In such a state, Judaism is a central component of the polity. Of course, those who insist on uniqueness must contend with the difficulties it generates: the more the state is designed to reflect the unique identity preferences of the Jewish majority, the more damage it inflicts on the sense of belonging, and to a certain extent on the rights, of non-Jewish citizens, as well as Jews who are not interested in a Jewish identity.

Israel's 1948 Declaration of Independence asserted "the establishment of a *Jewish state* in Eretz-Israel, to be known as the State of Israel" (italics mine). The term "democratic state" is absent, but the declaration's principles show an intent to establish one. Forty-four years later, during the legislation of two of the most important "Basic Laws" (which are considered part of a future Israeli constitution), the Knesset asserted that the State of Israel is "a Jewish and democratic state." The phrase represents a highly abstract political compromise that veils disagreements and postpones their resolution to the hour of concrete conflict. This definition, which Israeli law uses extensively and regularly, has long been accepted by the broad public. Most Israelis, including a significant number of Israeli Arabs, view the state as a dual entity: both Jewish and democratic.[17]

What is the significance of this two-pronged term?[18] Interpreters of "democratic state" may look to intellectual baggage and human experience that are not equally available to those wishing to interpret "Jewish state." A democratic state is a fairly widespread phenomenon in modern history, and its various modes have been at the center of human experience for centuries. There are disagreements over the scope of democracy's content: the narrower view sees it as a type of regime, a framework of rules for public decision-making. Its main tenet is the demand that the state's citizens elect the rulership of which they are subjects. This is formal democracy. The broader view, which supports substantive democracy, conceives of it as an idea and, moreover, an ideal. They believe that a state is not democratic if it is not pluralistic and tolerant. It must be committed to a concrete political doctrine (for example, liberalism) and to specific normative structures (for example, the Declaration of Human Rights). Thus, for instance, the relationship between the state and religion or nationality is conceived by the broader view as a litmus test for the very classification of a state as democratic. The same cannot be said of the narrower view, which does not gauge the democracy of a state by such measures. Any choice regarding the scope and depth of the democratic state affects the expanse available for influence by the values of a Jewish state.

The challenges inherent to comprehending both the theoretical and practical meanings of a democratic state are not unique to Israel. Communities around the world experience the blessings and promises of democracy and, simultaneously, the dangers it poses, insofar as it is perceived to be universal, to the particular nature of each community. This is a known and unresolved story in Western political heritage.

A Jewish state, by contrast, is a singular, young phenomenon, and its conception is still in an embryonic state. Although the roots of Jewish culture are deeper than those of democratic culture, Jewish culture existed for two thousand years without sovereignty. The Diaspora emptied Jewish memory of its political experience and left an enormous cogitative and legal lacuna regarding the meaning, conduct, and values of a Jewish state. While the path leading from democratic culture to a democratic state is relatively well-trodden, the application of Jewish culture as raw material for Jewish sovereignty is unprecedented.

"Judaism" has always been perceived as the designation of a people (a demographic criterion), a nation (a national criterion), and a religion (a religious criterion). The physical, spiritual, and cognitive existence of Jewish civilization in all its incarnations has always drawn from this triple source. It is reasonable, then, to assume that the term "Jewish state" should reflect the multifaceted nature of Judaism itself. It should be viewed as embodying a cultural criterion that contains all three components. The state of Israel is a Jewish state by virtue of being a political-organizational framework that preserves and nurtures central aspects of Jewish civilization in our generation—people, nation, and religion. The state is Jewish in the sense that most of its citizens are Jewish (people), that it serves as a nation-state for the Jews (nation), and that it has a Jewish religious ascription (religion), which is manifested in the assimilation of some parts of religious law into state law—for example, marriage and divorce, a religious state institution called the "Israel Chief Rabbinate," and more. Choosing among these components, which involves concealing one or more of them or markedly silencing its unique contribution, flattens out the Jewish nature of the state and creates a disconnect between historical Jewish memory, which is constructed on all three foundations, and the Jewish state.

Throughout history, most Jews have viewed the three components of Jewish culture as one discrete entity. Today, due to secularization and the establishment of the state, this entity has disintegrated. For many, the circles of people, nation, and religion are not overlapping, and at times they even experience friction. One must therefore ask what relative weight each of the three components should be assigned in areas that demand clarification of the Jewish state's values.

Fundamentalist interpretations of the concepts of "Jewish state" and "democratic state" thwart the possibility of conceptual (and practical) coexistence. Thus, for example, if a Jewish state must be a theocracy, which draws its authority from divine sovereignty, or if it must be a halakha state, in which case its regulatory norms have no popular source, then it cannot coexist with a democratic state, even in its formal definition, which must derive its authority from human sovereignty and wherein law is the product of a political system. Conversely, if a democratic state must adopt a pluralistic, liberal stance, if it is necessarily the state of "all its citizens" and rejects unique national identity, and if it must be culturally neutral, then it does not sit well with the classical concept of the nation-state, whereby the state itself has a national and cultural identity—in our case, Jewish.[19]

The more moderate interpretations also provoke a conceptual dissonance. Thus, for example, the demographic criterion for a Jewish state is problematic if it implies that the state is committed to preserving the Jewish majority by passing immigration and naturalization laws that give preference to Jews. The national criterion for a Jewish state is unacceptable if it means that, for the purpose of realizing self-determination, the state must allocate rights and resources in a way that prefers members of the Jewish nation over others. The religious criterion raises a problem inasmuch as it requires different treatment of those who are not Jews, and of women, and enforces religious obligations on secular Jews. All these arouse a measure of democratic discomfort, at least according to the interpretation that endows democracy with a richness of content. However, the belief that a democratic state requires full separation between state and religion, both in content and in symbols, or that a democratic state requires a liberal (as opposed to republican) outlook that emphasizes the individualistic ethos (while marginalizing the role of community)—these diminish the possibility of assigning Jewish content to a democratic state.

This tension between the state's two attributes must be openly acknowledged. As we have seen, each part of the two-headed beast is an open conceptual term. The intellectual and factual history of "democratic state" and of "Jewish state" leaves a variety of avenues—legal, social, and cultural—available to future generations regarding a possible combination of the two. One must not expect an intellectual breakthrough or a theoretical revelation. Rather, there will have to be a continuous process of mutual maturation, which will seek interpretations that do not sharpen and wrangle but rather round and complement. This is no reason to despair: in a profound sense, living with contradictions, with ideological and conceptual dissonance, is the mainstay of "the human condition."

BETWEEN JUDAISM AND LIBERALISM

Defining the state as Jewish and democratic reflects the cultural duality that characterizes Jewish society in Israel. As a rule, Israeli Jews identify—albeit with varying degrees of internalization and consciousness—with two cultures: traditional Jewish and Western liberal. Both serve as central identity components that mold their way of life. As we have seen, many secular and traditional people consume select symbolic and material products from Jewish culture, even from its religious facet. Likewise, religious and ultra-Orthodox people have adopted central values of liberal culture (such as equality, self-realization, liberty, and rule of law). Indeed, the vast majority of Jews in Israel carve their lives out of the rich resources of both cultures.[20]

This cultural duality could have been a fertilizing spring for Israeli society, but in actual fact it has had the opposite effect—one of paralyzing conflict. Instead of the blessing of diversity we have the curse of multiplicity. The influential agents of both cultures in Israel tend to dull the points of similarity and proximity between the two, preferring to represent them as alternatives geared up for inevitable battle—a culture war. They market each as an exclusive cultural-social product that "belongs" to one of the groups, underplaying the inclusive dimension of cultural duality. They divert the relationship between the two cultures from a dialogical route onto a decisive one. They reject a complex concept of reality in favor of a simplistic one. They refuse to conduct the cultural disagreement on a pluralistic basis, choosing instead a monistic basis.

What are the behavioral strategies adopted by the various groups in the light of the threatening duality? The Modern Orthodox community evades the decision by compartmentalizing, adopting different modes of conduct in different cultural contexts: at home, in synagogue, in educational institutes—they are Jewish; at work, as consumers, in the public sphere—they are Western. Modern Orthodoxy erects barriers between the two worlds and maintains a conscious separation between the two identity components. The ultra-Orthodox community chooses isolation and alienation. It is willing to engage in civic cooperation of an instrumental nature, but does not subscribe to the state's value system, and therefore rejects shared responsibility. The secular public, in a crude generalization, chooses to distance itself from any intimacy with its heritage. Israeli culture as a whole—as evinced in the educational system, in local art, in philosophy, morality, economics, law, language, media, politics, symbols, role models, and the array of social practices in Israeli life—is devoid of significant traces of Jewish culture. Direct engagement with Jewish studies in Israeli research universities is also dwindling. There is an emergent abandonment of the vibrant, contemporary, experiential use that could have been made of treasured experiences, memories, and meanings of Jewish existence through the ages. To paraphrase the German philosopher Gadamer, it is a relinquishing of the essential encounter between the horizon of the past and the horizon of the present.[21] The three strategies— Modern Orthodox compartmentalization, ultra-Orthodox alienation, and secular renunciation—have one thing in common: none contains an option for conceptually engaging with the reality of life in a cultural duality. None enables harmonious existence under the shadow of both cultures.

In the state's first three decades, Israel had a high level of internal Jewish accord: the Holocaust, the commitment to statehood, and security issues were the building blocks of the consensual democracy that prevailed. Against this background, one can understand how the three strategies, despite their practical deficiencies, enabled joint existence among the communities. But various processes, both internal and external, crumbled the traditional system of consent, and Israel long ago became a democracy in crisis. Public discourse today focuses on a sharp exposure of the cultural disagreements, resulting in continued pressure on each of the three strategies. If the past state of consensus enabled survival in cultural duality even without existential compromise, the current state of crisis has stripped the important groups in Israeli Jewish society of the thought patterns that would enable them to cope with the tension between two cultures.

The sad result is that everyone is pushing their way into an aggressive competition in the market of ideas. Both cultures face one another as at war, each side viewing the fulfillment of its position as a deterministic necessity. At stake are not only self-interests, but also components that, subjectively, establish reality and give meaning. The fanatics of liberal truth, who champion a universal democratic state, view the culture war as an essential rite of passage for the state on its way to normalcy. For them, the presence of Judaism, particularly the religious component (and for some the national component, too) in public life corrupts politics, violates human rights, makes rational discourse superficial, and diverts Israel from the central path of Zionism. The extremists of Jewish heritage in its religious-orthodox version, by contrast, who support a Jewish state free of "foreign" democratic influences, regard the fulfillment of Western cultural values in Israel as causing a loss of national identity, betraying Jewish history, and emptying the national revival of meaning. Each side is entrenched in one cultural truth.[22] Fulfilling one side's dream comes at the cost of a nightmarish reality for the other.

BETWEEN LAW AND POLITICS

The tensions mounting in the different strata—between Jewish continuity and Israeli revolution, religion and state, Judaism and democracy, and Jewish and Western cultures—position Israeli society in a crisis of identity with interpersonal aspects (in addition to the intrapersonal aspects, which are not our concern here). The shared living space, which is necessary in order to build a dialogue between the Jewish groups, has been reduced. It is now only a short distance to the aspiration to achieve cultural resolution through legal means. Turning to the legal system enables the parties to accomplish a complex goal: conducting a culture war while maintaining a purist image.

The judicial process seems suitable for the task because it projects professional cleanliness and sterile objectivity. We therefore see that the secular public, including members of the Israeli parliament, often need the courts' help to resolve ideological-cultural disputes. In a mirror image, the religious and ultra-Orthodox communities turn to traditional Jewish law—halakha—which they perceive as an ideal decision-making method that is, ostensibly, unaffected by the adjudicator's personal values. The experiential difficulty of the identity crisis leads Israelis to choose the legal arena as an ideal place to conduct their internal struggles. They align themselves with, on the one hand, Israeli law, with its liberal-secular bent, and on the other, the law of Jewish halakha, which has a traditional-religious nature. A significant part of the public debate over the appropriate relationship between the state's Jewish and democratic designations has been occurring for the last generation in Israeli courts. At the same time, more and more religious ideologues are formulating their positions on fundamental questions—the character of the state, the source of its authority, issues of war and peace—in the framework of halakha rulings.

Translating the cultural duality into legal language has severe repercussions. Legal judgment renders the disagreement more banal. It has a cutthroat quality that sharpens the resolution and encourages a discourse of "winner" versus "loser." It is conducted from within a drama of competition and often results in demonization of the other because of his or her views. It escalates the disagreements and fortifies the sides behind defense lines formulated in binary terms: rights versus obligations, commandments versus transgressions. It makes it difficult to develop educational options characterized by mediation, complexity, procedure, and experience. It demarcates camps, and undermines the possibility of establishing common denominators between them. It paralyses the market of ideas, and dilutes the social importance of the political process.

Furthermore, excessive use of the law corrodes the authority of the courts and the judges and damages the rule of law. Thus, for example, if in the past eighty percent of Israelis trusted the Israel Supreme Court, today only roughly half (!) of all Israelis do. Among the ultra-Orthodox and the religious, trust in the Supreme Court reaches only twenty percent and thirty-four percent, respectively. The loss of trust weakens the court and damages the democratic state's accepted avenue for resolving conflicts, especially in disagreements among sectors. The identity crisis is therefore corroding a strategic social asset of primary importance.[23]

POSSIBLE BALANCES

National identity distress cannot be resolved by means of normative resolution, and it is no matter for the courts. The courts are responsible for a discourse of rights that bears a monologist nature, which erases the other's face, and which wishes to subdue the other. By contrast, the identity discourse required for Israeli society is essentially dialogist, one that wishes to know the other, to enrich and be enriched by the other. As stated previously, the Jewish Israeli public has never settled the extreme identity tensions that divide it. Therefore, the decision-making process in Israeli society has trickled down over the past thirty years from the ideological systems, through the political systems, to the legal systems. What is required now is a reversal that entails educational, social, religious, and political work. I shall briefly outline possible courses of action that might alleviate the identity crisis in each of the three central components of Judaism: religious, national, and cultural.

Religion

For many years, the religious and ultra-Orthodox public in Israel has been trying to enforce the observance of certain religious commandments on the entire Israeli public. The reason is clear: secular identity is illegitimate from a religious perspective, and so religious coercion is perceived as an essential way to "repair" those who have strayed. Religious coercion is not intended to lead secular individuals to observe commandments in their own homes, but is rather focused on strengthening the Jewish nature of the public arena. For this purpose, some members of the religious and ultra-Orthodox communities seek to turn certain aspects of religious law into national law. They also wish the religious norms to obligate everyone in those domains—such as conversion, and marriage and divorce law—in which this is required from a religious point of view in order to maintain the Jewish people's unity.

The aggressive efforts of the religious and ultra-Orthodox, however, inflict severe damage on the quality of the encounter between religious and ultra-Orthodox people and their secular counterparts, and between religion and the state. The extreme cultural prominence of the struggle over religious legislation dulls the cultural value of the religious experience—a rich platform of thought and philosophy, poetry and art, mysticism and legend, from which Jewish Israeliness might have been woven. Many people identify religion itself with the political and rabbinical establishment that is trying to impose its beliefs on them. The belligerence and guile integral to the minority's desire to enforce norms in which the majority is uninterested is shaking the foundations of democracy in Israel.[24] In actual fact, history has shown that the concrete accomplishments of religious legislation in Israel are extremely meager. Alongside a prevalent preference for the traditional way of life, as described previously, there is also a rejection of and resistance to religious norms being dictated by the religious establishment.

Growing distant from religious norms is not a purpose in and of itself. If the State of Israel wishes to be more Jewish, it must ask itself how it can be built and enriched by the religious value system. I shall demonstrate this by examining the possible status of religious values in the Israeli legal system. Every legal system reflects particular social ideals and strives to establish certain values and cultural preferences. If the Israeli legislature draws primarily from American law, it serves as a cultural mediator that performs a deafening amplification of the American ethos and value system in the Israeli market of ideas. Is this appropriate? Many would argue it is not, and so there is a demand to "open up" the Israeli legal system to influences from diverse cultural voices. One of them—to my mind, a central one—is the religious Jewish voice.

According to this proposal, the role of halakha in Israeli society should not be an instrument of coercion but a critical model—a suggestion for "a good life" and "good society." Halakha can aid Israeli society to mold the civic-social ethos it deserves. It should serve as a point of criticism by an ideal-religious system for a practical-worldly system. Religious law would serve as a reflection for the prevalent law and enable a "promotion" of Israeli law in cases where most Israelis believe it appropriate. The legislature, the academy, the courts, and the public would face a choice—without coercion—between cultural proposals that are the fruit of a religious-halakhic debate and other cultural offers.[25]

Absent coercion, one could expect a dynamic intercultural discourse to develop in Israeli society. The belligerent communication would be replaced by a discourse of persuasion and mutual influence. Halakha would expose itself to the new possibilities contained in the existing legal system, and at the same time, Israeli law would be open to the reasonable notion that there is something in the world of halakha that sustained the Jewish people throughout the years and that is worthy of imitation and internalization. Mutual listening, apart from being a religious and democratic value, would fertilize all of Israeli society. When the critical model operates in both directions, it will give true meaning to the term "Jewish and democratic state."

Nation

The Mandate from the League of Nations, and subsequently the United Nations, validated the historical bond between the Jewish people and Eretz Yisrael and asserted the Jewish people's right to establish a national home. The main tenet of the Declaration of Independence was to set forth the connection between the Jewish people and the State of Israel, and to determine "the natural right of the Jewish people to be masters of their own fate, like all other nations, in their own sovereign state." But Israel is home to a significant minority of non-Jewish citizens, most of them possessing a different national identity—Arab. Defining the state as Jewish embodies real injury to this population.[26] How? One must distinguish between the private sphere and the community sphere.

The democratic nature of the state, certainly according to the broader interpretation, diminishes the damage inflicted on Arab individuals. The Universal Declaration of Human Rights is supposed to apply to all people, regardless of national or religious orientation. The Arab Israeli citizen, as an individual, is entitled to full equality of rights in the Jewish and democratic state, including protection of life, dignity, liberty, security, opinions, religion, creation, privacy, property, occupation, and more. In a Jewish and democratic state, discrimination based on race, religion, or nation must be prohibited.

Every person, however, in addition to being an individual, is a member of a community. Arab citizens, as members of a national minority, may feel alienated from the state because it is Jewish. The alienation has both symbolic and practical backgrounds. Symbolically, the state defines itself in a way that excludes them, adopting an anthem, a flag, and symbols that are Jewish. Practically, it attributes special importance to the values of Israel as a Jewish state, it legislates a Law of Return intended only for Jews, and so forth. And so the Jewish majority bears the Jewish and democratic obligation to preserve the rights of the national minority in the Jewish state. Alongside strictly maintaining equal rights and opportunities for Arab citizens, the law must protect the right of every member of a national minority to preserve and develop his or her culture, religion, language, and heritage, alone or with the other members of the minority group. Similar protection is awarded to minorities by the European Charter for Protection of National Minorities, which Israel must adopt. As per the Charter, collective rights should not be given to the minority groups themselves, but to the individuals who belong to them.[27]

The European version of minority rights would enable the Arab minority to protect its unique culture, religions, language, and heritage, and to actively advance and endow them for future generations. Furthermore, the state must give the Arabic language a recognized and special status, since it is the mother-tongue of approximately one-fifth of the population. The use of Arabic in national institutes must be set forth in law. The proposed balance recognizes the uniqueness of the Arab national community, ensures the conditions for its prosperity, but does not allow it to acquire political or geographical autonomy—to be a state within a state.

Culture

The cultural duality in the Jewish and democratic state does not require resolution. On the contrary: it is precisely the existence of the cultural other that promises great benefit for all sides. On the one hand, secular Jewish society in Israel is searching for its uniqueness in the face of the West's cultural imperialism and the global trend of uniformity. On the other hand, religious and ultra-Orthodox Jewish societies are in need of renewal in order to contend with previously unknown phenomena, such as Jewish sovereignty. These larger trends indicate the advantages embodied in developing and deepening the discourse between the two foundation cultures of Jewish society in Israel. Each of them must recognize that it cannot exist as a closed autarchic system, but must act as a partner in a dynamic intercultural framework, wherein it both shapes and is shaped by the other.

Ideological discourse between Jewish culture and democratic culture, with one acting as a critical model for the other, is the key to a successful merging of horizons between Jewish historical memory and the Israeli present in a way that will justify the characterization of Israel as a Jewish and democratic state.

SUMMARY

Israeli identity is an unsolved issue. Beneath which flag might Israelis gather together, however uncomfortably? As is evident from this chapter, even if we focus on the Jewish majority in Israel and ignore what cannot be ignored—the non-Jewish citizens—it is difficult to answer this question. It transpires that the commotion of disagreement that regularly rises from the pages of traditional Jewish writings, in regard to the array of spiritual, ideological, and legal questions in which Judaism has engaged for generations, still rages. The dispute has turned to face the central phenomenon of Judaism in the current era—the state. If the state is a womb within which (part of) Jewish identity is supposed to gestate, it is only natural to find that it contains various competing options, one grasping the heels of the next.

The large Jewish communities in Israel are profoundly affected by the legacies of Ben-Gurion, the Chazon Ish, and Rabbi Kook. The commonality of these three legacies is that they all treat the encounter between "Judaism" and the "state" in an intolerant and non-dialogical way. The reasons for this might be understood when we consider the meaning of the encounter. On the one hand, we have "Judaism." Although this is a definition of the entire collective, each of the three identity communities described here aims to appropriate it. Each imbibes the collective vessel with a different interpretive spirit and wishes to gather beneath it all Jewish people, not only those who belong to its own community. The other side of the encounter, the "state," also generates huge difficulties. The state is one political and territorial space shared by different identity communities. When the competing visions in Israel address the same exact space— the entire Israeli public sphere—they are impossible to reconcile. These circumstances diminish the chance for dialogue and severely challenge the aspiration to conduct the disagreement in a tolerant manner.

It is worth considering this fundamental problem in comparison to the multicultural approach. A basic condition for the success of multiculturalism is that the participating communities wish only to ensure that they exist and flourish. When this is their purpose, they can accept the neutrality of the common framework and the existence and flourishing of other identity communities alongside them. However, when the participating communities define their self-realization on the basis of an imperialist desire to enforce their identity on the entire public, multiculturalism cannot survive. Those who wish to read Israeli reality as a type of multicultural existence are failing to grasp the profound infrastructure of the dispute.

I have briefly raised courses of action that might alleviate the identity crisis. A condition for implementing these suggestions and others is that the various identity communities must avoid labeling the alternatives as illegitimate. The educational, political, social, and religious challenge is to understand that competing identities must not be viewed through reductive oversimplifications of absolute good against absolute evil. The members of each of the tribes that make up Jewish society in Israel, who seek refuge in the guise of exclusive concrete identities, must persist in their outlooks without being tempted to derive absolute claims regarding the illegitimacy of the competing identities.

NOTES

1   Anita Shapira, "Ben-Gurion and the Bible: The Forging of an Historical Narrative?" *Middle Eastern Studies* 33, no. 4 (October 1997). Avi Sagi, "On the Tensions Between Religious and Secular: From a Discourse of Rights to a Discourse of Identity" [Hebrew], in *A Good Eye: Dialogue and Polemic in Jewish Culture*, ed. Ilan Nahem (Tel Aviv: Hakibbutz Hameuchad, 1999), 408, 418–19; Michael Keren, *Ben-Gurion and the Intellectuals* [Hebrew] (Be'er-Sheva: Ben Gurion University, 1988), 103.

2   See Aviezer Ravitzky, "The Full Cart and the Empty Cart: The Secular Zionist in Orthodox Thought" [Hebrew], in *Freedom Inscribed: Diverse Voices of Jewish Religious Thought* (Tel Aviv: Am Oved, 1999), 222, 225–26.

3   For Ben-Gurion's state-based conception, see Nir Kedar, *Mamlachtiyut: David Ben-Gurion's Political-Civic Ideas* [Hebrew] (Ben-Gurion University Press and Yad Ben-Zvi, 2009). For the state-based considerations with regard to religion and the religious parties, see Ravitzky, "The Full Cart and the Empty Cart," 184–86. Zvi Zameret, "Jewish State—Yes; Clerical State—No; The Heads of Mapam and Their Approach to Religion and Religious People" [Hebrew], in *On Both Sides of the Bridge*, ed. Mordechai Bar-On and Zvi Zameret (Tel-Aviv: Yad Ben-Zvi, 2002), 175, 201–3.

4   See Menachem Friedman, *The Haredi Ultra-Orthodox Society: Sources, Trends and Processes* [Hebrew] (Jerusalem: Jerusalem Institute for Israel Studies, 1991), 53; Yair Tzaban, "Status Quo on Religious Issues," *New Jewish Time: Jewish Culture in a Secular Age*, vol. 4, ed. Yirmiyahu Yovel, Yair Tzaban, and David Shaham (Jerusalem:

Lamda—Association for Modern Jewish Culture and Spinoza Institute in Jerusalem, 2007), 434.

5   For the differences and disagreements between the two camps, see Benjamin Brown, "From Political Isolationism to Cultural Fortification" [Hebrew], in *On Both Sides of the Bridge* (Jerusalem: Yad Ben-Zvi, 2002), 367–413.

6   For a comprehensive discussion of religious Zionism's view of itself, see Avi Sagi, *A Challenge: Returning to Tradition* [Hebrew] (Ramat Gan, Israel: Shalom Hartman Institute, Bar-Ilan University Faculty of Law and Hakibbutz Hameuchad, 2003), chap. 7. For Kook's view, see, for example, Zvi Yaron, *The Philosophy of Rabbi Kook* [Hebrew] (Jerusalem: World Zionist Organization, 1974), 231–84. Rabbi Yosef Dov Soloveichik, one of the more prominent ideologues of religious Zionism in the twentieth century, thus believes that the religious aspect is immanent to Zionism and to the state. According to Dov Schwartz's analysis, Rabbi Soloveichik believed that God created the State of Israel in order to fulfill the inheritance of the land and the covenant He made with the forefathers and the People of Israel at Mount Sinai, to prevent assimilation, to implement halakhic categories in concrete reality, and more. See Dov Schwartz, "Rabbi Soloveichik's Doctrine as Viewed by Religious-Zionist Thought" [Hebrew], in *Faith in Changing Times: On the Doctrine of Rabbi Y.D. Soloveichick*, ed. Avi Sagi (Jerusalem: Elinar Library and Yaakov Herzog Center, 1996), 123, 132.

7   See "Eretz-Yisrael Takes Precedence Over the Commandments?" [Hebrew], in A. Sagi and Y. Z. Stern, *Barefooted Homeland: Israeli Reflections* (Tel-Aviv: Am Oved, 2011), 120. The common denominator between religious Zionists and ultra-Orthodox Jews is a religious perception of reality, but that reality's content is keenly disputed. From the perspective of religious Zionism, the ultra-Orthodox have abandoned their obligation to promote the redemptive process.

8   The data provided here are from a survey conducted by the Guttman Institute. See Shlomit Levi, Hanna Levinson, and Elihu Katz, *Beliefs, Observances and Social Interaction among Israeli Jews* [Hebrew] (Jerusalem: Louis Guttman Israel Institute of Applied Social Research, 1993). A later survey by the Guttman Institute reveals similar results: Shlomit Levi, Hanna Levinson, and Elihu Katz, *Israeli Jews, A Portrait: Faiths, Observances and Values of Jews in Israel* [Hebrew] (Jerusalem: Guttman Institute, 2002). In 2000, six percent of Jews in Israel defined themselves as ultra-Orthodox, nine percent as religious, thirty-four percent as traditional, and fifty-one percent as secular. See *Ha'aretz* Saturday supplement, October 6, 2000, 6. Data from a social survey conducted by the Central Bureau of Statistics in 2009 show that of the Jewish population in Israel, eight percent defined themselves as ultra-Orthodox, twelve percent as religious, thirteen percent as traditional-religious, twenty-five percent as not-so-religious traditional, and forty-two percent as secular (see press release, May 16, 2010). "Most of the public would like the state to ensure that life is conducted according to the religious Jewish tradition," according to Asher Arian, Nir Atmor, and Yael Hadar in *Auditing Israeli Democracy, 2007: Cohesion in a Divided Society* [Hebrew] (Jerusalem: Israel Democracy Institute, 2007), 82.

9   See Yair Sheleg, *The Jewish Renaissance in Israeli Society* (Jerusalem: Israel Democracy Institute, 2010). Quote from Bernard Susser and Charles S. Liebman, *Choosing Survival: Strategies for a Jewish Future* (New York: Oxford University Press, 1999), 101.

10   Baruch Kimmerling, "Religion, Nationality and Democracy in Israel" [Hebrew], *Zmanim* 50–51 (1994): 129.

11   On the belief in a civil war, see Uri Ram, "Between Arms and Economy: Liberal Post-Zionism in the GlobaLocal World" [Hebrew], in *Ethnocracy and Globalocalism: New Approaches to Study of Society and Space in Israel* (Be'er-Sheva: Negev Center for Regional Development, 1999). On poor relations between religious and non-religious people: Asher Arian, David Nachmias, Doron Nevot, and Daniel Shani, *Democracy in Israel: Followup Report 2003* [Hebrew] (Jerusalem: Israel Democracy Institute, 2003), 196.

12   Anita Shapira, *New Jews, Old Jews* [Hebrew] (Tel-Aviv: Am Oved, 1998), 237.

13   For a critical analysis of the religious, democratic and cultural significance of religious legislation, see Yedidia Z. Stern, "What Is Jewish in Israeli Law?" [Hebrew], in *The Jewishness of Israel*, ed. Aviezer Ravitzky and Yedidia Z. Stern (Jerusalem: Israel Democracy Institute, 2007), 13, 15–19.

14   "A decisive reinforcement of religious Zionist theology is found in the Six-Day War. The secular state fulfilled its mission: acting with no religious consciousness, it performed a religious act of liberating the historical-mythic homeland from foreign hands. The political Zionist act was interwoven with religious Zionist theology around the Land of Israel, and they became one, at least for a while" (Sagi and Stern, *Barefooted Homeland*, 122).

15   Report by the State Inquiry Committee on the Authorities' Treatment of Evacuated Settlers from Gush Katif and Northern Shomron (Jerusalem, 2010), 485.

16   Blurb on the back cover of Motti Karpel, *The Faith-Based Revolution: The Demise of Zionism and the Rise of the Faith Alternative* (Alon Shvut: Lechatchila Publishing, 2003).

17   For the democratic intent of the Declaration, see Uri Zilbersheid, "The Legal-Political Development of the Declaration of Independence: The Victory of the Bourgeois Democratic Concept" [Hebrew], *Democratic Culture* 12 (2010): 7. Knesset's assertion: Basic Law: Freedom of Occupation, Article 2, Book of Law 1994, 90; Basic Law: Human Dignity and Liberty, Article 1A, Book of Law 1992, 150. For postponement of conflict: Judith Karp, "Basic Law: Human Dignity and Liberty: A Biography of Power Struggles" [Hebrew], *Mishpat Umimshal* 1 (1993): 323.

18   There is a variety of literature on this topic. See, for example, "A Jewish and Democratic State: Six Perspectives," in *New Jewish Time: Jewish Culture in a Secular Age*, vol. 4, 499–520. Part of the rest of the discussion in this section appears in Stern, in "A Jewish and Democratic State," 515–19.

19   On theocracy: See Gershon Weiler, *Jewish Theocracy* (Boston: Brill Academic Publishers, 1988). Halakha state: See for example, Aviezer Ravitzky, *Is a Halakhic State Possible? The Paradox of Jewish Theocracy* [Hebrew] (Jerusalem: Israel Democracy Institute, 2004). The pluralistic, liberal state is the political vision advanced in Israel by the "Balad" movement, founded by former Knesset Member Dr. Azmi Bishara. See A.B. 11280/02 *Central Elections Committee for the Sixteenth Knesset vs. M.K. Tibi*, Court Ruling 57(4) 1.

20   For a more extensive discussion of this section's argument, see Yedidia Z. Stern, "Israeli Law and *Halakha* in Israeli Society," [Hebrew] *Bar-Ilan Law Studies* 19 (2002): 103.

21   See Hans-Georg Gadamer, *Truth and Method* (New York: Continuum, 1988), 273.

22   Compare, for example, the positions of Avraham B. Yehoshua in *Between Right and Right* (New York: Doubleday, 1981) and Motti Karpel in *The Faith-Based Revolution*.

23   Trust statistics: Asher Arian, Tamar Hermann, Yuval Lebel, Michael Philippov, Hila Zaban, and Anna Knafelman, *Auditing Israeli Democracy, 2010: Democratic Values in Practice* [Hebrew] (Jerusalem: Israel Democracy Institute, 2010), 110. For further discussion of the effects of the identity crisis, see Yedidia Z. Stern, "Let Your Curse Be on Me, My Son" [Hebrew], *Mishpat Umimshal* 12 (2010): 13.

24   Chaim H. Cohen, "Religious Coercion in Israel," in *Berenson Book*, vol. II [Hebrew], ed. Aharon Barak and Haim Berenson (Jerusalem: Nevo Publishing, 2000), 297–326. For recent political changes, see Chaim Oron, "Is Religious Coercion in Israel on the Rise?" [Hebrew], *Ha'aretz*, September 19, 2010.

25   For a discussion of this possibility, see Stern, "What Is Jewish in Israeli Law?," 13.

26   See for example Arian, Atmor, and Hadar, *Auditing Israeli Democracy, 2007* [Hebrew], 56–60.

27   Framework Convention for Protection of National Minorities, Council of Europe, 34 I.L.M. 351 (1995). Similar arrangements are offered by the draft constitution proposed by the Israel Democracy Institute in its "Constitution by Consensus." See, for example, Article 38: "Every person who belongs to a national-ethnic, religious, cultural or linguistic group has the right—alone or with the other members of the group—to preserve and develop his culture, religion, language and heritage."

2 What is Zionism?

GADI TAUB

Jews have dreamed of returning to their ancient homeland during the whole period of exile; but Zionism as a political movement is a new thing, which goes beyond the traditional yearning for Zion. Individuals and groups have always immigrated to the Land of Israel, but Zionism went beyond that too, in its demand for political institutionalization of Jewish life in that land. Antisemitism existed throughout the ages, but Zionism sought a state for reasons above and beyond the need for a physical sanctuary for Jews. Zionism is a modern phenomenon, and its novelty is part of modernity itself: the promise that all human beings, including the Jews, will be free and sovereign over their own fate.

This, indeed, is the cornerstone of Zionism: the right of Jews to be "masters of their own fate"—in David Ben-Gurion's famous words—without having to give up their Jewish identity. Though it is true that under the name "Zionism" there are many ideas and different shades of ideology, one can nonetheless articulate with some clarity the common framework for mainstream political Zionism. Theodor Herzl's and later David Ben-Gurion's concepts of Zionism sought to put an end to the dependence of Jews for their rights, their safety, often their very existence, on the goodwill of others. They sought to achieve this by applying the universal ethical principal of self-determination to the case of the Jews. The phrasing varied, but the content remained: it is "the natural right of the Jewish people," says Israel's Declaration of Independence, "to be masters of their own fate, like all other nations, in their own sovereign State."[1]

The aspiration for political self-determination led to the gathering of the Diaspora. There seemed to be no place else to gather it but in the Land of Israel. Because the Love of Zion (*hibat tziyon*), which was present all along, provided a powerful emotional force, it became the inevitable conclusion of the political logic of Zionism: only in the Land of Israel, early Zionists came to believe (based on their experience in Europe), would Jews be able to achieve political independence *as Jews*.

Just how inevitable this conclusion was, many (including Herzl himself) realized only gradually. But once this became clear, other ideas that the movement entertained—different territories, limited collective autonomy for Jews within other states—lost their appeal. Modern Zionism, the aspiration for liberation from dependence on others, met the age-old longing for the old homeland, and produced a social force so immense it was able to move millions, create a functioning society and economy, wage a war for independence, gain wide international legitimacy, and finally establish a democratic nation-state for Jews. But it all began with liberty.

To see how the desire for liberty led to the momentous enterprise of gathering the Diaspora in the land of Israel, we would need to distill the internal ideological logic of the movement from the plethora of its variations. Such a rendering misses much of the movement's diversity of thought and sentiment, but it can serve to clarify the ideas that were to become the movement's moral and political grounding. We may speak, then, of four links in an ideological chain, which we shall order not according to the sequence of their appearance in the work of any single Zionist thinker, but rather by the internal logic that led from one to the other:

- Individual liberty
- Democracy
- National identity
- The Land of Israel.

The connection between these, into which we will later look in more detail, can be sketched as follows:

a) First, the desire for equality and individual liberty is only secured when political sovereignty resides with those individuals.

b) A democratic form of government is where this sovereignty has its only stable grounding.

c) Democracy is never only a formal social contract. It is almost always a national creature, dependent on a sentiment that binds individuals into a collective and creates a sense of collective responsibility. The bitter experience of Emancipation in Europe demonstrated to Jews that within the existing nations of Europe they would remain an alien element in the eyes of gentiles. Emancipation therefore presented Jews with an impossible dilemma: either they could take part in the march of democratic progress at the price of giving up their Jewish identity and fully assimilating, or else they could preserve their identity at the price of exclusion from the march of progress. The Zionist solution to this dilemma stemmed from this connection between national identity and democracy. Zionism applied this logic to "the Jewish question" in a new and modern way: Jews will be able to become sovereign over their own fate without giving up their Jewish identity, if they perceive their own identity in national terms and create their own democratic nation-state.

d) For this, a territory would be needed. Many such territories were suggested and then dismissed. It turned out that the Land of Israel alone could serve as home for a Jewish nation-state. Any other territory would not do because the Jews in their multitudes would not immigrate there. This was never only a practical consideration. There are deeper reasons for it. The Land of Israel is such a foundational element in Jewish identity that a Jewish state would not make sense to Jews without it, for the same reasons that a British nation-state would not make sense outside Britain. Englishmen and women who seek political independence elsewhere eventually stop seeing themselves as English and become American, or Australian, or Canadian. Jewish national (as opposed to religious) identity is bound with a territory, as is the case with most other nations.

Since political Zionism begins with liberty, the democratic form of government was, in fact, a given from the movement's very inception. After all, Jews will not be free—sovereign over their own fate—if they are subjects of a Jewish monarchy, dictatorship, or theocracy. They would be free only as enfranchised citizens. For Zionism, the "democratic" and the "Jewish"—the two components that define Israel's character as a state—were far from presenting a contradiction in terms, as some argue today. Rather, the Jewish character of the state and its democratic form of government were, according to Zionism, two faces of the same coin: a democratic state where the decisive majority of the citizenry are Jewish would be Jewish since, when free, citizens shape their public sphere according to their culture and tradition. Hebrew would be the state's (first) official language, Jewish holidays would be the official calendar, the Sabbath would be the day of rest, and the national culture would be based on the Jewish heritage. For Zionism, Judaism would be Israel's national identity, not the state's religion.[2] Israel would, therefore, be Jewish in the sense that Poland is Polish, not in the sense that Poland is Catholic. As long as Israel has a Jewish majority, the only way to make it non-Jewish, in the Zionist sense, is by disenfranchising its citizens. Abolishing the Jewish nature of the state would depend, then, on abolishing democracy.

This does not mean that the idea of a democratic Jewish nation-state is free from problems and internal tensions, but the Jewish national character of the state does not stand in opposition to the democratic logic of the Zionist movement; it stems from it. Since this logic is not exclusive to the case of the Jewish nation-state, but is rather the norm on which most democracies are based, it may be useful to look first at the general ideological context in which such national democracies emerged.

LIBERTY, DEMOCRACY AND NATIONAL IDENTITY

We identify the term "modernity" with many things. The scientific revolution, the age of Enlightenment, rationalism, the American and French revolutions, the Industrial Revolution, secularism, urbanization, the replacement of "organic" with "mass" society, and much else. But at the heart of modernity lies an idea that emerged from the cluster of innovations we identify with the term "Enlightenment": the idea of human sovereignty over human fate.[3] This is not a simple idea, nor is it free of problems even in theory (let alone in practice).

One of its first difficulties has to do with subject of sovereignty: who is this human subject that is entitled to rule over its own fate? Is it the individual who is the bearer of sovereignty, or is it a human collective that should assume it? On the face of it, one must choose: if it is the individual, would this not make the very existence of society illegitimate (as Ralph Waldo Emerson, and later Friedrich Nietzsche implied)? And if the collective is sovereign, would this not mean that the liberty and sovereignty of individuals would be voided (as Hobbes thought inevitable)?

But between these two poles—the individual and the collective—there is also a relation of mutual dependence, and it is from this dependence that most progressive ideologies would emerge: society's authority not only limits personal autonomy, it also enables it. True, in a social context no individual can be free to do whatever he or she chooses without limits. However, it is also true that individual liberty collapses without society, and for two different sets of reasons: first, because, without social organization, human beings have no control over the public dimension of their lives; and second, as seventeenth and eighteenth-century political thinkers have already pointed out, because without political authority to keep public order, the safety and liberty of each will be constantly threatened by all.

This, indeed, was the assumption behind early social contract theories: government is necessary in order to protect each person against all others. Gradually, this idea was extended from security to liberty. Government is not just responsible for safeguarding the life and property of citizens; it is also entrusted with protecting their freedom.[4] This is the origin of modern liberalism, but not necessarily of modern democracy: it centers around individual rights, which are the very reason for the creation of government and the only valid justification for its existence, but it does not invest the citizenry with effective political sovereignty. Enlightened despotism is, in principle, legitimate on this view.

From there to full-fledged democracy, the distance turned out to be theoretically small. As early as John Locke's liberalism we find something akin to the right to dismiss the government, though not by means of any orderly political procedure. If, as Locke believes, government's legitimacy depends on its protection of "natural rights," then, if it fails to protect them, citizens are justified in rebelling against it. This relies on the idea of natural rights itself: those are rights humans have based on their very nature, which means they precede society—historically, morally, and logically. This is why society has no right to void them; if it does, it defies the social contract itself and citizens too are no longer bound by it.

It was only one further step from the idea that the public can dismiss a government to the idea that it is also entitled to appoint it. This revolutionized the very conception of government for early modern thinkers. Under the new conception, it was no longer supposed that governments were to rule over their subjects, but rather they were to execute the will of their citizens. It is not their master but their servant. The democratic social contract is in this way not just a limit on individual liberty, but also a way to enhance it. Without society, the individual is helpless to protect himself or herself and, devoid of organized social power, unable to develop many aspects of his or her life. Whether it is a need for a bridge or a school, a law, a trade agreement, or a war, the democratic form of government enables individuals to do more than just protect themselves: it is able to extend their control over life to the public sphere, which determines so much in their private lives. Democratic sovereignty is thus not a negation of individual sovereignty, it is a sum, or an aggregation, of the individual sovereignties of all, based on an effective procedure of subordinating government to the will of citizens.

All this presupposes a complex conception of the relations between public and private life. It assumes interdependence between the two, as well as a separation of the realms (a question that, as we shall see, turned out to be crucial in the bitter experience of Jews in Europe). Individual life is embedded in a public sphere, but there are also aspects that remain private. In the private sphere, the individual alone is sovereign, and his or her decisions require no one else's consent. In the public sphere any decision requires the joint consent of the public.[5] In both spheres, the same principle applies: those affected by a decision are the ones entitled to take it. We call this "government with the consent of the governed."

Of course the consent of all to decisions that affect all is an ideal that can only be approximated. Large groups are unlikely to reach unanimous decisions. But the way to approximate the ideal is by taking such decisions as would satisfy more people than they would frustrate. This is the basis for the majoritarian principle: it is the way to approximate the theoretical "will of all" as much as possible.

Such a description of the democratic form of government is formal and schematic, and misses a great deal. Though it seems coherent and rigorous, it was not at all clear, on the eve of the great democratic revolutions, that it is workable in modern states.[6] Though investing the masses with the power to elect their government would be a realization of those noble principles, it was not clear to eighteenth-century thinkers that the masses would be able to use this power responsibly. What will make ordinary citizens, simple peasants or artisans, use their power in light of the common good, as opposed to their petty egotistic interests? For example, how can we guarantee that able-bodied men, eligible for draft, would decide about wars according to the public interest, rather than their own fear of being drafted or killed in battle? How would the multitudes be taught to overcome their private sentiments and use their reason to discern the common good?

When the great democratic revolutions erupted in America and France, it turned out that such worries were in vain, and that the very terms used to express them missed the point. The public interest, it turned out, was actually dear to the hearts, not just the minds, of individuals, and not because they were educated to prefer reason to passion, nor because they were brought to see that private interest depended on the public good (which, indeed, is not always the case), but rather because emotional bonds tie the individual to the collective. A national sentiment, patriotism, binds individuals together, and it this sentiment, rather than some pure reason, that makes them care about the fate of the community. It is also this sentiment that enables the formal democratic scheme to function. It turned out, for example, that many able-bodied men would support a draft, even volunteer to sacrifice their own lives, for what they saw as the common good.

A democratic society is thus much more than a legal social contract. It is based on identification with the common. As in the French Revolution's rallying cry, the third pillar that supported the republic, along with "liberty" and "equality," was "fraternity"—solidarity. Patriotism was the foundation of modern democracy from the very beginning, and democracy, from its inception, was a national creature.

JEWS AND THE IDEA OF HUMAN SOVEREIGNTY OVER HUMAN FATE

The question of how Jews would be integrated into the new political order that promised new liberties ran parallel to (though slightly behind) the development of liberal and democratic thought. In its first versions, the *haskala*—the Jewish Enlightenment—saw the question of liberty in terms that fitted the formal conception of republicanism, that conception which still did not see a connection between liberty, democracy, and national identity. It rested on a universal idea of citizenship, and understood the political realm in terms of a pure formal social contract. Jewish thinkers such as Judah Leib Gordon and Moses Mendelssohn, typical representatives of the *haskala*, believed that the question of identity could be limited to the private sphere, whereas in the public sphere Jews would be citizens like all others. Be a human being in public, and a Jew at home, Gordon taught.[7]

When it turned out that in reality democracy and liberalism were not pure contractual creatures, that they depend on a national identity, it also became clear that Gordon's formula was unworkable. Worse, it was damaging to Jews. If democracy depended on national identity, and Jews wished to take part in it based on an abstract universal conception of citizenship, outside the identity of the nation, this would mean that they were a cosmopolitan, transnational element. As such, they were automatically suspected of undermining the cohesion of the social body. They were, then, inherently subversive. This idea of the Jews as a cosmopolitan subversive element would become central to the modern antisemitic mind. The forged *Protocols of the Elders of Zion* captures this trope clearly: Jews are members of no nation, yet they reside in them all. Loyal not to their country, but to each other, they form a transnational conspiracy designed to subjugate all nations.

The more the force of modern nationalism became manifest, the more urgent it became to abandon the formulas of Gordon and other *haskala* thinkers, and replace them with formulas that take nationalism into account. Jews would no longer be Jews in the private sphere and just human beings outside it. They would be Jewish privately, and share the national identity of gentiles in the public sphere. A Jew could then be a German of the Moses faith, an English man or woman of the Moses faith, a French man or woman of the Moses faith, and so on.

Countless Jews in Europe made relentless efforts to prove their patriotism in their countries of residence, and endeavored to show that their Jewish identity did not stand in opposition to their national one. They were deeply wounded when their declarations of loyalty crashed against a solid wall of disbelief. Their enemies, and often their friends too, still saw them as an alien element. Early Zionists repeatedly poured their wrath on their brethren, wallowing in vain at the feet of gentiles who would not accept their gift of love. So much blood, sweat, and tears, so much humiliation, was undertaken to prove Jewish loyalty to European nations, and Jews were still shunned and avoided. Reading Leon Pinsker's *Auto-Emancipation* (1882),[8] one is still struck by the pain of this proud man, a physician and decorated soldier of the Russian army, former advocate of Jewish assimilation, when he realized that no measure of devotion would ever be enough. Haim Nahman Bialik's chilling poems about the pogroms poured the poet's terrible wrath against his fellow Jews for their humility, their complete surrender, their lack of self-respect. He scorned their futile efforts to find favor with peoples who despised them, and would only repay them with rape and death.

Antisemitism is, indeed, the first thing that comes to mind when we consider what prevented Jews from taking part in the new social order of emerging modern nation-states. No doubt, antisemitism played a decisive role in this drama, and the fathers of political Zionism all emphasize it in the formation of their Zionist beliefs. But the other side of the story is no less important. It was not only external pressure, but also a powerful internal need, of which Jews were active agents rather than passive targets, that gave birth to Zionism. Zionism, we need to remember, emerged in a century that was relatively comfortable for Jews, an era when persecutions waned, and it was inaugurated in Western Europe, where Jewish life was more peaceful. In short, it was born when Jews had unprecedented opportunities of assimilation. There is a deep reason for this: the new opportunities also created a new problem, one that was born of the rights they enjoyed, not just the rights they were denied, from the opening of new doors, not from doors slammed in their faces.

If we want to understand the force of the Zionist movement, it will not do to look only at old and renewed persecution. We also have to probe a new and burning desire, an explicitly modern aspiration. Zionism aimed at more than securing existence. It aimed for a specific kind of existence: a modern life of independent, free people, who respected themselves in new ways. Jews sought to become free as Jews. The scorn early Zionists heaped on assimilating Jews had much to do with the obvious contradiction of attempting to gain self-respect only after giving up your own identity. How can one walk upright on the condition that one bend backwards to become what others expect one to be, after one is asked to scorn one's own identity? The assimilating Jew, early Zionists thought, might gain liberty only after giving up selfhood, and so, if the aspiration to self-sovereignty had to pass through its degrading opposite, did it not lose its very meaning in the process?

To understand the full weight of this aspiration to liberty, we must, therefore, remember the case of Theodor Herzl, who did not suffer from antisemitism, in addition to the case of Alfred Dreyfus, who was shunned by the nation of which he tried so hard to become a part. The problem that Jews like Herzl faced stemmed from the fact that the offer of full equality was accompanied by a latent demand that the Jews would "improve." That "improvement" would only be complete after Jews shed practically everything Jewish. Even in the eyes of those who meant well, assimilation into a nation meant that Jewish identity would give way to the national identities of gentiles, and finally all but disappear. Herzl understood that Emancipation in Europe failed not only when Europe refused to grant Jews their rights, but also when it kept its promise and granted them. The reason was that the separation between citizenship and identity in the first version (that of the Enlightenment), and between private identity and national public identity in the second version (that of the era of Emancipation) is artificial. In reality, in order to be fully German, Jews would have to give up their Judaism in their private sphere too.

As Shlomo Avineri has shown in the introduction to his *The Making of Modern Zionism*,[9] this was no theoretical dilemma, and was not limited to thinkers who understood the complexity of identity and politics. A Jewish boy who went to a German school, for example, felt it just as acutely. That boy could not keep the Sabbath, since the day of rest in German schools was Sunday; he could not eat with the rest of the students, because the food in school was not kosher. Even if he was not an observant Jew, he could not escape the predicament, because education does not provide one only with knowledge, or skills; it forms one's identity. And it does so by way of teaching a historical narrative. In a German school, one would be taught that one's forefathers were barbarian tribes who invaded the Roman Empire, and if that Jewish boy adopts the story as his own, he would need to give up the story of the Exodus of Egypt, which is the story of his own ancestors. Fully taking the national identity of another people, then, would mean forsaking the common tradition of Jews, the basis of Jewish identity, because Jewish identity can never be fully private and the national identity of the Germans, the French, or the English can never be only public.

All this lays bare the heart of a dilemma that modernity imposed on Europe's Jews: individual sovereignty over individual life and collective sovereignty over collective life turned out to be irreconcilable for them. A Jew would not be able to become fully free—a master of his or her own fate—in the context of European nation-states, except if he or she relinquished Jewish identity altogether.

The solution to the Jewish dilemma, the way to prevent the private and public spheres from clashing, seemed to lie in the creation of a Jewish public sphere. Such a public sphere would let Jews be themselves outside the private sphere as well as within it. Or, to borrow a metaphor from the later gay liberation movement, Jews would no longer need to be closeted Jews. If the problem was the rise of national identities in the political sphere, a national identity for Jews seemed to be the solution. Nationalism transformed both the Jewish question and the answer to it. Instead of separating Judaism from national identity, Zionism proposed to understand Jewish identity itself as a national identity. "The Jewish question," Herzl wrote in his *The Jewish State*, ". . . is a national question." Modern Jewish identity should therefore be no different than German, English, or French identity (not in opposition to religious identity, but separate from or supplemental to it[10]).

The consequences of this view were, for Zionists, explicitly political: national identity in the modern sense is at bottom, they believed, an aspiration to political independence. Only a Jewish nation-state, in their view, would enable Jews to reconcile the private and public dimensions of their existence. Only in their own nation-state would they be able to be masters of their own fate individually as well as collectively. This was not a surprising conclusion. After all, it was the same one that the pioneers of modern democracies reached: a national sentiment and a republican form of government were mutually dependent.

Zionism, however, was not the only plan for the realization of Jewish national identity. There were territorialists and autonomists as well. The autonomists (such as Shimon Dubnove or the Bund) believed that a limited autonomy with partial political authority within existing nation-states would suffice. Territorialists believed, as Zionists did, that nothing short of full political independence would do. But unlike Zionists, they did not think the Jewish state must necessarily be in the Land of Israel. A plethora of other locations rose and then fell: Birobidjan, Crimea, Madagascar, Argentina and scores—no less—of other places were suggested. Herzl himself is wrongly remembered as succumbing to the territorialist view with what was called the Uganda Plan. However, Herzl, who promoted that plan toward the end of his life in the Sixth Zionist Congress, never thought of it as more than an intermediary stage on the way to a permanent national home in the land of Israel. Convinced— prophetically, as it turned out—that Jews faced mass massacre in Europe, he sought to get them out of there, even if only to a temporary refuge. In fact, Herzl flirted with territorialism at the outset, not at the end, of his political career. In *The Jewish State*, he wrote that he was still willing to accept Argentina as a viable alternative (as did Leon Pinsker in *Auto-Emancipation*) if the Land of Israel turned out to be a political impossibility. As he grew acquainted with the actual aspirations of actual

Jews, Herzl came to realize that nothing short of the Promised Land itself would do.

The internal logic of the Zionist movement finally led to the rejection of territorialism as well as autonomism. *Hibat tziyon* (which originally moved so many to join Herzl's movement) reasserted itself and imposed its sentiments on Zionism at large. To tell the story of the Exodus of Egypt, to preserve the Jewish narrative, was, after all, to remember not only where one came from, but also where one was going. It was the Promised Land for which Jews undertook that mythic forty-year journey through the desert. The Land of Israel was so thoroughly woven into Jewish identity—in Jewish prayers, in Jewish history, in Jewish symbols and collective memory—that without it the very narrative that preserves their identity would be, it seemed, lost. If narratives—the stories that peoples tell themselves to explain to themselves who they are—are the foundations of identity, then there seemed to be no Jewish narrative without the Land of Israel. If national identity is normally tied to a homeland, there was no other land the Jews could see as home. Jews can live in many places. A Jewish nation-state can only exist in the Land of Israel, as English identity—the colonial experience in the New World seems to confirm this maxim—can only endure in England.

For the religious, there is more beyond the historical ties of people to land. For them the bond is first and foremost based on a divine promise. Ever since God promised the land to Abraham and his descendants, the land belonged to the Jewish people, by virtue of a supernatural force, outside history, beyond the ability of human deeds to influence. Political Zionism did not share this view. This is not to say that it renounced the bond, or even that it gave up the Bible as its testimony. Ben-Gurion too saw the Bible as proof of the bond between people and land. However, for him it was a historical, rather than metaphysical proof. It was a question of human deeds and earthly human history, and herein, he believed lay its force. When he wrote Israel's Declaration of Independence he called the right of Jews to the land "the historic right," and by this he sought to establish a stronger, not a weaker, argument for the ties that bound the Jews to the historical Land of Israel. History was an anchor that all should accept—both the religious and the atheistic (he himself was an atheist through and through). Jews and non-Jews alike would see this histor-ical logic, since it was universal. Other peoples too are bound to their lands by history. The English do not need God to explain why they have a right to England, nor do the French, the Germans, the Turks, the Italians, or the Chinese. The peoples of the world might question the validity of the Jewish belief in a divine promise, but they will not deny that history establishes rights, for it is history in which they base their own. To a great extent Ben-Gurion was proven right. The Balfur Declaration, the Mandate Charter, and finally the United Nations Partition Resolution of 1947, all accepted this logic. This is also how Israel's Declaration of Inde-pendence opens:

> The Land of Israel was the birthplace of the Jewish people. Here their spiritual, religious, and political identity was shaped. Here they first attained to statehood, created cultural values of national and universal significance and gave to the world the eternal Book of Books.
>
> After being forcibly exiled from their land, the people kept faith with it throughout their Dispersion and never ceased to pray and hope for their return to it and for the restoration in it of their political freedom.
>
> Impelled by this historic and traditional attachment, Jews strove in every successive generation to re-establish themselves in their ancient homeland.

The political logic of the Declaration derives this specific right of Jews for a homeland in the land of Israel (which it calls "the historic right") from a universal right of all peoples to self-determination (which the Declaration calls "the natural right"). The universal right, then, precedes the historic right logically, morally, and chronologically. The historic right, which ties Jews to their homeland, is in this sense the specific fulfillment for Jews of a universally just demand: the right of all peoples to inde-pendence in their own homeland. Both rights were acknowledged by the international community in the United Nations Partition Resolution of

November 29, 1947. Thus the declaration sums up the justifications for the right of Jews to a state of their own in the Land of Israel as follows:

> We, members of the People's Council, representatives of the Jewish Community of Eretz-Israel [the Land of Israel] and of the Zionist Movement, are here assembled on the day of the termination of the British Mandate over Eretz-Israel and, *by virtue of our natural and historic right and on the strength of the resolution of the United Nations General Assembly,* hereby declare the establishment of a Jewish state in Eretz-Israel, to be known as the State of Israel. [Emphasis added]

If Zionism aimed to make Jews masters of their own fate as Jews—that is without giving up their Jewish identity—we may conclude that the natural right means "masters of their own fate" and the historic right means that they would be able to realize this as Jews; that is, without giving up the foundations of identity that tie them to their homeland. The fact that Zionism is akin to so many other national liberation movements in these aspirations is itself central to the Declaration's argument, and Zionism in general. Zionism, from Herzl on, indeed aimed exactly at this: normalizing Jewish existence so that Jews may live like "all other nations."

REVOLUTION AND CONTINUITY: PAST AND FUTURE IN ZIONIST IDEOLOGY

Zionism, then, offered a way to preserve continuity in Jewish existence under modern conditions. The rise of a national political order threatened to turn the Jews from one people into "seventy nations" if Jews remained in the Diaspora, because, under modern conditions, and the rise of a new national political order, modernization ultimately seemed to mean complete assimilation. Zionism's promise offered a way for Jews to become modern not only without giving up their private Jewish identity, but also without giving up the future of Jews as a people. It had, therefore, a strong claim to continuity.

But the Zionist vision of continuity demanded a thorough revolution in Jewish life, personal as well as public and political. The revolutionary element indeed stands out over the claim to continuity, because the revolution had to do not only with the Jewishness of human individuals but also with the humanity of individual Jews. It demanded the renouncing of a passive, fatalistic, otherworldly orientation and the complete dependence on others; in its stead, Zionism called for an adoption of a modern conception of humans as masters of their own fate. The two are not the same: to break the bonds of dependence does not, in itself, guarantee true independence. Jewish tradition has taught us this lesson vividly: forty years separated the exodus from slavery in Egypt from actual political independence. A whole generation of slaves had to die before a slavish mentality could be banished. Zionism was not quite that harsh, but the transition it urged was no less monumental, and demanded a tremendous feat from its adherents: Jews were to tear themselves from a whole fabric of life, and weave a new one for themselves. They were to leave their homes and families, the countries and climates and cultures in which they were born and bred, and the languages that they spoke as mother tongues; they were to shed habits of body and mind, and grow roots in new soil where they would become economically self-sufficient and politically independent, and where they would create a new culture in a new-old language. Only by re-creating themselves could they turn themselves from passive objects to active agents of their own history. To become masters of their own fate was not only the end of the movement, it was also its indispensible means. The fundamental assumption was that one could turn one's self from a passive to an active being by virtue—and only by virtue—of one's own powers.

Individuals can take control of their own lives in this way, but for a people to become a master of its own fate, it must reshape itself into an effective historical agent, which in the modern world means a nation. Herein lies the importance of substituting the old term "people" (am, in Hebrew) with the new term "nation" (leom). The term "nation" designates the modern political dimension of peoplehood, and it requires a functioning economy and a live common culture, which could then form a society, to be politically institutionalized in a state. Contrary to European right-wing conceptions of the nation as an organic whole, the nation as an effective historical agent need not be a mystical entity that exists above or apart from the wills of the individuals comprising it. What creates an active nation in the mainstream Zionist view is active individuals. As in democracy, where the common sovereignty is the sum total of individual sovereignties, not the negation of individual sovereignty, so the national subject is the sum total of individual subjects who create it by their own active engagement. This is why the ideal of pioneering was so central to the Zionist movement, and also why it is so deeply tied to the democratic worldview: active individuals orient their action for the public good—indeed for the very creation of the public—and so create the active nation through their own agency. It is no coincidence that Zionism finally coalesced around the desire for a democratic state, which is an embodiment of the active conception of human life, private and public.

We should, however, keep in mind that Jewish nationhood was, in the days of early Zionism, a vision of a possible future, not a political fact; a plan, not a reality. Although the term "The Jewish People" in the old religious sense was heterogeneous enough, its diversity and plurality become all the more crucial when one seeks to remake it along modern national lines. Because the very things that tie individuals and groups into a nation—and above all a common territory and a common language—did not exist. Or more precisely, they were, to use Jacob Katz's apt term, dormant: the common language existed in holy books, but was not used for everyday life, and the territory existed as an object of yearning rather than a physical home. The national Jewish identity was therefore more potential than actuality.

It is one thing to demand of both Jews and non-Jews to conceive of the Jews of Galicia, Egypt, Argentina, Morocco, Russia and Germany (and many other places) as one nation. It is quite another to realize this conception in a functioning national society, to take the belief in a common past and the desire for a common future and wedge between them the material body that was to bear these conceptions. "Nation" was not just a new name for something old. It was a deliberate creation of a new thing out of the old. It was an identity that needed to be imagined before it could become an actual political fact.[11]

The idea that intentional action can give birth to a new historical subject, to create the nation that would then become master of its own fate, was extremely radical, since it implied not only a rebellion against the condition of exile, but also what seemed like a defiance of the laws of history itself, or what was generally perceived at the time to be history's laws. What seemed to Herzl's contemporaries to be the "natural" order of things, in the passage to modernity, was a process that began with territory, in which a national society was formed, and then created a state; only later would the nation awake from its presumed slumbers and break the shackles of tyranny to take its fate in its own hands (whether suddenly, by revolution, or gradually, by reform) to come into its own in a modern republic. The pioneers of Zionism dared to think that the process could be turned on its head: first Jews would decide they were a nation, then they would create a democratic government virtually hovering in the air without a territory or a state (such indeed was the World Zionist Organization) then this stateless government, comprised of elected representatives, would secure a territory and bring Jews from all over the world into it, in order to create a functional national democratic society, which only at the end of the process would create an independent state. The plan was unprecedented, and Herzl's novel *Altneuland*[12]—with its dictum "if you will it, it is no fantasy"—must have seemed no less unrealistic than other science fiction utopias of the day.

Gathering the Jews into one territory seemed utopian enough in Herzl's time. However, though necessary, it was far from being a sufficient condition. The real challenge would then be turning the immigrants, if they came, into a functioning national society. And such a society could only become a reality if the dream of a common national identity was realized—hence the centrality of the melting pot ideal to the Zionist enterprise.

Today the very term "melting pot" has become synonymous with oppression and discrimination, with the forced imposition of uniformity on plurality. Many now consider it one of the original sins of the Zionist movement. The truth is that without a melting pot Zionism would have made no sense. The whole enterprise depended upon the creation of a new national identity, a sense of "we," without which republics cannot function.

This is not to say, however, that the implementation of the melting pot policy did not have grave faults. A melting pot can be the imposition of one group's identity on all others, and it can be a plurality that converges into unity, a creation of a common fabric out of the many different cultural threads. There is a great difference between the two and the question of who gets to have a say in the creation of the common identity is by no means a minor one. Part of what the founding groups laid down as foundational to the pre-state society (the *Yishuv*), and later to the state, was accepted by most others who came along later. Though some of the traits of the new society were of explicit European origin, they can be described as essential to the Zionist vision: democracy, a European-style national identity, and legal equality between men and women (in terms of gender equality, Zionism was indeed a pronounced progressive force: the Zionist congress gave the vote to women before all other European parliaments). All these were imposed by the founding groups, and were not seriously contested by later newcomers.[13] Other aspects of the ethos of the founders were later rejected. The founders' socialism, for example, lost its dominance after two decades of statehood, and was later marginalized. It is nevertheless a fact that Labor Zionism—mostly comprised of eastern European Jews—established the social framework of the future society, its modern economic structure, and also the basis of its cultural identity. It was indeed an unarticulated presupposition of the enterprise that later immigrants would have to fit a mold already shaped for them. For many later immigration waves, and most poignantly for immigrants from Arab countries, this added insult to the injury of immigration, which itself should not be underestimated. Any immigration is a tremendous feat. If it is also a transition from a traditional agrarian society to a modern industrial one, the difficulties are enormously compounded. However, condescension, discrimination, and cultural arrogance were now piled on top of those difficulties, when many among the founders' groups looked down on Middle Eastern Jews as "natives" requiring thorough "civilizing." All this left deep scars.

Those who felt marginalized or trampled over by the melting pot policy mostly rejected parts of its specific content (and the condescension that came along with them), not the idea of creating a common national identity itself. This was most clearly manifest in the stormy election campaign of 1977 that ended up ousting the Labor government and replacing it with the right-wing Likud. The massive vote of the *mizrahim*, Jews of Middle Eastern origin, for the Likud was a result of a strong sense of marginalization and discrimination by the Labor establishment, but it was nevertheless a vote for a clearly national, even nationalistic, party. The voters did not seek to protect their specific identity from the melting pot, or seclude themselves from the hegemonic center. Rather they demanded to be a part of its formation, to reform the melting pot so as to create a common identity that would include the ingredients of Middle Eastern Jewish culture, and recognize the cultural contribution of the *mizrahim*. It was a demand for an equal share in the project of nation building, not a protection from it.

There was, then, a wide agreement on the need to create a new common identity. The basic Zionist sentiment, the desire to remake Jews into masters of their own fate, and the dependence of this project on a common national identity led the vast majority of immigrants—from both West and East—to the realization that the project could not succeed if it tried to preserve intact the identities of their countries of origin. One can speak of diversity and multiculturalism as positive ideals only after the common ground is secure, after a sense of "we" has become a living experience. Diversity can enliven the common ground, but in the absence of the common, it threatens the possibility of solidarity and shared purpose. In truth, multiculturalism was, at first, Zionism's problem, not the solution for social ills. What separated Jews who came from so many countries was far more pronounced than what they shared: there was no common culture, no common language, no common family structure, and no common mores. One cannot create a society when, for example, half the population are accustomed to the idea that wives are their husbands' property while the other half espouses gender equality.[14] One cannot create a functioning society if some of its parts would speak Yiddish, and others Ladino, Polish, Spanish, or various dialects of Arabic. This is surely true even under the most favorable conditions, but the extreme conditions that Zionism had to operate under—war, mass immigration, economic crisis—made it abundantly clear: only by creating a strong sense of solidarity, a genuine feeling that there is such a thing as "we," could the *Yishuv* undertake the formidable tasks it faced on the way to statehood. This sense of "we" with all its problems drew on a strong desire of the vast majority for a new common identity, on which a new future for Jews could be established. Contrary to some claims currently in vogue, the common identity was not simply imposed from above. If it were, the surge of voluntary energy needed to sustain the common effort would never have emerged. Without some form of "hegemonic narrative" to which the majority subscribed, it would probably not have been possible to achieve the immense feat that brought the Jewish national liberation movement its success in the form of political independence.

In immigrant societies, unlike other national societies, a common narrative is not a given. It has to be created consciously and deliberately. In most national societies—democratic and undemocratic alike—the sense of "we" flows (or subjectively seems to flow) from the experience of a common past. It seems to be a "natural" result of a succession of generations (real or imagined). In an immigrant society such a succession does not exist and there is no (immediate) common past. We may, then, attempt to define the difference like this: in most national societies, the sense of "we" stems from an *experience* of a *common past*. In immigrant societies, the sense of "we" depends on a *plan* for a *common future*. "We" in such societies is projected on the future, rather than flowing from the past. As the case of Zionism shows, such a projection on the future can draw much from a common past, real or mythical. It can blend such past elements in its forming identity and claim continuity with them. Still the common identity does not flow, nor does it seem to flow, "naturally" from the past. Zionism is thus strongly oriented toward the future: the new identity is a conscious decision to subscribe to a common plan for the future. The moral and political outlines of this plan are sketched in Israel's Declaration of Independence (as those of the United States are sketched in its Declaration of Independence). But there is much more that a new society would need to fill in, as the plan takes shape in reality.

What about those who do not subscribe to the plan for that common future? There are, after all, many in the Jewish state—both Jews and non-Jews—who are not Zionists.

Zionism saw itself as a voluntary movement. One is not born a Zionist, nor can one be forced to become a Zionist. Zionism is a conscious choice. Herzl suggested to many rabbis, including those who believed Judaism was a faith, not a national identity, that they join the movement. But he respected the choice of those who did not want to take part. Self-determination is at the sole discretion of each self. A movement that inscribed self-determination as its moral base could not impose its conception of Judaism on those who did not share it. Israel walked in Herzl's footsteps in this regard. It does not force its non-Zionist ultra-orthodox Jewish citizens to partake in the newly created identity, and allows them the latitude of cultural and educational autonomy. Israel's Arab citizens, a large national minority, also never wished to take part in the creation of a common identity, nor to assimilate into that of the Jewish majority. This is why all suggestions that seek to create a common national identity inclusive of the minority completely miss the point. The problem is how to protect the minority from the majority culture, not how to assimilate them into it. The real question is, then, how to preserve the separate identity without compromising equality, civil rights and social benefits. The Jewish nation-state did not demand such assimilation, of course, and sought (in its legal framework, though sadly not always in its shifting policies) to secure equal rights without it.

Such a solution is short of perfect, as it is so in all cases where nation-states have national minorities (and most of them do). For Israel these problems are compounded by the fact that the minority is a native one, and that its relations with the majority must be managed under the extreme stress of the conflict between Israel and the Arab world in general, and the Palestinian national movement, of which the minority is a part, in particular. We may assume that once Palestinians achieve a nation-state of their own, these tensions will be greatly eased. Still the problem of national and religious minorities is not an easy one for Zionism. After all, Zionism itself emerged from the realization that a Jewish minority would not be able to achieve full liberty, full self-determination, within European nations. Was Zionism not, then, reproducing for Arabs the same predicament that it tried to alleviate for Jews? Were not Arabs in Israel doomed to suffer a re-enactment of the failure of Emancipation in Europe?

The solution, the founders of Israel envisaged, came from the same experience that gave rise to the question in the first place: the experience of the failure of Emancipation. The Emancipation in Europe offered Jews as individuals, it was said, everything, and the Jews as a collective nothing (this view was already apparent in the national assembly of revolutionary France, in 1791). From their own bitter experience, Jews learned that the denial of the public dimension of their identity amounted, finally, to denial of liberty itself.

Israel's constitutional structure attempted to minimize this problem for its minorities by rejecting the idea that one can split one's private identity from one's public identity. If the problem was that Jews were forced to be closeted Jews, the solution must lie with granting minorities collective as well as individual rights. Only in this way can they safeguard their separate identity without compromising their civil rights. Therefore, Israel's Declaration of Independence sought to guarantee for Israel's minorities, apart from full and equal citizenship, a large measure of collective autonomy, so that apart from the promise (which was not always fulfilled) for "complete equality of social and political rights to all [Israeli] inhabitants irrespective of religion, race or sex" Israel also inscribed in its founding document a collective dimension of minority rights: Israel, says the Declaration "will guarantee freedom of religion, conscience, language, education and culture." This may not fully answer the needs of all minorities, but it does offer what nineteenth-century Europe denied the Jews, and what contemporary Europe grants its Jews and its other minorities (in fact, the European Council articulated in 1995 principles along the lines of Israel's Declaration of Independence, in a paper outlining the rights of national minorities).[15]

The realization of the Zionist idea was far from perfect. It is nevertheless striking that despite its daring, unprecedented ambition to gather a dispersed people and create an independent state for them, and despite the fact that the state absorbed in its first seven years twice as many immigrants as the size of its population at the time, the regime remained stable, and what is more, it retained its democratic character. And all this, under a constant state of military emergency. What understandably seemed like a mere fantasy to Herzl's generation was carried out successfully and was secured and stabilized over time.

Should we then conclude that, having achieved its central goals, Zionism is no longer relevant? The answer, it seems, is no. On Herzl's terms, regardless of Israel's existence, anyone who believes that the Jewish people has a right to democratic national self-determination is a supporter of Zionism, and anyone who denies that Jews have such a right, is an anti-Zionist. Such a question, as it pertains to most nations, has become not so much irrelevant as dormant. We do not usually ask whether the Italians or the Japanese have such a right. We mostly realize we support it when it is contested, and in the case of most nations it is not contested.

Zionism would be relevant even if Israel's right to exist was not contested. But it is. This makes Zionism not just relevant, but very much alive. There were, since Zionism began, and there still are, vigorous campaigns bent on undermining the right of Jews to national self-determination. Moreover, there are powerful political forces bent on Israel's destruction, while others (within Israel and outside it) wish to abolish either its national Jewish character, or its democratic basis. So long as such forces exist, Zionism would continue to be a vital, important, and a central answer to "the Jewish question."

NOTES

1   The declaration is formally entitled "The Declaration of the Establishment of the State of Israel." See http://www.knesset.gov.il/docs/eng/megilat_eng.htm (accessed June 6, 2012). I will nevertheless refer to it here as Israel's Declaration of Independence, as much of the literature on Zionism does. All quotes are from the official English version as it appears on the Knesset website.

2   There is a second official language in Israel, Arabic, which is the minority's national tongue. Unlike some other democracies—the United Kingdom, or Greece, for example—Israel does not, in fact, have a state church.

3   It is worth noting that in this sense, what we call "postmodernism," contrary to the testimony of its adherents, is a typical modern view, based as it is on the idea of the social construction of knowledge. This idea presupposes, in a rather facile way, that human beings create themselves, indeed, create their world, through their discourse.

4   In Hobbes's early formulation, the social contract is a trade-off: individuals give up liberty in exchange for public order and security; see Thomas Hobbes, *Leviathan* (New York: Penguin, 1985). John Locke, who argued against Hobbes, believed that no such trade-off was necessary. On the contrary, government must preserve individual liberty, as well individual security; see John Locke, *Two Treatises of Government* (Cambridge: Cambridge University Press, 1967).

5   We may note that the principle of government with the consent of the governed applies not only on both the private and the public levels, but also on all intermediary levels, which may vary from co-op houses to municipal government to states under federal structures.

6   Eighteenth-century thinkers often believed that only small city-states, where the public sphere is relatively intimate, could inculcate their citizens with the public spirit required for republican government. See, for example, Charles Louis de Secondat, Baron de Montesquieu, *The Spirit of the Laws,* vol. 1, bk. 8, chap. 16, trans. Thomas Nugent (London: Hafner Press, 1949), 120–21. Rousseau went even further in his conception of direct democracy, where a condition for democratic government is "a very small state, in which the people may be readily assembled"; see Jean-Jacques Rousseau, *The Social Contract,* in *The Social Contract and Discourse on the Origin of Inequality,* ed. Lester G. Crocker (New York: Washington Square Press, 1967), 70.

7   The original Hebrew phrasing is more picturesque. Literally translated it reads: be a human being when you exist, and a Jew in your own tent.

8   The full text is available on the web: MidEastWeb, http://www.mideastweb.org/auto-emancipation.htm (accessed June 6, 2012).

9   Shlomo Avineri, *The Making of Modern Zionism: Intellectual Origins of the Jewish State* (New York: Basic Books, 1981).

10 Theodor Herzl, *The Jewish State,* http://www.mideastweb.org/jewishstate.pdf (accessed June 6, 2012), 5. Herzl realized that one could conceive of one's Jewish identity in purely national terms, or in purely religious terms, or combine both. He did not think Zionism should impose a national conception of identity on those who saw their Judaism as a faith only. It was a choice individuals were free to make. This too was testimony to his belief in self-determination: identity should be a choice, not a fate.

11 We now often talk about nations as "imagined communities" following Benedict Anderson's theory of their modern formation. These terms have led many to assume that "imagined" amounts to something like "fictitious," or "not-real." But, as the case of Zionism clearly demonstrates, what is imagined can and often does become a very real political fact.

12 The radicality of intentionally creating a new nation was especially pronounced in the socialist wing of the movement, who espoused what they called "constructive socialism" as opposed to revolutionary socialism. Revolutionary socialism, which often claimed scientific status for itself (based on its analysis of the laws which governed history and which presumably would lead human society, inevitably, from capitalism to socialism) assumed an eventual rebellion of the proletariat against their bourgeoisie oppressors. But Zionist socialism faced an awkward situation: it lacked a Jewish proletariat. It therefore had to deliberately create one by turning the Jews into workers and farmers. If society itself would be built from scratch, by that proletariat itself, it would be free of oppression to begin with. A revolution would thus not be necessary. Society would be constructed anew on socialist principles, hence the term "constructive socialism." The issue of pioneering was thus central to Zionism, though not all agreed on its role: some believed, as did Herzl, that the state should precede society and economy, while others believed that society and economy must first be established before statehood could be realized (Theodore Herzl, *Old New Land* [*Altneuland*], trans. Lotta Levensohn [Princeton: Markus Wiener Publishers, 2007]).

13   The exception to this rule was the objection of Orthodox Jews within and outside
      the movement to political equality of the sexes.
14   Family structure is not, of course, just a legal issue; it is a deeply embedded view of
      life, grounded in both beliefs and sentiments.
15   Quotation from Declaration, http://www.knesset.gov.il/docs/eng/megilat_eng.htm;
      see the Council of Europe's *Framework Convention for the Protection of National
      Minorities*, http://conventions.coe.int/Treaty/en/Treaties/html/157.htm (accessed
      June 6, 2012).

PART II

HISTORICAL AND PHILOSOPHICAL CONTEXTS

Democratic First, Jewish Second: A Rationale

3

FANIA OZ-SALZBERGER

$\mathbb{A}$ common error ascribes the epithet for Israel, a "Jewish and democratic state," to the Declaration of Independence of 1948. In fact, the term
did not surface prominently in the public arena until well into the 1980s.
It was carved onto two civil rights-related Basic Laws even later, in 1992,
and became prevalent in Israeli discourse since then. Rather than clarifying the issues of cultural and political identity, the "Jewish and democratic" formula has often served to obfuscate the complex matter of Israeli
self-definition.[1]

The two adjectives opened up a cluster of questions: *is* Israel "Jewish
and democratic"? Can it be both? Does "Jewish," under any definition,
support or undermine "democratic"? And, when push comes to shove,
would "Jewish" trump "democratic," or vice versa?[2]

It is a muddy discussion, often simplistic about what democracy
means, and conceptually entangled about what "Jewish" means. It would
have been so even without a Palestinian nation living in Israel and in its
occupied territories. Even had Jews accomplished a ninety-seven percent
majority (akin to the main ethnic group in modern Greece), some of the
questions would still prevail: Is Judaism a religion, a nation, or both?

Should the Jewish state live by ancient Hebraic law, the halakha? If not, in what sense is it Jewish? Who is entitled to citizenship? And who, for heaven's sake, is a Jew?

I submit that "Jewish" and "democratic" are neither parallel concepts nor do they belong on a single conceptual plane. The simplest reason is that democracy is a form of government, and Jewish is an appellation for nation, religion, or culture, singly or jointly. So they are two very different things. They are not a conceptual seesaw, neither dichotomous nor mutually balancing. They belong in different spheres, akin to different parts of speech.

Of course, if "Jewish" and "democratic" function like different parts of speech, they could work quite well together, as nouns and adjectives usually do. We would talk, for instance, about a Jewish democracy. Indeed, every nation-state hinges on the mutually complementary elements of the nation and its form of government. Isn't the Jewish and democratic state the equivalent of the French Republic or the Kingdom of Denmark? Some people would probably say, very reasonably, that if we understand "Jewish" as a national appellation, then the Jewish state is no exception to a host of other nation-states, many of them good democracies, around the globe.

This could work. But not now, not where we stand today. Rather than clarifying the issues of cultural and political identity, the "Jewish and democratic" formula has often served to obfuscate the complex matter of Israeli self-definition. And it has given too much license to play down democracy.

Israeli public discourse, ever since it took on the Jewish and democratic formula, has been steadily fattening the concept of Jewish and thinning the concept of democratic. In prevalent political rhetoric, "Jewish state" has become dangerously overladen and ambiguous, while "democratic" has become dangerously simplistic and frail. To use a biblical metaphor, Israel's Jewish character looks like seven fat cows of Pharaoh's famous dream, while its democratic character is one rather thin cow. In the Jewish-democratic sphere of discourse, "Jewish" has become so laden with specific meanings that it cannot stand on par with "democratic" without threatening to compromise it.[3]

Israel's Jewish character is increasingly seen, in recent years, as amorphously blending nation, religion, culture, and sometimes mystical and meta-historical claims, into a unique concoction of faith and identity. Far more than a simple national claim, it now stands for a series of impassioned, and often mutually incompatible, ideas of the good, of how life should be lived. Several meanings of the Jewish state today straightforwardly contradict democracy. Other meanings stand for particular world views that democracy ought to defend, *vis-à-vis* other legitimate world views.

Thus, Jewish supremacist legislation or halakhic jurisdiction might be seen as patently anti-democratic due to their ethnocentric nature.[4] By contrast, privileging Jewish holidays and public symbols, or business closure on the Sabbath, or Judaism-oriented school curricula, while obviously controversial, are well within the legitimate democratic interplay of cultural preferences. Israel as a nation-state cannot be neutral about its symbols, language, holidays, or narrative, otherwise it will lose its national identity. Nevertheless, it must respect the collective rights of its minorities.[5]

It is a staple of the thickened discourse of Jewish national identity among right-of-center Israeli politicians and law-makers that the line between democratic and anti-democratic claims and proposals has become increasingly blurry. Still, the line is not difficult to demarcate: it is crossed wherever "Jewish" is purported, intentionally and unapologetically, to trump "democratic."

In an austere little assembly room, over sixty years ago, David Ben-Gurion declared the establishment of the State of Israel. Drafted by a distinguished group of lawyers, some of them sporting heavy German accents, and ratified by the provisional People's Council on May 14, 1948, the Declaration of Independence was read out by Israel's first prime minister to an audience of 250 people, as many as the quaint Bauhaus building that housed the Tel Aviv Museum could hold. A crowd gathered outside, eager to rejoice but emotional to the point of tears. No one came from Jerusalem:

it was besieged by Arab militias immediately after the United Nations General Assembly granted Jews and Arabs their respective sovereign states on November 29, 1947.

Significantly, the term "democracy" does not appear in Israel's Declaration—known in Hebrew as the Scroll—of Independence. The term "Jewish" and its derivatives appear twenty-five times, and the combination "Jewish state" five times. The reason for this multiplicity of Jewish derivatives is clear enough: here was the groundbreaking novelty of the document, its tangible edge of historical drama. The formulation "a state for the Jewish people"[6] was precious, its implementation touching on the incredible.

For many of the actors and listeners in Tel Aviv and across the globe, perhaps even the majestically confident Ben-Gurion himself, a historical miracle was in the making. That the Jews, whose irreversible loss of political liberty was described by Josephus just after 70 CE, would regain sovereignty and proclaim their independence in revived Hebrew on reclaimed Israelite soil, beggared belief. In the hall and out on the streets, many adults were crying openly. Any historian who puts on record, justifiably and rightly, the tears of the Palestinians in their moment of disaster, but fails to note the tears of the Jews, is making a shambles of historical explanation. We should remember that on that moment on May 14, 1948, it was not at all clear that the Israeli state that Ben-Gurion was establishing would survive the attack of its neighboring states, Egypt, Jordan, and Syria, alongside Iraq, who joined the local Arab fighters immediately after the Declaration.[7]

Alongside the enormous moral power of the concept of a Jewish state in the late 1940s, it is important to stress that the Jewish state came into the world as a democracy. The Declaration of Independence, in clear and beautiful Hebrew, also speaks to non-Jews, loudly, liberally, and humanely. Indeed, it is one of the most democratic documents in Israel's constitutional history, in many ways an admirable text that should have carried far more legal and political weight than it actually does today.[8]

Its best-known passage, often proposed as a viable opening clause for Israel's yet-unwritten constitution, says that "the State of Israel will foster the development of the country for the benefit of all its inhabitants; it will be based on freedom, justice, and peace as envisaged by the prophets of Israel; it will ensure complete equality of social and political rights to all its inhabitants irrespective of religion, race, or sex; it will guarantee freedom of religion, conscience, language, education and culture; it will safeguard the Holy Places of all religions; and it will be faithful to the principles of the Charter of the United Nations."[9]

Intentions are notoriously difficult to fathom, all the more so from historical distance and in the dense fog of domestic and international politics, escalating bloodshed, and animated ideological rhetoric. If Israel's Declaration of Independence, and most (though not all) of its legal history, is taken at face value, then the Jewish state has always sustained a strong liberal-democratic intention. From its inception, its democratic record has been different from that of an "ethnocracy" granting civil liberties to Jews alone, as suggested by some recent scholarly critique. Israel has yet to succeed in fully implementing its declared intention, but the intention is inscribed on its founding scroll in language crisp and clear: a state for the Jewish people and for all its citizens. A state founded on freedom, equality, justice, and civil rights.[10]

Why, then, did the Declaration of Independence not use the term "democracy"? Several explanations spring to mind. Its authors may not have wished to deploy a Greek term, even the best of Greek terms, in this grand re-enactment of Jewish sovereignty. More likely, the founding fathers and mothers took Israel's democratic nature to be self-evident. Democracy was already an institutional fact and an established feature of the Zionist movement. For the leaders of the Yishuv (the pre-state Jewish community in Palestine), including, across a broad political spectrum, Ben-Gurion and Yitzhak Ben-Zvi, Golda Meir and Zerah Warhaftig, Pinhas Rosen and Meir Wilner, the democratic nature of the new state was nothing novel. For the delegates of no fewer than ten political parties, representatives of a dozen pre-statehood institutions, and civil society organizations, democracy was no news. But a Jewish state, *that* was news. Political freedom for the Jews was anything but self-evident or granted. The Declaration thus dwells on the Jewishness of the nascent state more intensely, but it nevertheless projects it as a modern liberal polity. Far from being a theocracy or an ethnocracy, it is conceived as the sovereign state of the Jews as a nation, rather than a religion, alongside a non-Jewish citizenry.[11]

The Zionist movement had been democratic from its very inception, evolving in a series of congresses where hundreds of elected delegates from numerous Jewish communities deliberated and voted. Ever since the late nineteenth century, the embryonic Jewish polity was based on the principle of equal representation, with both men and women given the vote. Indeed, women had full voting and elective rights at the second Zionist congress in 1898, before any state in the world legislated female suffrage (the only exceptions were South Australia and New Zealand, then still colonies). Of course, since the Zionist congresses were attended by Jews alone, it was a democratic game among Jews. Nevertheless, Theodor Herzl stipulated, in his *Altneuland* of 1902, that Jews and Arabs, men and women, would all be citizens of equal standing with full voting rights in the Jewish state to come. Israel's Declaration of Independence reiterated and expanded this Herzlian intention.[12]

Consider the official name the country was given, after some debate. It is "The State of Israel." Interestingly, very few countries in the world contain "State" in their official titles. Israel is in company with the States of Eritrea, Kuwait, Qatar, and Vatican City. Two others are officially named "The Independent State of": Papua New Guinea and Samoa. Two other cases incorporate further elements, "The Plurinational State of Bolivia," and even "State of Brunei, Abode of Peace" (in Brunei Malay, "Negara Brunei Darussalam"). In a few instances, the plural form "states" denotes a federal structure. Most other countries that are not kingdoms, and that added a further tag to their official names, have opted for Republic. Many took their cues from *La République Française*.

The reason that Israel's founders did not opt for "The Republic of Israel" is, I surmise, twofold: "Republic" is an alien, more specifically Roman, term; and the republican nature of Israel's regime, like its democratic government form, was deemed self-evident. But why was "State" inserted at all? Why not just "Israel"? Again, my explanation is twofold: Ben-Gurion and his counterparts wished to distinguish the modern State of Israel from ancient Israel. The second reason is possibly emotional: reveling in the miracle of modern Jewish statehood, its founders wished to engrave this great historical novelty into the name of the newborn country.

Returning to our key concept, democracy: although it went unmentioned as a term, democracy as a set of values was safer with Israel's Declaration of Independence than it has been with recent Israeli legislation. In the Declaration, its nominal absence derived from palpable presence. On today's political stage, some Israeli politicians tend to ignore democratic values, demote them, or delegate them to Jews alone. It is the thin-cow democracy they have in mind, the solely procedural notion of democracy that enables the Yisrael Beitenu party to declare itself proudly democratic, and in the same breath offer to ban Arab citizens from publicly observing the Nakba day of mourning. Comparably, the National Union party defines the State of Israel in its platform as Jewish and democratic, and a few paragraphs later promises "to fight anti-Jewish and anti-Zionist trends in the judicial branch."[13]

Let us explore the democratic-Jewish quandary further. Modern democracy is a form of government and a civic state of mind. Democracy depends on two inherent pillars: procedure and essence. Procedure is made of free and fair elections, of majority rule counterbalanced by specific non-majoritarian institutes. The essential pillars of democracy are the rule of law, separation of powers, an independent judiciary, and due process, maintaining civil rights that apply equally to all citizens, and safeguarding the human rights of all denizens, citizens and non-citizens alike.[14] As a form of government, democracy is universally applicable to Israel's citizens, Jews and Arabs. Yet the state's Jewish character, the privilege of its Jewish majority, historically well earned and culturally much debated, cannot be forced upon its non-Jewish minority in ways that encroach on their individual liberty.[15]

It is precisely this essence of democracy that has not yet materialized in Iran, in Pakistan, Gaza, and Egypt after their quasi-democratic shifts of regime. Important as may be the procedural pillar of democracy—majority rule, divorced of essential democracy and its core values—many observers have pointed out that the West, particularly the United States, erred in pushing for procedural democracy in societies that may not yet be ripe and ready for essential democracy. No democracy can rest on procedure alone. Remove the core values, the essence, and you have no true democracy, but a fake and a phantom. Democracy in its essential sense offers the sort of institutional justice requisite for a numerous and variegated citizenry to pursue its plural and diverse notions of the good life. In the terminology of John Rawls, whose political philosophy resonates strongly in Israel, human beings have many ideas of the good, and some of them are mutually incompatible. Only democracy—"essential" democracy or liberal democracy in the Rawlsian sense—can handle our disparate notions of the good, allowing us to compromise and to prioritize rather than to clash, to oppress or to be oppressed.[16]

Israeli political discourse tends to emphasize the procedural aspect of democracy rather than its essential aspect. Yet essential democracy prescribes that the state of the Jews must guarantee equal civil and human rights for all its citizens, be they members of the national majority or not. Herzl understood it; some Knesset members today do not.

As for the adjective "Jewish," here we trudge in a fascinatingly murky terrain. What, exactly, does this "Jewish" refer to? The nation? The religion? The legal structure? The mores? The mentality? Is it the modern and secular State of the Jews, as in Herzl's *Der Judenstaat*, or a more mystical being residing in the realm of theology and meta-history? What is the main business of a Jewish state: granting Jews citizenship, or keeping them within the religious fold, or ascertaining a Jewish majority in the country, or guarding against the real and imagined enemies of the Jews? Or perhaps a heady mixture of all of the above? In the early 2000s, the Israeli parliament offered a dazzling variety of interpretations for the Jewish state as it is or as it ought to be: a divinely ordained halakhic state, a country where Jewish symbols and holidays define the public sphere, a society bluntly exercising Jewish supremacy.

However, the simplest meaning of a Jewish state, which is still prevalent among the moderate left, right and center in Israel, is that this is state of the Jews (Herzl's original *Judenstaat*) is a national home for the Jews, a haven for every Jew who seeks its citizenship. This definition is about persons, not about laws or symbols or rituals. It is essentially a secular and national definition. It posits Israel as a modern nation-state, such that does not bar minorities hailing from other ethnic or religious groups. Herzl certainly did not intend non-Jewish citizens to be precluded or ousted, nor did Ben-Gurion and a majority of the co-signers of the Declaration of Independence.

Israelis argue incessantly about the meaning of a Jewish state. It is a debate of the highest public and cultural order. Profound disagreements about being a Jew and about being a citizen, about the good state, the good life, the good person, about faith and truth and human nature itself, are constantly acted out in the Israeli public sphere, vocally but usually peacefully. Nevertheless, Israelis are increasingly concerned that the "Jewish" and "democratic" conceptions are headed for a showdown, in which case, "Jewish" would trump "democratic," or "democratic" would trump "Jewish."

If democracy is understood only in its thin-cow version, procedural democracy alone, then Israel's Jewish majority is entitled to play out its own numeric advantage against its non-Jewish minority. Unlike in Pharaoh's dream, the thin cow cannot eat the seven fat cows; it can only join them by turning against essential democracy—human rights democracy—and devouring it to the bone.

But the fat cows are not so well off, either. Because if we take "Jewish" in any of its substantial senses, as a religion, or as a Mosaic-halakhic legal system, or as a unique set of cultural goods, then no possible democratic theory can accommodate Israel's Jewish character with democracy. Jewish faith, Jewish symbols, halakhic law, all these can only represent certain forms of the good life—perhaps good and respectable forms, but still particular forms—that ought to make room for other faiths, symbols, and legal cultures under the neutral guidance of democracy. Any prior claim to superiority would be plainly undemocratic. If "Jewish" is more than a national appellation for the State of Israel, if it makes religious or legal or cultural claims, then these claims must be subjected to the democratic process, in the full meaning of democracy, and fairly compete with other claims. They must also pass the test of non-interference with everyone's civil and human rights, alongside the prodecural test of representing the majority group in society.[17]

The only viable way to keep both "Jewish" and "democratic" on par, to keep the "Jewish and democratic" formula in working order, is therefore to fatten one cow and slim down the other. Israelis must look far deeper into the concept of democracy, recalling its essential component and understanding its implications for the procedural, majoritarian component. "Jewish State" ought to mean, in the political field, mainly what it meant for Herzl and Ben-Gurion: the state of the Jewish people, based on a national concept of Jewish. All other meanings might be valuable and interesting, but they should be played out in the public, intellectual, and cultural arenas, where they belong, and not in the constitutional centerfield.

Israeli democracy is frail and flawed, but it is still a democracy. Its best chance to survive and thrive is for Israelis to understand it far better. Along the way, they may wish to reread and recollect the essential democracy prescribed to the Jewish state in its own Declaration of Independence. As to Israel's Jewish character, it would not be impoverished by deflating the constitutional nature of the Jewish state to its basic national meaning. It may even gain a new horizon of cultural renaissance. Beyond that, in the thriving arena of public debate, let a thousand cows bloom.

NOTES

1   The dual adjective "Jewish and democratic" ensued from the debate regarding High Court's decision that made the racist Kahana Hai party qualify to be elected in the 1984 general elections. In 1985, Amendment 9 to the Basic Law: the Knesset enacted that a political party that denies Israel's status as the state of the Jewish people or its democratic character cannot run for election. In 1992, Art. 1a of Basic Law: Human Dignity and Liberty declared that "the purpose of this Basic Law is to protect human dignity and liberty, in order to establish in a Basic Law the values of the State of Israel as a Jewish and democratic state." Basic Law: Freedom of Occupation opens with an identical purpose clause. See *Knesset*, "Basic Law: The Knesset—1958," http://www.knesset.gov.il/laws/special/eng/basic2_eng.htm (accessed June 23, 2012), and the two Basic Laws of 1992 at Knesset, "The Existing Basic Laws: Full Texts," http://www.knesset.gov.il/description/eng/eng_mimshal_yesod1.htm (accessed June 23, 2012).

2   For an interesting review to some of these questions see Amnon Rubinstein, "The Curious Case of Jewish Democracy," *Azure* 41 (2010): 33; Ruth E. Gavison, "Can Israel Be Both Jewish and Democratic?" in *Israel as a Jewish and Democratic State*, ed. Asher Maoz (Liverpool: Deborah Charles Publications, 2011), 115; and Joseph E. David, ed., *The State of Israel: Between Judaism and Democracy* (Jerusalem: IDI Press, 2003).

3   Pharaoh's dream is in Genesis 41:1–7. Recent legislation controlling issues pertaining to Israel's Jewish character, such as citizenship, right of entry into the country, and the selling of non-kosher meat, displays an accumulation of preference for "Jewish"

over "democratic." For a major critique see Daphne Barak-Erez, "Law and Religion Under the Status Quo Model: Between Past Compromises and Constant Change," *Cardozo Law Review* 30 (2009): 2495.

4   It is important to note that, on the legislative level, religious monopoly in Israel is not granted only to Jews but to other major religious groups as well, and it was authorized by a secular authority, the Knesset.

5   In general, Israeli legislation indeed respects the collective rights of minorities, especially on cultural matters. For example, the Hours of Work and Rest Law enables every person to choose their own day of rest according to their religion. Similarly, Arabic is the language of about 20 percent of Israeli citizens, and it is an official language alongside Hebrew and English. Its speakers have the right to schooling in their language. However, while in both cases the legal arrangements are reasonably democratic, practical applications of the laws are still encumbered with inequity and discrimination.

6   *Knesset*, "The Declaration of the Establishment of the State of Israel," May 14, 1948, http://www.knesset.gov.il/docs/eng/megilat_eng.htm (accessed June 23, 2012).

7   Titus Flavius Josephus (Yosef ben-Matityahu), *Wars of the Jews*, c. 75 CE; Benny Morris, *1948: A History of the First Arab-Israeli War* (New Haven, CT: Yale University Press, 2008).

8   Even after the amendment of section 1 to Basic Law: Human Dignity and Liberty and Basic Law: Freedom of Occupation that states that "Fundamental human rights . . . shall be upheld in the spirit of the principles set forth in the Declaration of the Establishment of the State of Israel," the Declaration appears to be used merely as a secondary source of law, and mainly as a tool of interpretation. See HCJ 73/53, Kol Ha'am v. Minister of the Interior, IsrSC 7 871 (1953), and Aharon Barak, *Purposive Interpretation in Law*, trans. Sari Bashi (Princeton: Princeton University Press, 2005).

9   *Knesset*, "The Declaration of the Establishment of the State of Israel."

10 Recent scholarly critique: see Oren Yiftachel, *Ethnocracy—Land and Identity Politics in Israel/Palestine* (Philadelphia: University of Pennsylvania Press, 2006), 211. See also Tony Judt, "Israel Must Unpick Its Ethnic Myth," *Financial Times*, December 7, 2009. As no nation-state can be fully neutral in selecting its public symbols, some of these critical claims may well be applied to any nation-state. The sociologist Baruch Kimmerling, among others, asserted that a big step toward democracy would be to change the policy of immigration to Israel, namely to cancel the Law of Return. This proposal is only a part of the demand that Israel finally acknowledge its multicultural nature. See Baruch Kimmerling, *The Invention and Decline of Israeliness: State, Culture and Military in Israel* (Berkeley: University of California Press, 2001), and Yossi Yonah, "Israel As a Multicultural Democracy: Challenges and Obstacles," *Israel Affairs* 11 (2005): 95–116.

11 On Jewish nationhood, rather than religion, as the core concept of the Zionist ideal and the State of Israel, the basic text is of course Theodor Herzl, *Der Judenstaat* [The State of the Jews], (Leipzig and Vienna: M. Breitenstein's Verlags-Buchhandlung, 1896). For modern analyses, see especially Shlomo Avineri, *The Making of Modern Zionism: Intellectual Origins of the Jewish State* (New York: Basic Books, 1981); and the essays by Yedidia Stern and Gadi Taub in this volume.

12 Theodor Herzl, *Altneuland* [German] (Leipzig: H. Seemann Publishing, 1902).

13   Yisrael Beitenu initiated the Budget Foundations Law (Amendment No. 40) 2286, 674–2011 (The Nakba Law). The National Union party platform is available at: http://sites.azilevon.com/general/IchoodLeumi/index.php-option=com_content &task=view&id=6463&Itemid=55.htm [Hebrew].

14   See especially David Held, *Models of Democracy*, 3rd ed. (Cambridge: Polity, 2006); Arend Lijphart, *Patterns of Democracy: Government Forms and Performance in Thirty-Six Countries* (New Haven, CT: Yale University Press, 1999).

15   The Jewishness of Israel cannot justify violations of human rights, which include the minority's collective rights. It is legitimately disputable, however, whether Israel as a country must sustain certain collective rights of minority groups. While sizable minorities indisputably deserve the right to education (also) in their native languages, the scale of governmental finance for such programs, when the national core curriculum is in Hebrew, may reasonably remain negotiable.

16   John Rawls, *Political Liberalism* (New York: Columbia University Press, 1993), especially Lecture IV.

17   Cf. Fania Oz-Salzberger, "But Is It Good for Democracy? Israel's Dilemma," *World Affairs* 176 (May–June 2010): 62–70.

Cosmopolitanism versus Normative Difference: From Habermas to Levinas—Is Israel an Exception?

4 SHIRA WOLOSKY

The question of the status and indeed the very justification of Israel continues to be an urgent and contested one. In this, the Jewish state, as the Jew so often does in history, emerges as a fault line for contemporary issues in culture, ethics, and politics. In the discourses of universalist post-nationalism, Israel stands for nationalist deviance; in the discourses of cultural difference and the Other, Israel represents imperialist imposition. What neither form of politics grasps is the full ethical claim of difference itself as the basis for moral thinking. Isaiah Berlin, noting that Zionism is described as "imperialism, colonialism, racialism and so on," defended Jewish cultural and political difference against the dangers of universalizing reason. As he wrote in "Democracy, Communism, and The Individual," "one can, in the name of reason, impose it ruthlessly on others, since if they are rational they will agree freely; if they do not agree, they are not rational. This denies that different ideals of life, not necessarily altogether reconcilable with each other, are equally valid and equally worthy."[1]

This contest over Israel as betraying both universalism and the Other governs discussions of the Levinasian philosophy of the Other in ways that miss the radical ethics of difference that he offers. Almost everyone who has discussed Levinas's politics judges it to be self-betraying. Especially in his commitments to Israel, Levinas is said to contradict his own ethics of the "Other," of irreducible difference as the foundational ethical principle. To Howard Caygill, Levinas's Zionism "reduces his ethical mission to politics" in that statehood "betrays to racism." Michael Shapiro sees Israel as an "egregious blind spot" in Levinas. "Levinas's attachment to state sovereignty makes him veer away from his commitment to an ethical bond that precedes all such ontological/spatial attachments . . . he does not heed the other's stories of self and space." Sarah Hammerschlag, in her study of *The Figural Jew*, reviews the ways in which the "Jew" has in postmodernity been made into a symbol for the "Other" and its ethical treatment. However, Levinas's Zionism betrays this "otherness" of the Jew and of ethics; "deracination becomes the condition for ethics." The Jew is an ethical figure only as it symbolizes "uprootedness"—a traditional suspicion against Jews that, she argues, Levinas adopts but reverses from an antisemitic charge into an ethical claim. Indeed, quite contrary to Levinas, she insists that only as offering an "underlying universal message" can the Jew retain his ethical place: that is, as "detached from the particularism of tradition and ethnicity or as a possible prophetic." Michael F. Bernard-Donals similarly claims that the Jew fulfills his ethical role as "exiled on the earth," in an "uprooting from context" and "particularism," such that he remains "a person outside peoplehood."[2]

As Alain Fienkelkraut sums up in his interview with Levinas after the Sabra and Shatila massacres of 1982: "E Levinas, you are the philosopher of the 'other.' Isn't history, isn't politics the very site of the encounter with the 'other,' and for the Israeli, isn't the 'other' above all the Palestinians?" Yet Levinas's answer is telling: "My definition of the other is completely different. The other is the neighbour, who is not necessarily kin, but who can be. And in that sense, if you're for the other, you're for the neighbor. But if your neighbor attacks another neighbour or treats him unjustly, what can you do? Then alterity takes on another character. In alterity we can find an enemy, or at least then we are faced with the problem of knowing who is just and who is unjust. There are people who are wrong."[3]

"My definition of the other is completely different." The readings of contradiction and betrayal in Levinas's politics represent a significant misunderstanding of his ethics, of the meanings of the Other in his work, and of his philosophical critique. This is fundamentally a critique of universalism—in political terms, as it attacks particularist cultural identifications and their political expression. The ethic of the Other is one that affirms the particular, the unique, the different, including both individuals and communities; deriving norms exactly from difference and Otherness. This is to oppose the long idealist tradition that regards the universal as normative ground. Levinas describes "the history of philosophy as an attempt at universal synthesis, a reduction of all experience, of all that is reasonable, to a totality wherein consciousness embraces the world, leaves nothing other outside of itself, and thus becomes absolute thought."[4]

To Levinas, universalism, instead of representing an ideal, poses ethical problems and ethical dangers. It is one of his central claims that ethics has been secondary in the tradition, derivative of questions of metaphysics and of knowledge based in universals. Levinas instead sees ethics as "first philosophy," and the universalism privileged by traditional metaphysics as weakening rather than grounding ethical norms, threatening violence against the difference and multiplicity that makes up the human world.[5]

To accuse Levinas of betraying the Other, contradicting his ethics with his politics, is to misread his notion of the Other in important ways. It miscalculates the radical nature of his critique of universalism and his defense of the particular, including particular cultural identities, as these recast fundamental assumptions traditional to Western thought and their political implications. The Other, which has emerged as a key term in contemporary political discussions, instead tends to be reabsorbed into universalist ideals in ways that run counter to Levinas's uses of the term. This can be seen in discourses of cosmopolitanism and post-nationalism, as in the work of Jürgen Habermas.

COSMOPOLITAN DISEMBODIMENT

In Habermas's *Inclusion of the Other* and *The Postnational Constellation*, cosmopolitanism emerges as the ideal of ethical politics. It commands the moral high ground, from which particular attachments look at best partial, at worst like obstacles to peace and indeed causes of war. Difference is the reason for conflict; overcoming difference must therefore be the solution to conflict. Especially dangerous is difference in the form of what Habermas calls "barbaric nationalism," the obstacle blocking the path to peace through "decentered perspectives . . . as a motive for overcoming particularisms."[6]

Habermas's anti-nationalism is a response to National Socialism; and also to the nationalist wars that erupted with the fall of the Soviet empire (one reason for Hobsbawm's lamenting its demise). As such it is the opposite of democratic politics: "The integral nationalism of the twentieth century (not to speak of the racist policies of the Nazis), illustrate the sad facts that the idea of the nation did not so much reinforce the loyalty of the population to the constitutional state but more often served as an instrument to mobilize the masses for political goals that can scarcely be reconciled with republican principles." The antidote, then, to nationalist fascism is to "transcend boundaries of limited national public spheres" in ways that do away with national cultures and their political expression: "The majority culture must become sufficiently detached from its traditional, historically explicable fusion with the political culture shared by all its citizens."[7]

Habermas frames his post-national cosmopolitanism through a number of core terms. While conceding that "the democratic process must always be embedded in a common political culture," he asserts that this does not imply "the exclusivist project of realizing national particularity." What is required instead is "a collective political existence [that] keeps itself open for inclusion without enclosing others into the uniformity of a homogenous community . . . A previous background consensus on the basis of homogeneity . . . becomes superfluous to the extent that public, discursively structured processes of opinion and will formation make a reasonable political understanding possible, even among strangers . . . Thanks to its procedural properties, the democratic process has its own mechanisms for securing legitimacy; it can, when necessary, fill the gaps that open in social integration."[8]

Habermas in this passage wishes for "collective existence" but without "uniformity;" "consensus" without "homogeneity," "strangers" but with "integration." As Will Kymlicka sums up the dilemma, there is the need "to show respect for diversity in a pluralistic society without at the same time damaging or eroding the bonds and virtues of citizenship." Or, as Habermas himself puts it, there must be "unity within national diversity."[9]

Yet Habermas's argument clearly tilts away from "diversity" and toward "unity," almost paradoxically, since he also wishes to avoid "the exclusivist project" that he identifies with nationalist particularity. His unity is not that of a particular national community, which he identifies, reductively and unnecessarily, with "homogeneity." It instead reaches beyond particular political communities, transcending them in a cosmopolitan society. Such a society would be neutral regarding specific cultural forms, emerging instead out of democratic "procedural properties" that are essentially abstract. The communicative theory on which Habermas bases democratic procedures, the "discursively structured processes of opinion and will formation" that make a "reasonable political understanding possible, even among strangers," relies on reason itself to unite across difference, filling the "gaps" between people. This presupposes a unity in reason itself, to which all have access beyond any differences. Habermas's ideal is thus "the practice of deliberation between participants in communication who want to arrive at rationally motivated decisions" through a "consensus" based "on . . . democratically structured opinion and will-formation [that makes] possible rational agreement even between strangers."[10] Here, strangers enter only to shed their strangeness. Habermas does not give any positive function to difference. The inclusion of the Other of his title is based on its becoming part of cosmopolitan society by ceasing to be other, by erasing its difference into an integration that absorbs and dissolves otherness.

There are many criticisms that can be made of this Habermasian model: in its claims to neutrality, in its repetition of problematic aspects of liberal theory; as self-contradictory in undercutting principles required for its own fulfillment; as faulty, in the discourse theory and its linguistic models on which its deliberative democracy is based; as severely remote from the historical and human contexts it purports to address; and finally, in Levinasian terms, as problematic in ethical terms.

With regard to its replication of weaknesses in liberal theory, Habermas's view that democracy can be conducted without a common cultural community—"without recourse to common value orientations and shared conceptions of justice"—abstracts both the people who participate in politics and the cultural contexts of political structure and action. As Michael Walzer, Charles Taylor, William Galston and others have argued, democracy itself is not, in Walzer's terms, a "neutral procedure but a way of life," embracing "a view of the human good that favors certain ways of life." Taylor similarly claims that it is not possible to "ground political identity purely in republican elements, without any reference to national or cultural identities." Even apparently formal democratic features are substantive in the sense that they emerge from, and reflect, specific historical processes, cultural practices, religious backgrounds, and at times foreground territorial, ethnic, and other histories and patterns. These affect the forms that representation takes, the sorts of parties and other political organizations that are set up, and the motives and relationships of the people who join and are active in them. As Isaiah Berlin wrote: "Nationalism is often painted only negatively, as xenophobic; but all values and standards must be intrinsic to a society and its unique history: in terms of which the individual sees all values and purposes."[11]

Habermas's is ultimately an "unencumbered" politics, akin to the "unencumbered selves" of pure liberal theory that has been critiqued by Michael Sandel and others. Habermas claims to deny the "metaphysical assumption of an individual who exists prior to all socialization and as it were comes into the world equipped with innate rights." But his individuals, disjoined from cultural matrices, resemble just such abstracted, metaphysical persons, acting in an abstracted, dehistoricized politics. His cosmopolitan individuals in fact resemble the atomized selves he fears as a negative effect of globalization, which he describes as scattered "like discrete monads, across global, functionally coordinated networks, rather than overlapping in the course of social integration, in larger, multidimensional political entities." His post-national state, with its "post-national networks with new forms of political regulation" and "global actors" required "to consider one another's interests mutually and to perceive general interests," is difficult to distinguish from the "post-political global, functionally coordinated networks" he criticizes.[12]

Habermas's vision of post-national democracy further denies the foundations necessary to its own success. Both distributive justice, and the procedures of democracy themselves, depend on a civil solidarity that Habermas fails to account for or construct. In particular, the redistributive justice he sees as integral to democratic equality requires exactly the solidarity he has dissolved. As he writes, only citizens who "feel responsible enough for one another . . . are prepared to make sacrifices, as in military service or redistributive taxation." However, just this mutual commitment depends on a sense of belonging to a common cultural world that Habermas would disband. David Miller, for example, argues that that the democratic possibility to legislate, authorize, and execute political action rests on "shared beliefs of a set of people: a belief that each belongs together with the rest; that this association is neither transitory nor merely instrumental but stems from a long history of living together which (it is hoped and expected) will continue into the future; that the community is marked off from other communities by its members' distinctive characteristics; and that each member recognizes a loyalty to the community." Only shared attachments make members of a community willing to sacrifice personal gain for a common good. National community is moreover what grants them the political autonomy to institute and execute their decisions democratically—a power to shape environment that is most effective in the form of sovereign nationality. "If a community is to make claim on my allegiance," Miller writes, "it must represent a distinct way of life."[13]

Similarly, Dworkin claims, writing from the side not of communitarianism but of liberal individualism: "People are members of a genuine political community only when they accept that their fates are linked in the following strong way: they accept that they are governed by common principles, adopted in 'a theater of debate' and recognizing that each member's rights and duties arise from the historical fact that his community has adopted that scheme." Solidarity within a particular community grounds distributive justice and the respect for authority to enable execution of actions in the democratic community's name. Charles Taylor underscores the idea that free societies especially require "trust" and "a higher level

of commitment and participation than despotic or authoritarian ones."
Only if "citizens feel a strong bond of identification with their political
community" will they accept its decisions as representing them as well.
Democracy—Dworkin's "theater of debate"—requires "more solidarity
and commitment to joint political projects than authoritarian or hierarchical governments do;" in order to form a deliberative unit, "the modern
democratic state demands a 'people' with a strong collective identity."
The willingness to accept the outcomes of democratic decision-making
depends upon the sense of having taken part in its processes as members
of its community. Michael Walzer, arguing for the "Moral Standing of
States," insists that particular political communities have "not been transcended," for "politics depends upon a shared history, communal sentiment, accepted conventions."[14]

Habermas concedes that the "civil solidarity" of the nation-state has
until now been the ground for the willingness for citizens "to take responsibility for each other." His call, however, for post-national forms posits
that all will "learn to mutually recognize one another as members of a
common political existence beyond national borders." But Habermas's
vision of a "cosmopolitan democracy" of "world citizens no longer medi-
ated through their nationality" in fact dissolves the solidarity on which it
continues to depend.[15] Democratic processes themselves cannot generate
solidarity separate from context, location, history, and language in the
way that Habermas assumes.

What Habermasian post-nationalism proposes is a form of disembodiment. It disembodies political life by dissociating it from the cultural
forms in which social life takes place and the histories that gave rise to
them: "The level of shared political culture must be uncoupled from the
level of subcultures and their pre-political identities." It disembodies
from the citizens themselves, their histories, attachments, commitments,
dissolving them into rationality as providing "the general accessibility
of deliberative process whose structure grounds an expectation of rationally acceptable results." For, as Paul Kahn writes, "Reason leads beyond
particularity to a domain of abstract ideas in which the uniqueness
of the self is either irrelevant or a distraction."[16] Finally, the model of
communication on which Habermas grounds democratic procedure is

disembodied in a linguistic sense, abstracted from the very language(s) in which it takes place.

The ideal communicative community or ideal speech situation on which Habermas bases his model of political deliberation has been widely criticized. As feminists in particular have protested, it ignores the social and political contexts that determine who has access to deliberation: the way wealth, gender, education, socialization and culture very much affect both its composition and the conduct of its discourses.[17] As in critiques of abstract liberalism, Habermasian deliberation assumes individuals without the interests, affiliations, histories, and commitments that define them.

Deliberation itself becomes emptied of all the issues that politics addresses, conflicts as well as confirmations, compromises and trade-offs. Habermasian deliberation is in effect circular. The ideal speech situation ultimately assumes the conditions it itself must produce, the agreements it purports to accomplish. As Michael Walzer argues, Habermas's ideal speech situation implies an already given "social structure, political arrangements, distributive standards," presupposing "the institutional arrangements which are, however, one of the things that conversation is supposed to decide." Or, as Levinas puts it, "it would be necessary to find a dialogue to make these beings enter into dialogue." What the ideal speech situation idealizes is a "preordained harmony" as opposed to the "adversarial" quality inherent in democratic exchanges. Indeed, speech itself would have no role other than conveying the rational positions that all already subscribe to, merely conveying universal, impersonal reason— "public discourses oriented to rational acceptability in light of generalized interests." To Habermas discourse is a vehicle delivering ideas the way trucks deliver merchandise. Language is nothing more than a "medium" for information that has been pre-formulated. Although Habermas speaks of "how communication participants . . . can achieve an understanding," in the "cooperative communicative practice" he outlines, the speakers "already tacitly accept the condition of symmetrical or equal consideration for everyone's interests." Habermas's model presumes an agreement it also claims to obtain, and does so, as Walzer comments on Rousseau, in ways that ultimately dispense with language altogether, where citizens, already united in their will, need "have no communication with each other."[18]

Habermas ignores how deliberation itself takes place in cultural words as well as worlds: how language both frames and forms what people say, how they address each other. It is not surprising that Habermas is basically indifferent to what language politics may be conducted in, or the need for a common language at all, claiming that meanings remain identical in diverse languages.[19] Yet discourse is not a neutral, transparent, instrumental conveyer of meanings. Language itself densely shapes experiences and understandings that do not exist as pure disembodied ideas. The power of language in politics is not only to transmit knowledge, or to persuade, but to establish the shared forms in which deliberation itself takes shape and that help to define and to connect the participants as belonging to a shared community of authorities, responsibilities, and concerns. Habermasian deliberative discourse finally reverts to metaphysics, assuming abstract ideas that he claims to have elided.

Habermas is sensitive to the need for "a symbolically embodied, culturally contextualized, historically situated reason" rather than the pure idealism of disembodied reason. His discursive reason, he claims, grounds itself not in metaphysical universals but in democratic procedures that remain embedded in historical and cultural contexts—the "interpersonal relationships and cultural traditions in which they can maintain their identities." While conceding that "communicative reason too is embedded in contexts of different forms of life," he adds that these "symbolic structures of the lifeworld preserve an internal relation to communicative reason," building toward an "abstract self-identity" where "the processes of social integration are increasingly uncoupled from established traditions" (cf. "one that has thrown off the shackles of any exclusionary community").[20]

Habermas's model ultimately remains supra-historical, as it is supra-linguistic. Despite his disclaimers, his model abstracts from selves and cultures—selves in cultures—in their particularity. His cosmopolitanism bypasses historical and cultural forms, appealing instead to a "form of reason that can transcend its own context" reaching into the "context-transcendent force of truth claims . . . that speakers raise with their utterance in general." These abstract truth claims take place in an equally abstract language as a "universal medium for embodying reason." Intersubjectivity itself, through which Habermas attempts to bridge even while retaining individual subjectivies, ultimately works to absorb them. They become a kind of hall of reflecting mirrors of reason in "reciprocal recognition" grounded in the participation in universal reason.[21]

Habermas's appeal to discursive reason is in part motivated by fear of a fall into relativism. If there is only difference—different cultures, different subjectivities—without a unifying shared reason, then fragmentation and conflict could result, without reference to any fixed standard. "Destroying an unconditioned and pure reason" threatens to rob ideas of "self-consciousness, determination, self-realization, and normatively binding force." This relativist danger Habermas sees as realized in postmodernism. Its critique of "unconditioned, pure, context-independent and generalizing reason" as "transcendental illusion," Habermas feels leaves "only the contingent networks of a natural history or a language game." History and language here are not only contingent, but disruptive. Lacking any universal trait, all that remains is "selective and hence prejudiced perspective."[22]

Habermas's goal, then, is to avert relativist anarchy or conflicts of difference without, however, falling back into idealist abstraction. And yet, this is what Habermas does, proposing ideal systems that can be critiqued as undermining the very project of democracy that Habermas seeks to defend. Democratic communities are embedded within concrete historical and cultural contexts, as are individual humans. Politics arises from and appeals to these attachments, and takes place within cultures and languages; democracy itself depends on the commitments and participations of individuals in particular communities.[23] These are what Habermas desires ultimately to detour. While conceding that a "cosmopolitan democracy" has yet to develop the solidarity of "collective identity . . . of citizens of a particular democratic life," he desires a different model of "legitimacy" on the basis of "organizational forms of an international negotiation system," ultimately drawing "legitimizing force . . . not from political participation and the expression of political will," but rather from "a deliberative process whose structure grounds an expectation of rationally acceptable results."

Habermas's ideal is a "form of deliberation in which each participant is compelled to adopt the perspective of all the others." In Levinasian terms, this in effect erases the perspective of both individual and Other.

Just so, the ideal of inclusion involves absorption of each into an "enlarged first person plural perspective of a community that does not exclude anybody." Selves merge, difference is effaced. "First and second person perspectives" unite "in symmetrical relations of reciprocal recognition" so that "what initially appears as incommensurable can always in principle be bridged."[24]

Besides the fact that this cosmopolitan picture is utterly remote from any political reality that has ever existed in the world, it raises severe moral problems instead of solving them. Although Habermas insists that he intends to respect difference—that "citizens who share a common political life also are others to one another, and each is entitled to remain Other"— his model grants no positive value to such otherness. What is normative is what overcomes it. Difference figures as a threat to be dispelled, cast in the role of villain: as religious schism, regional fragmentation, war between nations. At most it can contribute to a "decentering of perspectives" that provides a "motive for overcoming of particularisms" which Habermas equates with "prejudices and biases." As Habermas himself concedes, his "communicative reason . . . retains portions of the idealist heritage": the politics it imagines is disembodied from culture, community, and particulars, which is to say from different selves and difference itself. In its place would arise a global public sphere, transcending boundaries of social space and historical time. Popular sovereignty becomes "desubstantialized." As against "embodiment in the people," there would be a "decentered society." Decision-making would move from "concrete embodiments of sovereign will in persons, votes and collectives to the procedural demands of communicative processes." This is a democracy where community has been dissolved, and the Other is included only at cost of his/her own erasure.[25]

NORMATIVE DIFFERENCE

Levinas's work marks a radical break from the traditions of universalism that continue to underlie cosmopolitan discourses, despite, as in Habermas, the adoption of a discourse of the Other. Where Habermas sees difference as a problem to overcome, Levinas sees it as the ground for ethical responsibility. Instead of its being the cause of violence, recognizing difference and Otherness becomes in Levinas the guard against violence. Instead of transcending difference, Levinas urges not only the impossibility of such transcendence, but sees retaining the transcendence of the Other as guarding it from coercion, violation, and erasure. The self in Levinas remains embodied and embedded in history and society rather than abstracted from them. This particularity distinguishes each unique self from every other. Honoring it preserves each self and Other in their particularity. Thus difference is not what must be transcended but what cannot be. Difference in this sense emerges in Levinas in place of universal absorption as a normative principle, neither relativist nor idealist.

In Levinas, not difference, but universalism's desire to overcome it, is what signals violence and violation. Habermasian claims for reciprocal comprehension represent for Levinas not the guard against violence, but the form it takes. The notion of a universal opens the possibility of imposing one claim, model, or pattern on others, exactly in the name of normativity. Assuming a single truth of reason to which all must accede, universalism devalues argument and difference. Its assumption that each one can take the viewpoint of the other—such that "each participant is compelled to adopt the perspective of all others"[26]—risks imposing one's own understanding and interests and erasing those of others.

Levinas's ethic, no less than—although in opposition to—that of Habermas, arose from the shadows of National Socialism. As he sums up in his retrospective *Ethics and Infinity*, "critique of the totality has come in fact after a political experience that we have not yet forgotten." The roots of his suspicion of universalist reason are visible in a 1934 essay, "Reflections on the Philosophy of Hitlerism." Written well before the Holocaust, it presumably registers the shock of Heidegger's joining the Nazi Party in 1933, Levinas having studied with and been deeply influenced by him in Freiburg.[27]

The essay marks a radicalization of Levinas's philosophical critique of Western tradition. At the center of the "Reflections on Hitlerism" is a kind of history of dualism, which Levinas claims to have structured Western philosophical and religious traditions even in their Enlightenment and secularized transformations. In his account, dualism demotes concrete earthly life, the material world, history itself as philosophically unreal. In its Enlightenment form, an abstract, disembodied truth above history, culture, and context is identified with reason. Levinas argues that this is a continuation of idealist philosophies that go back to Plato, which place truth and value itself in an abstract world of Being made up of ideas that are eternal, unchanging, immaterial, and unitary, as against the world of time, change, material body, and multiplicity. Throughout Western culture, these two worlds of Being and Becoming have been regarded as not only separate but, varying with the dualist mood, radically opposed, with the material world dismissed or disdained as against the abstract realm of ideas. Value and truth are placed in the higher abstract world, not the concrete historical one. Body as materiality becomes, in Levinas's words, "foreign," "inferior," "something to be overcome," an "obstacle," a "tomb," an "eternal strangeness."[28]

This dualist abstraction carries for Levinas seeds of evil: as he writes in his preface to the "Reflections on Hitlerism," the "barbarism of National Socialism lies not in some contingent anomaly within human reasoning, but . . . from the essential possibility of elemental Evil into which we can be led by logic [itself] and against which Western philosophy had not sufficiently insured itself." It was not some error in philosophy and its elevation of reason above phenomena that gave rise, as it turned out, to the dangers of Nazism, but rather the very structure itself in which reason is defined in purely abstract and absolute ways, above all historical conditions and human limitations. Nazism in turn is seen as caught in such dualism, albeit in an inverse way. For Nazism retains a kind of abstract claim to absoluteness that Levinas sees as profoundly immoral. The "whole philosophical and political thought of modern times," writes Levinas, "tends to place the human spirit on a plane that is superior to reality and so creates a gulf between man and world. It makes it impossible to apply the categories of the physical world to the spirituality of reason, and so locates the ultimate foundation of the spirit outside the brutal world and the implacable history of concrete existence."[29]

How, however, does the problem of locating "spirit outside the . . . implacable history of concrete existence" reflect on Hitlerism? How is racist nationalism a form of universalist "spirituality of reason"? Or, as

Levinas asks in *Beyond the Verse*, "How is universality compatible with racism?" He continues: "the answer [is] to be found in the logic of what first inspires racism"—a logic that embraces notions of uniformity of race as against the distinctions, mixtures, and multiplicities of the historical world. Racism is then an inverted claim of universality, for "the general can be inverted in [its] application."[30] Just so, the Nazis pursued and imposed uniformity within their own polity and in its ambition for extension. What was to be eliminated or subordinated was difference: Jews paradigmatically, but all Others as well, as deviations from the ideal Aryan. This is not an embrace of the particular, but its erasure for one form, claimed as absolute. It is the attempt of one particular to universalize itself, to become the norm to be imposed upon all others.

Habermas in *The Postnational Constellation* concedes that the "universal can hide power," as postmodernists such as Foucault claim.[31] Habermas, however, is more suspicious of postmodern critiques of universalism as leading to relativism than he is of universalism itself. Levinas, conversely, was himself a formative figure in postmodern critique of universals, notably Derrida's. Levinas points this critique in normative directions that respond to the problematic dangers of universalism, yet are not simply relativistic. Levinas in this offers what may be the most incisive response to the urgent question of contemporary politics and ethics: How, without universals, can normativity be constructed? how can plural viewpoints be distinguished or restrained from mere relativism, from a pure subjectivity of competing views without the possibility of adjudication or moral judgment? If there is no one truth, are there only lies? This indeed is the postmodern dilemma. With the challenge to universalism—an ideal, however, as Levinas is central in exposing, that itself carries the possibility of violent imposition—what other normative structures can be specified?

A Levinasian ethics of difference and the Other, of multiple particulars in place of universalist reductions, can be constructed. In place of unity as the ultimate good, the presumption since Plato, Levinas radically proposes that multiplicity, difference, and Otherness are good. For one thing, multiplicity is the given of earthly existence, and eliminating it would require the suppression or elimination of human and all other forms of life. As Madison said in the *Federalist*, uniformity is a cure worse than the disease of dissension it would remedy.[32] However, in Levinas difference is not a flaw to be tolerated, but rather is itself a moral guard, preventing the unlimited appropriation of another by the self or of one culture by another. The defense of difference thus denies justification for any person or cultural community to suppress or destroy in the name of unity or unitary truth.

The ethical priority of difference, multiplicity, and Otherness becomes normative rather than relativist or anarchic when regarded as regulatory in a number of ways. On one side, what emerges is an ethical principle of limitation. A given particular—whether a person or a cultural community (or a self in a cultural community)—does not have the right to impose itself on other given particulars, whether on the basis of presumed common traits or claims of superior truths or knowledge. The "multiplicity of humans and the uniqueness of persons," Levinas writes in "The Rights of Man and the Rights of the Other," requires something beyond "the formalism of universality," but rather "upholding justice itself in its limitations" as a mode of "reciprocal limitation"—not, however, merely as a negative, but also as a "positivity."[33]

For Levinas's ethic is not only a negative ethic of restraint, preserving and respecting the Other from the self's own claims, not to mention appropriation or violence. Levinas's ethic is also a positive ethic of responsibility. The self limits itself as to what it can impose on others, but is also positively responsible for sustaining others. If Otherness, difference, multiplicity is a good, then not only not destroying, but also positively sustaining it is a good.

These regulatory principles apply both to individual selves and to communities: that is, selves in relation to other selves, selves in relation to communities, and communities in relation to other communities. Habermas portrays nationalism as homogeneous and exclusionary, defining national identities in reified, even racial terms. But this equation of nationality with homogeneity is a straw man: as many have argued, national groupings need not be ethnically consistent or ethnically constituted at all. They can be historical, civic, and cultural, sharing memories and civic principles, commitments, and projects without common descent (with whatever validity such a category may in any case carry). A homogeneous notion of nationality would not be one that embraces an ethic of difference, but rather one that asserts and attempts to impose a homogeneity that will never exist, since nations are more or less plural in their constituency in ethnic as well as other terms.[34]

Communities emerge through shared references to histories, narratives, heritage(s), practices, texts, legal traditions, and territories, in varying combinations, and associations, which are also always partial and individuated. These multiple configurations need not defeat either the notion of national political community, or of normative difference. What would be required instead is to extend principles of normative difference both to individuals within communities and to relations between communities as well. In traditional liberal terms, this would mean upholding an exit principle: that is, the right of exit for any individual from a given subcommunity within a nation or from a national community. Rather than speaking (only) of rights, however, Levinasian ethics embrace, on the one hand, ethical limitations against negating the difference of Others, and on the other hand, ethical responsibility for sustaining the Other in his or her difference: what he calls "a proximity" of "one facing the other," not as an "identity of the universal," but as a "freedom in which the responsibility of one-for-the-other is affirmed."[35]

Levinas is in fact among the early critics of a pure liberal individualism, both as a phenomenology of the self and as an ethic. In "Reflections on Hitlerism," Levinas describes liberal liberty as both a fantasized and a faulty model. It would leave a man "absolutely free in his relations to the world and the possibilities that solicit action from him," but this would assume a condition in which "he has no history." Levinas rejects a human "freedom which is infinite with regard to any attachment." People are attached. They are born into families, cultures, languages. Removing selves from their cultural histories—the families, locations, the social structures, the religious, historical, cultural, political traditions in which they grew up and that give them both context and formation, is in fact to remove the very selfhood of each, what constitutes him and her as him- and herself. Levinas insists that selves cannot be defined or reduced to abstract reason—"the sovereign freedom of reason," which erases difference and joins all in universal structures. Rather, selves are embedded in relationships, histories, and cultures. This in no way effaces their uniqueness and particularity. On the contrary, it is what constitutes their particular personhood.[36]

The self is never simply unitary. Inevitably, a person participates in and identifies with more than one community—cultural and national, but also professional, civic, social, religious, and so on.[37] These need not be identical or harmonious with each other, and in fact cannot fully be; they may be in various relations of tension or conflict. Nor does this multiplicity erase identity. Rather, it constitutes it. Selves are the complex, shifting intersections between their various affiliations and experiences. The self is thus situated rather than abstract, plural rather than unified. The same can be said for a national cultural identity: that is, a culture organized civically with powers of government, constituted of differences among its citizens and their communities, and in relation to other national cultures and communities, in an ethic in which such difference is normative through limitations of claims by any one particular to universality, while also sustaining difference as a good.

A government consistent with normative difference—adopting difference rather than unity as its normative principle—must be democratic. Only then are voices of difference able to express themselves, to participate and be heard in the exceedingly complex decision-making that normative difference requires. How to distribute goods in order to sustain differences is a legal and civic challenge that only those involved can decide through negotiation, which may not and indeed need not involve the sharing of viewpoints, as Habermas requires. Habermas's notion of reciprocal recognition as embracing the "viewpoint of the other" demands symmetrical structures in the attempt to reach understanding; through "universal discourse of an unbounded community of interpretation" and "conflict-free networks." However, to Levinas, embracing the viewpoint of the other is either an oxymoron or an imposition. Levinas insists that the viewpoint of the other can never be fully grasped or entered into. "The ultimate experience of relationship [is] not in synthesis;" but a withholding of synthesis in the intersubjective relation as well, which remains "non-symmetrical." Each Other is unique,

Other to any other. Yet this is not relativist, since each other is limited as to what it can impose, as well as responsible to others. Participation and negotiation are thus not grounded on common universal reason but the value of difference itself, a difference which each is responsible for respecting and sustaining. To say each "other" is unique is not to say it is autonomous or isolated. Levinas insists that the "self begins in relation," is "both unique and in-relation." Like communitarians, Levinas sees the self emerge out of sociality itself, in responsibility to others: "I speak of responsibility as the essential, primary and fundamental structure of subjectivity . . . the very node of the subjective is in ethics understood as responsibility." But such responsibility equally inheres in respecting difference, between both selves and communities.[38]

In the essay "Peace and Proximity," Levinas turns these norms of difference to politics. Levinas names his ethic of relation and Otherness "proximity." This he opposes with ideals of "peace" where, in the tradition strongly evident in Habermas and other cosmopolitan writers, "the diverse agrees with itself and unites . . . where the other is reconciled with the identity of the identical in everyone." This notion of peace would try to gather "humans participating in the same ideal truths," idealizing a "unity of a Whole" promised on the "basis of a universal knowledge" and reason. Such ideals are mirrored in "millennia of fratricide," where it is hard to separate "universalism or imperialism." The turn—Levinas's turn—to "innumerable particularisms" instead is one that turns from a Hegelian dialectic, whose project of "absolute thought" is "indifferent to wars, murders, and suffering as these are necessary for the unfolding of rational thought," where peace is, as Hegel writes, "the identity of the identical and the non-identical." As "comprehensive structure," this peace demands "conforming to the ideal of the unity of the one which every alterity disturbs," in which each "human multiplicity would be reduced to part of the whole."[39]

Levinas offers not a Hegelian dialectic, but what might be called a dialectonic, where particulars encounter and confront each other without synthesis. Here Otherness, alterity, has an "absolute character" not reducible to synthesis. Multiplicity then would not be a "privation of unity" but the very situation of ethics, the "relation with the inassimilable other, the

irreducible other, the other, unique." This "proximity" of irreducible difference does not unite in identity but rather questions and limits unitary
identity, constraining its claims to "limitless freedom and its power." As
a basis of law and politics, responsible difference, not unity, is regulatory.
The political remains necessary, but not where the universal and unity,
with its impetus of assimilation and imposition, is its ground and goal.
Rather, "responsibility for the other human being is, in its immediacy,
anterior." Difference, its ethics of restraint and responsibility, govern—and
limit—selves and communities as a normative principle.[40]

THE STATE OF LANGUAGE

In "Peace and Proximity," Levinas characteristically and significantly
describes his ethics in terms of a "call to responsibility" and "a summons."
An ethics of the Other is an ethics of language: that is, language not only as
a conduit in which relationships are negotiated and enacted, but also as a
fundamental model for Levinasian ethics of both relation and difference,
responsibility and Otherness. The notion of address is pivotal. Throughout
Levinas's writings, the relation of language is a relation across difference,
what he calls an "unrelating relation," a "relationship to the Other . . . that
does not become correlation . . . a relationship and a non-relationship."
Relation in fact entails separation and difference: otherwise it would be
identity.[41]

This relation of difference is exemplified as well as enacted in
language. In language each self acts as "absolutely other in relation to the
other, without common measure or domain available for some sort of
coincidence." "Despite the relations among individuals" there remains
an "ontological separation between human beings and . . . the transcendence that gapes between them." Yet there is also an "approach" that is
best described in terms of self and other as interlocutors: "The distance
of absolute alterity of transcendence signifies by itself the difference and
the relationship between the I and the You as interlocutors . . . who form
no totality," regarding each other not through abstract supra-linguistic
reason, but in the "concrete [as] the absolute distance and relationship of
dialogue." As interlocutors, self and other remain apart, yet also address

each other—an address already invoking response: what Levinas calls responsibility as being "answerable," in which the "I frees itself from its auto-affirmation to answer for the other."[42]

In Habermas's communicative model, language conveys thought, which is carried and then absorbed as thought, uniting participants in communicative reason. Thought is privileged and prior to language, which has itself no shaping role in communication. Neither is it granted formative cultural force as a carrier of historical meanings that bind together those who speak and share it. Indeed, as Levinas exposes, language in this model is not only ideally transparent, but is ideally dispensable. The granting to language no role other than that of conveying the subjectivities that are joined together in discourse makes language itself secondary at best. Indeed, there would be no need to exchange words in language at all if thought were shared in unity. Writes Levinas, "a universal thought dispenses with communication."[43]

But language in Levinas does not merely convey thoughts that are first formulated without it, before they come to the embodiment of expression. Nor does Levinas idealize a unitary reason that all language would simply reflect and to which it would conduct its speakers. Instead, thought takes shape in language, in its very exteriorization and embodiment as verbal forms that address others. There is "no thought without language." Nor is unity as universal reason idealized. Rather, it is multiplicity, as it assumes difference, that is required and affirmed in linguistic action. Multiplicity is not the problem to be overcome, but the necessary, given, and indeed ethical context for democratic community and its discourses. In this affirmation of multiplicity, language is both conduct and model. As Levinas writes in *Totality and Infinity*: "Language presupposes interlocutors, a plurality. Their commerce is not a representation of the one by the other, nor a participation in universality, on the common plane of language." In an essay on "Dialogue" in *Of God Who Comes to Mind*, he reiterates this essential link between language and multiplicity: "It is through the empirical multiplicity of thinking men that language circulates." Language does not, as in idealist models, consist "in entering into the thought of the other, in coinciding in reason, and in internalizing itself," where "reason would be the true inner life. Reason is One."

Nor does language attempt to bring "interlocutors to reason, establishing peace in unanimity, and suppressing proximity in coincidence." Dialogue is not where "interlocutors enter into the thought of the others."[44]

Likewise linguistic interchange is not the "effect of some fall or ontological catastrophe of the One. The social existence that language establishes between souls is not compensation for a unity of thought lost or missed. And sociality is not the unity of multiple consciousnesses that have entered into the same thought in which their reciprocal alterity is suppressed."[45]

"Sociality" in Levinas is itself intricately invested in language. People are born into language, as they are into culture, and never subsist as purely independent or autonomous from the specificities of this cultural birth. Yet this by no means posits a unitary cultural identity, either in a self, in a community, or in the political organization of a nation. Nor, alternatively, does it posit a universal reason that unites all selves above particularities. Rather, as in language, Levinas posits separate, distinct selves who relate above all by addressing each other. There is, Levinas writes, an "original sociality produced in dialogue" out of the "multiplicity of thinking beings, the plurality of consciousness." The linguistic relation does not require agreement or shared reason, is not "reducible to transmission . . . of knowledge raised to universal intelligibility into which these thinking I's would be absorbed." Rather, it requires the address and response itself: "in the summons of a You by an I."[46]

This "difference and relationship between the I and the You as interlocutors" retains an "absolute alterity" that Levinas calls transcendence, "a difference that is never itself transcended." The ethics of language takes place above all in the "vocative," "the relationship with the Other that is cast in the relation of language, where . . . the other is maintained and confirmed in his heterogeneity as soon as one calls upon him . . . he is the one to whom I speak." It is this construction of "discourse or more exactly response or responsibility which is the authentic relationship with the other." This discourse structure in fact points to a needed rethinking of the very term or notion of "identity," which carries with it a sense of static, unchanging, unitary essence rather than the continuous negotiation among multiple relationships within and between selves. Levinas writes of the words "I

am" having "a signification different from the Eleatic or Platonic signification," and of "multiplicity and a transcendence in the verb to exist." Signification itself points to models of the articulation of meanings not as static
references but in relations and distinctions as they multiply and unfold.
One possible alternative term might be "signature," the title essay for Levinas's own brief memoir, as marking the trace of the self as it unfolds in the
actions it has performed and is performing.[47]

Levinas points to a different democratic discourse theory from Habermas's model. It does not presuppose ideal speech situations or dissolution
of difference in shared universal reason. Instead, Levinas sees in language
the necessity and affirmation of difference, as well as the structure of
relation across it that never absorbs or erases difference in address and
response. This applies within a polity in which individuals participate,
and also between communities or polities. It takes place not as a kind of
abstract linguistic disembodiment, but in a particular language in particular locations in time, place, and culture. As Michael Walzer writes in
Thick and Thin, "there is no neutral (unexpressive) moral language, no
Esperanto of moral discourse."[48]

Rather than either cosmopolitanism or even a politics of recognition,
Levinas's is a politics of address and response.[49] Neither universalist nor
relativist, it affirms norms of difference as regulating proximity between
selves and others, both as individuals and as communities. This affirms a
"transcendence or relation according to its double meaning of absolute
distance and the crossing of this by language . . . [This] concept of the
ethical . . . is separated from the tradition that derives the ethical from
knowledge and from reason as the faculty of the universal."

A political community based in an ethics of the Other is not "collectivist and exclusionary," as Habermas defines the nation. Conducted
through democratic discourses and practices that negotiate but do not
absorb difference, individuals within a polity as well as distinctive cultures
can retain their particular characters without what Levinas calls that
"suppression of alterity" that becomes a mask for domination: where
unitary claims—whether in the guise of rationalist cosmopolitanism
that transcends cultural distinction, or that of a single culture that seeks
to impose itself on others—devour difference. Levinas's ethics instead

affirms difference as limiting the self from imposing on others, but in relationships that demand responsibility to others. His support of Israel is not contradictory to his ethics. Levinas sees Israel as a democratic polity of distinctive cultural commitments in which, to return to Isaiah Berlin's pluralism, as he writes, values "can be incompatible between cultures, or groups in the same culture, or between you and me" not as a failure of an ideal unity, but as a valuation of plurality itself as a good. This was the basis of Berlin's defense of Israel: "Nationalism, including Zionism, is an awareness of oneself as a community possessing certain internal bonds which are neither superior nor inferior, but simply different in some respects from similar bonds that unite other nations."[50] Difference here is not only descriptive but prescriptive: where pluralism is enacted, inevitably, both within and between cultural communities, and embraced as the moral ground for community and political life.

NOTES

1   Isaiah Berlin, "The Achievement of Zionism," Isaiah Berlin Virtual Library, http://berlin.wolf.ox.ac.uk/lists/nachlass/achiezio.pdf (accessed June 9, 2012); and "Democracy, Communism, and The Individual," Isaiah Berlin Virtual Library, http://berlin.wolf.ox.ac.uk/lists/nachlass/demcomind.pdf (accessed June 9 2012).

2   Howard Caygill, *Levinas and the Political* (New York: Routledge, 2002), 163. Caygill sees any state as colonialist, 170; Michael Shapiro, "The Ethics of Encounter: Unreading, Unmapping the Imperium," in *Moral Spaces: Rethinking Ethics and World Politics*, ed. David Campbell and Michael Shapiro (Minneapolis: University of Minnesota Press, 1999), 69; Sarah Hammerschlag, *The Figural Jew* (Illinois: University of Chicago Press, 2010), 120, 18, 147. "Uprooted" in Levinasian discourse, as used by Hammerschlag, is taken out of context here, and is not a recommended or ideal state of true Jewish existence either historically or ethically: *Figural Jew*, 159–60; cf. 132, 142, 144, 147, 159 (the figure of the Jew has of course been a widely treated topic, including the ways it continues into postmodernity, carrying with it antisemitic elements); Michael F. Bernard-Donals, "'Difficult Freedom' Levinas, Language and Politics," *Diacritics* 35, no 3 (2005): 69, 75.

3   "Ethics and Politics," *The Levinas Reader*, ed. Sean Hand (Oxford: Blackwell, 1989), 294.

4   *Ethics and Infinity* (Pittsburgh: Duquesne University Press, 1985), 75; philosophy as the "nostalgia for totality," ibid., 76.

5   For example, *Ethics and Infinity*, 77: "morality comes not as a secondary layer, above an abstract reflection on the totality. . . First philosophy is an ethics."

6   Jürgen Habermas, *The Postnational Constellation* (Cambridge, MA: MIT Press, 2001), 103; *Inclusion of the Other* (Cambridge, MA: MIT Press, 1999).

7   Habermas, *Inclusion of the Other*, 116, 160.

8   Habermas, *Postnational Constellation*, 73, cf. *Inclusion of the Other*, 139, 140, 145.

9   Will Kymlicka and Wayne Norman, eds., "Introduction," in *Citizenship in Diverse Societies* (New York: Oxford University Press, 2000), 17; Habermas, *Inclusion of the Other*, 161.

10 Habermas, *Postnational Constellation*, 73, 137–38.

11 Ibid., 109; Michael Walzer, "Education, Democratic Citizenship and Multiculturalism," in Yael Tamir, *Democratic Education in a Multicultural State* (Oxford: Blackwell, 1995), 23–32. Walzer argues that each democracy "has its own particular history and points towards its own culture." Democracy has a "substantive character." As Walzer writes elsewhere, even Habermas's "democratic procedure" turns out to be "rather more than minimal . . . the rules of engagement constitute a way of life." They arise out of "history: they have been worked on for many generations" (*Thick and Thin: Moral Argument at Home and Abroad* [Notre Dame: University of Notre Dame Press, 1994], 14–15). Cf. Paul Kahn: claims of sovereignty reflect a community's understanding of itself as embodying a distinct set of meanings that are substantive not formal, realized at a particular historical moment and limited to members (*Putting Liberalism in its Place* [Princeton: Princeton University Press, 2005], 11). Cf. William Galston, *Liberal Purposes* (Cambridge: Cambridge University Press, 1991), 3, 28: he argues that one "can't ground political identity . . . without any reference to national or cultural identities. There is no pure liberalism without reference to identity"; Charles Taylor, "Democratic Exclusion in Multiculturalism," in *Multiculturalism, Liberalism and Democracy*, ed. Rajeev Bhargava, Amiya Kumar Bagchi, R. Sudarshan (New York: Oxford University Press, 2007), 158–59; Isaiah Berlin, *Against the Current* (London: Penguin, 1979), 344.

12 Michael Sandel, *Democracy's Discontents* (Cambridge, MA: Harvard University Press, 1996); Habermas quotations from *Postnational Constellation*, 126, 88, 81, 110, 81. Cf. Kahn associates the liberal rational self with the "plastic and disembodied conception of a subject who locates the self in a variety of networked relationships: economic, informational, communicative: ie postmodern world" (*Liberalism*, 9).

13 Habermas quotation from *Postnational Constellation*, 64–65. On disbanding of common cultural worlds, Habermas offers the European Union as an "exemplary" case, but he concedes that the legitimacy of the governing capacities of the EU "is unthinkable without an expansion of their formal democratic basis of legitimacy," *Postnational Constellation*, 88, 99. David Miller, *Market, State and Community* (Oxford: Clarendon Press, 1990), 235, 231 (cf. Miller, "The Ethical Significance of Nationality," *Ethics* 98, no. 4 [1988]: 648). For, as Miller goes on to say, "loyalty to the human race as a whole is meaningless" (238).

14 Ronald Dworkin, *Law's Empire* (Cambridge, MA: Belknap Press, 1986), 175; Taylor, "Democratic Exclusion,"145–46; Michael Walzer, "The Moral Standing of States," *Philosophy and Public Affairs* 9, no. 3 (1980): 225–28.

15 Quotations from Habermas, *Postnational Constellation*, 99, 107.

16 Habermas quotations from *Inclusion of the Other*, 118, 110; Kahn, *Liberalism*, 16.

17 Habermas's public sphere has been critiqued by feminists as ignoring the inequalities that make access to this sphere unequal, in which case the speech setting is not ideal. "Consensus" defined as arising "under conditions of freedom, equality, fairness," writes Nancy Fraser, ignores gender and other distinctions in which people are not

equally free and for whom conditions are not equally fair. If Foucault equates all relationships to power, with reason itself only an instrument of domination, Habermas ignores power and how it enters into relationships, in the public sphere as well as in the family. "To reclaim Habermas," Fraser writes, "there is a need to reconstruct the unthematized gender subtext of his material," *Unruly Practices: Power, Discourse, and Gender in Contemporary Social Theory* (Minneapolis: University of Minnesota Press, 1989), 119. Cf. Marie Fleming, "Women and the 'Public Use of Reason,'" that critiques Habermas's fundamental structure of public and private as remaining gendered, 130–31: *Feminists Read Habermas,* ed. Johanna Meehan (New York: Routledge, 1995), 117–37.

18   Walzer, *Thick and Thin,* 12, 14–15, and "A Critique of Philosophical Conversation," in *Hermeneutics and Political Theory in Ethics and Politics,* ed. Michael Kelly (Cambridge, MA: MIT Press, 1991), 185, 187; speech as neutral conveyance for reason, Habermas, *Inclusion of the Other,* 138; language as medium quotations, Jürgen Habermas, *Between Facts and Norms* (Cambridge, MA: MIT Press, 1996), 18; participants achieving understanding, Habermas, *Postnational Constellation,* 151; cooperative practice, Habermas, *Inclusion of the Other,* 24; Walzer, "Conversation," 187; Emmanuel Levinas, *Of God Who Comes To Mind,* trans. Bettina Bergo (Stanford: Stanford University Press, 1998), 142.

19   Habermas, *Between Facts and Norms,* 500, 15.

20   Quotations from Habermas, *Postnational Constellation,* 143, 126, 152, *Inclusion of the Other,* 26. Cf. this last statement with *Inclusion of the Other,* 222, conceding that the "identity of the individual is interwoven with collective identities" but insisting on the "normative" necessity not to protect "forms of life and traditions" of groups but only "the recognition of their members."

21   Quotations from Habermas, *Postnational Constellation,* 150, 151; *Between Facts and Norms,* 8 (in this, attempts to go beyond a Kantian isolated individual by extending the universal to be "accepted by everyone from the perspective of each individual" which remains the normative formula [*Inclusion of the Other,* 31] to a discursive structure he feels answers to social and historical context). Intersubjectivity from Habermas, *Inclusion of the Other,* 137–38; reciprocal recognition, Habermas, *Inclusion of the Other,* 139.

22   Quotations from Habermas, *Postnational Constellation,* 146; final quotation ibid., 150. Natural history, language game: positions Habermas attacks as postmodern, including Wittgenstein's views of language games as context-dependent. Habermas is concerned with resisting Foucauldian reduction of all institutions and interactions to power. Against those who claim that normative language "can supposedly reflect nothing else but the factual claims to power of political self-assertion," he counters "sheer power can be domesticated by legitimate law" (*Postnational Constellation,* 120). Yet he does not acknowledge the ways in which communicative community in fact reflects, reproduces, and reinforces cultural and historical contexts rather than transcending or correcting them.

23   For democratic procedures that are embedded beyond deliberative discourse, see Michael Walzer, *Passion and Politics* (New Haven: Yale University Press, 2004). Following quotations are from Habermas, *Postnational Constellation,* 107, 110.

24   Quotations from Habermas, *Inclusion of the Other,* 33, 30; *Postnational Constellation,* 151.

25 First quotation from Habermas, *Postnational Constellation*, 19; difference as villain, Habermas, *Postnational Constellation*, 103; following quotations from Habermas, *Postnational Constellation*, 103; *Between Facts and Norms*, 8 (cf. *Postnational Costellation*, 107–08); the rising global sphere, Habermas, *Inclusion of the Other*, 176; remaining quotations from Habermas, *Between Facts and Norms*, 486; *Inclusion of the Other*, 251; *Postnational Constellation*, 111.

26 Habermas, *Inclusion of the Other*, 333. Even Habermas's stated goal to reformulate Kant in intersubjective terms that are not unhistorical (ibid., 33) results in the dismissal of "substantive background consensus" for the "neutral fact" of participation in communication itself as "reciprocal recognition" (ibid., 39).

27 Emmanuel Levinas, *Ethics of Infinity*, 79, and "Reflections on the Philosophy of Hitlerism," *Critical Inquiry* 17, no. 1 (Autumn 1990): 62–71.

28 Levinas, "Philosophy of Hitlerism," 67–68.

29 Ibid., 66.

30 Emmanuel Levinas, *Beyond the Verse* (Bloomington, IN: Indiana University Press, 1994), 79, 70, 191.

31 Habermas, *Postnational Constellation*, 120, 147–48. Kymlicka raises the question to what extent reasonableness itself "does not simply reflect the majority's cultural traditions, languages, religion" (*Citizenship*, 9).

32 James Madison, " The Utility of the Union as a Safeguard against Domestic Faction and Insurrection (continued)," *Federalist* 10 (November 22, 1787), http://www.constitution.org/fed/federa10.htm (accessed June 28, 2012).

33 Emmanuel Levinas, *Outside the Subject*, trans. Michael Smith (Stanford: Stanford University Press, 1994), 122–24.

34 Habermas's portrayal of nationalism: *Postnational Constellation*, 74, 76, 84, 100, 102; cf. Habermas, *Inclusion of the Other*, 107, 116, 119, 130, 148 152 et al. Nationality without common descent: there are many discussions on the complex compositions of civic nationalism, for example, Donald Horowitz, *Ethnic Groups in Conflict* (Berkeley: University of California Press, 1985), 589; David Miller speaks of the "historical fluidity of national identities" as a condition, not an impossibility, of national polities (*Market, State and Community*, 239).

35 Levinas, *Outside the Subject*, 125.

36 Quotations from Levinas, "Philosophy of Hitlerism," 64, 65, 66.

37 Cf. William Galston who defines liberal pluralism as one that acknowledges and indeed supports multiple identities.

38 Quotations from Habermas, *Postnational Constellation*, 151; *Between Facts and Norms*, 16, 18; from Levinas, *Ethics and Infinity*, 77, 98, "From Ethics to Exegesis," in *The Time of Nations* (Bloomington, IN: Indiana University Press), 111; *Otherwise Than Being: or Beyond Essence*, trans. Alphonso Lingis (Pittsburgh: Duquesne University Press, 1998), 158; *Ethics and Infinity*, 95.

39 Opening quotation from "Peace and Proximity" in Emmanuel Levinas, *Basic Philosophical Writings*, ed. Adriaan Peperzak, Simon Critchley, Robert Bernasconi (Bloomington, IN: Indiana University Press, 1996), 162; the notion of "proximity" rather than "peace," cf. Alain Badiou, *Saint Paul: The Foundation of Universalism*, trans. Ray Brassier (Stanford: Stanford University Press, 2003); Ulrich Beck *Cosmopolitan Vision* (Cambridge: Polity Press, 2006), Amartya Sen, *Identity and Violence* (New York: Norton, 2006). Remaining quotations from Levinas, "Peace and Proximity," 162–3, 164, 165.

40 Quotations from Levinas, "Peace and Proximity," 165, 167, 168.
41 Quotations from Levinas, "Peace and Proximity," 167; the relation of language in Emmanuel Levinas, *Totality and Infinity*, trans. Alphonso Lingis (The Hague: M. Nijhoff Publishers, 1979), 295, and Levinas, *Of God*, 107.
42 All quotations from Levinas, *Of God*, 144–45, except for last sentence, where quotations are from Levinas, *Outside the Subject*, 125.
43 Levinas, *Totality and Infinity*, 72.
44 First quotation from Levinas, *Of God*, 140: Levinas here is critiquing Husserlian phenomenology, which places consciousness before language, as Derrida follows him in doing in his *Speech and Phenomena*, and in accord with many twentieth-century philosophers of language in ways that Habermas specifically critiques, see "Philosophy of Hitlerism." Other quotations from Levinas, *Totality and Infinity*, 73; *Of God*, 140
45 Levinas, *Of God*, 141.
46 Quotations from ibid., 143.
47 Quotations from Levinas, *Of God*, 145, *Totality and Infinity*, 69 (cf. *Otherwise Than Being*, 144); *Ethics and Infinity*, 88—cf. Tariq Modood in "Anti-essentialism, Multiculturalism and the Recognition of Religious Groups," in *Citizenship in Diverse Societies*, ed. Will Kymlicka and Wayne Norman (New York: Oxford University Press, 2000), 175–98, discusses identity as a process of change and adaptation, borrowings and influences, through the continuation of a subject that undergoes change. Culture "is made through change. It is not defined by an essence which exists apart from change, but possibility of making historical connections of being able to see change and resemblance" (ibid., 179). Quotations in final two sentences, Levinas, *Ethics and Infinity*, 72.
48 Walzer, *Thick and Thin*, 9. Cf. Rajeev Bhargava, "Introduction," *Multiculturalism, Liberalism and Democracy*, 7, defined by language. Identification with beliefs and desires is impossible without language, located in a common world of meanings, a culture, 8; language and the meanings it bears are an integral part of a particular network of meanings, 7–8. In a feminist context, cf. Allison Jagger in *Setting the Moral Compass*, ed. Cheshire Calhoun (New York: Oxford University Press, 2004): small communities, whose members are known personally to each other, have been indispensable "in developing a language to make themselves heard," since "language is a public construct," and "creating a new language is by definition a collective project" based on "creating a collective identity with other women in similar situations"; "Articulating women's distinctive interests requires a language and this, in turn, requires a community" (Jagger, *Setting the Moral Compass*, 238).
49 It is not possible to enter here into a fuller discussion of Levinas in comparison with the wide variety of multicultural discourses that also recognize difference, but often in ways that either reify it in groups or dissolve it into its own forms of post-nationalism. Tariq Modood describes this as the tendency to claim essentialist identity yet to reject identity altogether as if lack of essence entails that there is "not identity at all, no unified self, deconstruction, no culture or self,"—"Anti-essentialism," 177. Following quotation from Levinas, *Of God*, 149.
50 For Habermas's definition of nation, see *Inclusion of the Other*, 139; quotation from Levinas, *Of God*, 141; Isaiah Berlin, "On The Pursuit of the Ideal," *New York Times Review of Books* 35, no. 4 (March 17, 1988); for Berlin's defense of Israel, see "Achievement of Zionism."

The Holocaust as the Zionist and Anti-Zionist Narrative of the State of Israel

5

ANITA SHAPIRA

In 1992, Ehud Barak, then Chief of Staff of the Israel Defense Forces, paid a visit to Auschwitz. In his speech at the camp memorial he declared: "Here, at the end of March 1942, the gas chambers were first operated on a massive scale. And we, soldiers of the IDF, have arrived 50 years later, perhaps 50 years too late."[1]

These words bespeak a view of the Holocaust held by many Israelis: a gnawing sense of guilt over their failure to save European Jewry, mingled with a certain naivety about the European arena in which the catastrophe occurred, and an anachronistic historical perspective, ascribing post factum to the tiny 1940s Yishuv in Palestine the twenty-first-century capabilities of the IDF in particular and the State of Israel in general. The covert assumption: had the State of Israel been born before World War II, it would have been possible to save European Jewry. This is a characteristic assumption of the Zionist narrative of the Holocaust.

The Holocaust was incorporated within the founding myths of the State of Israel virtually in real time. Though none could foresee the Holocaust, in retrospect it was understood as the very same cataclysm that Zionism had darkly prophesized for Europe's Jews. Most survivors had not been Zionists, but the years of terror had kindled in them a sense of ethnic and national identification with the Jewish people. Their Zionism was intuitive, articulating recognition of a shared fate. The fight for a Jewish state provided Jews in Palestine, in the United States and in the displaced persons camps in Germany and Austria, with a positive goal to battle for, a lodestar to counter incipient inclinations to nihilism and desires for revenge that had surfaced in various circles. The Holocaust was the nadir of despair, the state the antipode of hope, symbolizing the brightening future.

At the war's end, the creation of a Jewish State was perceived by Jews as a kind of compensation for the huge tragedy that had befallen European Jewry. Jews held on to the belief that the democratic world was an enlightened and just tribunal: it was inconceivable that Jews would not be compensated for all that had been perpetrated. The basic material and political foundations for establishing a Jewish state in Palestine had been laid before World War II. However, the Holocaust infused the fight for independence with its emotional intensity, spiritual energy, and determination. The battle for opening the gates of Palestine to the *She'erit ha-Pleta*, the surviving remnant of European Jewry, forged the link in Jewish public consciousness between "Holocaust" and "Rebirth" (*tekumah*). Without that rebirth there would be no solution for the survivors.

The political event that clearly melded the Holocaust with *tekumah* was the UN General Assembly vote on November 29, 1947. The fact that thirty-three members, more than two-thirds of those voting, balloted in favor of partition and the creation of two states—one Jewish, one Arab— was interpreted by many Jews as a direct consequence of the Holocaust's impact on world public opinion. The joint support of Soviet Russia and the USA was seen as signaling the shared insight into the fundamental justice at stake here. Current research does not bear out such an optimistic reading of Assembly members' motives: their votes were driven by political considerations and individual national agendas. Jews were reassured, eager to retain their belief in a world of morality and justice. The Israeli Declaration of Independence cites the Holocaust as one of the reasons for the state's creation, strung between the Balfour Declaration and the UN partition resolution of November 29, 1947. The text also underscored the struggle of "survivors of the Nazi holocaust in Europe, as well as Jews from other parts of the world" to immigrate to Palestine: they "never ceased to assert their right to a life of dignity, freedom and honest toil in their national homeland." Yet nowhere did it assert that the establishment of the State of Israel was the *result* of the Holocaust.

As the turbulent events of the 1940s receded into the past, there were more and more people who forged a direct link between the state's establishment and the Holocaust. Two simultaneous processes were afoot: on the one hand, the memory of the struggle for the establishment of the state and even of the War for Independence was now receding. On the other, the place of the Holocaust in collective memory became much more pronounced. The Holocaust became the standard justification for the state's creation, seemingly held out to the Jews at the end of the war in Europe on a kind of silver platter. As we will see, this innocent assumption became the foundation for an anti-Zionist myth.

From day one, the State of Israel claimed for itself the right to represent the memory of the Holocaust. As the state of the Jews and the polity that had absorbed the largest number of Holocaust survivors (almost two-thirds) and Jewish refugees from eastern Europe, Israel claimed the right to speak in the name of all Jews, living and dead. The proposal to bestow Israeli citizenship retroactively on all those who died in the Holocaust and the Resistance, though never implemented, articulated Israel's desire not only to lead the Jewish people in the present, but to speak for and represent the millions of Jews who had perished.[2]

The growing centrality of the Holocaust in collective memory was now drawn on ever more by politicians, intellectuals, and the media, and created a bond between the Zionist narrative and the Holocaust. Concomitantly, post- and anti-Zionists eager to undermine the Zionist narrative seized on that link between the Holocaust and the national revival.

The readiest argument against Israel's legitimacy to represent the memory of the Holocaust was the charge that the leaders of the Yishuv had failed to rescue European Jewry. During the war in Europe, there had already been analogous criticism: while Jews are being slaughtered, you stand idly by. Such charges came largely from the camp that disavowed the Yishuv's leaders, in the main the right wing in Palestine, particularly the underground IZL. Protesting against the Jewish Agency's policy of cooperation with the British during the war, they drew a double analogy: just as the British were similar to the Nazis, the leadership of the Jewish Agency resembled the ghetto Judenrat. Just as the Judenräte had stooped to collaborating with the Nazis, the JA leadership had degraded itself in dealings with the British.

After the establishment of the state, two political episodes provided the political ammunition for an attack on Ben-Gurion and the ruling party more generally, denouncing them as guilty of complicity in cooperating with the Jewish people's enemies: namely, the storm over reparations and the Kasztner affair. In the first episode, Begin succeeded in tapping the vehement emotions that any mode of cooperation with Germany aroused in that period. His determined struggle against negotiations with West German representatives helped Begin regain the place he had lost in Israeli politics in the aftermath of the Herut defeat in the July 1951 elections to the Second Knesset. The *cause célèbre* around Israel Kasztner in the mid-1950s was to generate bitter feelings for many years within Israeli society. Kasztner, a Zionist leader of Hungarian Jewry in 1944, was affiliated with Mapai. His close relations with Nazi officials had saved the lives of thousands of Jews but also gave rise to accusations of collaboration. The libel suit brought by Kasztner in 1955 against one of his accusers, Malkiel Gruenwald, turned into a trial against Kasztner himself. In the court proceedings, Shmuel Tamir, the young, aggressive, and viciously anti-Ben-Gurion lawyer for the defense, again raised the assertion that Mapai equaled Judenräte. He crystallized the anti-exilic stereotypes, reinforcing the contrast between the Jewish fighters in Palestine and occupied Europe on the one hand—and those "diasporic Jews" who had failed to resist (and even collaborated with the enemy) on the other, going to their death "like sheep to the slaughter."

The same political line was also espoused by elements on the Israeli left at a time of heightened rivalry between Mapai and Mapam, the latter then a Moscow-friendly Marxist party. The pro-Western orientation of the Social Democratic Mapai was perceived by the left as a betrayal of socialist principles and a deviation from the correct line. In both these episodes, the extreme left claimed it was the true representative of the ghetto fighters and partisans, denouncing Mapai as a party continuing in the tradition of the Judenräte.

The accusation of collaboration between Zionists and Nazis sprang in the main from internecine struggles between feuding Zionist camps, but was quickly seized upon by the Soviet propaganda machine against Israel. Not only did Israel have no right to represent the victims of the Holocaust, it was also guilty of collaborating with the murderers. Here was an avenue for invalidating the very legitimacy of the Jewish State. The Soviet accusations that the Zionists had worked hand in glove with the Nazis warped into vulgar analogy: Zionism equaled racism. That equation gained great popularity in the Arab camp, and was even given a stamp of global approval by the notorious resolution in the UN General Assembly in 1975.

The gravest accusation against Ben-Gurion and his associates came from Shabtai Beit Zvi, a Mapai Zionist from its right wing, who in 1977 published his *Post-Ugandian Zionism in the Crucible of the Holocaust*.[3]

He asserted that the Zionist movement, since the sixth congress in 1903, the famous Uganda controversy, had linked its destiny exclusively to Palestine, rejecting any solution and salvation for the Jews outside the ancient homeland. Beit Zvi argued that the Zionists had been opposed to proposals that opened an opportunity for saving Jews outside Palestine, concentrating their efforts only in the land of Israel. This, he alleged, stemmed from the notion of "negation of exile" (*shlilat ha-galut*), which had prevented the Zionist leadership from identifying with European Jewry and from saving them.

Beginning in the 1970s, there was a marked shift in emphases in Israeli memory of the Holocaust: from glorifying valor and heroism to emphasis on the sheer struggle to survive, to preserve one's basic human dignity. In a symbolic sense, Kasztner's image underwent a kind of rehabilitation in Israeli public opinion with Moti Lerner's popular stage play *Kasztner* and the television series based on it that followed. These presented the tale from the perspective of Kasztner and his associates. However, the concept of "negation of exile," as one of the causes underlying the failure to save European Jewry, continued to seep into scholarly works, and especially into public discourse through the media, providing the basis for the popular anti-Zionist narrative.

Beit Zvi outlined a *fundamental* contradiction and clash of interests within Zionist ideology: the good of the Jewish people versus the Zionist cause in Palestine. At critical moments, he claimed, the Zionist movement gave priority to the *summum bonum* of the tiny Yishuv in Palestine over what was best for the Jewish people as a whole. As he saw it, this clash of interests was rooted in the "negation of exile" ideology, and was the reason that the Zionists had not rescued European Jewry.

Beit Zvi's *Post-Ugandian Zionism* became a veritable cult book, dug out every few years and "rediscovered" by various journalists. Established academic historians were berated for having "buried away" the book and sidestepped its disconcerting thesis.

Over the years, Beit Zvi's thesis has penetrated into feature articles in the press and books on the fringe between historical inquiry and journalism, such as the fascinating and controversial work by Tom Segev, *The Seventh Million: The Israelis and the Holocaust*. Yet the thesis also made its way into historical inquiry, both as a research topic for analysis and a supposedly self-evident hypothesis.[4] In common with other cult works, the book reinforces hidden assumptions and bolsters popular prejudices. Research has long ago refuted Beit Zvi's factual arguments with regard to various rescue schemes that did not work out. Facts notwithstanding, his thesis persists. Beit Zvi played on intuitive thought patterns among Jews, whose sense of guilt for their lost family members and fellow Jews deepened as the Holocaust became ever more central in collective memory. Contingency is difficult for the mind to accommodate. The notion that historical events are in large part an accidental collection of arbitrary happenings subverts the trust human beings have in a logical ordered world governed by cause and effect. Faced with cataclysmic events, we search for some key, all-inclusive explanation, so the view that the concept of negation of exile was the real "reason" behind the failure to save European Jewry persists long after its factual basis has been invalidated.

Moreover, the more the State of Israel demonstrated its military prowess, political and diplomatic skills, the harder it became even to conceive of a time when Jews were completely powerless. From that perspective, Ehud Barak's words at the ceremony in Auschwitz unwittingly served to reinforce the anti-Zionist narrative: even the IDF Chief of Staff believes it was possible somehow to save the victims!

One of the factors that contributed to the acceptance of Beit Zvi's thesis was the reserve and arrogance with which Holocaust survivors were received by Israeli society more generally, and the younger generation in particular. The new immigrants looked different, they talked and behaved differently. Among Yishuv youth during the 1930s and 1940s, that attitude towards new immigrants had been quite common; now, in the context and aftermath of the Holocaust, it took on a sinister significance. Was that same arrogant contempt at the basis of the indifference that had impeded the rescue of Jews in the years of the Holocaust? The parallelism between later attitudes toward the survivors and the earlier relation to possible rescue of European Jewry is neither inevitable nor logical, yet it corresponded to psychological needs of the Jewish public and thus was adopted as a post-factum proof of the criminal negligence.

David Ben-Gurion is the founding father of the State of Israel. If the aim is to undermine the state's foundation myth, he is a prime target for attack. Ben-Gurion was a staunch and steadfast "negator of exile." From the 1920s on, he often articulated his strong views on the topic; even in the wake of the Holocaust, he did not revise his thinking. In his speeches, he always referred to the Holocaust in an elevated tone, but displayed no special interest in the survivors. Nor did he ever claim direct involvement in rescue activities, averring he had been busy with the business of establishing the State. Before the war, on at least one occasion, he expressed views interpreted as reflecting his preference for bringing a limited number of immigrants to Palestine over the rescue of a larger number of Jews in other lands. At the time, the discourse of "rescue" signified delivering Jews from a life without hope—not physical survival. In the postwar context, his pronouncement had a chilling resonance. While the war raged, Ben-Gurion did not make immigration to Palestine a condition for offering Jews assistance to get out of Europe: they should go wherever they could as long as they were rescued. Yet with war's end, he returned to Palestinocentric politics. Ben-Gurion viewed the DPs (displaced persons) as the lever that would help alter the status quo in Palestine, and did not balk at using the survivors as an instrument in the battle for a Jewish state.

Two key issues emerge from this brief account of Ben-Gurion's politics. The first: the use of the survivors as an expedient for advancing the Zionist cause. Whoever disavowed Zionism was quick to denounce Ben-Gurion's policy, depicting it as a cynical utilization of survivors to further an ideology alien to them. The second: the inference from Ben-Gurion's policy on the survivors and his general attitude to the Diaspora to the issue of the physical rescue of Jews during the war. If someone wants to find evidence to substantiate Beit Zvi's thesis, they will contend that Ben-Gurion's actions and omissions reveal his underlying motives. It was the ideology of the negation of exile that motivated him to refrain from rescue activities and persevere in a single aim: furthering the establishment of the state.

Is the fact that Ben-Gurion was not actively involved in attempts to save Jews during the Holocaust empirical proof that he was basically indifferent, an attitude driven by his rejection of the Diaspora? This conclusion seems far-fetched. Whoever claims this must demonstrate, first, that there was a genuine possibility, not seized upon, to save the Jews, and second, that the ideology of exilic negation was the reason no action was taken. Even if we assume there may have been missed opportunities for rescuing Jews, it is doubtful whether that convincingly establishes the connection between negation of exile and the failure to save European Jewry. The link between espoused ideology and everyday action is never direct, as between input and output. If reality were indeed all that simple, religious or revolutionary movements would not find it necessary to glorify the few true believers who live and die according to their principles. This is all the more so when an ideological tenet clashes with a matter of survival. As a rule, when confronted with the prospect of life or death, ideology gives way. Thus, many Zionists who were sworn rejecters of exile and lovers of Zion did not stand the supreme test of making *aliyah*. Similarly, in 1914 the devotees of cosmopolitan solidarity abandoned the slogan "workers of the world unite," departing to the ramparts to defend home and country. There is no proof whatsoever that when individuals were confronted by the possible fates of their family, friends, *shtetl*, or people, the "negation of exile" proved more powerful. Far more reasonable is the assumption that the Zionist Executive, with Ben-Gurion at its helm, were at times mistaken in their judgment and failed to properly gauge the unprecedented enormity of the Nazi Holocaust. Errors were of course made, but their origin lay in circumstances of the time and place—not in some inherent quasi-mythological disability of the Zionist movement deriving from the controversies sown at the Uganda Congress of 1903.

The more research brought to light the actual efforts made to rescue European Jews and the formidable dilemmas they entailed, the weaker the argument of imputed indifference and inaction. At the same time, the claim that the survivors had been exploited as an expedient was elaborated by those bent on undermining the state's legitimacy. The survivors were cast not as enthusiastic participants in the struggle to establish the state, but as some sort of marionettes controlled by the grand manipulator Ben-Gurion, responding in accordance with his wishes and schemes.[5] That argument entails a secondary assertion: had the gates of the United States not been closed, many of the survivors would never have emigrated to Palestine. Though not baseless, that hypothesis cannot be proven. In the years prior to the state's establishment, there was no certainty as to whether the United States would be willing to absorb Jewish refugees. Actually, it accepted only a limited number, and quite late, after the emergence of Israel. *De facto*, the survivors' struggle to open up immigration to Palestine was a fight for their own future. At that specific conjuncture, the interests of the survivors and the Zionist movement intermeshed.

Immediately after the war, two dominant currents emerged in the interpretation of the Holocaust's meaning: the national orientation, focusing on the lesson of Jewish isolation and the imperative need for self-reliance; and the socialist current that viewed the Holocaust universally, interpreting the catastrophe as a result of the racism and prejudice that had plagued and scapegoated Jews for centuries. Over the years, these currents radicalized: the first moved toward isolationism and hatred of the Other, transforming all enemies into the emblematic image of Hitler. Under its impress, anxieties about a renewed Holocaust bolstered refusal to recognize the rights of the Palestinians. The second universalizing paradigm seeks to dilute the specifically Jewish character of the Holocaust: the Holocaust was reconceived as a global metaphor for man's inhumanity to man. This expropriation of the Holocaust from Jewish history, transposing it into one chapter in the long annals of universal atrocities and injustice, had a specific agenda: to eradicate the Holocaust as justification for the Jewish state.[6]

This also impinges on the issue of the Holocaust and the Palestinians. Azmi Bishara argued that the Holocaust was the reason behind the establishment of the state—perpetrated by the Europeans, while the Palestinians were the ones compelled to pay the price. Ilan Pappe has commented: "The State of Israel was created with the aid of Western colonialism. It uprooted the Palestinian population deliberately, justifying it post factum on the basis of 'Jewish uniqueness' deriving from the singularity of the Holocaust."[7] Thus, the binary "Holocaust–Rebirth" is supplanted by a new triad: "Holocaust–Rebirth–Arab disaster."

The extraction of the Holocaust from its historical context and its moral universalizing, as reflected in post-Zionist ideology, are designed to serve as an ultimate retort to the Zionist argument that the Holocaust validated the Zionist prognosis. The Jewish state cannot protect the Jews from a second Holocaust—only the resolve to transform the world in the spirit of tolerance and pluralism, *tikkun olam*, holds out that hope. This is an old argument that accompanied the Zionist project from its very inception: should the Jews dedicate energies to improving human society at large, or concentrate on the particularistic and provincial project in Palestine? In the wake of the Holocaust, that question was dismissed from the agenda for several decades. It gained renewed relevance as time receded, pluralism took hold in Western society, and voices critical of Israel grew more vociferous.

Today we are witnessing an attempt to turn the axis "Holocaust–Rebirth" on its head: not only did Zionism not rescue the Jews, not only were the survivors exploited and the memory of the Holocaust erased, but even more, it transformed the Jews from victims into perpetrators. This burden of guilt awakens in Jews nostalgia for a pre-state era unencumbered by sovereignty, its obligations and constraints—when they were powerless but righteous. Ultimately, the Holocaust becomes an alternative explanatory paradigm to the nationalist narrative of the state's birth: not created because Jews had become a bona fide nation—but rather because the Europeans wished to *compensate* them for the catastrophe.

In the 1980s, the crux of the accusations against Israel had to do with the memory of the Holocaust. Why did it take so long for the state of Israel to internalize the memory of the trauma and to accord it the rightful place in the collective memory? Today the trend has reversed: the fear of extinction, based on the memory of the Holocaust, that has accompanied Israel since the Eichmann trial, is now presented as the reason for the Six-Day War and as the obstacle to the peace process. The condition now for reconciliation between Jews and Palestinians is hence the neutralization of the memory of the Holocaust, or at least the transformation of its lesson from a nationalist to a universalist one. The connection between the establishment of Israel and the Shoah, between memory and politics, changes according to the world view of the speaker and the expediencies of the moment. But we should not forget that the Jewish state was not given to the Jews by the Europeans or the Americans, Holocaust or not, but was won on the battle-field. Indeed, considering the enormous demographic, economic, and spiritual losses suffered by the Jewish people in the Holocaust, it is legitimate to ask how, in spite of the Holocaust, the State of Israel was established.

NOTES

1   "'Auschwitz—Never Again,' Speech Delivered by the Chief of Staff in the Auschwitz Extermination Camp, April 7, 1992," *Ba-Mahane*, no. 32 (April 15, 1992) [Hebrew].

2   "Independence Day Message of the Prime Minister," *Davar*, April 21, 1961 [Hebrew].

3   Shabtai Beit Zvi, *Post-Ugandian Zionism in the Crucible of the Holocaust* (Tel Aviv: Bronfman, 1977) [Hebrew].

4   Tom Segev, *The Seventh Million: The Israelis and the Holocaust*, trans. Haim Watzman (New York: Hill and Wang, 1993). One example of the spread of the thesis is Yehi'am Weitz, "David Ben Gurion: From Class Leader to Leader of the People," a critique of Shabtai Teveth's book *Kin'at David* (The Zeal of David), vol. 3, in *Zemanim* 29 (Autumn 1988) [Hebrew].

5   See Segev, *The Seventh Million; Idith Zertal, From Catastrophe to Power: The Holocaust Survivors and the Emergence of Israel* (Berkeley: University of California Press, 1998).

6   Yosef Grodzinski, "To Fight Against the Zionisation of the Holocaust," *Ha'aretz*, July 15, 1994 [Hebrew]; Amnon Raz- Krakotzkin, "Exile within Sovereignty: Toward a Critique of the 'Negation of Exile' in Israeli Culture," *Teoriyah u-Vikoret*, no. 4 (1993): 23–55 [Hebrew].

7   See Azmi Bishara, "The Arabs and the Holocaust: Analysis of the Problematics of the Conjunctive," *Zmanim*, no. 53 (1995); reply by Dan Michman, *Zmanim*, no. 54 (1995); response by Moshe Zuckerman, *Zmanim*, no. 55 (1996); reply by Bishara, ibid.; reply by Dan Michman, *Zmanim*, no. 56 (1996) [all Hebrew]; Ilan Pappe, "Lesson in Modern History," *Ha'aretz*, Supplement, June 24, 1994 [Hebrew].

PART III

STATE AND NATION

The Constitutional Significance of the Jewishness of Israel

6

ARIEL L. BENDOR

"There are many democratic states. Only one of them is a Jewish state . . . This nature is central to its existence, and it is . . . an 'axiom' of the State."

—Chief Justice Aharon Barak in Central Elections Committee for the Sixteenth Knesset v. Tibi (2003)

"It is impossible to separate Judaism from democracy. There is no such animal."

—Shimon Peres, President of the State of Israel

INTRODUCTION

The Declaration of Independence of the State of Israel, issued on May 14, 1948, defined Israel as a "Jewish state" and determined that "The State of Israel will be open for Jewish immigration and for the Ingathering of the Exiles." The Declaration went on to state that "[The State of Israel] will be based on freedom, justice and peace as envisaged by the prophets of Israel; it will ensure complete equality of social and political rights to all its inhabitants irrespective of religion, race or sex; it will guarantee freedom of religion, conscience, language, education and culture; it will safeguard the Holy Places of all religions; and it will be faithful to the principles of the Charter of the United Nations." The Israeli Basic Laws on human rights— Basic Law: Human Dignity and Liberty and Basic Law: Freedom of Occupation—state that Israel's values are those of a "Jewish and democratic state," and that human rights may not be prejudiced other than by means of a statute befitting the values of the state. The same Basic Laws also state that "fundamental human rights in Israel are founded upon recognition of the value of the human being, the sanctity of human life, and the principle that all persons are free; these rights shall be upheld in the spirit of the principles set forth in the Declaration of the Establishment of the State of Israel"—that is, the Declaration of Independence. Israel's Basic Laws also include additional provisions that express the affinity of the State of Israel to the Jewish people. Thus, Basic Law: The Knesset states that "A candidates' list shall not participate in elections to the Knesset, and a person shall not be a candidate for election to the Knesset, if the goals or actions of the list or the actions of the person, expressly or by implication, include . . . negation of the existence of the State of Israel as a Jewish and democratic state."[1]

Against the background of this legal infrastructure, this chapter will consider the constitutional significance of the Jewishness of Israel, focusing on the legal limitations that apply to the Knesset itself—as the legislative branch, and perhaps even the Constituent Assembly, of the State of Israel—in light of Israel's nature as a Jewish state. Accordingly, the principal objective of the chapter is not to determine the legal manifestations of the Jewishness of the state in practice, and certainly not to determine the cultural, social, and political extralegal manifestations of the affinity of the state to the Jewish people. Rather, it is intended to clarify the legal limits of the Knesset's power to make changes that will derogate from the Jewishness of the state.

As may be seen in the Declaration of Independence and the Basic Laws, Israel's affinity to the Jewish people is not its sole characteristic. In both the Declaration of Independence and the Basic Laws, Israel is defined as a "Jewish and democratic state." This calls into question the relationship between the Jewish nature and the democratic nature of the state, and especially the limits that apply to the Knesset, on the basis of democratic considerations, in passing legislation intended to promote the Jewishness of the state.

In this chapter I shall argue that, first of all, there is a constitutional core of Jewishness, which Israeli law does not empower the governmental authorities of the State to set aside; and, secondly, that this core must be understood as reconcilable with Israel's nature as a democracy, which also cannot be set aside by any authority, but which also must be interpreted in a way that is reconcilable with Israel's nature as a Jewish State.

THE DECLARATION OF INDEPENDENCE

In addition to the provision by virtue of which the Constituent Assembly operated, the Declaration of Independence also stated Israel's affinity to the Jewish people and its democratic nature (which results both from the determination that the Constituent Assembly will be elected by means of a national election and that the governmental authorities to be established by virtue of the Constitution will also be elected, and from the series of human rights listed in the Declaration). Admittedly, shortly after the establishment of the state, the Israel Supreme Court rejected the concept pursuant to which the provisions of the Declaration of Independence have a binding constitutional status.[2] In my opinion as well, not all of the details of the provisions of the Declaration should be viewed as binding, because this was not the intention of the People's Council. Nonetheless, the normative principles of the Declaration of Independence—that is, the affinity to the Jewish people and the democratic nature of the state—are not merely interpretive tools. They are binding legal provisions, to which all of the authorities of the state are subject, including its Constituent Assembly, which exists and operates by virtue of the Declaration of Independence. The People's Council certainly did not consider either the possibility that the Constituent Assembly would establish a Constitution that would sever any affinity between the State of Israel and the Jewish people, or that it would establish a non-democratic system of government for the state, as legitimate. Israel's nature as a Jewish and democratic state, as set forth in the Declaration of Independence, is not a mere recommendation or hope. Even those of Israel's citizens who reject the fundamental elements anchored in the Declaration of Independence will have difficulty denying that those elements embody the State of Israel. From the legal standpoint, it is not possible—not even through a constitution—to set aside the fundamental elements of the state as they appear in the initial legal document that established it.

The Knesset, even in its role as the Constituent Assembly, is accordingly subject to the binding basic values that are set forth in the Declaration of Independence. This does not mean that any deviation from Jewish or democratic characteristics that appears in a Basic Law will be considered as an unauthorized action. Only a Basic Law that cannot be reconciled with the element set forth in the Declaration of Independence—that is, which bears a significance tantamount to the abolition of the state—will be rejected.

THE BASIC LAWS ON HUMAN RIGHTS

Israel's two Basic Laws that concern human rights are Basic Law: Human Dignity and Liberty and Basic Law: Freedom of Occupation. Section 1 of each of these Basic Laws—the sections are identical, and both are captioned "Basic Principles"—includes the following words: "Fundamental human rights in Israel are founded upon recognition of the value of the human being, the sanctity of human life, and the principle that all persons are free; these rights shall be upheld in the spirit of the principles set forth in the Declaration of the Establishment of the State of Israel." This section, which was added to both of the Basic Laws in 1994, has not been given a great deal of attention in the legislative process in the Knesset, and the Israel Supreme Court also frequently ignores it. It seems to be perceived as a declaration of the ideological origins of human rights in Israel and the relationship between the rights set forth in the Basic Laws and the Declaration of Independence, with no practical legal meaning. This is shown, for example, in a statement by Justice Itzhak Zamir, to the effect that "this is merely an impressive declaration which in fact says nothing new, for we have long since acted in this way."[3]

At the same time, in his 1994 book on constitutional interpretation, Justice Aharon Barak stated that "respect for basic human rights, in the spirit of the principles set forth in the Declaration of the Establishment of the State of Israel, has become a constitutional imperative. It has been found that not only do the principles of the Declaration of Independence have legal force, but also the duty of respecting the basic rights in the spirit of the principles of the Declaration of Independence has become a constitutional duty, against which an 'ordinary statute' cannot stand. What we have before us, then, is a material change in the legal status of the Declaration of Independence." These words were consensually cited in a judgment handed down by the Israel Supreme Court in 1994 by Justice Dov Levin, who went on to state that "this introductory declaration in the Basic Laws . . . was not written into the law-books for the glory of the flowery phrase; rather, it was intended to express—and, this time, not as a wish or an abstract credo—that the Declaration of Independence has become a basic, binding constitutional principle."[4]

As set forth above, case law has neglected this section, and, in fact, it is almost never mentioned—and certainly not as the basis for imposing limits on the legislative power of the Knesset. It appears that the supreme legal status of the principles of the Declaration of Independence is not only—not even principally—conferred upon them by virtue of the Basic Laws; rather, their status primarily results from the fact that the Declaration of Independence is the supreme legal norm of the State of Israel, and the constituent powers of the Knesset that result therefrom and are subject thereto.

Section 2 of each of Israel's two Basic Laws on human rights—the sections are nearly identical, and both are captioned "Purpose"—reads as follows: "The purpose of this Basic Law is to protect human dignity and liberty [in Basic Law: Freedom of Occupation—to protect the freedom of occupation], in order to establish in a Basic Law the values of the State of Israel as a Jewish and democratic state." In Israel's first years, this section was given considerable attention in case law, in academic articles and, to a great degree, by the general public. Its interpretation gave rise to profound legal and ethical disputes. Nonetheless, as time went by— once it transpired that the practical legal significance of the section was limited—the debate on it died down. Today, the courts only infrequently cite it in substantiation of their rulings, especially those that concern the constitutionality of statutes. No statute has ever been rejected by the Israel Supreme Court on the grounds that the statute in question does not befit the values of the State.

The wording of the section is puzzling and seems to be poorly phrased, in a way that is inappropriate for any constitutional provision, especially one that determines the purpose of two particularly central Basic Laws. Is the purpose of the protection of human dignity and liberty, or of the freedom of occupation, really "to establish in a Basic Law the values of the State of Israel"? After all, establishment in a Basic Law—like establishment in any other legal provision—is a means of achieving a social purpose. The very act of establishment in a Basic Law does not constitute a purpose *per se*. The true significance of the section therefore appears to be that the protection of human rights shall be carried out in the spirit of the values of the State of Israel as a Jewish and democratic state.

BASIC LAW: THE KNESSET

An additional central provision of a Basic Law, which reflects the supreme constitutional values of Israel as a Jewish and democratic state, is Section 7A of Basic Law: The Knesset, which states, *inter alia*, that "A candidates' list shall not participate in elections to the Knesset, and a person shall not be a candidate for election to the Knesset, if the goals or actions of the list or the actions of the person, expressly or by implication, include: (1) negation of the existence of the State of Israel as a Jewish and democratic state; (2) incitement to racism; (3) support for armed struggle by a hostile state or a terrorist organization against the State of Israel." This section considers the Jewishness and the democratic nature of Israel as jointly characterizing its very existence, and eliminates any possibility that members of lists of candidates, or individual candidates, who oppose the existence of Israel as a Jewish and democratic state will be elected to Israel's legislative body.

It appears that the rationale behind this section, which negates the right to run for election to the Knesset, even for candidates who are entitled to freedom of expression—a freedom that, as a general rule, can only be prejudiced in Israel when there is a near-certainty level of probability that harm will be done to the security of Israel or to public peace—is, in the words of Justice Dalia Dorner: "The limitations on the exercise of the power of disqualification, pursuant to Section 7A, are not [based] . . . on the probability that running in elections will cause harm to the State, but rather, on preventing lists and candidates, whose purposes and political activity cannot be reconciled with membership in the legislative body of the State of Israel, from running. It is inconceivable that in the Knesset— which is the supreme governmental authority of the State of Israel—lists and candidates who devote their political activity to the destruction of the State could be allowed to stand as candidates and to be elected."[5]

Indeed, there is a problem with the exploitation of membership in the legislative body of the state in order to undermine its very existence—which, in the case of Israel, is reflected in its nature as a Jewish and democratic state. At the same time, "the disqualification of lists and candidates merely because they are not ideologically bound by the basic values of the State is likely to remove significant minority groups from the political game. Thus, most of the members of the Arab minority do not seek to promote the values of the State as a Jewish state. On the other hand, among the Jewish population there are groups which are not bound by the values of the State as a democratic state which treats its Arab citizens with full equality." Accordingly, "an ideology which remains at the level of a mere theory or ideal, and which is not accompanied by political activity intended to give rise to the attainment thereof, does not constitute cause for disqualification . . . A list of candidates shall [only] be disqualified if its political activity is principally devoted to striving to harm the protected values."[6]

WHAT ARE THE CONSTITUTIONAL VALUES OF ISRAEL AS A JEWISH STATE?

What are the values that, from a constitutional point of view—and, by virtue of the Declaration of Independence, even from a supra-constitutional point of view—reflect the Jewishness of Israel? These, in the words of Chief Justice Barak, are values that "are centered on the right of every

Jew to immigrate to the State of Israel, in which the Jews will constitute a majority; Hebrew is the central official language of the State, and most of its holidays and emblems reflect the national renaissance of the Jewish People; the heritage of [the Jewish people] is a central component of the religious and cultural heritage [of the state]." It may perhaps be possible to dispute some of the details in this definition. At the same time, although there is nothing that prevents Israel from also recognizing the collective rights of the non-Jewish minorities which live in it—and, to a certain degree, it recognizes those rights even today—it appears that the State cannot be defined as a multinational state.[7]

There is not necessarily a contradiction between a Jewish state and a state for all of its citizens. This depends on the meaning of "a state for all of its citizens." Indeed, "if the purpose of Israel's being 'a state for all of its citizens' is directed exclusively toward ensuring domestic equality among citizens and recognizing the rights of the minority which lives within our midst, this does not negate the existence of the State of Israel as a Jewish state. On the other hand, if the purpose ... seeks to detract from the rationale which underlies the establishment of the State, and thereby to negate the nature of the State of Israel as the State of the Jewish People, this is capable of prejudicing the minimal core characteristics which characterize the State of Israel as a Jewish state."[8]

Accordingly, within the framework of the State of Israel, it is not possible to cancel the right of return (although it is possible to modify various details of the existing Law of Return), or the central status of Jewish and Hebrew culture—just as it is not possible to eliminate the fundamental elements of democracy: free elections, separation of powers, and basic human rights.

In this context, the restriction to the core concept of the Jewish and democratic nature of Israel does not result from any diminution of the values of the state. Rather, it results from recognition of their supra-legal status. Precisely that status calls for considerable abstraction in defining the values, while refraining from setting a plethora of detail in supra-constitutional stone. In this way, the public will be able, at any time, to shape Israeli society as it pleases, while preventing a situation in which the founding fathers and mothers will rule Israel from their graves.

The core approach is also based on the need for a broad—though probably not absolute—consensus among the citizens of the state with respect to the nature of its values. The public has different ways of understanding the Jewishness of the state, and it is fitting and proper for the constitutional—not to mention the supra-constitutional—understanding thereof to reflect a broad common denominator. This also applies in light of the significance of a constitution as limiting the legislative power of the majority. This is because it is appropriate, wherever possible, to interpret constitutional rules in a way that does not limit the power of the elected authorities, which represent the public, where such a limitation is unnecessary.

A core interpretation of the constitutional values of Israel as a Jewish state is also required for a coherent understanding of its nature as a Jewish and democratic state without giving rise to a contradiction between the Jewish values and the democratic values. I shall consider this point below.

IS THERE A CONTRADICTION BETWEEN ISRAEL'S JEWISHNESS AND ITS DEMOCRATIC NATURE?

Many of the disputes as to the constitutional significance of the definition of Israel as a Jewish and democratic state have to do with the contradiction that is likely to arise between Israel's values as a Jewish state and its values as a democratic state. In cases of conflict or collision, which should be preferred: the Jewish values, which are mentioned first in the combination "Jewish and democratic state," or the democratic values? However, the assumption that the purpose section of the Basic Laws on human rights, such as Section 7A of Basic Law: The Knesset and a number of statutes in which the phrase "Jewish and democratic state" appears,[9] contains an internal contradiction—which is likely to necessitate a choice between the values of Judaism and those of democracy—is baseless. This is not because it is impossible to interpret Jewish values as likely to collide with democratic values or vice versa, but because no legal rule should be interpreted as simultaneously establishing two opposites.

The interpretation of a legal rule necessitates the attribution of a coherent meaning to the rule under interpretation. This means that there is a duty—one might say a professional legal duty—of interpreting the purpose section, like any other section of a Basic Law or of any other law, in a way that attributes a meaning to it, and not in a way that renders it meaningless. Indeed, as Chief Justice Aharon Barak has pointed out, "an interpretive concept which is common to all of the provisions is the concept which considers the expression 'the State of Israel as a Jewish and democratic state' as a single cause which consists of two components (Jewish and democratic). It is fitting and proper for these two components to exist in synthesis and harmony. Judges, as faithful interpreters of the constitutional text, must do everything possible in order to uphold that synthesis."[10] Therefore, when interpreting the expression "the values of the State as a Jewish and democratic state" in the Basic Laws, the question is not the historical, philosophical, or ideological meaning of Judaism or of democracy. The question is the meaning of the provision in which the expression appears. For this purpose, it is necessary to choose, from among the various meanings of Israel's values as a Jewish state, a meaning that is in line with its values as a democratic state; and, from among the various meanings of Israel's values as a democratic state, it is necessary to choose a meaning that is in line with its values as a Jewish state.

As set forth above, an interpretation that, in the constitutional context, reconciles Judaism with democracy is a core interpretation—a relatively narrow and thin interpretation—of both Judaism and democracy. This is because, in the words of Chief Justice Barak, "it is only natural that, if a broad and comprehensive deployment is given to each of these components, the areas of friction and dispute between the two components will prevail. This gives rise to the concept that is necessary to focus exclusively on the minimal 'core' elements of these concepts."[11]

The purpose section of the Basic Laws on human rights is likely to be significant in interpreting the limitation clause, which is common to both Basic Laws, which states that a human right can be limited only by means of a statute befitting the values of the State of Israel. Those values, as may be seen from the purpose section, are the values of Israel as a Jewish and democratic state. The section does not separate or distinguish between Jewish values and democratic values of the state. It concerns the values of the State of Israel as a Jewish and democratic state. These are the ideals that are reflected in the Declaration of Independence, which combine the objective of the state as a national home for the Jewish people with its democratic nature, as a state that also respects the rights of minorities. In fact, the explanatory statement that accompanied the limitation clause, as it appeared in Draft Basic Law: Human Dignity and Liberty, pointed out that its purpose was to establish the values of the State of Israel in a Basic Law. Moreover, it appears that a "proper purpose"—which, pursuant to the Basic Laws on human rights as a precondition for the legality of any law that limits human rights, also includes a purpose that has to do with Israel's nature as a Jewish and democratic state.[12]

Furthermore, the intuition that was once—and perhaps, at times, is still—generally accepted, to the effect that an expansive interpretation of Israel's values as a Jewish state would enable *limitation* of human rights to a greater extent than would be permissible under its democratic values, is not correct. This is because the limitation clause deals with the question of when it is permissible to limit human rights, and not with the question of whether it is permissible to grant them. It reads: "There shall be no *limitation* of [rights] except by a statute befitting the values of the State of Israel," and not "There shall be no *granting* of [rights] except by a statute befitting the values of the State of Israel." A law that limits a right—and not a law that grants one—must be commensurate with all of the values of the state. Accordingly, the more expansive an interpretation that is given to Israel's values—whether its values as a Jewish state or its values as a democratic state—the more limited the possibility of limiting rights will be. For example, the laws of evidence under Jewish law are more stringent with the prosecution than the laws of evidence that are generally accepted today in democratic legal systems. Thus, as a general rule, under Jewish law two witnesses are required for the purposes of proof. According to an expansive approach, which identifies the values of the State of Israel as a Jewish state with Jewish religious law, the existing laws of evidence—which enable a person to be convicted, even of serious offenses, on the strength of a single witness—are likely to be disqualified. On the other hand, the rules of Jewish law, which obviously prohibit the desecration of the Sabbath, will not prevent the raising of an argument to the effect that any law that determines that travel on the Sabbath is a criminal offense deserves to be repealed. As set forth above, expanding the significance of Israel's Jewish values, in the context of the limitation clause, can only have the effect of expanding (and not of restricting) the protection of rights. Obviously, the outcome will be similar if the democratic values are broadly interpreted as ruling out, for example, the constitutionality of the Work and Rest Hours Statute. Thus, for example, the Israeli Supreme Court rejected the argument that held that a section of the Work and Rest Hours Statute, which prohibited the employment of Jews on the [Jewish] Sabbath, runs counter to Basic Law: Freedom of Occupation. The opinion by Justice Dalia Dorner stated as follows: "Determining the Sabbath as the day of rest for Jews fulfills the values of the State as a Jewish and democratic state. Both of these values combine, in complete harmony, in the statute in question. A day of rest for workers has a social and societal purpose; on the other hand, Judaism, which conferred the concept of a weekly day of rest upon human kind, sanctified the Sabbath as the day of rest for members of the Jewish People. The Sabbath is a national value no less than a religious one."[13] The approach adopted by the Supreme Court—which takes care to avoid over-expansion when interpreting the values of the state and seeks common denominators, and not conflict, between them—is accordingly a worthy one.

In light of that set forth above, the application of the limitation clause is focused on other requirements set forth therein, primarily the requirement that limitation of rights must be for a proper purpose and to an extent no greater than is required. It is difficult to imagine many cases in which a law that limits human rights upholds those requirements, and in which such a law would be rejected solely and exclusively because it does not befit the values of Israel as a Jewish and democratic state.

THE CONSTITUTIONAL SIGNIFICANCE OF THE JEWISHNESS OF ISRAEL IN PRACTICAL TERMS

Legislation

Many Israeli statutes reflect values that are founded on Israel's nature as a Jewish state. Thus, *inter alia*, besides the Law of Return—which, as set forth above, reflects a super-constitutional principle that was first set forth in the Declaration of Independence—the nature of the state as a Jewish and democratic state is mentioned, in various contexts, in a series of statutes. At the same time, these statutes do not necessarily reflect the *constitutional* significance of Israel's Jewishness, and the constitutionality of some or all of them may be disputable.[14]

Case Law

Against the background of the devaluation of the narrow legal meaning of the purpose section of the Basic Laws on human rights, the Supreme Court has referred to the constitutional definition that appears therein as a general expression of basic values of Israeli society—not necessarily those that are closely related to the Basic Laws and the rights set forth therein. Here are several examples from recent years.

In Holon Municipality v. Minister of Transport and Road Safety, Justice Elyakim Rubinstein writes as follows: "The State of Israel is a Jewish and democratic state, and insofar as Israeli society—not to mention the state in which it holds a 'golden share'—adjusts its flights to the keeping of the Sabbath . . . it is not appropriate for the State authorities not to consider that fact in determining its flight schedule.[15]

In Soriano v. Minister of Defense, Justice Neal Hendel writes as follows: "There is no need to expand upon the importance of the role of the Chief Military Rabbi of the State of Israel—which is a Jewish and democratic state."[16]

In Rayek v. Prison Service, Justice Rubinstein writes as follows: "The fair assumption is that bread is definitely an important component in the customary diet; and at the same time . . . there is no lack of proportionality in the fact that, for a period of a few days, bread is replaced by a satisfying amount of another food. Accordingly, no violation of constitutional rights, and a Jewish and democratic state, is involved in not supplying bread on the days of Passover in wings where non-Jews dwell together with Jews, provided that another food is properly supplied; there is no need to take up the constitutional banner at all times, when it is possible to reach an arrangement peacefully, with no harsh words and by proceeding along the middle course."[17]

At times, the Supreme Court uses the phrase "Jewish and democratic state" as a constitutional stock phrase, with no clear affinity to the subject under discussion. Thus, in Schlittner v. Pension Officer, Justice Ayala Procaccia writes as follows: "An amendment to the Statute, which improves the situation of middle-aged Israel Defense Forces discharged veterans, by way of a change in the *status quo*, in which their right to a pension was not recognized, to a situation in which they acquire the right to a pension as a result of an arrangement for the freezing of rights which is implemented at age 67, is an arrangement which befits the values of the State [as a Jewish and democratic state], because it is an arrangement which significantly ameliorates the status of those discharged veterans."[18]

CONCLUSION

One may wonder what value there can be to legal limitations that are imposed upon the very nature and definition of a state. Such limitations, after all, cannot prevent a revolution, which manifests as the replacement of the basic norm of the state. The basic norm, in fact, is a situation of power—a social fact, and not a legal rule. The basic norm is replaced upon the change of the source of authority of the entire legal system. In such a situation, all of the legal rules of the previous system expire. This is especially true of the rules that defined the nature of the state and limited the powers of its governmental authorities.

In the State of Israel, the basic norm is the power that, on May 14, 1948, was vested in the People's Council, headed by David Ben-Gurion, enabling it to establish the state and to replace the legal system and the source of authority. The People's Council did not operate by virtue of any legal authority that was conferred upon it under the previous regime—the British Mandate. The power to impose its will resulted from a revolution that ended the Mandatory State and led to the establishment of a new state—Israel. The supreme legal norm of the State of Israel, which the People's Council created by virtue of the basic norm—the non-legal power that it had at that moment—was the Declaration of Independence.

In just the same way as the legal rules on which the British Mandate was based could not prevent the establishment of the State of Israel, there is no guarantee that Israel's legal rules, basic as they may be, will secure its continued existence as a Jewish and democratic state. This is especially true in light of the fact that the enforcement of law is entrusted to the judicial branch—the weakest of the governmental authorities, which neither wields a sword nor holds the purse strings.

At the same time, even if it is not certain that legal rules—even those that purport to be eternal—that shape the nature of the State of Israel will stand forever, they have a significant, albeit not absolute, practical value in securing Israel's existence. The more armor-plated the rules of law, the more difficult it is to launch a revolution and overthrow the regime.

Accordingly, the value of the constitutional—or, more precisely, supra-constitutional—anchoring of Israel's Jewishness, as well as of its nature as a democratic state, is not merely symbolic. It is important to the very survival of the State of Israel in its present format, as set forth in the Declaration of Independence, under which Israel was established by virtue of "the natural right of the Jewish People to be masters of their own fate, like all other nations, in their own sovereign State."

NOTES

1   "Jewish and democratic"—Basic Law: Human Dignity and Liberty, Section 1a; rights not be prejudiced—Basic Law: Freedom of Occupation, Section 2. Fundamental human rights—Basic Law: Human Dignity and Liberty, Section 8; Basic Law: Freedom of Occupation, Section 4. Basic Law: Human Dignity and Liberty; Basic Law: Freedom of Occupation—Section 1 of both basic laws. Final quotation: Basic Law: the Knesset, Section 7A.

2   Provision for operation of Constituent Assembly: "We declare that, with effect from the moment of the termination of the Mandate being tonight . . . until the establishment of the elected, regular authorities of the State in accordance with the Constitution which shall be adopted by the Elected Constituent Assembly . . . the People's Council shall act as a Provisional Council of State, and its executive organ, the People's Administration, shall be the Provisional Government of the Jewish State, to be called 'Israel.'" Upon the election of the Constituent Assembly in 1949, it changed its name to the First Knesset and was given the powers of the legislative branch of government. The Knesset has not yet adopted a complete Constitution; it exercises its constitutional powers by enacting Basic Laws. To date, twelve Basic Laws have been passed, representing chapters of the Constitution that is to be active in the future; even today, however, their status transcends that of ordinary parliamentary laws. See Ariel L. Bendor, "Is It a Duck? On the Israeli Written Constitution," *Yale Israel Journal* 6 (2005): 53. Israel Supreme Court decision: see HCJ (High Court of

Justice) 10/48 Zeev v. Acting District Commissioner of the Urban Area of Tel-Aviv, 1 IsrSC 85 (1948). For the official English translation of the judgment, see http://elyon1.court.gov.il/files_eng/48/100/000/Z01/48000100.z01.htm.

3 HCJ 453/94 Israel Women's Network v. Government of Israel (1994), opinion by Justice Itzhak Zamir. For the official English translation of the judgment, see http://elyon1.court.gov.il/files_eng/94/530/004/Z01/94004530.z01.htm.

4 Aharon Barak, *Interpretation in Law* (Jerusalem: Nevo Publishing House, 1994), vol. 3, *Constitutional Interpretation*, 305 [Hebrew]; HCJ 726/94 Clal Insurance Co. Ltd. v. Ministry of Finance, 58(5) IsrSC 551 (1994), p. 464, Section 27 of the opinion by Justice Dov Levin.

5 For extent of freedom of expression, see HCJ 73/53 "Kol Ha'am" Company Limited v. Minister of the Interior (1953). For the official English translation of the judgment, see http://elyon1.court.gov.il/files_eng/53/730/000/Z01/53000730.z01.htm. EC 11280/02Central Elections Committee for the Sixteenth Knesset v. Tibi, 54(4) IsrSC 1 (2003), at p. 95, Section 5 of the opinion by Justice Dalia Dorner.

6 Ibid., at 94, Sections 2 and 3 of the opinion by Justice Dorner.

7 Quotation—ibid., at 22, Section 12 of the opinion by Chief Justice Barak. For recognition of minority rights today, see Zeev Segal, "Do Israeli Arabs Have Collective Rights?" *Journal of Law in Society* 12 (2001): 94–115.

8 Central Elections Committee v. Tibi, p. 23, section 13 of the opinion by Chief Justice Barak.

9 See Aharon Barak, *Proportionality: Constitutional Rights and Their Limitations* (Jerusalem: Nevo Publishing House, 2010), 308–17 [Hebrew].

10 Central Elections Committee v. Tibi, p. 19, section 7 of the opinion by Chief Justice Barak.

11 Ibid., p. 20, section 7 of the opinion by Chief Justice Barak.

12 See Barak, *Proportionality*, 308–17.

13 LCA (Leave for Criminal Appeal) 10687/02 Handyman Do It Yourself Ltd. v. State of Israel, 57(3) IsrSC 1 (2003), p. 5, section 5 of the opinion by Justice Dalia Dorner.

14 Statues mentioning Jewish and democratic nature: see, for example, the Terminally Ill Patient Statute, 2005 (Section 1(b): "This Statute is based upon the values of the State of Israel as a Jewish and democratic state and on fundamental principles in the realm of morality, ethics and religion"); the Culture and Art Statute, 2002 (Section 2(c): "The [Israel] Council [of Culture and Art] shall act toward promoting a policy of culture and art, which expresses creative and spiritual life in the State of Israel, while ensuring creative freedom and providing an expression for the cultural variety of society in Israel, the various views which prevail therein and its values as a Jewish and democratic state"); the State Education Statute, 1953 (Section 2(2): "The purposes of State education are: . . . to inculcate the values contained in the Declaration of the Establishment of the State of Israel and the values of the State of Israel as a Jewish and democratic state and to develop an attitude of respect for human rights, the basic freedoms, democratic values, compliance with the law, the culture and views of others, and to educate toward striving for peace and tolerance in the relations between human beings and between peoples"); The Budget Foundations Statute, 1985 (Section 3B(b): "Should the Minister of Finance see that an entity has made an expenditure of which, by nature, is one of those set forth below . . . he is entitled . . . to reduce the amounts which are to be transferred from the State budget to that entity under any law: (1) negation of the existence of the State of Israel as a

Jewish and democratic state; (2) incitement to racism, violence and terrorism; (3) support of an armed struggle or an act of terror, by an enemy state or a terrorist organization, against the State of Israel; (4) the designation of Independence Day or the date of the establishment of the State as a day of mourning; (5) an act of desecration or physical contempt which injures the dignity of the State flag or the State emblem"). Disputable nature: thus, as this chapter is written, a petition against the constitutionality of the section of The Budget Foundations Statute cited in note 22 above is pending before the Supreme Court.

15   HCJ 3835/10 Holon Municipality v. Minister of Transport and Road Safety (2011), section 28 of the opinion by Justice Elyakim Rubinstein.
16   HCJ 3194/10 Soriano v. Minister of Defense (2011), section 5 of the opinion by Justice Neal Hendel.
17   LPA (Leave of Prisoners Appeal) 4201/09 Rayek v. Prison Service (2010), section 13 of the opinion by Justice Rubinstein.
18   HCJ 6784/06 Schlittner v. Pension Officer (2011), section 77 of the opinion by Justice Procaccia.

Reflections on the Meaning and Justification of "Jewish" in the Expression "A Jewish and Democratic State"

7

RUTH GAVISON

In November 1947, the General Assembly of the United Nations debated the report of the commission that had been formed to address the question of Palestine–Eretz Yisrael, and recommended that two states should be founded in the territory between the Mediterranean Sea and the Jordan River: a Jewish state and an Arab state. The lines of partition were set mainly on the basis of demographic concentrations. The resolution stated that both states would be democratic and that both of them would not infringe the civil or political rights of those members of the other group, who should remain in their respective territories. The partition resolution was based on the recognition of the rights to self-determination of the Palestinian-Arab and Jewish collectives and also on the fact that at that time, the two collectives were incapable of living together peacefully or of reaching an agreement on essential subjects, such as immigration, security, or foreign policy.

The Jewish leadership accepted the partition resolution, and the night of the UN vote was a night of celebration in the Yishuv. The Arab and Palestinian leadership rejected the resolution, claiming that it infringed the right of Arabs and Palestinians to self-determination in the whole of the territory. But the Arab refusal led to the Jewish state being founded in 1948, while the territory allotted for the establishment of an Arab-Palestinian state was divided, at first, between Israel, Jordan, and Egypt, and then in 1967 was occupied in its entirety by Israel. About two-thirds of the Palestinian residents of what became the State of Israel in 1948 left and became refugees. Those who remained in Israel enjoy civil and political rights. Within the areas that fell under the control of Arab states, not one Jew remained.

The Declaration of Independence of May 1948 stresses the duality of the state's commitment to being the nation-state of the Jews, on the one hand, and its democratic character and commitment to the human rights of all its inhabitants, without distinction of ethnicity or religion, on the other. This duality received an explicit constitutional grounding in a series of laws, culminating in the Basic Laws of 1992. Israel is defined in these laws as a "Jewish and democratic state," and a vast majority in the country would like to continue that way. Moreover, this majority believes that there is no contradiction between Israel's character as the nation-state of the Jewish people and its commitment to democracy and to the defense of the human rights of all its residents.

In the past I have made the case that it is possible to justify Israel's existence as a state that is both Jewish and democratic.[1] In this essay I would like to flesh out those arguments.

In the first part of the chapter, I clarify my point of departure: namely, that the Jewish collective is entitled to state-level self-determination in (part of) Eretz Yisrael. In the second part, I argue that common claims according to which Jewishness and democracy are incompatible, or arguments against the justification of Israel as a Jewish state, should be rejected. In the third part, I elaborate on the statement that the state's Jewishness cannot justify the violation of basic rights. From there I proceed to a concise discussion on a few particular, central issues concerning which the Jewish character of the state and the justified desire to preserve it may have implications for political, legal, and social arrangements in Israel.

A BASIC JUSTIFICATION FOR A JEWISH NATION-STATE
IN (PART OF) ERETZ YISRAEL

The case for justifying a Jewish nation-state in (part of) Eretz Yisrael is based on the universal right to national self-determination, which is recognized in international law and international human rights law. The right to self-determination is not necessarily a right to a state. In a complex world such as ours, most ethnic groups will not be entitled to state-level self-determination, since state-level self-determination for one group would always burden the members of other ethnic groups living in the same state. An ethnic nation-state (as opposed to a civic state) is not neutral *vis-à-vis* the choice of symbols, narrative, or culture. Thus, a special justification is required to support a demand that one group's self-determination be implemented through the state.

Supporting a right for state-level self-determination requires us to recall the reasons that lie at the foundation of the right for self-determination, and to determine if it is possible to secure effective self-rule for the group in question without granting them control of state institutions. The right to self-determination is the quintessential collective right, and is not reducible to individual rights.[2] It is intended to guarantee for significant groups (or "all-encompassing groups") the possibility of sustaining themselves by ensuring the physical and cultural security of their members, as well as the possibility of passing their culture onto subsequent generations.

Jews lived for hundreds and thousands of years with no state. Nonetheless, they enjoyed various degrees of cultural self-determination in many diverse societies, and their separate existence was the product of both the choice of the Jews themselves and the preferences of the peoples with whom they dwelled. However, the fact that the Jews were a minority within other peoples led to great vulnerability, and over the course of time they suffered repeatedly from persecution, deportations, massacres, discrimination, exclusion, and pressures to convert, occasionally leading to forced conversion. With the beginning of the Enlightenment, and the accompanying processes of secularization in the different European societies, a new vulnerability was added to the former vulnerability of the

Jews: it was in fact the open society, which had granted the Jews civil and political equal rights, that subjected them to pressures to assimilate, but at the same time left them with the status of foreigners. Those Jews who desired integration (such as Herzl) experienced a bitter disappointment. The integration and achievements of Jews in all fields of life and creativity did not lead to their acceptance as equal and acknowledged citizens in the European societies in which they lived; there always remained the feeling that they were foreigners and objects of suspicion. Needless to say, this situation made it more difficult for the Jews to preserve their identity, since extremely strong incentives were created for Jews to convert or at least to obscure the Jewish features of their identity. In such a situation the ability to pass Jewish identity down from generation to generation is reduced, and the strength of the Jewish communities—which is a precondition for Jewish existence—is diminished.

Zionism developed in the context of the combination of these two types of Jewish vulnerability. It became clear that a group that is a small minority everywhere cannot hope to generate for itself either physical security or security of identity. Zionism was intended to do two things: to concentrate Jews in one location so that they would constitute a large portion, or even the majority, in that place, and—as a result of this demographic dominance—to enable the Jews to live a complete Jewish existence, in a place where they did not depend upon the goodwill of other peoples, who would always see them as different and foreign. The idea of Zionism was that only such self-determination would, in the long run, make possible the preservation of a strong Jewish community that is a prerequisite for the complete, secure, and stable Jewish existence of its members.

It was no coincidence that the United Nations resolution on the foundation of a Jewish state came so soon after the scope of the Holocaust became known, and after it had become clear how helpless the Jews had been in those countries, where the governments of the day either encouraged or did not punish those who persecuted and harmed the Jews. Similarly, the establishment of the state of Israel appeared necessary in light of the fact that the nations of the developed world had not hastened to take in those fleeing the menace of the Nazi regime and also had not been overly eager to take in the displaced survivors in Europe, who could not (or did not wish to) return to the places from which they had been sent to be murdered.[3] These circumstances of life and existence of Jews as permanent minorities in communities that considered them outsiders, constituted the first component of the justification of their claim to state-level self-determination.

The second element of the right to state-level self-determination for Jews in Eretz Yisrael pertains to the living conditions of Jews within Eretz Yisrael itself. If Jews had been able to immigrate freely to Eretz Yisrael and live there a complete and secure Jewish existence, it would have been possible to make do with sub-state self-determination for Jews in Eretz Yisrael, under the political rule of the Arab majority. This vision would have made it possible to avoid partition. Indeed, the vision of one state has accompanied the Zionist enterprise from its inception. The Arab residents of Palestine–Eretz Yisrael demanded it from the Mandate authorities and from the international community up until the partition resolution, and vehemently rejected propositions for partition such as that included in the Peel Commission report. The Jews, for their part, refused to give up their dream for a national home in the entirety of western Eretz Yisrael. The agreement of the Jewish leadership to the principle of partition did not stem from a concession on the ideological level. It stemmed from the realization that, in the demographic conditions that prevailed at the time, the Jews would not be able to be a stable majority in the whole of Eretz Yisrael, and that in order to establish a Jewish state they would have to agree to its establishment in those areas where there was such a majority and in those where it would be possible to stabilize one by means of immigration (*aliyah*).

Even in the UN special committee on the question of Palestine (UNSCOP), there was a minority recommendation that one state should be founded in Palestine–Eretz Yisrael on the basis of a federation of national communities. Fortunately for the Jews, the Arabs rejected the plan, and thus paved the way for the adoption of the partition resolution in 1947 ("fortunately" because the majority of the UN committee had determined that this solution did indeed address the needs of the Jews living in Eretz Yisrael at that time, but clearly would limit Jewish *aliyah* in the future). In this situation, the establishment of one state would not have satisfied the will of those Jews who were not yet residents of Eretz Yisrael to live in a state in which Jews could exercise effective self-determination. According to this proposal, the demographic statistics would have caused the Jews, in the best case, to be a recognized national minority possessing some extent of autonomy in the Arab state of Palestine. A more likely outcome would have been that Jews would have become the subjects of the Arab state, dependent on its preferences and determinations with respect to the nature of the regime and the status of the Jews. The vision of *Brit Shalom*— the vision of a binational state—would have given way fairly quickly to the vision of Palestine as an Arab state with a sizable Jewish minority.

Indeed, those Palestinians who uphold the vision of one state do not speak of a binational state. They speak of "a state of all its citizens" or of "a democratic and secular state." In both formulas the denial of Jewish national rights is clear. In both is implied the idea that while the state will appear neutral in terms of its official character, the vast Arab majority within it and in its surroundings would ensure its inclusion in the Arab world. The Jews might enjoy different degrees of autonomy with respect to their own affairs, but they would not enjoy political independence.

The vision of one state, in which Jews and Arabs live side by side and each group develops its own historical connections to the common homeland in its own way, is easier to justify than the idea of two states for two peoples. The Peel Commission recommended partition, more than seventy years ago, because it had reached the conclusion that this vision was not viable due to the significant cultural differences between the groups, and because of the enmity and emotionally charged history between them. Only British rule enabled some kind of coexistence between them. It was apparent that these groups could not administer a joint policy concerning internal and external security, immigration, settlement, or nation-building.

What was true in 1938 was also true in 1947, and unfortunately appears to be true today as well. Moreover, it is not clear if there is any process on both sides of accepting the necessity of coexistence within a single political entity or any move towards a readiness, resulting from that acceptance, to build common institutions or to make fundamental decisions with regard to managing the affairs of the single state that would be established.[4]

Thus the present reality establishes the right of Jews to self-determination specifically on the state level, at least as long as the deep conflict over the future of the region continues.

A FEW PRELIMINARY ARGUMENTS AGAINST THE JUSTIFICATION OF A JEWISH STATE

The case made above is a simple argument based on accepted international norms. It might seem natural to proceed directly to the primary discussion—the implications of Israel's existence as the nation-state of the Jewish people. However, Israel is unique among nations in that its very right to exist is persistently challenged. Moreover, in recent times it seems that these claims are arising anew in international forums, and even within Israel itself they are advocated with deep conviction by both Arabs and Jews alike. Against this background, I wish to briefly address the central claims made against the basic justification of the Jewish state, and to emphasize that the general argument made above does not evade or ignore them.

The first basic claim against the right to a Jewish nation-state is that there is no justification for ethnic nation-states in general. The second claim is that Jews do not satisfy the conditions that would justify recognition of their right to state-level self-determination, even in part of Eretz Yisrael. The third claim is that in actuality, Israel is not a nation-state but rather a theocracy and that religions do not have a right to self-determination. The final claim is that it is impossible to maintain Israel as a Jewish nation-state without an unacceptable violation of the individual and collective rights of the Palestinians living in it, and that this harm to the Palestinian citizens of Israel undermines Israel's justification as a nation-state. I will discuss the first three claims in this chapter; I will pursue the last claim elsewhere.

Justification for the Existence of Nation-States

There is a tendency in recent liberal scholarship to claim that the very idea of ethno-national nation-states, even if they grant full equality of civil rights to residents and citizens who do not belong to the ethnicity in question, is not justified. But it seems that, despite these claims, the strength of nationalism has not withered and in numerous regions throughout the world people are claiming for themselves national self-determination on a primordial, and not merely civic, basis.[5] It appears to be too early to pronounce the nation-state dead. In many of the nation-states in Europe, there are local minorities who do not belong to the ethnicity whose culture and history "define" the state.

It is particularly difficult to understand, and certainly to accept, principled arguments against the Jewish nation-state when they are put forth by people who adamantly support the establishment of a Palestinian state. It is true that Palestine is a territory and that one could think that a Palestinian state was simply a state in the territory of Palestine, at the disposal of whoever dwells in that territory. However, both the Palestinian charter and the draft constitution of the Palestinian state refer to it not only as the group of people living in Palestine, but as a portion of the greater Arab people in terms of culture. If the right to state-level self-determination applies to the Arab residents of Palestine, then it would seem that special justifications would have to be found for why it does not apply to Jews.

The Justification for the Existence of a Jewish State in (Part of) Eretz Yisrael

Three arguments are often suggested for the denial of the Jewish right to self-determination in general and to a nation-state in particular. The first is that the Jews are not a people but rather a religious community. The second is that the precondition for political self-determination in a given territory is presence in the country and being a majority population in it; Jews were never a majority in the country at any point prior to the founding of their state. The third is that the precondition for self-determination is that its actualization does not inevitably violate the rights of others, and that the Jewish state does violate the individual and collective rights of the

Palestinian people to political self-determination in the entirety of their historical homeland. All these arguments were raised, in various forms, from the very beginning of the political struggle between Arabs and Jews concerning the future of Palestine.

There is a certain irony in that, with respect to the two peoples laying claim to self-determination in the territory between the Mediterranean Sea and the Jordan River, it is said that they are not in fact peoples. Just as there are many Arabs who argue that the Jews are a religious community, since they have never had—even after the establishment of the State of Israel—the typical characteristics of a people, such as a common land, language, or culture, there has been no shortage of those (Jews and Arabs alike) who have claimed that "there is no Palestinian people." According to their argument, the Palestinians are an indistinguishable part of the greater Arab nation and, in any event, Palestine had never been a separate political entity: it became such only following the Balfour Declaration of 1917, which was actually made for the purpose of establishing the Jewish national home.[6]

There is no need to expand much on these arguments here, since they are to some extent circular. Nationalism is a combination of an internal nationalist sentiment with the external features supporting it. The will to work towards national self-determination supplies the "subjective" portion of the asserted nationalism. It is abundant among both Jews and Palestinians. With both groups, there is also an abundance of "objective" features that give each group a significant particularity that goes beyond religious affiliation (in the case of the Jews), or language and Arab ethnicity (in the case of the Palestinians).[7]

While—alongside the argument that denies Jews the status of a people—there is an analogous argument regarding the Palestinians, there is a distinct lack of symmetry between the Jews and the Palestinians with respect to the potency of the other two claims regarding the asserted right of the Jews to state-level self-determination in (part of) Eretz Yisrael. Indeed, at the beginning of the twentieth century, Arabs were the vast majority of the country's inhabitants, and even on the eve of the state's foundation they constituted approximately a two-thirds majority, after having failed partially in their efforts to forestall the Jewish immigration that threatened to make them a minority in their own country. Statements that Palestine was a country "without a people" should therefore be dismissed. Thus, I will address only arguments establishing state-level self-determination for the Jews, and I will assume, for the purposes of this essay, a right of self-determination for the Palestinians.

In a nutshell, this argument from history fails. In fact, the argument for the legitimacy of a Jewish state in a part of the land of Israel has become gradually stronger since the beginning of the Zionist move to settle Jews in the Land of Israel.[8]

I shall intentionally begin from the end. There are today more than six million Jews living in the State of Israel (and in the Judea and Samaria territories). Most of them have no other country to which they can go; Israel is their only home. They enjoy here an independent Jewish-Hebrew cultural existence, such as they could not have in any other place in the world. These Jews are without a doubt a collective with a right of self-determination in the place of dwelling. Removing them from their homes, or even bringing about a situation in which they are subject to the mercy of people with whom they have a long history of mutual enmity and suspicion, would constitute a serious violation of their rights.

These facts do not necessarily justify Jewish control of all the territory from the Mediterranean to the Jordan River, wherein dwell millions of Palestinians who are not citizens of the state. However, the Jewish collective does have a right to self-determination and self-defense, which it realizes—and which it is entitled to continue realizing—in the framework of the State of Israel.

Was there anything in the circumstances of the founding of the State of Israel, in the period between November 1947 and the armistice in 1949, that denies the Jewish people the right to a state in which they can rule themselves? I do not believe so. In effect, the opposite is the case. When the United Nations debated partition in 1947, the Arabs' arguments against it were voiced fully and eloquently. The General Assembly voted for partition, despite the fact that at that time Jews represented only a third of the country's residents between the Mediterranean and the Jordan River, because it was clear that one state in that territory, even if it were democratic, would not guarantee adequate protection of the Jews' right to security and self-determination. This situation has not changed since then, and perhaps it has even gotten worse. Moreover: in 1947 the question was whether or not to establish the Jewish state; today the question is whether or not to dismantle an existing state against the will of the vast majority of its inhabitants. The UN resolution would not have saved the Jewish state if it had not withstood the test of war with the Arabs. The United Nations—without detracting from its importance—similarly cannot dismantle the Jewish state, which has one of the strongest armies in the world, against its will.[9] The continued resistance of Arabs to the Jewish state, even in a part of Eretz Yisrael, is understandable. It is important, however, to distinguish between understanding and justification. Because this resistance is not justified, one should not tolerate the Arab refusal to accept what should be accepted: a Jewish state's right to existence.

Indeed, the international stance is clear and consistent: the international community embraces the solution of "two states for two peoples" in western Eretz Yisrael. By doing this it reaffirms its position that Jews are entitled to state-level self-determination in part of the territory.

The State of Israel Is Not a Jewish Theocracy

Those who acknowledge that Judaism is not just a religion, but rather a combination of religion and ethnicity, and therefore Jews can have a right to national self-determination, may deny the right of Jews to a state on the grounds that they have in fact (and perhaps as required by their religion) created a Jewish theocracy.

On the face of it, there is something infuriating in raising this objection specifically in a region in which not a few Arab countries declare themselves to be Muslim countries that impose *shari'a* law. We have not heard that as a result these collectives have forfeited their right to political self-determination.

Nonetheless, theocracy, including Jewish theocracy, is indeed incompatible with democracy. But those who claim that the State of Israel is not democratic, and that it cannot be democratic, for these reasons, need to prove that the State of Israel is in fact a theocracy. It is not sufficient to show that there are religious texts and even attitudes within Judaism that are inconsistent with democracy. It must be shown that such texts, or the views expressed in them, govern as binding over central areas of life in Israel.

The strongest claim in this direction is that put forth consistently by Baruch Kimmerling, who argued that the religious monopoly over matters of personal status in Israel prevents Israel from being a democracy. Indeed, there is no Western democracy in which there is religious monopoly over matters of personal status (although one should remember that even in Western democracies such as Italy and Ireland, it is only recently that the Catholic prohibition against divorce has ceased to be in effect). Indeed, such a monopoly does violate basic rights such as freedom of religion, which includes freedom from religion.[10] However, I do not think that the religious monopoly in Israel in this area disqualifies it as a democratic country. It certainly is not connected to the fact that it is a Jewish state, since this monopoly holds for all the residents of the country, Jews and non-Jews alike. In fact, when the Mandate government reviewed the Ottoman system for matters of personal status, the Jews requested that civil marriages be introduced into the country, but it was actually the Arabs who demanded a continuation and preservation of the *Millet* system, according to which these subjects fell under the religious jurisdiction of the different religious communities.

The State of Israel is considered Jewish because it is a nation-state of the Jewish people. The Israeli Declaration of Independence took great care to specify the non-religious meaning of the Jewishness of the state, and this is also the reality that prevails in it.

THE JEWISH STATE AND HUMAN RIGHTS

The final preliminary argument that I will address is the one that states that a Jewish state, by definition, cannot respect the human rights of all its residents, in particular those who are not Jewish. Accordingly, the argument goes, the State of Israel, even in the territory in which there is a Jewish majority, must give up its special Jewish features.

However, something must be wrong with this argument. As we have seen, the case for the Jewish nation-state itself invokes the same human rights discourse. The issue cannot be that human rights as such point against the legitimacy of nation-states. Tensions between nation-states and human rights of citizens who do not belong to the dominant ethnic group are internal issues of balancing between two human rights. Both the aspects of the Jewishness of the state on the one hand, as well as challenges of its legitimacy on the other, are grounded in the human rights discourse.

There is almost no worthy goal that can be promoted fully without limiting the liberty or infringing on the full enjoyment of some alleged human right or other. There are almost no human rights that are absolute. When prospective policy proposals are considered, their consequences with respect to various rights and interests must be identified and balanced so that an informed decision can be made. The test cannot be that a policy that infringes on the enjoyment of a right is thereby prohibited, irrespective of the goals it seeks to promote (which may also include the protection of rights). A commitment to a goal thus means also a willingness to accept that promoting that goal might involve some "proportional" infringements of other rights. This is a familiar argument in all discussions of rights.

It will be easier to demonstrate the point through the discussion of a conflict between rights that is less "emotionally charged" than the conflict between rights claimed by two peoples struggling over the same strip of earth. For instance, individuals have a right to freedom of expression; they also have a right to privacy regarding personal information pertaining to them. Both rights are very important, yet at times these two rights are in conflict with each other. Anyone who argues that the right to privacy is valid only on the condition that it never justifies any limitation to freedom of expression in effect states that there is no right to privacy.

The human rights discourse serves, as we have said, on both sides of our discussion. Perhaps this in itself shows that its use cannot be, in and of itself, decisive. Human rights do in fact have a special status, and they operate as binding constraints on what governments may do to citizens and groups. No state is permitted to *violate* the human rights of its inhabitants (that is, to infringe on them in a manner that is not justified). This principle does not become less obligatory if the purpose of the infringement is the preservation of the Jewish character of the state.

However, not every policy that individuals or minorities dislike or object to amounts to a violation of their *rights*. The distinction between a policy that a group or individual deems harmful, undesirable, unfair, or even dangerous, and one that constitutes an unjustified infringement of human rights and is therefore prohibited is one of the most difficult questions of practical politics. Too many people believe that any reasonable claim that frames a complaint in terms of an infringement of the rights of an individual is sufficient to obligate the state to refrain from the challenged policy; many also believe that the state must do everything necessary to protect its residents' rights to life and to security of persons. These beliefs are oversimplified. The human rights discourse does admit an extremely wide application. The practice of expanding it has been very noticeable in recent decades. However, to maintain the strength and credibility of the human rights discourse, as well as to maintain the legitimacy of both legislatures and courts, it is important to refrain from describing each political goal that is desired as one that is directly required by a commitment to human rights.[11]

Indeed, Israel must protect human rights. The Jewishness of the state does not justify violating them. However, not every hindrance to the *interests* of individuals or groups is also an infringement on *their rights*.[12]

If rights were deemed absolute, it would be implausible that a policy could infringe a right without violating it. To maintain both reasonable policy-making power and the status of rights, we would then need to append to every right an exhaustive list of its exceptions. Such drafting undermines the internal logic of bills of rights. One cannot determine at the outset all the exceptions to a right. This matter needs to be worked out dynamically through the examination of particular challenges and special circumstances. Accordingly, when a human right is invoked to justify a practice or a law (or when it is invoked to challenge them as inconsistent with it), we cannot avoid a careful examination of both the scope of the *prima facie* right as well as its possible exceptions. Only if this examination indicates that there is indeed an unjustified infringement of the right, the claim will act as a "trump" to defeat conflicting reasons. This holds in the case of freedom of expression as well as in the case of the conflicting rights of Jews and Palestinians to self-determination in Palestine–Eretz

Yisrael. It should be noted that all people living in the country, Jews and Palestinians alike, have common interests, such as security and stability. Working to fulfill these interests might also affect the extent to which the conflicting rights to self-determination may be recognized.

The need to examine in each case the conflicting rights and the general context exists with respect to both individual and collective rights. Both kinds of rights are pervasive in the context of our current concern. The right to self-determination, as we have said, is the quintessential collective right. The right to equality is usually an individual right, although it has significant consequences for the status of the group to which the individuals customarily subject to discrimination belong.

Since one of the main purposes of rights is to constrain the legislature itself, it is usually accepted that the authorized interpreter of the scope of rights is the court, which enjoys independence from the political branches. This is a strong and convincing argument, but it ignores the fact, noted above, that the human rights discourse may be interpreted in such a broad way that every question of policy would become a question of the correct balancing of different rights. Under this interpretation, making the courts the arbiters of rights may reduce the ability of the government and the Knesset to make effective policy decisions.[13]

This is true for individual rights; it is even truer for the scope and implications of collective rights, which naturally deal with the political and social arrangements concerning the relationships between the different groups living in the same country. On such questions, distinct from those of individual rights, it is less clear that courts have the special competence that justifies their reviewing the policy decisions of the political branches, which are usually ones made after deliberations and compromises, once the minimal constraints are met.

A relevant example may clarify this point: if Israel had not granted its Arab citizens the right to vote because they are Arabs, Israel would not be a democracy. This is a matter of the core human rights of each member of the minority, and of the core meaning of democracy, and these rights should be protected by the courts. The question of whether the Arab minority has a right to a school system in its own language financed by the state is different. In Israel, this is indeed the reality, and most

Arab youngsters attend public elementary and high schools with Arabic as the main language of tuition. However, if the state had decided to prefer a unitary public education system taught in Hebrew, it is not at all clear that the Arab minority would have a right, enforceable by the courts, to demand the present reality. Or that it should have such a right.[14]

In short, it is not true that the nation-state of Jews cannot, by definition, protect all the personal and group *rights* of minorities living within it. True, an (ethnic) nation-state cannot give its minorities a full sense of membership and belonging, because part of the sense of membership is indeed connected to the history and the culture of the majority. However, if we conclude that this sense of partial difference from the majority is by definition a violation of rights, we will have to reject the possibility that any ethnic nation-state could be legitimate. We have argued above that this conclusion, in itself, does not reflect the reality of many states that are considered fully legitimate. Moreover, it by definition prohibits the fulfillment of the right of peoples to self-determination on a state-level.

The principled compatibility of an ethnic nation-state and the protection of the personal and group rights of minority citizens is not enough, however. It must be shown that the reality of the challenged state does not in fact consist of a flagrant violation of such rights. A detailed analysis of the actual situation of minority rights in Israel is beyond the scope of this chapter. The reality of legal and social arrangements in Israel is mixed and complex. Efforts should be made to integrate members of the Arab minority more fully. At the same time, it is fair to say that the status of the Arab minority in Israel is not worse, and in many respects is better, than the status of national minority groups in other democratic nations. This is especially the case if we recall that Israel still is in the midst of an ongoing conflict and debate concerning its very legitimacy and its right to exist, in which its neighbor-adversary is the very same people to whom the Arab minority in Israel belongs.[15]

CONSEQUENCES OF ISRAEL BEING A JEWISH NATION-STATE

For many participants in the larger debate about Israel as a Jewish and democratic state, it is relatively easy to remain in the preemptory and generalized part of the debate. It is precisely those who—like myself—seek Israel's continued existence as a Jewish state who cannot afford these luxuries. Nonetheless, in many states such questions of identity are so difficult that an effort is made to avoid them as much as possible. Thus, in Israel, at the beginning of the twenty-first century, there is no systematic, orderly, and informed discussion on these issues. In this brief chapter, I will not be able to address in a systematic and detailed way the important literature that has accumulated in the last few years. I will make do with a few comments on some of the main topics.

First, we should recall that all the justifications advanced here assume that Palestinians too enjoy effective national self-determination. This is inconsistent with Jewish control over the whole territory west of the Jordan. Clearly, a state over this land cannot be either Jewish and democratic or justified.

Moreover, as we have said, Israel's identity as a nation-state of the Jewish people does not justify the violation of the *human rights* of its non-Jewish citizens and residents. However, within these constraints, the Jewishness of the state is apt to justify the implementation of policies that are preferential to the interests of the majority group, when such policies are needed to defend the vital interests of the ethnic group—the same interests that justified the recognition of the right to self-determination in the first place.

Ranking first in this matter is *the physical safety of the citizenry*. It is not always easy to see this, since it is customary to emphasize these two requirements—human rights and physical safety—specifically with respect to minority groups who are in need of protection from the majority of the country in which they dwell. In not a few cases, however, including the case of Israel, the state-level right to self-determination of the majority group stems also from the need to defend the security of its members, security that could not be ensured without the establishment of the state.

Beyond these primary interests, which come up clearly when there is a situation of armed conflict between Israel and some of its neighbors, there are other important issues. I will deal in this essay only with issues of public culture, with a special emphasis on language. These concerns apply to Israeli policy and affect it in times of peace as well.

Culture

Ernest Gellner defines the principle of nationalism as the striving for unification between political power and cultural identity.[16] He thus emphasizes the centrality of the cultural basis, with all its components, in defining groups as nations. An ethnic nation-state is different in this sense from a civic state, in which "the people" is the collective of citizens. When the United Nations decided to establish a Jewish state, it intended to create a political entity that would contain a Jewish majority not only so that the latter would be able to decide the issues of immigration and security, but also in order to establish the dominant culture. Control over the dominant culture is an important means for ensuring that the state will facilitate securing the group's identity, and this is one of the bases for the justification for state-level self-determination. Israel's Jewishness, in cultural terms, means that Israel does not aspire to be, and cannot be, a multicultural state in the neutral sense, in which there is no preference for a particular cluster of cultural identities. One of the consequences of the state's Jewishness is that Israel is permitted to take actions that strengthen the cluster of Jewish cultures, and make Jewishness the dominant culture in Israel—again, so long as this action does not violate the rights (and not just the interests) of other individuals or groups. As we have said, special attention needs to be given to the rights of the local Arab population.

Today, most of the countries in the developed world recognize that they contain communities whose culture is different than the majority culture, and that this requires an approach other than the standard policy of simple assimilation that has been practiced in the past. There is a growing debate, however, about just what this approach should be. Some advocate neutrality: a situation in which the state recognizes the equal worth of all subcultures (or at least the principal subcultures) and treats all of them equally. Such legal neutrality may in principle be possible concerning some non-civic affiliations. It is possible, for instance, to reach official neutrality regarding religions by means of a strong separation of religion and state and the complete privatization of all religions. However, even if we achieve legal or constitutional neutrality in this way, the social reality might be the hegemony of one religion. Thus, for instance, the

United States is neutral regarding religion in constitutional terms, but it is without a doubt a Christian society. Other aspects of public culture, like language, state symbols, or days of rest, cannot reflect all groups and cultures in an equal way, both because of practical necessity and in order not to undermine some civic cohesion. This means that a strong multiculturalism can only be incomplete in the best-case scenario. Moreover, some shared commitment to the constitutional arrangements and the welfare of the state, for instance, must be part of the civic identity that members of all subcultures should share.

In the case of Israel, the argument for multiculturalism usually comes from two sources: the Arab minority and *Haredi* Jews. In recent years, there have been those who argue that Israel should indeed adopt an egalitarian positive attitude towards all cultures within it, so that no important cultural group will be excluded or feel that it is a second-class group in the Israeli public space. This statement holds, in their opinion, for both non-Jewish cultures and the different Jewish subcultures.

This symmetry of attitude is attractive, but for the purposes of examining the possibility or the justification of preserving Israel as a Jewish state, we need to distinguish between these two kinds of cultural plurality. The issue raised by non-Jewish cultures is very different from the challenge of Jewish cultural pluralism.

The recognition of plurality in Jewish cultural life, combined with the recognition of the value and worth of the different cultural strands, and promoting the awareness to the fact that they are all instantiations of Jewish culture, is not only possible but is rather essential to the preservation of the cultural Jewishness of the State of Israel. After all, the wish to maintain and transmit cultural identity is at the basis of the argument for (state-level) self-determination. This right to self-determination is granted to the national collective and not to different groups of people with a historical link to a particular religion. It is a precondition to the Jewish right to national self-determination that Jews are a people. This claim of peoplehood must have an objective external component, and cannot rely only on the subjective feelings of belonging. It is precisely because Jews come from different cultural civilizations in which they lived for many years, and precisely because Judaism is undergoing a widespread process of secularization, that the project of Jewish national restoration must be based on a cultural unity that goes beyond the observance of ritual law in one style or another. It follows that the Jewish Zionist groups have an existential interest in the development of a common Jewish culture. However, every Jew who wants Israel to be strong in general, and as a Jewish state in particular, also has such an interest.

Of course, Jewish groups also have a "right to culture" in the sense of protection from religious coercion and the freedom to develop their own style of Jewish culture together with the lifestyles that result from it. A state is permitted to assist in the development of such subcultures, and it must do so on an egalitarian basis. It is important to note these things, because at times it seems that in the Jewish communities, or at any rate among their political deal-makers, there are those who are willing to make electoral gains through emphasizing the differences between the different Jewish groups and through the presentation of the relations between them as a zero–sum game that must be won at all costs.

Relations among Jewish and Arab cultures are different. It is easy to see that there is an enormous difference. While there are also relations of cultural-national complementarity among the Jewish subcultures, the relations between Jewish and non-Jewish cultures are likely to reflect tension, or even conflict. Culture includes language, religion, and ways of life, as well as a historical narrative. In the relations between Jews and Arabs in Israel, there is in some of these components not only difference, but at times even direct collision and conflict, open or concealed.

These conflicts between the national cultures and narratives make many choices concerning the public sphere in Israel problematic. It is natural for Israel, a young state established after struggle and war as the nation-state of the Jews, to want Israel's public culture to reflect Jewish aspirations and narratives. Thus it is not surprising that the flag and the anthem are Jewish; that Saturday is the official day of rest; that Holocaust Remembrance Day, the memorial day for fallen soldiers in Israel's wars, and Israeli Independence Day are all national holidays. At the same time, under the historical circumstances of Israel and its relation to the Arab minority within it, especially against the background of the unresolved conflict with the Palestinians, these arrangements are likely to exacerbate the feeling of alienation on the part of Arab citizens.

Yes, Israel and Israeli Jews should seek ways to mitigate this alienation. But does the Arab minority in Israel have a *right* that these symbols and holidays should be changed to accommodate them? I do not think so. This stems from the justification that I have given above for the existence of a Jewish nation-state in (part of) Eretz Yisrael. A nation-state cannot "privatize" its national identity or the events connected to its national history. Under the circumstances, Israel cannot be neutral with respect to the narrative of Independence Day versus that of the *Nakba*. There needs to be sensitivity to the difficulty that this causes Arab citizens; but there is a vast difference between such sensitivity and a renunciation on the part of the state of some of the essential characteristics that give expression to the fact that Israel is the realization of the Jewish dream national revival in its historic homeland.

The wish to maintain and transmit Jewish cultural identity has many implications on Israeli policies and the regulation of the Israeli public sphere, but the most important one relates to the structure and content of public education. It is impossible to overstate the importance of education in general and of the formal and public education in particular in the establishment of the state's cultural identity and of the attitudes of its inhabitants. By means of the educational system, the state conveys to all those affiliated with it (students, teachers, and parents) its fundamental values and the basic obligations of social and political organization. The educational system passes on values and creates mechanisms for social integration, both on the level of teaching basic skills to find one's way in the society as well as on the level of socialization mechanisms, which establish the normative framework in which the members of the group operate. In a homogenous society, the educational system will pass on skills and values that are acceptable to everyone, and thus will contribute to the continued societal stability and cohesiveness. In such a society there will be no gap or tension between education for the values of the community and education for citizenship and democracy. As we saw, this is not the reality in any state today, especially not in the developed world. Here, too, it is one thing to deal with differences and another to deal with conflicting realities and narratives. Israel's challenge here is to maintain an acceptable balance between transmitting to all the shared values of civic equality, human rights, and democracy, while at the same time respecting differences and conflicts.

Language

Language is of course a part of culture, but its enormous importance justifies a separate treatment. It is difficult to overstate the importance of the medium through which we think, speak, read, and write (and at times dream and fantasize) to our spiritual and cultural universe. With regard to language, it is normal to distinguish between two levels: the symbolic-cultural level, which creates a profound connection between individuals and the members of their linguistic and cultural community and the unique cultural tradition of the community; and the instrumental level of the effective communicative ability of individuals with their environment and their ability to integrate into the social, economic, political, and cultural world around them. Both are important, and together they determine the acceptable arrangements for language in those states in which there is a plurality of linguistic groups.

Every country in which there is more than one linguistic group needs to deal with the question of language policy. It is very rare that the majorities in such countries become bilingual or multilingual. Usually in each country there is one dominant language, and the minorities living there adopt it while they either preserve or abandon their own language. In some of the countries, the dominance of a national language is a matter of convenience, but in many of them language unity is a central ideological tenet, it is a component of national identity, and it is often mentioned as such in the state's constitution.

Language is one of the most basic components of a separate and unique culture. It therefore is unreasonable and wrong to demand that a local population give up its language. In Israel, the Declaration of Independence includes an explicit commitment to grant the country's inhabitants freedom of language. In fact, however, the status of Arabic in Israel is much stronger than that. During the British Mandate period, there were three official languages in the country: English, Arabic, and Hebrew. When Israel was established upon the termination of the Mandate, it refrained from a new regulation of the issue. Instead, the English language was taken out of the list of official languages, leaving only Arabic and Hebrew (in this order) on the list.

The law, however, never reflected the reality. The establishment of the state therefore represented a most significant change—Hebrew became the *de facto* language of the state, and Arabic became the minority language. Because large portions of the Arab population worked in the Jewish sector, the study of Hebrew, however basic, became a necessity. In Israel, knowledge of Hebrew is normally essential for integration into the work force, for academic study, and for effective communication in the Israeli public. At the same time, Israel offers to the Arab minority public education at the elementary and high school level, in which Arabic is the language of tuition.

The State of Israel grants full protection of *freedom of language* for Arabs. It also appropriately grants the Arabic language a special and unique status. In Arab communities, it is very easy to get by even if one only knows Arabic, and it is very difficult if one does not know Arabic. Nonetheless, Israel *is not a bilingual country*. In practice, the language of the state is Hebrew. Official government publications do not usually appear in both languages. The level of Hebrew study in Arab schools is much higher than the level of Arabic study in Jewish schools. The assumption is that all residents know Hebrew. There is no assumption that all the country's inhabitants know Arabic.

I believe that Israel should not be a bilingual country, but rather a country where the language is Hebrew, and that respects the right of the Arab minority to their own language, recognizes the special status of Arabic, does its best to supply Arabs services in Arabic, and demands and encourages high-level Arabic studies in all its schools. There is no question that the language of the future Palestinian state will be Arabic. If Jews live in Palestine, this will not, and should not, affect the language of the state. At best, Jews will be allowed to have Hebrew schools. The revival of Hebrew as a cultural characteristic of Jews is of huge significance to the ability of Jews to maintain and transmit their culture. The dominance of Hebrew in Israel is the direct and necessary result of the fact that Israel is a country in which the Jewish people realizes its right to self-determination and in which there is a significant Jewish majority.

Of course, Israel's language policy must respect the *rights* of Arabs, as individuals and as a native group. Such rights do have implications for language policy. For example, the right to freedom of language prohibits a policy of a Hebrew monopoly in the public sphere. In fact, there is no principle in Israel's present language policy that violates the language rights of Arabs.

The political and cultural importance of this issue is reflected both in the fact that the vision statements of the Arab minority in Israel explicitly demand a bilingual definition of the state; and by the fact that the issue of language was the first one mentioned when a recent bill to anchor Israel's identity as the nation-state of Jews in a Basic Law was presented to the Knesset in August 2011.[17]

CONCLUSION

I present here a vision of a Jewish state that does not deny or conceal the fact that it is a state in which the Jewish people realizes its right to self-determination and its will to act in order to maintain this situation. This is the sense of a "Jewish" state that I affirm. That same Jewish state wishes to be part of the family of nations, and has complete and full commitment to the values of democracy and human rights. In many of the subjects that I address here, we must develop an informed policy. The policies implemented up until now have frequently been marked by an unacceptable discrimination. Such discrimination must stop. At the same time, Israeli policy has at times ignored the legitimate need to preserve the basis for the Jewish state's survival. Political correctness must not undermine policies designed to improve the chances for a viable Jewish self-determination in (part of) Eretz Yisrael.

If a majority, or even a sizable minority of Israel's citizens, will believe that there is no reason to preserve the special Jewish character of the state, and that it might well be a neutral liberal democracy with no particular commitment to the fate of the Jewish people, Israel will probably gradually cast off its Jewish characteristics.

But at the moment this is not the case. The large majority of the Israeli public not only wishes for the continued existence of the State of Israel, but also for its continued attachment to the realization of the self-determination of the Jewish people. In this case, democracy requires that the will of the majority be respected, subject to the obligation to protect the rights of the minority. Thus, the state's Jewishness at the moment is not a component in conflict with democracy, but rather a characteristic required by it. At the same time, democracy makes the Jewish character of the state contingent on the preferences of the majority, and requires that the state should grant the minority actual freedom to convince the majority to change its opinion.

This conclusion does not necessarily imply that the state should be defined, in law or in constitution, as a Jewish state, or that explicit declarations will be made about the implications of the state's Jewishness. In fact, it seems to me preferable that such definitions not be included in law or constitution. These questions are not a legal matter, and frequently declarations are unnecessarily alienating when the reality of the situation is sufficient. Additionally, the inclusion of declarations such as these in laws transfers the power to decide such issues to the courts invoking the human rights discourse or constitutional interpretation. Ideally, these questions should not be resolved by courts in this manner. Ironically, declarations like these may seem needed precisely as a legislative response to judicial interpretation that should have been avoided in the first place. Alas, it may well be that since Israel has already been defined as "Jewish and democratic" in the 1992 Basic Laws there is now no choice but to continue on this path, despite its disadvantages.[18] Be that as it may, it is critical to repeat the policy implications: Israel has the liberty to act in ways that will promote it as the nation-state of Jews. Israel must not promote this legitimate cause in ways that violate the basic rights of its inhabitants and citizens, Jews and non-Jews alike, or in ways that violate the rights of those living under its effective rule.

Thus the desire to continue maintaining the Jewishness of the state does not justify discrimination against the non-Jewish citizens or residents of the state, especially the members of the native Palestinian people. It also does not justify a religious monopoly with regard to matters of personal status, or the privileging of the Orthodox establishment in respect to Jews.

The goals derived from this analysis are clear: Israel needs to undertake clearly and unambiguously those obligations that stem from democracy, human rights, and the principle of non-discrimination. Nonetheless, if a certain policy is needed in order to protect the Jewish state, and is compatible with these obligations, Israel may adopt it even if it does not pass the test of political correctness according to certain parties.[19]

We need to think through such issues in seriousness and integrity, listening attentively to critics in Israel and abroad. We must reject the claim that international criticism should be dismissed because it is motivated by hatred toward us. Not every criticism of Israeli policy is antisemitism, and not every claim that Israel violates human rights is unfounded, or made cynically by the enemies of Israel. To be sure, there is certainly an element of politicization in some of the more vocal and sweeping claims against Israel, and there are among them many cases of double standards. There are indeed those who believe that Israel was born in sin, and that its continued existence is a perpetual threat to world peace, so that the only moral path open to it is to surrender its continued existence as a Jewish nation-state. This fact does not exempt us from doing what we must do. We must examine challenges to our policies on their merits. We should avoid two dangers: resorting to sweeping disqualifications of the validity of such challenges; or accepting sole responsibility for the woes of the region, moved by a sense of blame to unending apology for our existence. If we do wrong, we must correct it. However, no state is required to forgo its own existence as a punishment for its deeds, and there is no reason that the Jewish state should be asked to do so.

Israel should act, within the constraints of human rights and morality, to ensure that it will be a place, the one place in the world, where Jews exercise their right to self-determination. It may do this. And it must do this.

NOTES

1   Ruth Gavison, "The Jews' Right to Statehood: A Defense," *Azure* 15 (Summer 2003): 70–108.

2   The right to self-determination is explicitly recognized in human rights law. See for example, Chaim Gans, *The Limits of Nationalism* (Cambridge: Cambridge University Press, 2003).

3   Nonetheless, it would be a mistake to argue that Israel was established only because of the Holocaust. If there had not been at the time a critical mass of Jews in Israel who had succeeded in building a strong and vibrant community with a strong culture and economy, there would have been no basis for the claim of Jews to a state of their own.

4   This statement is bolstered by recent developments, from the rise of Hamas, with its blatant charter and its aspirations to eradicate the State of Israel, to the statements by the president of Iran (Mahmoud Ahmadinejad) and the clear positions of the Hezbollah organization *vis-à-vis* Israel. It is the case as of the current revision of this article—at the end of 2011. Despite the increasing popularity of the vision of one state in certain circles, its typical advocates among both the Jews and the Palestinians are concerned with the need to defend the self-determination of both national groups and not their mutual civilian identity in one state. It is possible that the vision of two states is no longer something easily realized, but the alternative of one state for two peoples appears to be unrealistic in the existing circumstances. This does not inspire much optimism with respect to the conflict's future, but it is possible that just such a situation with no apparent way out will lead to creative ideas.

5   See for instance Gans, *The Limits of Nationalism*, and also the comprehensive and important book by Alexander Yakobson and Amnon Rubinstein, *Israel and the Family of Nations: The Jewish Nation-State and Human Rights* (London and New York: Routledge, 2009).

6   The Balfour Declaration, and even the original Mandate document of the League of Nations, included in the Mandate even parts of Eastern Eretz Yisrael (that is, from the eastern side of the Jordan River). Only in 1922 was it decided to restrict the extent of "the national home" to Western Eretz Yisrael.

7   For a comprehensive discussion of Jewish nationalism and its relation to Jewish religion, see Yehezkel Kaufmann, *Exile and Estrangement: A Socio-Historical Study on the Issue of the Fate of the Nation of Israel from Ancient Times until the Present* (Tel Aviv: Dvir, 1930) [Hebrew]. For a discussion of Palestinian identity, see Rashid Khalidi, *Palestinian Identity* (New York: Columbia University Press, 1997); Baruch Kimmerling and Joel S. Migdal, *The Palestinian People: A History* (Cambridge, MA: Harvard University Press, 2003).

8   For a development of this argument, see my analysis in "The Jews' Right to Statehood."

9   On this General Assembly vote, see the fascinating description by Yakobson and Rubinstein, *Israel and the Family of Nations*, chap. 1. Despite the UN's inability to dismantle Israel, I do not share David Ben-Gurion's dismissive attitude to the United Nations. [The UN is referred to in Hebrew with the acronym *Um*. Ben-Gurion derided the organization's significance by rhyming it with a nonsense word: *Um Shmum*—trans.] This is a matter of both prudence and political morality. Israel must do its best to maintain international legitimacy, even if some UN institutions are

biased against it. Even if resolutions against Israel cannot be enforced, Israel should seek continued international recognition and endorsement.

10   Kimmerling's claims: Baruch Kimmerling, "Religion, Nationalism and Democracy in Israel," *Constellations* 6 (1999): 339; see also Baruch Kimmerling, *Immigrants, Settlers and Natives: Israel Between Plurality of Cultures and Cultural Wars* (Tel Aviv: Am Oved, 2003) [Hebrew]. On monopoly violating basic rights: I have indeed argued that Israel should change the state of its law on this matter. See Ruth Gavison and Rabbi Yaacov Medan, *The Gavison–Medan Covenant: Main Points and Principles* (Jerusalem: Avi Chai Foundation and the Israel Democracy Institute, 2004), chap. 2.

11   I cannot go here into these general statements, which are central in contemporary discussions of political philosophy. For some general background see my article, "Immigration and the Human Rights Discourse: The Universality of Human Rights and the Relevance of States and Numbers," *Israel Law Review* 43 (2010): 7–48, available at http://ssrn.com/abstract=1862907.

12   All individuals have a great interest in limiting the amount of taxes that they have to pay. It does not follow that every increase in tax rate is an infringement, much less a violation, of a right. In a matter closer to our concerns, minority groups have an interest, a very important interest, that they will be able to transmit their culture and language to younger generations. They do have the right to the state not burdening this capacity and not prohibiting the use of their language or transmission of their culture. They do not have the right, however, to the state financing their efforts to transmit their separate culture.

13   For a more detailed discussion, see Gavison, "On the Relationship between Civil and Political Rights, and Social and Economic Rights," in *The Globalization of Human Rights*, ed. Jean-Marc Coicaud, Michael W. Doyle, and Anne-Marie Gardner (Tokyo and New York: United Nations University Press, 2003), 23–55.

14   Indeed, the Supreme Court in Israel held, in a majority opinion, that local authorities with a sizable Arab minority had to add Arabic to all road signs, including those in purely Jewish neighborhoods. The idea that public signs should be in Arabic as well as in Hebrew is a laudable goal, but I think the dissenting judge was right in saying that this arrangement should not have been decided as a matter of rights.

15   The best sign that this is indeed the case is the fact that most Arabs reject the idea that within negotiations with the Palestinians, some of their villages would be transferred to Palestine.

16   Ernest Gellner, *Nations and Nationalism* (New York: Cornell University Press, 1983).

17   For the vision statements of the Arab minority, see *The Democratic Constitution*, (Shafa'amr: Adalah, 2007), available at http://www.adalah.org/eng/democratic_constitution-e.pdf; Ghaida Rinawie-Zoabi, ed., *The Future Vision of the Palestinians Arabs in Israel* (Al Woroud: The National Committee for the Heads of the Arab Local Authorities in Israel, 2006), available at http://www.adalah.org/newsletter/eng/dec06/tasawor-mostaqbali.pdf. The proposed Basic Law can be found at http://www.knesset.gov.il/privatelaw/data/18/3541.rtf [Hebrew]. For commentaries stressing the implications for the status of Arabic, see Jonathan Lis, "Lawmakers Seek To Drop Arabic as One of Israel's Official Languages," *Haaretz*, August 4, 2011, http://www.haaretz.com/print-edition/news/lawmakers-seek-to-drop-arabic-as-one-of-israel-s-official-languages-1.376829.

18 I have addressed this topic at length in a number of other places. See especially Ruth Gavison, and Democratic? A Rejoinder to the Ethnic Democracy Debate," *Israel Studies*, 4, no. 1 (1999): 44–72.

19 Israel should not be deterred by the fact that there are those who will consequently charge it with racism. Unfortunately, a resolution that Zionism is a kind of racism was adopted by the General Assembly of the United Nations in 1975 and was only repealed in 1991. Many also spoke in this spirit at the world congress against racism in Durban, South Africa, in September 2001.

Israel as a Nation-State in Supreme Court Rulings

8 AVIAD BAKSHI AND GIDEON SAPIR

INTRODUCTION

The State of Israel is a Jewish nation-state. This was determined by the United Nations Partition Plan as well as by the Declaration of Independence and by two Basic Laws dealing with human rights. The national identification of Israel is anchored also in a great deal of legislation as well as in practices common in many fields.[1]

In this chapter, we shall describe the attitude of the Supreme Court over the past twenty years toward various components of national identity rooted in Israeli law. We examine rulings on the right of return; review rulings on political participation; examine the rendering of the court over the question of the status of the Hebrew language, and deal with its attitude toward allotting land for Jewish settlement and its approach to the provision of economic incentives for such settlement; describe rulings concerning the institutions of the Jewish people; and, finally, examine decisions regarding the naturalization of non-Jews. From the review, a judicial approach is depicted that erodes many of the components of national identity that were customary in Israel before the intervention of the court. The purpose of this chapter is positivist and not normative, we shall thus suffice with a description of the court's activity on this issue without evaluating it.

RETURN

The Law of Return grants almost every Jew the right to immigrate to Israel and become its citizen. This policy has parallels in other nation-states, but there is no precedent in the world of such a sweeping right as that awarded by the Law of Return.[2]

Many times, the Supreme Court has stressed the importance of the law as reflecting the national identity of Israel. Yet, despite its generally sympathetic approach, on two issues of secondary importance the court ruled in a manner that somewhat reduces this right. The first matter relates to the status of Jews' spouses, who, according to the Law of Return, are also eligible to become citizens of the country. The court determined, in contradiction of the plain language of the Law of Return, that the right to naturalization in Israel will not apply to spouses of Jews, if the Jews are Israeli citizens, with the explanation that granting it would discriminate between Jewish and non-Jewish citizens, in the sense that the former could provide their spouses with automatic citizenship, by virtue of the Law of Return, while the latter would be forced to suffice with conditional arrangements for naturalization that are determined in the Citizenship Law.[3]

The second issue concerns a qualification determined in Section 2(B)(3) of the Law of Return, according to which the right to return is denied to a person with a criminal past who is liable to be a danger to the public welfare. In the first three decades of the state, this paragraph was used only in extremely exceptional cases, with regard to people deeply involved in organized crime who wanted to exploit the country for the continuation of their criminal activity. From the close of the 1990s, the section was applied also to those who have committed serious crimes against persons, as well as to persons whose criminal experience accumulated after they arrived in Israel but before they requested Israeli citizenship. In recent years there have been signs of an additional expansion in the application of the section. The court considers minor offences—such as crimes against property or street fighting—in which the person requesting the Right of Return was involved, as sufficient reason for denying this right.[4]

Thus, one must distinguish between the core of the Right of Return—which concerns a critical mass of millions of immigrants—which the Court does protect, and two secondary issues—criminals' Right to Return and for the spouses of Jews who are Israeli citizens—in which the court in recent years has weakened the weight of the national consideration.

POLITICAL PARTICIPATION

In 1965, for the first time, a slate was disqualified from running in the Knesset elections, on the basis of its outlook. The Central Elections Committee invalidated the "Socialist List," whose main aims were to "achieve equality for the Arab nation and the granting of all opportunities to the Arab nation, even on Israeli territory, to express solidarity and part-nership with the national liberation waves in the Middle Eastern arena to the same extent that the Jewish nation in this country demanded and obtained this right for itself, and all of this for the benefit of the state."[5]

The Supreme Court rejected the petition of the Socialist List against the decision to disqualify it. Court President Agranat and Justice Zussman determined, in the majority opinion, that even though at that time Israel did not have legislation enabling the disqualification of political parties for their ideological basis, it was possible to invalidate a slate interested in harming the very existence of the country or its character as the state of the Jewish people, even with such legislation lacking.

In 1984, toward the elections for the Eleventh Knesset, the Central Elections Committee decided to disqualify the "Progressive List for Peace," with the rationale that it wished to negate the Jewish identity of the state. The decision was overturned by the Supreme Court,[6] which determined that in the absence of proper legislation it was permissible to disqualify only a list seeking to lead to the destruction of the state and to endanger the lives of its inhabitants, as distinct from a list that wishes to cancel the national character of the state by peaceful means.

As a result of the court's decision, the Knesset amended the Basic Law: The Knesset and added to it Section 7a. The relevant part of the section, as formulated then, determined that "a list of candidates will not participate in elections to the Knesset if its aims or actions, expressly or by implication . . . deny the existence of the State of Israel as the state of the Jewish people."[7] Yet, from the time this reason for disqualification was accepted to today, the court has barred every attempt to make use of it.

In the first elections held after the aforementioned amendment, in 1988, a request was submitted to the Central Elections Committee to disqualify the "Progressive List for Peace," arguing that it denies the existence of the Israel as the state of the Jewish people. The petition was rejected, as was an appeal on the decision made to the High Court of Justice.[8] The court applied the most stringent evidentiary tests and determined that these had not been met, even though it had been presented with explicit statements by the list's candidates that denied the Jewish character of the state.

In 1992, the Parties Law was passed in the Knesset.[9] Section 5 of the law set the tests for Section 7a of the Basic Law: The Knesset as the threshold for registration of a party. From then on, denying the Jewish nature of the state has prevented parties not only from running in the Knesset elections, but even registering (which is a prerequisite for the possibility for presenting a slate of candidates).

In 1996, an appeal was submitted, on the basis of section 5, against the decision of the Registrar of Parties to authorize the registration of the Arab Party for Change, lead by Ahmad Tibi.[10] The petition was rejected, but during the course of the discussion, the court dealt with a number of important questions relating to the cause for disqualification by virtue of denying the existence of the State of Israel as the state of the Jewish people. It was determined that support for the right of Palestinian return is not considered a call for a change in the Jewish nature of Israel. The panel of justices was divided over the question of whether calling for Israel to become "a state of all its citizens" contradicted its being a Jewish state. Justice Heshin thought there was no contradiction, since the meaning of the call is that one must treat all citizens of the country equally. In contrast, Justice Tal felt that one may assume that whoever supports turning the country into "a state of all its citizens" intends thereby to negate its Jewish character.

Toward the elections to the Fifteenth Knesset, a petition was submitted to disqualify the Balad list. The petition relied upon the positions of the list's leader, Azmi Bishara, who had been quoted in a newspaper interview as saying that in his opinion the Jewish public had no right to self-determination. The Elections Committee rejected the petition and the court denied the appeal. The court determined that in his statements, "MK Bishara had come dangerously close to the border that should not be crossed."[11] Yet, it decided that it could not disqualify the list, owing to other things that Bishara had told the Elections Committee, on the basis of which doubts had been raised that the evidentiary requirements necessary for disqualifying a party had not been met.

In 2002, an amendment was made to Section 7a of the Basic Law: The Knesset, that determined *inter alia* a possibility for personal disqualification of a candidate, when the candidate's actions comprise one of the reasons for disqualification, even without invalidating the list of which the candidate is a member. Another addition was a cause for disqualification of a candidate or list that supports armed struggle against the State of Israel. After the amending of the Basic Law, a number of petitions for disqualification were submitted against lists and individuals for the elections to the Sixteenth Knesset, for the various reasons determined by the law. The Elections Committee decided by a small majority to disqualify the candidacy of MK Tibi for the reason of his support for an armed struggle against Israel, and the Balad list and MK Bishara, who headed that list, by reason of supporting armed struggle and denying the existence of the state as a Jewish state. The Supreme Court invalidated these decisions.[12]

In his ruling, President Barak discussed the meaning of the reason for disqualification owing to denial of the existence of the state as a Jewish state. Barak clarified that this also applies to the desire to harm the Jewish identity of the state, and not only to the wish to harm its security or its existence. Barak further asked, "What are . . . the 'core' characteristics shaping the minimum definition of the State of Israel as a Jewish state," whose negation would be considered denying the Jewish identity of the state? He determined that at the center of these characteristics "stands the right of every Jew to immigrate to the State of Israel, where the Jews will constitute a majority; Hebrew is the official and principal language of the State and most of its fests and symbols reflect the national revival of the Jewish people; the heritage of the Jewish people is a central component in its religious and cultural legacy."[13]

From the above quote, one could deduce that in the *Tibi* case Justice Barak halted *de jure* the trend to limit Section 7a. Yet, *de facto*, the court refrained yet again from effecting Section 7a, while applying strict evidentiary tests and determining that the factual data presented did not meet these tests.

In 2009, on the eve of the elections for the Eighteenth Knesset, the Central Elections Committee discussed a petition to disqualify the Balad slate, based both on the reason of denying the Jewish identity of the state as well as supporting terrorist organizations.

The petition was based on a collection of statements by the Balad leaders against the Jewish state; on their support for the previous leader of their movement, Azmi Bishara, who had fled the country after being suspected of espionage and aiding the enemy in time of war; and for utterances on the right to a violent struggle by terrorist organizations against the State of Israel. The petition was likewise based on parts of Balad's platform, which supported a state "of all its citizens" and the repeal of the Law of Return. In its response to the petition, Balad denied its endorsement of an armed struggle by terrorist organizations, but did admit wholeheartedly that it opposed the definition of Israel as a Jewish state. It did not deny the Jewish right to self-determination in the State of Israel, but argued that it should be limited to a sub-state level within the framework of a neutral state that allows equal self-determination to different national groups.[14]

The Elections Committee decided to disqualify the list by the most sweeping majority in the history of such decisions: twenty-four members voted to support the disqualification and only three against. Balad appealed to the Supreme Court, which reversed the decision by a vote of eight justices to one.[15]

A central place in the discussion was devoted to the term "a state of all its citizens." The declaration submitted by the party chairman to the

Central Elections Committee avowed that the "vision of a state of all its citizens is not a vision that refers solely to freedoms of the individual but sets out from the starting point according to which no single cultural or national group is superior to another and for this reason Balad supports the principle of complete equality among all groups and peoples."[16] The Balad chairman stated that in line with this vision "not only Hebrew will be the official language. The symbols will not be only Jewish" and the same applied to the days of rest and the state holidays.

In the rendering on the *Tibi* case of 2003, President Barak determined that

> If the purpose of Israel's being "a state of all its citizens" is intended to insure equality between the citizens within its own house, while recognizing the rights of the minority living within it, it does not constitute a denial of the existence of the State of Israel as a Jewish state. If, however, the purpose of Israel being "a state of all its citizens" is aimed at more than that, and it is seeking to harm through the rationale of the term [as] the basis of the establishment of the state, and thereby negate the character of the State of Israel as the country of the Jew people, then it does constitute a means for harming the minimal and core characteristics of the State of Israel as a Jewish state.[17]

Reading the Balad chairman's 2009 declaration in light of the decision of President Barak in 2003 must lead to the disqualification of the list, for Balad explicitly negates many of the "core and minimal" characteristics of the State of Israel as a Jewish state. The refusal of the majority justices to disqualify the Balad list must, therefore, be interpreted as a refusal by the Supreme Court to make use of the cause for disqualification through denial of the Jewish identity of the State of Israel. The question as to whether this refusal is justified and legitimate goes beyond the scope of this chapter. Important for our issue is only the fact that the Supreme Court's refusal to disqualify lists that negate the Jewish character of the state means the *de facto* annulment of a component of Israel's national identity, which is anchored in a Basic Law.

LANGUAGES

In contrast to the two previous areas reviewed, in which the Israeli legislature explicitly granted preferred status to the Jewish national components, the situation in the sphere of languages is not clear. Par. 82 of the "Palestine Order in Council" granted Hebrew, Arabic, and English equal standing as official languages. The Law and Administration Ordinance, enacted immediately after the establishment of the state, annulled the official status of the English language and declared the continuation of Mandatory law.[18] Joining these two facts leads ostensibly to the conclusion that Israel has two official languages with equal status: Hebrew and Arabic. This conclusion is somewhat shaken when one considers various laws that grant exclusivity to the Hebrew language for main issues, a fact from which one may conclude that even though Par. 82 was not directly cancelled, later legislation weakened the official status of the Arabic language. Either way, this chapter focuses on the position of the court, so we will refrain from a detailed analysis of the legislative arrangement and suffice with a review of the court's rulings.

In the early years of the state, the court awarded Hebrew a clearly senior status. For example, in a petition submitted to the High Court of Justice in 1955, a Jewish petitioner, a resident of a Jewish neighborhood in Jerusalem, argued for an exemption from the municipal fee for the construction of infrastructure for sewage, owing to the fact that the municipality had not fulfilled its obligation, as determined by a Mandatory bylaw, to publish an announcement about the obligation to pay the fee in the Arabic language as well. Judge Zilberg rejected the petition. The court examined a thesis according to which the establishment of the State of Israel (as a Jewish state) led to an evident cancellation of the official status of Arabic, leaving Hebrew as the single official language. However, eventually the court based its judgment on a different view, according to which only someone who understands no language other than Arabic is eligible to raise arguments against the authorities refraining from making use of it, a situation that did not exist under the circumstances discussed in the petition. Rulings from the 1960s and the 1970s again anchored the concept according to which Arabic does not enjoy equal status with Hebrew, and the possibility to receive remedy for breach of duty to publish in Arabic is conditional upon proving that this violation actually prevents the citizen from having access to information.[19]

From the beginning of the 1990s, the trend changed and in a series of rulings the Court eroded the status of Hebrew. We shall now describe in brief a number of milestones indicating this trend.

The *Kastenbaum* case dealt with a stipulation in a contract—made between relatives of a deceased person and the Hevra Kadisha—that forbade the use of Latin letters on a tombstone.[20] During the proceedings the judges addressed, *inter alia*, the question of the status of the Hebrew language. Deputy President Elon and Justice Barak agreed that the Hebrew language enjoys special status in Israel as a national value, yet they were divided as to the bottom line. Elon felt, in a minority opinion, that the value of Hebrew overrode the rights of the deceased and her relatives, so he authorized the paragraph on exclusivity. Barak held, in the majority opinion, that the rights of the individual overrode the interest of protecting the status of Hebrew.

About a year and a half after the ruling in *Kastenbaum*, the court again had chance to deal with the same issue, in the *Re'em* case.[21] This time, the court invalidated a bylaw, passed by the municipality of Upper Nazareth, that determined that private posters published on city bulletin boards must devote at least two-thirds of their space to Hebrew.

Justice Barak determined that freedom of speech includes the right to choose the language in which expression will be carried out, and therefore the request to add a Hebrew caption is detrimental to this right. Opposite the *right* to freedom of speech, Barak set the *interest* in nurturing the Hebrew language as a national value, but he determined that on balance, the right takes precedent.[22]

A comparison between the two rulings informs us of the erosion in the status of Hebrew. In *Kastenbaum*, Justice Barak determined explicitly that if the matter under discussion was a requirement to include an epitaph in Hebrew in the tombstone—rather than an absolute prohibition against adding a foreign-language epitaph—he would have defended it. This was precisely the requirement treated in *Re'em*—a requirement to add a Hebrew phrase alongside an Arabic one—and Justice Barak still decided to nullify the bylaw. Moreover, in *Kastenbaum*, the value of the Hebrew language was rejected owing to severe harm to human dignity, a right that the court considers extremely important. In contrast, in *Re'em*, the value of the Hebrew language was rejected in favor of freedom of commercial expression, a right that the Supreme Court considers as relatively slight.

The Language on the Paper Election Ballots

The Knesset Elections Law requires the use of a Hebrew letter on the paper ballots in the general elections. A similar arrangement also applies in the elections to the Local Authorities. Towards the end of the 1990s, the court was requested to determine the outcome of elections in a certain local authority that were decided by one vote.[23] One paper ballot on which there was only a handwritten Arabic letter for a given ticket, without the addition of a Hebrew letter on it, had been counted in these elections. Justice Heshin determined, with the majority opinion, that the main purpose of the legislation is the realization of the voter's will, so one is required to respect the wish of the voter who expressed his opinion in the Arabic language. This ruling, too, erodes the senior status granted by the legislature to the Hebrew language.

The *Adalah* Case

In this instance,[24] a petition was discussed to obligate municipalities in which the Arab minority is 6 percent or more to have the street signs throughout the city also in Arabic. The responding cities agreed to include Arabic on street signs in the major thoroughfares and in the side streets in which the Arab population lives. The dispute, therefore, was limited to signs on side streets in areas in which Arab population does not reside. The court granted the petition by a majority opinion.

This petition came after a previous one, submitted against the Public Works Authority, in which the state had pledged to change all the signs directing traffic on intercity highways in Israel, with signage that included the Arabic language, a pledge that led to the petition's withdrawal. In the *Adalah* case, the court accepted as a given the state's previous voluntary pledge, without having recourse to the question of whether this agreement was required by law. The majority justices stated that—given the state's consent to include an inscription in Arabic on intercity signage, despite the damage to the Jewish identity of the state involved in this decision—it was not justified in refusing similar inscriptions on city signs in which the damage to the state's Jewish identity was less severe.[25]

The minority justice, Mishael Heshin, thought that the petition should be rejected. Heshin explained that underpinning the petition was a request to acknowledge the right of the Arab minority to recognition of its right to culture. He argued that granting this new right was an issue to which the legislature should respond and not the court.

Use of Arabic in the Courts

In 2002, the *Adalah* organization petitioned the High Court of Justice with a request to regularize the use of Arabic in proceedings before the courts in Israel. *Adalah* demanded, *inter alia*, that court proceedings could be conducted in Arabic.[26] In the end, *Adalah* withdrew its petition at the advice of the court, while preserving its rights. However, the fact that the petition was withdrawn and that no order nisi was issued shows us that the court had reservations about this petition.

On the surface, this reservation is at loggerheads with the court's decision on the petition concerning municipal signage in mixed cities, where the court decided that the government must allow Arabic speakers maximum linguistic accessibility. This consideration is no less relevant in relation to court proceedings. The reservation also counters Par. 82 of the "Palestine Order in Council," which makes obligatory the use of the two official languages in "official notices." In the petition on municipal signage, the court raised doubts as to whether street signs are considered official notices. No such doubt arose about judicial proceedings, since Par. 82 determines explicitly that "The three languages may be used . . . in the Government offices and the Law Courts." One may perhaps ascribe the different atmosphere in this decision to the specific composition of the justices, absent from which was President Barak, who sat in judgment on all the renderings described above in which the court eroded the standing of the Hebrew language. It may also be that this is a classical instance of the "principal-agent problem," according to which the agent—in our case, the court—finds it difficult to reach the same results when the discussion concerns its own realm.

In summary, this description attests to the consistent trend of the Supreme Court to reinforce the status of Arabic in comparison to Hebrew, along with hesitation about taking the final step of granting official, equal status to Arabic.

SETTLEMENT

The issue of land is an example of an area in which the court acted decisively against the long-standing policy of preference for the Jewish nation, while relinquishing what had been considered, at least in the past, a main component in the characterization of Israel as the Jewish nation-state.

The Jewish National Fund (JNF) served for decades as a main instrument in the activity of the Zionist movement for the establishment of the State of Israel. The Fifth Zionist Congress, convened in Basel in 1901, decided to establish the JNF. The JNF was a proprietary limited company and was registered in England in 1907. The JNF Corporate Charter determines that its main aim is to acquire land for the purpose of Jewish settlement in Israel.[27] The Charter likewise instituted a prohibition against transferring the ownership of its lands. The JNF goals were realized to the letter. It purchased tracts in the Land of Israel, refrained from selling them, and leased them solely to Jews.

In its first thirty years, the State of Israel continued with a policy of land administration in the spirit of the JNF goals and allotted a great deal of land for settlement intended for Jews alone. On occasion, the state even expropriated land of Arab citizens for the purpose of founding settlements that were only for Jews. The state granted the JNF statutory status and even authorized it to expropriate land. The state and the JNF signed a pact declaring joint interests, and the administration of the JNF lands was transferred to the Israel Land Administration.[28]

The question as to whether the state was permitted to allot land solely for Jewish settlement was first placed on the Supreme Court's agenda only in 1978. A government company, which dealt with the restoration of the Jewish Quarter in the Old City of Jerusalem, turned to the public with a proposal to purchase apartments that it had built. The appeal was directed toward an "Israeli citizen who lived in the country and had served in the IDF or had received an exemption from IDF service, or had served in one of the Hebrew organizations that pre-dated May 14, 1948, or was a new immigrant who was a resident of Israel."[29]

Muhamad Said Burqan, an Arab citizen of Jordan who was a permanent resident in Israel, asked to lease one of the apartments in that offer, and his request was denied owing to his not meeting the criteria that had been set. Although the offer did not explicitly state that an Arab was not eligible to lease an apartment in the Old City, Burqan insisted that the practical meaning of the criteria was exactly that. Burqan petitioned the High Court of Justice with the argument that the criterion that prevented him from purchasing an apartment was marred by prohibited discrimination, owing to nationality or religion.

The court rejected the petition unanimously, based on five arguments. Two of these were based upon the fact that the petitioner was not an Israeli citizen, and as such the state was permitted to discriminate against him in relation to an Israeli citizen. The third argument referred to the unique history of the Old City. The court explained that the "need to rehabilitate the Jewish Quarter of the Old City arose only after the Jordanian armies invaded it and drove out the Jews and stole their property and destroyed their houses. Naturally, this rehabilitation was meant to restore the glory of the Jewish Yishuv in the Old City, so that the Jews will again, as in the past, have their own quarter, alongside the Muslim, Christian, and Armenian Quarters." The fourth argument recognized the right of separate housing on the basis of nationality for members of all religions, including the members of the Jewish majority group. The fifth argument was based on the fact that the petitioner considered himself obliged to the commandments of Islam, which forbid him from selling land to Jews. The court decided that the petitioner had thereby lost his right to demand that the State of Israel refrain from discriminating against Muslims in allotting land.

A bit more than two decades later, the court again discussed this topic, but this time it adopted a different approach. The Kaadans, an Arab couple who were citizens of Israel, sought to lease a house in the town community of Katzir. Katzir was established on state land that had been allotted to the Jewish Agency, through a cooperative association whose aim was to establish a rural community settlement that would be based on organizing its members as a community, maintaining cooperation among its members. The request by the Kaadans was refused with the explanation that they did not meet the regulations of the cooperative association, which stipulated acceptance of a person to the association on his having "completed mandatory military service according to the Security Service Law 1959 [Consolidated Version] or exempted from mandatory service according to this law or that his military service was postponed according to this law."[30] The Kaadan family petitioned the High Court of Justice, which granted the petition.

The heart of the decision was written by President Barak. Barak set on one side of the equation the principle of equality, which in his opinion supported the position of the Kaadan family, and examined whether there were any values that were likely to tilt the balance in favor of the respondents. First, Barak traced the specific goals standing at the basis of the legislation regularizing the activity of the Israel Land Administration and determined that the main goal of the relevant legislation was the preservation of the lands of Israel in the ownership of *the state*. Barak ignored the fact that at the foundation of the JNF policy lay another principle: namely, preservation of the land in the ownership of the Jewish *people*. This principle is stressed at the opening of the pact signed between the JNF and the State of Israel: "Since its founding over fifty years ago, the Jewish National Fund has worked to acquire lands in the Land of Israel and transfer them to the ownership of the [Jewish] people . . . The government of Israel and the Jewish National Fund have reached a decision . . . to support the Jewish National Fund in achieving its goal."[31]

Barak also mentioned in brief the interest in preventing the transfer of the ownership of the land to "undesirable elements," but he did not make clear who those elements were. The same goes for other aims that Barak cites, such as "security policy," "national projects," "population distribution," and "agricultural settlement." These purposes do not receive elucidation in the statements by Barak, who chose to ignore the fact that in their basic meaning they are closely connected to the interests of the Jewish nation. By ignoring this, Barak was enabled to reach the conclusion that the terms of the relevant legislation do not contain any goal that justified, let alone obligated, allotting land for settlement intended solely by Jews.

At this stage, Barak moved on to the identification of the general purposes at the base of the Israeli legal system, which owing to their supreme status stand also at the basis of all legislation derived from this system. In this context, Barak mentioned the principle of equality, but ignored the possible claim that Israel's status as the Jewish nation-state results in another general purpose of encouraging Jewish settlement in the country. Barak determined that the Jewishness of the state had influence on its main language, on the days of rest customary in it, on its cultural and religious heritage, and even on its immigration policy, but the national nature of Israel could not justify any discrimination among its citizens, including even the area of settlement.

The ruling on the Kaadan matter served as an introduction to a series of decisions that reinforced and expanded the prohibition against allotting land for Jewish settlement. Owing to limitations of space, we will mention briefly, without going into detail, two issues. First, the court tended to extend its policy not only to state land but also to JNF land, which at least in the past had been described as a kind of trust, the purpose of which was settlement of Jews only. As a result, the attorney general published a directive that led to a change in JNF policy in a manner that insures equal participation of non-Jews in tenders for its lands. The second ruling determined severe criteria for participating in government tenders in a manner that prevents even a private association that wins a tender for residential projects from marketing apartments to only one national group. Such renderings led cumulatively to complete erosion of the practice customary in Israel for more than fifty years of allotting lands for exclusive Jewish settlement, a practice underpinned by the premise that this was necessary owing to the national character of the state.[32]

INCENTIVES FOR SETTLEMENT

Another issue related to settlement is that of providing economic incentives for Jewish settlement in outlying districts, among other things by granting the status of national priority areas for settlement in these regions.

The State of Israel grants priority to settlement in certain areas in a variety of ways. It invests in the development of infrastructure, assists in private building, gives supplements to the salaries of civil servants, and provides tax benefits for all workers living in these areas, and supplies subsidized education for preschoolers. In the past, this policy was adopted many a time, declared as a means for realizing the goal of "Judaizing" parts of the country—mainly in the Negev and Galilee. Yet, also in the past, the government refrained from setting national identity as a criterion for eligibility for the benefits, but rather fashioned the criteria in a manner that insured preference for the Jewish settlements located in those regions of the country.[33]

The court invalidated the government decision whereby the settlements included in areas of national priority are determined, by its deciding, inter alia, that the criteria posed for it contradict the principle of equality between Jews and Arabs. The court explained that the criteria should be examined not only by its aim but also by its result. Hence, even if the court had been convinced that the criteria had not been "custom-made" with the aim of preferring Jews, this would not have changed its decision, because the application of the criteria had led in reality to an unequal result.[34]

The political system acted according to the directives of the court, and the Knesset adopted a map of national priority regions that led to the result that from then on, 40 percent of those eligible for incentives were Arab citizens.[35] It turns out, therefore, that here too, the court's decision led to an erosion of the Jewish characteristics of the state in that it resulted in the cancellation of the policy of encouraging Jewish settlement in outlying regions or in areas with a definite Arab majority, which stimulates the possibility for irredentism. It can also be argued that the state "helped" the court lead to this result by its refraining from openly declaring the national consideration.

NATIONAL INSTITUTIONS

The State of Israel granted special statutory standing to institutions of the Jewish people as they were fashioned by the Zionist movement. In 1952, the Knesset enacted a law on the status of the World Zionist Organization and the Jewish Agency for Israel that determines principles for cooperation between the State of Israel and the Zionist Organizations.[36]

The beginning of the law states the following: "1. The State of Israel considers itself as a creation of the entire Jewish people, and its gates are open, according to its laws, to every Jew who wishes to immigrate to it," and "2. The World Zionist Organization since its establishment fifty years ago has led the movement of the Jewish people and its efforts to realize the vision of generations to return to its homeland, and with the help of other Jewish circles and bodies bore the main responsibility for the establishment of the State of Israel." From the law, one sees that the State of Israel considers the Zionist bodies as a type of emissary for the promotion of the goals to which it is obligated. One of the means for effecting the aims of the law is the pact made between the state and the Zionist bodies, which is granted the status of secondary legislation. The pact was signed in 1954 and was accepted again with a few changes in 1979.[37]

The special status of the Zionist organizations was anchored in the wording of a great deal of legislation. They are considered "a public institution" for certain matters, exempted from taxes, a representative on their behalf serves on various governmental bodies, their workers are permitted to vote in Knesset elections at the Israeli representations abroad, similar to civil servants, and even the Israeli penal code acknowledges their special status by setting up a specific prohibition (extended even abroad) against damaging, "the property, rights or orderly functioning of . . . the World Zionist Organization, the Jewish Agency for Israel, the JNF and Keren Hayesod . . . The public status not only provides them with rights but also levies upon them quite a few obligations.[38]

From all the foregoing, a picture is depicted according to which the Zionist institutions enjoy a "quasi-governmental" status. However, this reality reached a turning point with the decision over Beit Rivka.[39] In this instance, the court was requested to decide whether the Jewish Agency was "a body fulfilling a public role according to law," a relative piece of data for deciding the question of whether the agency was obliged to honor a series of human rights. The court decided that the law recognized Zionist bodies, but only in the guise of voluntary organizations working on behalf of themselves to encourage *aliyah* (immigration to Israel). As for the agreements made between the state and Zionist institutions, the court attributed to them the status of a private law contract, and even the exemption from taxes was not considered by the court as sufficient for recognizing the agency as a body fulfilling a public role. In our opinion, the court's stance does not coincide with the variety of legislative arrangements sampled above, from which, as noted, one gains a clear picture of mutual relations and mission. The ruling on Beit Rivka thus constitutes another step in the gradual process, led by the court, of erosion of Israel's identity as a nation-state.

IMMIGRATION

The issue of immigration has serious implications for the national identity of Israel. The interesting fact regarding the court's treatment of this issue is that on this matter, the court did not reject the national consideration, or weaken its standing on balance with other considerations, but rather chose to ignore it completely. The conduct of the court in this field expresses, in a sense, a further step in the erosion of Israel's national identity.

Israeli legislation in the area of immigration deals, *inter alia*, with the situation called in jargon "reunification of families," in which a citizen of the state requests to bring into the country a foreign spouse and grant that person citizenship. The Citizenship Law facilitates the naturalization processes of the spouse and releases him or her from most of the conditions that must be met for regular naturalization.[40] The law leaves to the discretion of the Minister of the Interior, in this case too, whether to accede to the request for citizenship, but, in reality, the Minister of the Interior usually approves the vast majority of these requests, and, following the directives of the High Court of Justice, even designated clear criteria on this matter.

After the signing of the Oslo Agreements between Israel and the PLO, a very sharp increase occurred in the number of marriages between Palestinian residents of the Territories and Arab citizens of Israel. Under these circumstances, the lenient family reunification policy led to a highly significant rise in the number of Palestinians who became naturalized citizens of Israel. According to Ministry of Interior statistics, between 1994 and 2002 some 130,00–140,000 Palestinians became naturalized citizens of Israel.[41]

In March 2002, the Minister of the Interior froze the graduated process of family unification of Israelis with Palestinian spouses. The declared motivation was security, after a Palestinian who held an Israeli identity card, which was given to him as a result of his parents' family unification process, carried out a terrorist act that injured many. In May 2002, the policy was anchored by a government decision, against which a number of petitions were submitted to the High Court of Justice. While the proceedings in the High Court of Justice were pending, the Knesset anchored the policy in law.[42] The law was enacted as a temporary order and explained through the exigencies of security. During the period of the law's validity, the Minister of the Interior and the military commander are prohibited from granting temporary permits to state in Israel, residency permits, and Israeli citizenship to residents of the Territories, other than in the most limited exceptional cases as specified in the law. The law established an apparatus for extending the validity of the temporary order by the government with the approval of the Knesset.

The government made use of this apparatus a number of times, and each time extended the validity of the law for a few months. A number of petitions against the legality of the law were submitted to the High Court of Justice, which discussed them with an expanded panel of eleven justices and rejected them by a difference of one vote (the *First Reunification of Families* decision). Taking into consideration the court's comments during the course of the discussions of the petitions, the Knesset amended the law even before the decision was rendered, and relaxed a number of its conditions. After the decision was given, the Knesset amended the law again (the third version). The third version of the law further expanded the exceptions to the prohibition, defined precisely the security considerations that the Minister of the Interior was permitted to take in account, and ordered the establishment of a committee that the Minister of the Interior is to avail himself of when he is about to authorize family reunification for humanitarian reasons.[43]

A number of petitions were submitted to the High Court of Justice against the third version of the law. The court heard the petitions in an expanded panel of eleven justices, and on January 2012 handed down its decision, rejecting them, again by a difference of one vote (the *Second Reunification of Families* decision).[44] Let us turn now to summarize the various opinions in the *First Reunification of Families* decision.

The minority justices thought that the petition should be granted and invalidation of the law should be declared. The main minority opinion was written by Justice Barak. Barak examined the issue from the viewpoint of the Israeli spouse, while noting the need to investigate the question of whether the foreign spouse has relevant constitutional rights as well.

In the first part of the ruling, Barak examined whether the law infringed upon constitutional rights. He argued that the right to dignity, anchored in the Basic Law: Human Dignity and Liberty, should be interpreted as also including the right to establish a family. Barak argued further that this right entails the right of the Israeli citizen to bring his or her spouse to Israel and to conduct their mutual life there. In light of this, Barak determined that the law was detrimental to the constitutional right to establish a family. He further decided that the law infringed upon the right to equality of the Arab citizens of Israel, since in practice it was directed almost exclusively toward them.

In the second part, Barak examined whether it is possible to justify the infringement on rights to a family life and equality. The state argued that that the purpose of the law was to prevent terror attacks, and Barak determined that this goal was worthy. It should be noted that the state did not present any other goal, and especially not the demographic one, to which we shall return shortly. At this point Barak turned to the proportionality balancing test. There are three assessments of proportionality: the means-goal link, selection of the means that achieves the goal while harming the right to the smallest extent, and benefit—in terms of attaining the goal (which overrides the harm)—in terms of infringement upon the right. Barak determined that a rational link exists between the means adopted by the law—sweeping limitation of the entry of Palestinians—and the goal—prevention of terror. Barak also determined that it was, of course, possible to employ less harmful means—individual examination of requests for family reunification—but this means would not yield the same degree of security as sweeping limitation on immigration, so the law passed the second assessment of proportionality. Yet, in Barak's opinion, the law failed the third test, in the sense that the increase in security deriving from the mechanism that the law determines, in comparison to the alternative of individual examination, was not of greater weight than the additional harm deriving from the mechanism rooted in the law. In other words, Barak felt that it would be worthwhile to pay in terms of security so as to lower the detriment to human rights.[45]

Concurring with Barak's minority opinion were four justices, among whom Justice Procaccia's opinion deserves note as it differed from those of her colleagues over the question of the purpose of the law. Procaccia did not accept the state's claim according to which the law's goal was only security, and she referred—as a reason for her lack of belief—to a discussion held in the Knesset as part of the legislative process in which various Knesset members presented demographic considerations as the purpose of the law. As additional support for her doubt, Procaccia indicated the fact that the state was refraining from instituting a sweeping prohibition against the Palestinians who were seeking temporary work permits in Israel and the fact that the state managed to cope with the danger of terror among Israeli Arabs with methods of individual treatment. These facts led Procaccia to the conclusion that defending the security of the state was not the only aim the law was seeking to promote and that, in addition, it aimed to maintain the demographic balance between Jews and Arabs among the citizens of the state. Procaccia refrained from expressing an unequivocal opinion over the question of whether the demographic goal could serve as a proper one, and she sufficed with the incongruence between the declared aim and the goal that could be deduced (as stated, in her opinion) as the reason for determining that the law did not pass the test of a worthy goal.

What did the other members of the panel think about the demographic aim? On the surface, one cannot know, since they did accept the state's claim that the purpose of security, and not the demographic one, lay at the base of the law; therefore, they did not have recourse at all to the issue of the legitimacy of the demographic purpose. Support for this reply can be found in the words of Justice Heshin, who rebuked Justice Procaccia for having incidentally touched upon the demographic issue.[46] Yet, on second thought, it may be that the refraining of the justices from referring to the question of the legitimacy of the demographic aim can inform us somewhat about their position on the subject. Had they been convinced that the demographic goal was legitimate, they would have said so explicitly.

Two facts reinforce this possible conclusion. First, the court rejected the request of an association called The Jewish Majority in Israel to join the case as a respondent. This association argued that the demographic consideration definitely underpinned the foundation of the law, that this consideration constituted a worthy goal and that the law effected this aim proportionally. Second, in his response to the High Court of Justice, the attorney general indeed argued that "even if the dominant goal of the law was demographic—which does not seem to be the case—then this goal is likely to coincide with the values of the State of Israel as a Jewish and democratic state."[47] The fact that the court chose to ignore this statement strengthens the feeling that the demographic consideration hovered in the courtroom, but the judges were afraid to deal with it. This conclusion should be moderated in light of the fact that the state was the one that refrained from pressing the demographic consideration. Conversely, one may argue that this avoidance derived from the state's presumption that presenting this consideration in an explicit manner would greatly weaken the chance that the court would authorize the law.

Either way, the state's not raising of the demographic goal in the context of immigration policy has become a pattern. In April 2011, the Supreme Court invalidated an accepted practice of the Ministry of the Interior, according to which a foreign worker who gave birth in Israel had to leave the country within 90 days of the birth. The State Attorney's office sought to justify the practice by arguing that it was intended to prevent permanent settlement of foreign workers in Israel beyond the period of their work permit, and that giving birth and raising children in Israel were a recipe for long-term settlement.[48] The state, however, explained the need to prevent the permanent settlement in Israel of foreign workers by the necessity of preserving available jobs for Israelis and by the necessity of enforcing the laws of immigration into Israel. As a result, the court dealt only with these arguments, which are correct for every country and not necessarily to a nation-state, and completely ignored the consideration of preventing a blow to the Jewish majority in the State of Israel.

Before concluding this point, it should be noted, though, that the majority opinion in the *Second Reunification of Families* decision might signal a change in the court's attitude towards the demographic goal. Indeed, operatively, the majority based its conclusion again on the security goal only. However, this time, several justices emphasized clearly that their lack of reference to the demographic goal stemmed from the state's abstention from relying on this rationale. These justices pointed out that should the state explicitly raise the demographic aim in the future, they would consider it favorably.[49]

CONCLUSION

The picture formed from the rulings examined in this chapter is of a court that is eroding components of national identity that existed in Israel before its decisions. Yet the various issues are distinct from one another in the extent of erosion evident in each of them. On the issue of return, which perhaps constitutes the main component in the identity of Israel as a nation-state, the court refrained almost entirely from eroding the national dimension. The court has gradually eroded the superior status of the Hebrew language but avoided granting equal status to Arabic, formally and practically. On four issues the court almost totally wore away the component of national identity: on the matter of invalidating political parties that deny the Jewish identity of the state, on the matter of allotting land for Jewish settlement, on the matter of providing economic incentives for Jewish settlement, and on the question of the public status of the institutions of the Jewish people. In the area of immigration of non-Jews, a new phenomenon seems to be forming, according to which the court completely ignores the consideration of maintaining the Jewish identity of the state, although a recently published decision might indicate that the court will consider the national goal positively in the future, should the state explicitly rely on it.

The fact that the state has chosen in recent years to bypass the national consideration and to justify before the High Court of Justice the decisions of the Knesset and the government for other reasons is likely, perhaps, to serve as one explanation for the change in the direction of the High Court of Justice rulings. In our opinion, however, the tendency toward erosion of the components of national identity in the decisions of the Supreme Court cannot be ascribed only to a change in the mood of the political branches (the Knesset and the government). This tendency also expresses a change in the outlook of the court itself. Even if the regime is no longer certain of the justice of policy the aim of which is the preservation of the national character of Israel, the court constitutes a leading factor in the conceptual and practical change, in a manner that points the way for the political system and the public in Israel. Does the court deserve praise for having taken this role upon itself, or should it be criticized for doing so? We shall leave discussion of this question for another time.

NOTES

1   Partition Plan: UN General Assembly Resolution 181, November 29, 1947. See also at *The Knesset: The Israeli Government*, "UN General Assembly Resolution 181," http://www.knesset.gov.il/process/docs/un181_eng.htm (accessed June 12, 2012). Declaration of Independence: Declaration of the Establishment of the State of Israel, 1 Laws of the State of Israel [L.S.I.] 3, 4 (1948). Basic Laws: Section 1A of Hok Yesod: Kevod Ha-Adam Ve-Heruto (Basic Law: Human Dignity and Liberty), Sefer Ha-Hukim S.H. 150 (1992); Section 2 of Hok Yesod: Hofesh Ha-Issuk (Basic Law: Freedom of Occupation), [S.H.] 114 (1992). Legislation: see, for example: Section 1 of Hok Hashvut (Law of Return), 5710-1950; Section 2 of Hok Haezrachut (Citizenship Law), 5712-1952; World Zionist Organizations and Jewish Agency for Israel Status Law, 5713-1952; Jewish National Fund Law, 5713-1953; Hok Yesodot Hamishpat (Law of Legal Foundations), 5740-1980; section 18a(1) for government and law order, 5708-1948. Common practices: many formal announcements, for example, are published only in Hebrew and most government forms are in Hebrew only. See Ilan Saban "(Bilingual) Sound Alone In the Dark?," *Iyunei Mishpat* 27 (2003): 109n1 and text near it.

2   See section 1 of Law of Return for the right to immigrate to Israel; for other nations, see Alexander Yakobson and Amnon Rubinstein, *Israel and the Family of Nations: The Jewish Nation State and Human Rights* (New York: Routledge, 2009).

3   Examples of law reflecting national identity: HCJ 442/71 Lanski v. Minister of the Interior, PD 26(2) 337, 399 (1972). Limitation of rights for spouses: HCJ 3648/97 Stamka v. Minister of the Interior, PD 53(2) 728 (1999).

4   Use in exceptional cases: HCJ 442/71 Lanski v. Minister of the Interior, PD 26(2) 337 (1972); HCJ 48/58 Yanovici v. Minister of the Interior, PD 12 646 (1972); HCJ 94/62 Gold v. Minister of the Interior, PD 16 1846 (1962); HCJ 186/62 Vaider v. Minister of the Interior, PD 16 1547 (1962). Application to serious crimes: HCJ 1227/98 Malevski v. Minister of the Interior, PD 52(4) 690 (1998). Application to active criminals before citizenship application: HCJ 5067/02 Gulaiev v. Government ministry of the Interior, Tak-Al 2003(3), 1100 (2003). Extension to minor offences: HCJ 5033/06 Gilvanov v. The State of Israel, Tak-Al 2007(2), 3342 (2007); HCJ 6624/06 Peshko v. Government Ministry of the Interior, Tak-Al 2007(2), 2183 (2007).

5   Disqualification of slate: HCJ 1/65 Yardor v. Chairman of the Sixth Knesset Central Elections Committee, Tak-Al 2003(3), 1100 (2003) (Yardor). The Central Elections Committee is headed by a Supreme Court justice and consists of representatives of the various political parties. Final quotation from Yardor, at 371.

6   EA 2/84 Neiman v. Chairman of the 11th Knesset Central Elections Committee, PD 39(2), 225.

7   Hok Yesod: Hakneset (Basic Law: The Knesset), as amended at S.H. 5725-1965. This version was revised later on.

8   EA 2/88 Ben-Shalom v. Chairman of the 12th Knesset Central Elections Committee, PD 43(4), 221.

9   Parties Law 5752-1992.

10 CA 2316/96 Isakson v. The Political Parties Registrar, PD 50(2) 529.

11 EA 2600/99 Erliche v. Chairman of the Knesset Central Elections Committee, PD 53(3), 38, 41–42 (quoting an interview with Bashara in Haaretz, May 29, 1998), 44.

12 EA 11280/02 16th Knesset Central Elections Committee v. Achmad Tibi et al., PD 57(4), 1 (Tibi).

13 Ibid., 22.

14 Written answer on behalf of Balad in FR 1/18 Furman et al v. Balad. The document [Hebrew] is available at The Knesset: The Israeli Government, http://knesset.gov.il/elections18/heb/list/6.pdf (accessed June 12, 2012).

15 EA 561/09 Balad Group v. 18th Knesset Central Elections Committee (unpublished, March 7, 2011).

16 Written answer on behalf of Balad in FR 1/18 Furman et al v. Balad, sections 8–9.

17 Tibi, Justice Barak's Ruling, section 13.

18 Three official languages: Article 82 of the Palestine Order-in Council, 1922–1947. English no longer official: Section 15(2) for Government and law order, 5708-1948 and for continuation of Mandatory law, section 11.

19 1955 case: CA 148/54 Khaa v. Jerusalem Municipality, PD 9, 1247. 1960s ruling: HCJ 297/65 El-Chuari v. Chairman Of Nazareth Municipality Election committee, PD 19(3), 279 (1965). 1970s ruling: HCJ 527/74 Chalaf v. The North County Committee for Planning and Construction, PD 29(2) 319 (1975).

20 CA 294/91 Jerusalem Community Burial Society v. Kastenbaum, PD 46(2) 464 (1992) (Kastenbaum).

21 CA 105/92 "Re'em" Engineers v. Nazareth Eilit Municipality, PD 47(5) 189 (1993) (Re'em).

22 Ibid., 209.

23 Requirement for use of Hebrew letter: Sections 61 and(3)ec 2(a) 76(b) of The Knesset Elections Law (Consolidated Version) 5729-1969. Knesset Elections Law—

Arrangements for local authorities: Section 51 of Local Authorities (Elections) Law, 5725-1965. Contested case: PCA 12/99 Mareei v. Savek, PD 53(2) 128 (1999).

24 HCJ 4112/99 Adalah v. Tel-Aviv-Jaffa Municipality, PD 56(5) 393 (2002) (*Adalah*).

25 Previous petition: HCJ 4438/97 *Adalah* v. Public Works Authority (petition deleted, February 25, 1999) (*Adalah v. PWA*). Majority justices opinion: section 24 of Justice Barak ruling in *Adalah*.

26 HCJ 792/02 *Adalah* v. Courts Administrator (unpublished).

27 JNF background: see JNF reply to the petition at HCJ 9010/04 Arab Center for Alternative Design et al v. Israel Land Administration. Jewish National Fund Corporate Charter, Yalkut Hapirsumim [Y.P.], 5714-1954, 345, section 3a.

28 Authorization for expropriation: Jewish National Fund law, 5713-1953. Joint interest pact: Y.P. 5728, 1597. Transfer of administration: Israel Lands Administration Law, 5720-1960.

29 HCJ 114/78 Muhammad Saaid Burqan v. Finance Minister, Tak-Al 2003(3), 1100 (2003) (*Burqan*).

30 HCJ 6698/95 Adal Kaadan et al. v. Israel Land Administration, PD 54(1), 258 (*Kaadan*), 265

31 Goals of the legislation: ibid., 272. The Treaty between JNF and the State of Israel, Y.P. 5728, 1597.

32 Further decisions expanding on *Kaadan*: see, for example, HCJ 8060/03 Kaadan v. Israel Land Administration, Tak-Al 2(2006), 775 (2006); HCJ 9818/02 Abu-alhigga v. Minister of Finance et al., (unpublished, 2003); HCJ 7574/06 Hasolelim Young Maccabi Group for Agricultural communal settlement Ltd v. Israel Land Administration, Tak-Al 2007(1) 758 (2007); FHCJ 1107/07 Hasolelim Young Maccabi Group for Agricultural communal settlement Ltd v. Israel Land Administration, Tak-Al 2007(1) 4183 (2007). Extension to JNF land: HCJ 9010/04 Arab Center for Alternative Design et al. v. Israel Land Administration et al. (decision from October 11, 2004). Attorney general's directive: see documentation of state commitment facing the High Court of Justice at HCJ 9010/04 Arab Center for Alternative Design et al. v. Israel Land Administration et al. (decision from October 20, 2004). Criteria in government tenders: APA 1789/10 Esther Saba v. Israel Land Administration (unpublished, November 7, 2010).

33 David Kretzmer, *The Legal Status of the Arabs in Israel* (Boulder, CO: Westview Press, 1990), 107.

34 HCJ 11163/03 Supreme Supervision Commission for Arab Issues in Israel v. Prime Minister, Tak-Al 2006(1) 2562(2006); section 23 for Justice Barak's ruling.

35 See Economic and Efficiency Law (Legislative Amendments to implement the economic program for 2009-2010) chap. 26; The 32nd Government Decision No. 1060 dated December 13, 2009.

36 World Zionist Organization and Jewish Agency Status Law, 5713-1952.

37 Ibid., sections 1-2. YP, 5715, 386, 187; YP, 2172.

38 Special status in legislation: examination of the legislation in Israel as updated for April 2010, found 54 occurrences of the World Zionist Organization and 88 occurrences of the Jewish Agency. Representative on government bodies: see, for example, Section 8 of Authority for the Development and Advancement of Culture, Tourism and Foreign Relations of Jerusalem Law, 5766-2005. Voting rights: Section 116g of the Knesset Elections Law (Consolidated Version) 5729-1969. Special status in penal

code: sections 13(1)(5) and 13(3) of the Penal Law, 5737-1977. Oligations: see, for instance, section 13(8) of Defamation (Prohibition) Law, 5725-1965; sections 1(1)(4) (3) and 1(1)(4)(4) of the Income Tax Ordinance [New Version].

39   HCJ 4212/91 "Bet-Rebecca" Educational Institution v. The Jewish Agency, PD 47(2) 661(1993).

40   Section 7 of the Citizenship Law. For this purpose it is immaterial whether their spouse citizen is Jewish or not. See, HCJ 3648/97 Stamka v. Minister of the Interior, PD 53(2) 728 (1999).

41   From Deputy Attorney General, Menachem Mazuz, presentation in a session at the Knesset Interior Committee on July 14, 2003 regarding to The Citizenship and Entry into Israel (temporary provision) bill 5763-2003. See *The Knesset: The Israeli Government*, http://www.knesset.gov.il/protocols/data/html/pnim/2003-07-14-01. html [Hebrew] (accessed June 12, 2012).

42   Government Decision No. 1813 dated May 12, 2002. Petitions: see, for instance, HCJ 4022/02 Association for Civil Rights in Israel v. Minister of the Interior, Tak-Al 2007(1) 188(2007). Law: The Citizenship and Entry into Israel Law (temporary Order) 5763-2003. For background and critical analysis, see G. Davidov, Y. Yuval, A. Saban, and A. Reichman, "State or Family? The Citizenship and Entry into Israel (Temporary Order), 5763-2003," *Mishpat U'mimshal* 8 (2005): 643 [Hebrew]; Amnon Rubinstein and Liav Orgad, "Human Rights, National Security, and Jewish Majority—the Case of Migration for Marriage," *Hapraklit* 48 (2006): 315 [Hebrew].

43   *First Reunification of Families* decision: HCJ 7102/03 Member of Knesset, Zehava Galon v. Attorney General; HCJ 8099/03 Association For Civil Rights in Israel v. Minister of the Interior; HCJ 8263/03 Aschafi v. Minister of the Interior; HCJ 7052/03 Adalah v. Minister of the Interior, Tak-Al 2006(2), 1754 (2006). Relaxed conditions: the Citizenship and Entry into Israel Law (Temporary Order) (Amendment), 5765-2005. Third version of the law: Section 3d of the Citizenship and Entry into Israel Law (Temporary Order) (Amendment) 5767-2007.

44   HCJ 466/07 Galoen v. Attorney General (forthcoming).

45   For similar ruling of Justice Barak on another case, see HCJ 7102/03 Beit-Surick Village Council v. Israel Government (June 30, 2004).

46   Section 135 for Justice Cheshin's ruling.

47   Section 169 of the State summary dated December 13, 2003 in HCJ 7052/03 Adalah v. Minister of the Interior, Tak-Al 2006(2), 1754 (2006) as quoted in section 14 for Justice Procaccia's ruling.

48   HCJ 11437/05 Kav LaOved v. Ministry of the Interior (forthcoming); section 7–11 for Justice Procaccia's ruling.

49   See, for example, *Second Reunification of Families* decision, section 16 for Justice Rivlin's ruling.

A Jewish Majority as the Leading Criterion for Shaping Immigration Policy to Israel

9

YAFFA ZILBERSHATS

AN OVERVIEW

This chapter considers a very complex issue, namely, immigration to the State of Israel. Israeli law explicitly prefers the immigration of Jews while making it difficult for non-Jews to immigrate to the state. In this chapter, we shall try to defend this approach. Our defense is based on both legal and political philosophical arguments, drawing comparisons with cases around the world at different times.

The population of the State of Israel is about seventy-five percent Jewish, twenty percent Arab, and five percent other non-Jews. Whoever resides in Israel and is a citizen of the state holds full and equal rights, whether or not he or she is Jewish. This means that non-Jews may vote and be elected to the Israeli parliament—the Knesset—and if economic resources are not distributed to them on an equal basis, they have the right to claim what is due to them. Non-Jewish citizens of Israel have the right to pursue their culture, language, and religion. As citizens, they also have an equal right to enter Israel.

However, immigration is different. Immigration rules apply to people who are not yet citizens of the state. In this context, Israeli law draws a distinction between Jews and non-Jews. While Jewish immigration is almost automatic, stringent restrictions are imposed on non-Jews wishing to immigrate. This legal arrangement protects the existence of a considerable Jewish majority in the State of Israel.

The biggest risk to the maintenance of a Jewish majority, in terms of non-Jewish immigration to Israel, is the alleged Palestinian right to return to the State of Israel. Another problem is that of indirect rolling return through family unification where non-Jews—mainly Arabs of whom the majority are Palestinians—demand to immigrate to Israel by virtue of having married Israeli citizens, primarily of Arab origin.

Non-Jews, whether or not Arab, effectively immigrate into Israel as a result of the application of the overly broad Law of Return. As the Israeli Law of Return aspires to enable any Jew to immigrate to Israel, it also confers this right upon non-Jewish spouses and non-Jewish children; such children might be non-Jews if the mother is not Jewish. This law has also been used to open the doors of the state to the grandchild of a Jew and that grandchild's spouse, thereby further increasing non-Jewish immigration to Israel. The law has been criticized, but, as yet, it has not been amended. The number of non-Jewish immigrants entering by virtue of this law is considerable, yet it is not as large as the numbers of Palestinian Arabs demanding to immigrate to Israel.

Another pressing issue is that of migrant workers, people who arrive on a temporary basis to work in Israel, with the object of sending money to support their families back in their homeland. The policy of allowing migrants to stay permanently depends on government decisions. There is no law on this matter, but there are Supreme Court decisions regarding the naturalization process of migrant workers married to Israeli citizens. Currently, the number of the latter class of migrants is not very large and it does not threaten to lower the rate of the Jewish majority in Israel.

The main threat to the Jewish majority at present is Arab, and more specifically Palestinian, immigration. This chapter will focus on that threat. We will provide justifications for both the preference given to Jewish immigration to Israel and the non-recognition of the alleged Palestinian right to enter Israel or return to it. Some of the arguments in this discourse may also be used in the future when discussing limiting the Law of Return and the policy of imposing restrictions on migrant workers.

INTRODUCTION: RETURN AND RETURN—*SHVUT* AND *SHIVA*

In Hebrew two words can be used to describe "return": *Shvut* and *Shiva*.

Shvut is the term used when describing the right of Jews to immigrate to the State of Israel. This right, which is almost absolute according to Israeli law, is enshrined in the Law of Return enacted in 1950.[1] This law provides that "Every Jew has a right to immigrate to Israel." The term used in the Law of Return for the act of "immigrating" is *la'alot*, meaning to climb or to go up, the same term used when we go to Jerusalem from any part of Israel. One always "goes up" to Jerusalem. One never just "goes." By analogy, Jews do not just come to Israel, they "go up," they "climb" to it.

It may be seen, therefore, that this is a very powerful right and even though it has not been formally entrenched in a Basic Law, it is considered a constitutional right in Israeli Law.

The other term of return, *Shiva*, is used when describing the alleged Palestinian right to come back to the State of Israel.

The "right of return" claimed by the Palestinians is an outcome of the Palestinian refugee problem that arose after the War of Independence waged in Palestine from the end of 1947 to the beginning of 1949. On November 29, 1947, the UN General Assembly adopted Resolution 181 regarding the termination of the British Mandate and the partition of Mandatory Palestine into two states—Jewish and Arab—on the basis of the nationality of their respective populations. The Arab inhabitants of the land and the Arab states, apart from King Abdullah of Jordan, rejected the Partition Plan. As long as the British Mandate continued, their rejection of the plan was expressed by a violent struggle within the area of western Palestine. Upon the termination of the Mandate, the leadership of the Jewish *yishuv* declared the establishment of the State of Israel and the armed forces of the Arab states invaded the newly declared state. These events led to the departure of hundreds of thousands of Arabs from the territory of Mandatory Palestine occupied by the Jews. The number of people who left has been estimated at about 750,000. Other estimates range from 500,000 to 900,000 people.[2]

In the past, the reasons for the departure of the Palestinian Arab inhabitants of Palestine were disputed. Today, the detailed description given by Benny Morris[3] is commonly accepted, to the effect that some of the refugees fled the area while others were deported, albeit these acts of deportation were not part of a preordained plan.

These refugees were not protected by the UN General High Commissioner for Refugees, but by the UN Relief and Works Agency for Palestine Refugees in the Near East, known in by its acronym—UNRWA.

The role of UNRWA in creating the Palestinian refugee problem is immense. Discussion of this issue is beyond the scope of this chapter, but it should be noted that UNRWA's definition of a "refugee" is far broader than that of the UN High Commission for Refugees, which deals with all the other refugees in the world. As a result of this expanded definition, the number of Palestinian refugees registered today with UNRWA has reached 4.9 million.[4]

It can therefore be understood that two concurrent demands exist to return to the State of Israel: that of Jews—*Shvut*—and that of Palestinians—*Shiva*.

We will now proceed to explain why Jews have a right to return to the State of Israel while Palestinian refugees do not.

RETURN—*SHVUT*

Justifications According to International Law

The main criticism of the Israeli Law of Return is that it is discriminatory. The law refers explicitly to the immigration of Jews to Israel, while it places many obstacles to the immigration of non-Jews.

This charge may be refuted in a variety of ways. The Law of Return does not contravene international law. Current understanding of international law holds that states have a sovereign right to determine who will be allowed to immigrate. States control their borders; not every person has an inherent right to enter the state. The various human rights conventions proclaim the right of persons to enter a state of which they are nationals ("no one shall arbitrarily be deprived of the right to enter his own country"). The *travaux preparatoires* of the conventions, like the authoritative literature, explain that the term "his own country" includes citizens and permanent residents. These are the only categories of people to whom a sovereign state is obliged to allow entry.[5] Insofar as all other persons are concerned, the state has the discretion to restrict or even prohibit entry.

The claim that the Palestinian refugees and their descendents have a right to return, based on Article 12(4) of the International Covenant on Civil and Political Rights, relies on the following: first, the territory of the State of Israel is "his own country" from the point of view of the refugee, and therefore the article vests the refugee with the right to enter Israel; second, preventing the return of Palestinian refugees (and their descendents) to the State of Israel is an arbitrary deprivation of this right.

The Palestinian interpretation of Article 12(4) may be challenged on the following grounds:

- Neither of the two statements applies to someone who left the territory of the State of Israel during the war and was not present there at the time of the determinative census.
- Article 12(4) deals with the rights of individuals, but is not intended to apply in cases of the mass displacement of people because of an ethnic conflict.
- There is no ground for the argument that Article 12(4) vests a right of return or entry to the descendents of those who left their homes.

As we have shown, most of the Palestinians who currently demand to return are the descendants of those who left their homes in areas within the borders of the State of Israel.

It should be noted that Article 1(3) of the International Convention on the Elimination of All Forms of Racial Discrimination provides that "nothing in the Convention may be interpreted as affecting in any way the legal provisions of State Parties concerning nationality, citizenship or naturalization provided that such provisions do not discriminate against any particular nationality."[6]

Questions of citizenship and nationality are the second phase of immigration. First, a person immigrates to a state and then he asks for citizenship. The Convention against Discrimination provides explicitly that state laws that prefer the grant of citizenship to certain people or groups are not discriminatory. This means that laws that grant the right to immigrate to a certain group but not to others are also not discriminatory.

Article 1(3) of the Convention against Discrimination contains one exception: "discrimination against a particular nationality." Accordingly, the Israeli amendment to the Law of Citizenship and Entry to Israel (Temporary Order) 2003, which absolutely prohibits Palestinians from occupied territories and subsequently citizens of enemy countries from entering Israel for family unification purposes, became the subject of judicial review. It was contended that this law was unconstitutional by reason of being discriminatory. The Supreme Court rendered its decision on May 14, 2006, and, by a majority of five to four, the court decided not to invalidate the amendment.[7] The judgment is extremely long and elaborate (263 pages) and it is beyond the scope of this chapter to analyze it. The principal argument validating the amendment was based on security considerations and the fear that the entering population might harm the Israeli public. The counter-argument (not in effect today) was that the prohibition should not be all-embracing, but that each case should be examined individually with the person only barred from entering upon showing probable cause that he or she might pose a danger to state security.

It is noteworthy that immigration resulting from unrestricted family unification could bring into Israel a volume of immigrants capable of undermining the state's Jewish majority. This would be dangerous to the existence of Israel as a Jewish state and as a democratic state, since most of the potential entrants neither believe in nor adhere to the democratic way of life. This is Israel's national security problem in the broad sense.

This argument was neither raised nor discussed in the Supreme Court. It will be interesting to see whether these points will be put before the Court when the constitutionality of this law is again examined and how the court will react.

To conclude this point about Jewish return and international law, we have shown that the concept of Jewish return, *Shvut*, to the State of Israel and the prohibition against allowing the unrestricted entry of Arabs from the occupied territories and the neighboring Arab states do not violate international law.

Justifications According to Theories of Justice

Even if, by framing such an immigration policy, Israel is acting according to international law, it still remains to be discussed whether the rules of international law reflect basic theories of justice. Our answer is positive for a number of reasons. The preference given to Jewish immigration to Israel may be justified on the ground of the principle of affirmative action. Jews lived in the Diaspora for two thousand years; they were persecuted and could not live freely in accordance with their religion, nationality, and culture. The international community now has an obligation towards the Jewish people to ensure the restoration of their national and cultural life and identity. This argument was proffered by Professor Asa Kasher, who also claimed that it is a temporary rationale, since after a certain period of time the Jews will have established their national identity and culture, and at that point there will no longer be any justification for affirmative action. In such cases, according to Kasher, another justification exists for the preference given to Jewish immigration to Israel and this is the inherent right of the Jewish people to national self-determination. This right, enshrined explicitly in Article 1(1) of both 1966 Human Rights Covenants, encompasses the right of the Jewish people to strive for a majority within the borders of its state.[8]

There are political philosophers who support this approach and assert that, in order to pursue an exclusive culture, a significant majority has to be established and preserved within a national state. Others look at it from a slightly different perspective and argue that a majority must be preserved within a state, since individuals possess a right to their unique culture or that there is a right to the existence of continued culture. Self-determination of a significant majority within a national state is also viewed philosophically as a tool that enables the maximization of civic solidarity or the profound human need to belong.[9]

Recent years have witnessed a major discussion on global versus local justice. It has been argued that in an open, globalized world, we cannot only look at justice from a local perspective, but we must also examine it in a global context. In theory, we could have concluded from this that considerations of global justice might impose an obligation upon states to remove the fetters on their immigration policies, opening their borders to more people; yet considerations of global justice, as presented today by various scholars, do not necessarily impose duties upon states to change their immigration policies. This may be deduced from the writings of scholars who adhere to a statist approach to global justice and, indeed, even from the work of those who adopt a universalist approach.[10]

RETURN—*SHIVA*

Legal Arguments against the Alleged Palestinian "Right" of Return—*Shiva*

The previous section explained why the alleged Palestinian right of return cannot be based on the classical right to freedom of movement entrenched in the general human rights conventions. Nonetheless, the Palestinians contend that international law provides them, particularly, with a right to return to the State of Israel and they base this assertion on Resolution 194(III) adopted by the General Assembly on December 11, 1948.[11]

Resolution 194(III) was adopted following the submission of the Bernadotte report, within the framework of the UN attempt to reach a political solution between Jews and Arabs that would settle the conflict and end hostilities. The resolution deals with a proposal for mediation and conciliation between the parties and mentions the issue of the refugees in Article 11. Usually, Article 11 is quoted alone and out of context. In order to understand the content of this article, it is essential to recall the context and to look at the resolution as a whole.

In consequence of this resolution, efforts were indeed directed at mediation and conciliation, but important parts of the resolution were not implemented, such as the demilitarization of Jerusalem, a guarantee of free access to the city, and the imposition of an international regime there. Likewise, Article 11, relating to the problem of the refugees, was not implemented. Today, no one would contemplate continuing the mediation efforts of the Conciliation Commission nor would they persist in treating Jerusalem as an international city without the consent of both sides. It would seem, therefore, that Article 11 too should be seen as a part of the resolution that was not implemented and remains open for re-examination and not as a declarative article that will stand alone forever.

Moreover, even beyond this critical context, a perusal of Article 11 itself fails to support the argument that the article recognizes the *right* of the Palestinian refugees to return to their homes.

The first argument supporting the assertion that this resolution does not create a basis for the right to return stems from a scrutiny of the wording of Article 11 itself, which provides that the UN General Assembly:

> 11. Resolves that the refugees wishing to return to their homes and live at peace with their neighbours should be permitted to do so at the earliest practicable date, and that compensation should be paid for the property of those choosing not to return and for loss of or damage to property which, under principles of international law or in equity, should be made good by the Governments or authorities responsible;
>
> Instructs the Conciliation Commission to facilitate the repatriation, resettlement and economic and social rehabilitation of the refugees and the payment of compensation, and to maintain close relations with the Director of the United Nations Relief for Palestine Refugees and, through him, with the appropriate organs and agencies of the United Nations.

First, Article 11 states that refugees wishing to return to their homes and live at peace with their neighbors should be permitted to do so "at the earliest practicable date." It is important to note that the provision does not use the language of rights, even though Bernadotte's recommendations included a recommendation to recognize such a right. In other words, the article reflects a clear appreciation of the distinction between the language it actually uses and the non-existent determination that it is the *right* of the refugees to return to their homes.

Second, the UN resolution includes a condition whereby only refugees wishing to "live at peace with their neighbours" should be allowed to return to the State of Israel. The Palestinians denied the legitimacy of Resolution 194(III) for many years because of this condition, arguing that obligating them to live in peace with the Israelis would also indirectly compel them to recognize the existence of the State of Israel.[12] Israel, for its part, interpreted this condition as releasing it from the duty to allow the return of the Palestinian refugees to its territory. In Israel's view, so long as comprehensive peace has not been attained with all the Arab countries in the region, and so long as the return of the Palestinian refugees may endanger its security, the issue of return should not be discussed. The inclusion of this condition in the language of Article 11 greatly weakens the argument that it relates to a legal right to return.

Third, the resolution refers to the return of the refugees to their *homes*. As the Palestinians argue that everyone who has been defined as a "refugee" by UNRWA is entitled to return, it follows that the majority of Palestinians defined today as "refugees" are not persons who fled from their homes but are actually the descendents of those people. Accordingly, the return of the majority of these refugees cannot meet the condition of "return to their homes."

Fourth, such an interpretation of Article 11 of Resolution 194(III) is also consistent with the second part of the article, which deals with the Conciliation Commission's function not only to aid the return of the refugees, but also their resettlement and social and economic rehabilitation. The original goal was to deal appropriately with the refugee problem that had arisen, and certainly not to perpetuate the problem in such a way that not a single refugee would be allowed to be absorbed or resettled elsewhere.

The *second argument* against the assertion that Resolution 194(III) creates a basis for the right to return stems from the manner in which the resolution was perceived at the time it was adopted. We have seen that the Arab states and the Palestinians rejected the resolution because they saw it as a demand to recognize the State of Israel. At the time that the resolution was adopted, they still pursued the fundamental approach that led them to reject the Partition Plan and to launch a war to prevent its implementation. It is not reasonable to isolate the provision in the resolution granting permission to the Palestinian refugees to return to their homes in order to reduce the violence and end the war through the creation of two states, yet concurrently give that provision a construction that undermines the logic of two states. Similarly, when the resolution was adopted by the General Assembly, the State of Israel took the view that it was not binding. It is illogical to argue years later that a resolution that was rejected by the Palestinians and the Israelis at the time when it was adopted is the source of law binding these parties today.

After the Six-Day War, the Security Council took a completely different approach to the issue. Resolution 237 of June 14, 1967, sought to assist in the return of residents who had fled from the area after the outbreak of hostilities. The language of Resolution 237 is therefore soft, and refers only to refugees from the West Bank and from the Gaza Strip who fled from the region as a result of the Six-Day War. The resolution makes no mention of the refugees of 1948. After Resolution 237, Security Council Resolution 242 was adopted on November 22, 1967. This resolution was again adopted after the Yom Kippur War in Security Council Resolution 338 of October 22, 1973.[13] These resolutions call for Israel's withdrawal from territories occupied in the conflict, the end of the state of belligerency, respect for the sovereignty of every state in the region (including Israel) and achievement of a "just settlement" of the refugee problem. The phrase "just settlement" in relation to the refugee issue does not impose any obligation to arrive at a solution that is based on Resolution 194(III). Accordingly, the emphasis here is on the need to find a practical solution to the problem within the framework of a comprehensive political package that would ensure the existence of Israel, its recognition and defensible borders.

The issue of the Palestinian refugees arose in the discussions leading to the peace agreements signed by Israel with Egypt, Jordan, and the Palestinians. These agreements create binding legal norms. Each contains provisions relating to the right of Palestinian refugees who fled from the West Bank or from the Gaza Strip to return to those areas. They contain no agreement regarding the return of the refugees of 1948 or 1967 to the territory of the State of Israel.[14]

In the Oslo Accords that were signed in 1993, the Palestinian Liberation Organization, which was recognized as the representative of the

Palestinian people, undertook to adopt Security Council Resolutions 242 and 338 and repeal the sections in the Palestinian Charter calling for the destruction of the State of Israel.[15] Resolutions 242 and 338, which, as noted, determine the need for a "just settlement" of the refugee problem, but do not mention the right of return of the Palestinian refugees, are the only UN resolutions referred to in the Oslo Accords. Accordingly, only these resolutions, and not Resolution 194(III), create binding legal arrangements between Israel and the Palestinians regarding the refugees.

Political Precedents Regarding the Return of Refugees

An examination of various precedents concerning the resolution of political and ethnic conflicts in mixed societies also supports our contention that the Palestinians do not possess any right to return to the State of Israel.

When the Palestinian problem arose in 1948, the forcible transfer of populations after political upheavals and as a result of agreements between states was not considered illegal under international law. On the contrary, until the end of the Cold War, resolving ethnic conflicts through the exchange or transfer of populations was regarded as legitimate, just, and even the preferred solution. Exchanges of population that were intended to achieve ethnic homogeneity, by means of agreements after war, were accepted as a means of preventing the renewed eruption of hostilities.

Thus, for example, in the peace agreement signed between Greece and Bulgaria in 1919, it was agreed that there would be an exchange of populations. Some 46,000 Greek citizens of Bulgaria were forced to move to Greece, while 96,000 Bulgarian citizens of Greece were transferred to Bulgaria.[16]

An additional example of how ethnic conflicts after hostilities have been resolved by means of the compulsory transfer of populations is found in the Potsdam Declaration adopted by the Allies in 1945 at the end of World War II.[17] This declaration included an agreement to uproot millions of Germans who were living in Poland, Czechoslovakia, and Hungary and transfer them to Germany.

Population exchanges also took place in India. In 1947, when the British left British India, it was divided into two states: India and Pakistan. The division was intended to separate the Hindus, who originally came from India, from the Muslims who originally came from Pakistan, in an effort to prevent violent conflicts between the two groups. This division led to an exchange of populations in vast numbers. Estimates put the figures at between twelve million and thirty million people.[18]

It is interesting to note that the exchange of population solution was expressly referred to in the British Peel Commission Report of July 1937, which sought to offer a solution to the conflict between the Jews and the Arabs in Mandatory Palestine. The commission stated that in view of the wide gulf and great differences between the two national groups, it would be impossible to resolve the dispute between them within the framework of a single state, and therefore recommended the partition of the territory into two states—Arab and Jewish—as well as an exchange of populations and land between the two states.[19]

This pattern of activity, consisting of the exchange of populations and compulsory transfer, which was once regarded as desirable and legitimate, is now deemed to be "ethnic cleansing" and is completely prohibited by international law. However, it should be recalled that in 1948, when the Palestinian refugee problem was created, the exchange of populations was regarded as an appropriate solution in the case of ethnic conflicts in general and in the aftermath of war in particular. This solution had even greater legitimacy in the case of the Palestinian refugees. It should be recalled that the problem of the Palestinian refugees was caused by their flight to the nearby Arab countries, primarily Jordan, Syria, Lebanon, and the Gaza Strip, because of the war that they and the Arab states had launched in order to thwart the establishment of the Jewish state. At the same time, masses of Jewish refugees came to Israel from Arab states in numbers similar to those of the Palestinian refugees who left Mandatory Palestine. In retrospect, the process that took place can be interpreted as an exchange of populations. It might have been expected that this exchange of populations would help create an appropriate solution to the ethnic conflict in the region. This did not occur because of the asymmetry between the conduct of the State of Israel and that of its neighbors. Israel made enormous efforts to absorb and resettle Jewish refugees, whereas the Arab states to which the Palestinian refugees fled generally chose not to follow that course. As noted, their goal was to exert pressure on Israel and on the international community in the hope of forcing the return of the refugees, thereby undermining the stability and existence of the Jewish state.

In addition to the exchange of population solution, the Refugees Convention, after World War II, provided for the solution of settling refugees in countries reached by them as safe havens. The refugees had no wish whatsoever to return. The Refugees Convention of 1951 does not mention return as a possible solution to the refugees' problem.[20]

In the 1990s the dismantling of the Soviet bloc and Balkans caused large streams of refugees to flow from Eastern Europe to the more developed countries of Central and Western Europe. The developed states of Europe were neither prepared nor interested—economically or culturally —in absorbing large numbers of refugees in their territory. The developed and developing states in which the refugees arrived suffered from severe economic conditions that were reflected, *inter alia*, in high levels of unemployment. The refugees were a heavy burden on these economies, and therefore the states refused to absorb them. Thus, at the beginning of the 1990s a policy favoring the return of the refugees to their countries of origin developed, usually accompanied by a declaration that this was the preferred solution. The right of return of individuals has in fact become an insistence on the "duty to return" of the refugees as well as an obligation on the part of their country of origin to receive them.[21]

When a conflict is temporary and superficial, and it is possible to settle it in such a way as to guarantee stability and public order in the country of origin, it is reasonable to assume that people will prefer to return to their homes and cultures and not become refugees, but, in regions where there are active ethnic conflicts, the desire of the absorbing states to repatriate the refugees is not sufficient. Additional measures are required to stabilize the situation and rehabilitate the refugees.

The case of Bosnia and Herzegovina illustrates how return as a solution to a refugee problem ensuing from an ethnic conflict cannot in fact be implemented despite being agreed upon in the Dayton Agreement. The returning refugees have suffered from discrimination, their homes have been seized, they cannot find work, and they are the targets of numerous acts of reprisal.[22]

Another recent important precedent is Cyprus. A refugee problem arose in Cyprus as a result of the prolonged conflict between the Muslim Turkish Cypriots and the Christian Greek Cypriots that began in 1965. In 1974, Turkey invaded Cyprus and occupied a region in the north of the island. This action led about 200,000 Greek Cypriots who lived in the north of the island to flee to the southern half in which the Greek majority lived, whereas about 65,000 Turkish Cypriots who lived in the south left for the north and took over the vacated homes of the Greek Cypriots. Over the course of three years, most of the refugees were rehabilitated, integrated, and began to contribute to the economic and social life of Greek Cyprus, even though they did not stop regarding themselves as refugees or as entitled to compensation.

On April 1, 2003, Kofi Annan, then the UN Secretary General, published a report regarding his mission to Cyprus.[23] In this report, Annan referred to the difference between the refugee issue in Bosnia and Herzegovina and that in Cyprus and explained why repatriation and the restitution of property, which had been suggested as a suitable solution in Bosnia and Herzegovina, was not an appropriate answer to the refugee problem in Cyprus.

Annan noted in the report that a distinction had to be drawn between the problem of the refugees in Cyprus and the problem in Bosnia and Herzegovina, and stated that it would be inappropriate to apply the solution of sweeping repatriation adopted in the Dayton Agreement to Cyprus. Annan explained the difference in terms of the appropriate solution by emphasizing the issue of the lapse of time; that is, the fact that the events in Cyprus had taken place thirty to forty years previously and that, during the interim period, the displaced persons had rebuilt their homes and become integrated into society and the economy. Accordingly, he asserted, it was impossible to restore the previous situation. Repatriation was only possible where it was proposed in response to a recently generated refugee problem. Anan also called for the creation of two separate political entities, wherein the governing ethnic group of each entity would preserve its majority.

It is important to note that the European Court of Human Rights in a decision adopted on March 5, 2010 accepted the approach taken by

Kofi Anan and rejected the Greek Cypriots' claim to return to their homes in northern Cyprus.[24]

CONCLUDING REMARKS

The unequivocal position that Palestinians do not posses a right to return to the State of Israel is based on three principal grounds. First, the legal analysis that we offered proves definitively that international law *does not* grant the Palestinian refugees a right to compel Israel to allow them to settle in its territory. Second, the experience of other ethnic conflicts, past and present, shows that return to a place where conflicts existed and are not completely resolved is not possible. The Cyprus case is a very strong precedent that explicitly counters the solution of return when decades have passed since the people demanding to return fled their homes. Third, if we look at the specific case of the Palestinian refugees, the entry into Israel of large numbers of Palestinian refugees and their descendents would undermine the continued existence of a Jewish majority in the state and would be contrary to the right of Jews to self-determination. Nor would returning to the State of Israel be in the best interest of the refugees themselves, since they possess personal and group characteristics that differ significantly from those of the majority population in the State of Israel. A political solution of two states for two peoples is needed to enable both the Jewish people and the Palestinians to pursue their right to self-determination. Jews have a right to return to the State of Israel, while Palestinians do not. They will have a right to return to their own state upon its establishment.

NOTES

1   Law of Return, 5710-1950, Sefer Hahukim (Statutes of the State of Israel) (No. 51) 159.
2   Resolution 181: A/Res/181 of 29 November 1947, http://www.knesset.gov.il/process/docs/un181_eng.htm (accessed June 12, 2012). Arab departures: see UNRWA, "Palestine Refugees," http://www.unrwa.org/etemplate.php?id=86 (accessed November 22, 2011).
3   Benny Morris, *The Birth of the Palestinian Refugee Problem 1947–1949* (Cambridge: Cambridge University Press, 1987).

4 See *UNWRA Statistics—2010: Selected Indicators*, no. 1 (November 2011), http://www.unrwa.org/userfiles/2011120434013.pdf (accessed December 7, 2011).

5 Quotation on arbitrary deprivation from Article 12(4) of the International Covenant on Civil and Political Rights, 1966, 999 U.N.T.S. 171; Paul Sieghart, *The Lawful Rights of Mankind: An Introduction to the Legal Code of Human Rights* (Oxford: Oxford University Press, 1985), 115; Jose Ingles, *Special Rapporteur: Study of Discrimination in Respect to the Right of Everyone to Leave Any Country, Including His Own and to Return to His Country*, U. N. Pub. Sale no. 64 XIV 2 (first issued as U.N. Doc. E/CN/4 Sub.2/220/Rev.I) (1963); Manfred Nowak, *U.N. Convention on Civil and Political Rights (CCPR)*, Commentary 219–20 (1993); UN Doc. CCPR/C/21/Rev.1/Add 9, 2.11.1999, at 5–6.

6 660 U.N.T.S. 195.

7 The Citizenship and Entry into Israel Law (Temporary Provision) 5763-2003, S.H. (1901) 544; decision on the amendment: High Court of Justice (HCJ) 7052/03 Adala v. Minister of Interior, PD 51(2) 202 (2006).

8 For the international obligation, see Ruth Gavison, "The Law of Return at Sixty Years: History, Ideology, Justification" (2010), 42, *Social Science Research Network*, http://ssrn.com/abstract=1951784 (accessed June 22, 2012); Asa Kasher, "Law of Return (Shvut), Justice and Affirmative Action," in *Man's Spirit* 73 (2000): 82–85 [in Hebrew]; International Covenant on Civil and Political Rights, and International Covenant on Social, Economic and Cultural Rights, 1966, 993 UNTS 3.

9 Philosophers in support: Michael Walzer, "Global and Local Justice," *Collegio Carlo Alberto* 15 (2008), http://www.carloandalberto.org/assets/events/slides/globalandlocaljustice.pdf (accessed June 22, 2012). Self-determination as a tool: Gavison, "The Law of Return at Sixty," 39.

10 Yaffa Zilbershats, "Sovereign States Control of Immigration: A Global Justice Perspective," *Israel Law Review* 43 (2010): 126.

11 G.A. Res 194(III), December 1948, "Resolutions Adopted by the General Assembly During Its Third Session," *United Nations*, http://un.org/documents/ga/res/3/ares3.htm (accessed November 22, 2011).

12 Yoav Gelber, *Independence Versus Nakbah: The Arab–Israeli War of 1948* (Or-Yehuda: Zmora-Bitan-Dvir, 2004) [in Hebrew], 73.

13 Resolution 237: A/Res/273(III) in United Nations, Security Council, "Resolution 237 (1967) of 14 June 1967," http://unispal.un.org/UNISPAL.NSF/0/E02B4F9D-23B2EEF3852560CB95A (accessed June 13, 2012). Resolution 242: S/Res/242 in United Nations, Security Council, "Resolution 242 (1967) of 22 November 1967," http://unispal.un.org/UNISPAL.NSF/0/7D35E1F729DF491C85256EE700686136 (accessed June 13, 2012). Resolution 338: S/Res/338 in United Nations, Security Council, "Resolution 338 (1973) of 22 October 1973," http://unispal.un.org/UNISPAL.NSF/0/7FB7C26FCBE80A31852560C50065F878, (accessed June 13, 2012).

14 Ruth Lapidot, "Israel and the Palestinians: Some Legal Issues," *Die Friedens-Warte* 76 (2001): 238.

15 See the Introduction and Article XXX (9) to the Israeli–Palestinian Interim Agreement relating to the West Bank and the Gaza Strip, September 28, 1995, *The Knesset: The Israeli Parliament*, http://www.knesset.gov.il/process/docs/heskemb_eng.htm (accessed June 13, 2012).

16   Treaty of Nueilly, November 27, 1919, http://wwi.lib.byu.edu/index.php/Treaty_of_
      Neuilly (accessed November 22, 2011).

17   See "A Decade of American Foreign Policy 1941–1949 Potsdam Conference," *Avalon
      Project*, http://avalon.law.yale.edu/20th_century/decade17.asp (accessed June 13,
      2012).

18   Jeffrey Weiss, "India and Pakistan: A Cautionary Tale for Israel and Palestine,"
      Connecticut Journal of International Law 18 (2003): 459–60.

19   The Report of the Palestine Royal Commission was submitted to the UK Parliament
      by the Secretary of State for the Colonies, at the order of His Majesty in July 1937.
      For a Summary of the Report see League of Nations, Mandates, Palestine, Report of
      the Palestine Royal Commission Presented by the Secretary of State for the Colonies
      to the United Kingdom Parliament (July 1937), Summary of Report.

20   "Convention Relating to the Status of Refugees," (1951) Office of the United Nations
      High Commissioner for Human Rights, http://www2.ohchr.org/english/law/refu-
      gees.htm, (accessed June 13, 2012).

21   According to publications issued by the High Commission in 2007, about 654,000
      people have sought refuge in 154 countries, of whom 210,000 received the status
      of refugee under the Refugees Convention or received alternative protection under
      the domestic laws of the country even though they did not meet the criteria of a
      "refugee" under the Refugees Convention. The proportion of people receiving
      asylum as refugees or for other humanitarian reasons under the domestic laws of the
      countries concerned out of the entire population of people whose applications were
      considered during that year, was about forty-five percent: see UNHCR, "Asylum
      and Refugee Status Determination," *UNHCR Statistical Yearbook 2007*, http://www.
      unhcr.org/4981c37c2.html (accessed June 13, 2012). In 2006, 605,000 new applica-
      tions for asylum were submitted in 151 countries around the world. During that
      year, 196,000 people were recognized as refugees under the Refugees Convention
      (or received alternative protection in the state concerned). The proportion of people
      receiving asylum as refugees or for other humanitarian reasons under the domestic
      laws of the countries concerned out of the entire population of people whose applica-
      tions were considered during that year, was about thirty-nine percent: see UNHCR,
      "Asylum and Refugee Status Determination," *UNHCR Statistical Yearbook 2006*,
      http://www.unhcr.org/478ce2bd2.html (accessed June 13, 2012).

22   See UNHCR, "Bosnia and Herzegovina," *UNHCR Global Appeal 2009 (Update)*,
      http://www.unhcr.org/publ/PUBL/4922d4300.pdf (accessed June 13, 2012).

23   UNSC, S/2003/398, Report of the Secretary General on his mission of good office in
      Cyprus, *United Nations Peacekeeping Force in Cyprus*, http://www.un.org/en/peace-
      keeping/missions/unficyp/rep_mgo.shtml (accessed June 13, 2012).

24   See the judgment, *European Court of Human Rights*, http://cmiskp.echr.coe.int/
      tkp197/view.asp?action=html&documentId=864000&portal=hbkm&source= exter-
      nalbydocnumber&table=F69A27FD8FB86142BF01C1166DEA398649   (accessed
      June 13, 2012).

PART IV

STATE AND
RELIGIONS

Religion and State: A Critical Analysis of Meanings in Public Discourse

10

AVI SAGI

INTRODUCTION

My aim in this chapter is to analyze anew the symbolic meaning of the terms "religion" and "state" in Israel's public discourse. This chapter does not pretend to offer a theory about religion and state relations in Israel or to discuss the actual or ideal situation in this regard. Instead, it focuses on the semantic utterance as such, while attempting to decode the meaning contexts of the "religion and state" linkage. My starting assumption in the current discussion is that this conceptual linkage is a symbolic, metaphorical expression that, on the one hand, builds on previous contexts of meaning, and, on the other, shapes new ones. Each one of the terms in this linkage is loaded with historical, cultural, social, political, and ethical contexts, but their combination creates a powerful linguistic utterance that brings together different and even contradictory options into one conceptual scheme. Reality's complex picture converges into a symbol of either equivalence or antithesis, and the concepts of "religion" and "state" become either identical or contradictory.

The typical relationship between reality and the conceptual structure that denotes it—like that between signifier and signified—is frequently subject to modification. The conceptual structure thereby gradually loses its referential power and fashions an autonomous semantic area that creates a compelling linguistic utterance. This pattern has also prevailed concerning the semantic utterance "religion and state," whose power lies precisely in the possibilities it enhances and in the option it offers of bringing together equivalence and opposition. The compound "religion and state," then, functions in ways typical of what Clifford Geertz described as "metaphor":

> In metaphor one has, of course, a stratification of meaning, in which an incongruity of sense in one meaning, produces an influx of significance on another ... The power of a metaphor derives precisely from the interplay between the discordant meanings it symbolically coerces into a unitary conceptual framework ... When it works, a metaphor transforms a false identification ... into an apt analogy; when it misfires, it is a mere extravagance.[1]

The semantic utterance "religion and state" offers a symbolic expression that brings together contradictory meanings capable of shaping characteristic dispositions. What are these dispositions? Analyzing the rhetoric adopted by the advocates of equivalence or of opposition between these concepts will allow us to trace the sharply contrasting structuring of these dispositions. Supporters of an antithesis between these concepts endorse a secular and liberal semantics and promote a public discourse of rights that, by nature, is individualistic. The semantic that serves their purposes leans toward the present and the future and thereby minimizes the dimensions of the past and of tradition, which are confined to the private sphere. According to this discourse, the public sphere is a neutral domain that enables different and even contradictory practices.

By contrast, supporters of a conceptual equivalence between "religion and state" create a semantic at whose center are religion, nationality, and the collective. The discourse they promote is a discourse of identity, and at its core is a commitment to the past and to tradition as the main and perhaps the sole constitutive elements of identity. According to this discourse, certain dimensions in the private sphere and important practices in the public sphere are supposed to unfold according to meaning contexts in the identity discourse shaped by the inevitable juxtaposition of "religion and state."

The analysis of the semantic field at whose center is the "religion and state" linkage, then, leads to a metaphor that creates both antithesis and equivalence. Supporters of the antithesis develop a disposition of atomistic liberalism that places individuals and their rights at its core;[2] supporters of the equivalence develop a disposition centered on a conception of collectivist identity. The conclusion warranted by this analysis is that the "religion and state" question in Israel transcends the context of a typical political problem and is imbued with deep, thick, and tense symbolic meanings that make the controversy on this question even more charged.

A comparison between typical models of religion and state relations in democratic countries and the parallel discourse in Israel supports this conclusion. Benjamin Neuberger's comparison between arrangements regulating religion and state relations in Europe and Israel shows that the situation in Israel differs from any pattern currently known in democratic Europe.[3] Even in countries with a state church, such as England, the meaning of an equivalence relationship between religion and state is primarily formal. The state recognizes only one church as official, but the church is subject to the state—its leaders are the king or queen, who also appoint the bishops and other officials, and its rules must be ratified by the parliament.

Anglicanism, however, is not perceived in English public discourse as the body that determines the parameters of the discussion on questions about the equivalence of religion and state or on civil rights issues. As Neuberger notes, even in countries that support one official church, the status of the church is receding.

By contrast, the status of the official "church" in Israel—meaning Judaism—is the central theme in the discourse on religion and state relations. This discourse lacks basic shared understandings that can serve as starting points for discussion—it has never been agreed that an official "church" is necessary or that the "church" is or should be subject to the state. The Israeli discourse on religion and state is characterized by controversy and polarization. It rests on antagonistic dispositions and even creates them time and again, precluding a discourse based on accepted premises and on agreed rules of decision-making. In these circumstances, all that can be done is to devise political arrangements involving some dimension of compromise, but shared understandings or agreements are out of the question. These arrangements are therefore basically fragile, since political compromises convey recognition of the limitations of power, and not necessarily agreement with, or understanding of, the other's position. As expected, political compromises are repeatedly breached—the push of antithetical dispositions catalyzes confrontation processes meant to impose them, like magma sizzling in the depths of a volcano and threatening to erupt. It might be contained for a long time, but various circumstances—more or less noteworthy—lead to its renewed outburst, intensifying the symbolic meaning that is ascribed to the "religion and state" linkage in Israel.

What is the source of these antitheses? Why does the semantic field of the "religion and state" linkage evoke and create such inimical dispositions? Is this rivalry inevitable? To deal with these questions, I begin with a basic analysis of the conflicting dispositions and their attitude to the "religion and state" linkage.

CONTRADICTORY DISPOSITIONS CONCERNING THE "RELIGION AND STATE" LINKAGE

My starting assumption is that the State of Israel is a secular state. Its secularism is not a function of its founders' intention or of its leaders' identity, but of its quality as a modern state. In Eliezer Goldman's formulation:

> Secularism is essential to the modern state as a territorial state, the scope of whose authority overlaps a particular territory and extends over the entire population of the territory rather than being limited to part of it. It is the state of all its citizens. Furthermore, it is part of the state's essence that its powers, and only its powers, are authorized to exercise coercion. By definition, the state serves its entire population without discrimination. Such a state cannot have a religious regime if its population is religiously heterogeneous . . . Israel, which has a significant religious Jewish

minority, a considerable Moslem minority, a Christian minority, and most of whose Jewish inhabitants are secular, cannot be the Torah state. Such a state could become a Torah state only by enforcing means used by Iran's fundamentalist Islam.[4]

In this programmatic passage, Goldman notes several reasons for the secularism of the state. The first is that the State of Israel is a territorial state, and its authority and sovereignty extend to every person inhabiting its territory. The State of Israel is not "God's kingdom," it does not represent a church whose sovereignty and authority extend only to its believers; it is the state of its citizens, all its citizens. This determination rests on the character of the modern state, not on theological or philosophical considerations.

The second reason is linked to the power of the state. Only the state has the authority to legislate and coerce, and every authorized body within the state draws its authority from the state itself. Those officiating in a religious capacity, such as the rabbinate, the *shari'a* court or any other institution of religion, draw their power from the state rather than from the authority invested in them by the religious world. The power of the rabbinate to command and instruct does not derive from the biblical verse "according to the law which they shall teach thee" (Deuteronomy 17:11) but from the authority that the sovereign has granted them and within the limits it has set.

These are fundamental principles. Goldman, however, offers an additional argument: since most Israeli citizens are not religious Jews but secular Jews, Arabs, Christians, or Druze—establishing a Torah regime in the State of Israel would involve coercion. This argument is particularly important since, ostensibly, even if the State of Israel is a territorial state and even if the supreme sovereign is the state as such, the state can still establish a regime in which Jewish religious norms are dominant. This conclusion is correct not only for a state that is modern, secular, and non-democratic, such as a totalitarian state, but also for a state whose regime is democratic only in a formal sense, meaning it has not adopted the values entailed by a democratic world view, including freedom of thought and action and the protection of minorities' rights.

The State of Israel, however, is not democratic only in a formal sense. Israel has adopted since its foundation the basic values of a liberal democracy, so that the establishment of a Torah regime would only be possible at the expense of these values. These arguments show that both the supporters and opponents of separation have set up a dichotomy failing to fit the actual reality in the State of Israel.

Defending the claim concerning the failure of this dichotomy to fit Israeli reality is easy when confronting supporters of religion and state equivalence. Showing that the opposition between religion and state is also apparently inadequate to convey the signifier—signified relationship—that is, the reality—appears to be much harder. I will attempt to show that the problematic affecting the signifier-signified relationship characterizes all the contradictory possibilities latent in the "religion and state" linkage as it functions in the semantic field of Israeli society, whether it establishes an equivalence or an opposition. I begin with an analysis of the approach holding that this semantic utterance creates an equivalence.

The "Religion and State" Compound as Creating an Equivalence

The fundamental problem with the semantics accompanying the equivalence relationship between religion and state is that its supporters fail to clarify what they intend by this equivalence. One possibility is that the equivalence conveys the principle of sovereignty, meaning the theocratic conception of politics that is part of their religious world view. However, although theocracy as a political regime was an invention whose introduction into the philosophical discourse can be traced back to Josephus Flavius and Spinoza,[5] it never reflected either mainstream Jewish tradition or Jewish reality.[6] Spinoza assumed that theocracy is the only legitimate form of government for Jews, and still could not but add: "However, this state of things existed rather in theory than in practice."[7] No wonder, then, that this possibility was almost never formulated as a political platform by the supporters of the religion and state equivalence. A cursory review of the literature shows that supporters of a religion and state antithesis ascribe this option to those assuming equivalence, a finding that will prove extremely significant further in the discussion.

Another way of understanding the religion and state equivalence is to claim that supporters of this approach are concerned with what should be the ruling regime, that is, the norms in the State of Israel as a democratic state should be halakhic norms. Yeshayahu Leibowitz, who was among those who coined the term "Torah state," did mean by it the imposition of halakhic norms rather than the principle of sovereignty.[8] Yet, precisely within these circles, it soon became clear that halakhic tradition was far from ready for the creation of a modern territorial state. Attempts such as that of R. Neriah to derive the Halakhah relevant to the political-public domain from personal law proved inapplicable and irrelevant.[9]

Furthermore, norms called "religious" in the religion and state equivalence equation do not reflect halakhic tradition itself, as evident from an analysis of several examples typically used in this rhetoric. The first touches on the problem of imposing halakhic norms through the secular system—is the secular legal-political system in Israel halakhically worthy of this task? And even assuming the halakhic propriety of imposing observance of the commandments—is the duty to coerce them incumbent on the secular government? In halakhic sources, coercing the commandments is a task assigned to the courts[10]—is it plausible to ascribe to the secular legal system, whose halakhic validity is problematic at the very least, the status of a court enforcing observance of halakhic norms? Furthermore, is it halakhically proper to impose observance on a public that does not believe in the Torah and the commandments? R. Shaul Israeli was categorically opposed to coercion:

> The coercion rule applies only to one who wishes to comply with all the laws of the Torah and draw away from transgressions, but concerning those in our generation, where non-observance follows from a lack of faith in the Torah and the commandments … the law that the court (or those working as its representatives) will impose them by beating and so forth does not apply.… Even if we were stronger than them, they will not be persuaded of the truth of the commandments and will not agree to them willingly.[11]

Several matters could dictate a distinction between the coercion of observance and the imposition of halakhic norms in the public sphere in general, and in family law in particular. This is a halakhic question rather than an issue for political discussion, and positions in it derive from a complex halakhic and meta-halakhic set of considerations. Unfortunately, however, the political discourse of advocates of equivalence in the semantic compound "religion and state" shows no awareness of this complexity and creates a fictitious parallel between Halakhah and the politics of religion. The equivalence, then, is only apparent—it does not reflect halakhic "reality" and only creates it through the political discourse.

An analysis of political struggles that have sought to impose specific halakhic norms reveals a similar picture. In their politics, supporters of equivalence in the "religion and state" linkage consistently resist the introduction of civil marriage in Israel, insisting on marriage according to Jewish law.

I will not enter here the tangled halakhic discussion on this matter.[12] I will only note that, in the present reality of hastened processes of secularization on the one hand, and the collapse of the family on the other, it is not at all clear that marriage according to Jewish law is halakhically preferable to civil marriage. Indeed, marriage according to Jewish law could increase the number of *mamzerim*[13] should the couple fail to divorce according to Halakhah and should the woman become another man's partner. By contrast, civil marriage is a case of "doubtful marriage" (*safek kiddushin*). After a review of halakhic sources, Pinhas Schiffman writes:

> The problem of *mamzerut* due to doubtful marriage is particularly significant concerning the halakhic status of civil marriage. The question is whether the children of a woman fathered by a man she married following a previous civil marriage that was not dissolved through a divorce performed according to Jewish law could potentially fit the category of *mamzerim* . . . In light of the above [analysis of the halakhic sources], it appears that even those who take a stringent view of civil marriage and require that divorce be according to Jewish law, tend to be lenient regarding *mamzerut*. The question of whether rabbis will indeed be lenient

on this issue if civil marriage were introduced in Israel will largely depend on the social and ideological policy they will consider desirable.[14]

This analysis points to the gap between Halakhah and those who pretend to represent it in the political discourse by creating the "religion and state" equivalence. In this discourse, marriage according to Jewish law is not one more halakhic issue involving complex aspects that include contradictory positions. Instead, "Halakhah" becomes cut and dried, utterly denying the possibility of civil marriage not because it is halakhically impossible but because it contradicts the basic dispositions of the advocates of a "religion and state" equivalence. The issue of marriage, then, ceases to be a normative question and turns into a representative symbol within a dichotomous equation, where the recognition of other possibilities negates the basic dispositions themselves.[15]

One last example I will present is that of conversion. According to Halakhah, the conversion procedure can be performed by three fit laymen who constitute a conversion court, without need of an official court. Maimonides summed up this law as follows: "A proselyte who has not undergone an examination, or was not made acquainted with the commandments and the punishment for transgressing them, but was circumcised and immersed in the presence of three laymen, is deemed a proselyte."[16] Maimonides' formulation suggests that turning to three laymen rather than to the official court would not be the initial measure,[17] but a proposal raised in modern halakhic literature suggests that the official court refer halakhically "problematic" cases to non-institutional courts.[18]

Furthermore, according to the norm prevalent in Israel, the main meaning of conversion is a commitment to observance. On these grounds, most conversion courts refrain from converting individuals about whom they are not certain that they will be observant after undergoing conversion. This approach, however, is merely a new halakhic position adopted only in the modern era and does not reflect the halakhic stance that had prevailed in the past.[19]

Supporters of the "religion and state" equivalence, however, ignore this halakhic complexity. Conversion and its constitutive halakhic norms are no longer a halakhic problem; rather, they have become a symbolic issue in the political discourse, and the specific religious equivalence is poured into it. Although a conversion where a commitment to observance is not the central and constitutive component is halakhically valid, this possibility is rejected—not on halakhic grounds but because it contradicts the dispositions of adherents to the religion and state equivalence.

The symbolic meaning in the semantics of equivalence as it emerges in all the above examples is concretized in the image of Halakhah. Contrary to the concrete, pragmatic, and dynamic character of a Halakhah that contends openly and daringly with reality, Halakhah in this semantics is outlined as a closed, deductive system that operates according to an independent mechanism and is entirely dissociated from reality.

This analysis leads to the conclusion that supporters of the "religion and state" equivalence do not struggle for the imposition of Halakhah but for an entirely different cause. In their view, "religion" functions as a symbol signifying this cause and does not represent Halakhah as such. What is this cause? A more rigorous analysis of the struggle for the "religion and state" association will shed further light on this question. First, however, I need to explore the antithetical meaning of this linkage and the dispositions entailed by this stance.

The "Religion and State" Compound as Creating an Antithesis

Supporters of religion and state separation defend this thesis either on formal or on substantive grounds. The formal argument relies on Goldman's thesis above, whereby the modern state is secular by definition. Despite the importance of this argument, the dispositions assuming an antithesis or a dichotomy between religion and state convey an entirely different dimension. They reflect an approach stating that the equivalence of religion and state is detrimental to fundamental liberal values that place at the core the freedom of individuals to shape their lives without interference from state institutions. According to supporters of these dispositions, the imposition of religious norms within a liberal state harms the underpinnings of liberalism. The key question in this discussion is: what is the liberal approach—or more precisely the liberal disposition—at the basis of this antithesis?

The history of liberal thought and practice points to the development of two conceptions of liberalism: atomistic liberalism,[20] and communitarian liberalism. Atomistic liberalism centers on the individual autonomously shaping his or her life. Individuals have a right to think, to act, and to realize their aspirations as they wish. The hero of atomistic liberalism is the individual rather than the society or the community. By contrast, a communitarian approach has developed in recent decades that diverts the center of gravity from the autonomous individual to the community as the constitutive element of the person's existence and identity. Atomistic liberalism disregards the question of the person's identity and its modes of development in actual life, and views the individual as an abstract autonomous entity whose identity is created in the private sphere. The communitarian approach, by contrast, assigns decisive weight to the shaping of the person's concrete life within cultural and social contexts.[21]

In the public and political discourse prevailing in the State of Israel, the basic liberal disposition on religion and state relations is obviously that of atomistic liberalism.[22] This discourse tends to focus on the rights of individuals to realize themselves and live their lives as autonomous creatures. This atomistic liberalism is often shaped as the negative of the collectivistic national-religious disposition of the supporters of a "religion and state" equivalence.[23] Consider the following examples:[24]

An editorial in *Haaretz* (March 13, 1981) reacts to a bill of the religious factions to prohibit the marketing of pork in Israel:

> Needless to say, many Jews—and not only observant ones—consider pigs loathsome, and the ban on pork consumption as one of the most stringent halakhic injunctions. But is it appropriate to impose in state law a criminal prohibition prompted by a pure religious motivation, coercing secular Jews and non-Jews to adopt a lifestyle and eating habits they do not desire? This is actually an extreme case of interference with individual freedom and freedom of religion, which Israeli law is supposed to protect according to the principles of the Declaration of Independence. Should the Knesset pass these bills, it will move us one step closer to the imposition of religious norms through secular law ... The

Labor Party should also be told it must make a clear statement concerning individual rights and religious coercion even before the elections.

My concern here is not the contents of the argument presented in this editorial but its implicit dispositions. The writer knows that pigs have negative symbolic meanings for both religious and secular Jews, meaning that the ban on eating pork is part of meaning contexts that touch on the identity of Jews. In his view, however, the law is not meant to reflect or express these contexts but to protect the freedom of autonomous individuals to choose their lifestyle as they wish. The law, then, is supposed to reflect and express atomistic liberalism, which disregards these contexts.

The crucial role that the law plays in atomistic liberalism deserves special mention, and the approach presented in this editorial from the early 1980s would become increasingly dominant later. The law and the Supreme Court would become the venue to which the discourse of rights characterizing atomistic liberalism would be channeled.

Another *Haaretz* editorial (May 2, 1982) clearly traces the dispositions of atomistic liberalism and the mirror image ascribed to its opponents. The catalyst for the article is El-Al's flights on the Sabbath. The writer holds that this affair is a paradigm of the "shameful system that grants a small minority of the public the possibility of dictating to the vast majority how the country will be run." In his view, the question of El-Al flights is "another step towards the paralysis of the State of Israel on the Sabbath." But he goes even further. In his view, this matter is merely a further move in the transformation of the State of Israel into a theocracy. He repeatedly cautions against the danger of "surrender to the Orthodox," which "eats away more and more at the liberal, progressive, and free character of the State of Israel." In a warning tone, he adds: "Should this cancerous process persist, more and more of its enlightened citizens will find it hard to adapt to the prevailing atmosphere." From our present perspective, it is hard not to be slightly amused by this gloomy prognosis, since the State of Israel has become increasingly liberal in recent years. The importance of this article, however, is not in this "prediction" but in the "naïve" and uncritical expression of the classic liberal atomistic dispositions presented here as dogmas—enlightenment, progress, and freedom. This complex issue is examined here solely through the prism of these dispositions, whereas the question of the identity and culture of Israel's Jewish society never enters the assumed dichotomy between liberalism and theocracy.

Another editorial in *Haaretz* (February 3, 1984) deals with the public controversy surrounding the play *Messiah* shown at the Haifa Theater, and with the accompanying demands and threats to cancel it "due to several sentences uttered by the main female character, who inveighs against the Master of the Universe because of her suffering and the suffering of the Jews." The article criticizes the municipality of Haifa and others who intervened on the matter:

> Instead of unequivocally backing the theatre and freedom of expression, the Municipality of Haifa played a dubious role here . . . The involvement of the President [Haim Herzog] in this matter was interpreted as endorsing a position against freedom of expression and, for this reason, it would have been better had he not intervened. And yet, the most worrisome issue is not the President's initiative, but the very ability of religious circles to intervene in a play that was staged within the framework of the law and of the legitimate professional discretion of the Haifa Theater, to dictate what Israel's inhabitants will see or not see.

Typically, the familiar dichotomy is presented again: religion versus freedom. Furthermore, the public sphere, of which the theater is one element, mediates only through the category of freedom of expression. Except for the classic category of atomistic liberalism, no other category is suggested. The argument redraws the contrast between religion on the one hand and freedom and liberal civic rights on the other according to the symbolic semantic course of the "religion and state" linkage. In this semantics, whoever represents the position opposite to liberalism is portrayed in radically negative terms.

This editorial was not a lone voice. Another writer—Michael Handelsaltz—joined the fray (*Haaretz*, February 6, 1984) and described the scene and the two parties involved in this symbolic struggle. In his view, the struggle over *Messiah* is a *Kulturkampf*: "This is a war between humanism and Humeinism,[25] between tolerance and zealotry, between an enlightened and a backward world, between the twentieth century and the preceding ones."

Many ideologies are characterized by a sharp distinction between the good they represent and the evil represented by their adversaries: the lines are clear, and drawn in black and white.[26] The good that Handelsaltz describes in this equation does not include elements such as culture, identity, memory, feelings, and myths but only the basic dispositions of atomistic liberalism from which, as in a negative, the image of evil is derived.

But even this image is far from reflecting a real picture of individuals or of societies; the image of "the other" is created simply through the reversal of the liberal disposition. A *Kulturkampf* is not a struggle about the nature of a particular culture but a more fundamental war about dispositions positively or negatively calibrated solely through liberal atomistic lenses. As shown below, these findings entail interesting implications.

A later example is from a letter sent to *Iton Tel Aviv* (July 26, 2002), as part of a series of responses concerning acts of vandalism by students of the senior class at Municipal Tel Aviv High School D, and relates particularly to the response of the principal of Municipal Tel Aviv High School E.[27] In his letter, the principal noted that he had developed a program on the topic: "To be an Israeli Jew in the State of Israel." In response, Ronit Silver wrote:

> I hold that this is pure indoctrination at best or just racism at worst. How should an Israeli citizen who is not a Jew feel if he is a student at High School E? . . . It seems to me that in a program of this kind, they "explain" to the students what should be their Judaism or their Israeliness, without giving them a chance of interpreting their identity in the way they themselves understand it. It would have been better if he [the principal of the high school] had developed the topic "to be a person in the State of Israel" and then, perhaps, he would have prevented such phenomena as the vandalism at High School D.

This letter conveys the typical liberal dispositions built through processes denying the identity discourse. Here too we see a dichotomy: a discourse of rights or a discourse of identity. The writer recommends conducting a discourse of rights centering on the concept of the "person," in a classic liberal argument—consideration for the other's feelings. Like many people with liberal dispositions, she too holds that the liberal discourse grants some kind of immunity from violence and vandalism. Identity is repressed into the private realm since it is merely the realization of autonomy—individuals will interpret (or, more precisely, shape) their identity as they understand it, in a process entailing no implications for others.

The discourse on Jewish-Israeli identity is shaped as the antithesis of the liberal atomistic discourse of rights, and negative, almost demonic attributes are ascribed to it: it is indoctrinatory, racist, hurtful to the other's feelings, and, at least indirectly, responsible for the vandalism.

I do not pretend to claim that these examples exhaust the antithetical semantics. Serious methodological problems are involved in the extrapolation from specific texts written at specific times by individuals who are part of a defined cultural environment to a general claim about the semantics of the antithetical linkage "religion and state." And yet, a critical analysis of the processes affecting Israeli society points to an intensification of the atomistic liberal discourse. Completing the legislation of Basic Laws and the Supreme Court's involvement in a wave of litigation pursuing the realization of liberal rights and freedoms are signs of the strong entrenchment of atomistic liberalism in the public discourse bearing on religion and state relations.

The analysis I proposed could be countered by the claim that the quotations from journalistic passages show that atomistic liberalism does not represent an independent disposition but merely a reversal of the religious stance. The semantics of antithesis, then, is merely a by product of the threat lurking in the stance supporting equivalence, and does not reflect genuine opposition between the two.

A broad discussion of this claim is related to a basic question in the study of cultural phenomena: does a cultural phenomenon whose semantics is a response to another phenomenon reflect only a response or does it express independent cultural fullness? If it reflects only a response, several questions emerge: first, is it right to analyze a cultural fullness that creates contexts of meaning through a reduction to causal relationships? Geertz formulated this criticism in sharp terms: "The link between the causes of ideology and its consequences seem adventitious because the connecting element—the autonomous process of symbolic formulation— is passed over in virtual silence."[28] Second, if atomistic liberalism is only a response to a threat and does not reflect independent dispositions— why is it threatened by the advocates of a "religion and state" linkage? The assumption that this is a threat to someone or something warrants that something or someone exists independently of the threatening factor and that is why the threat can be made at all. Hence, atomistic liberalism is not only a "reaction" but an independent position expressing itself through the semantics of the "religion and state" linkage.

ATOMISTIC LIBERALISM

Neither the position that supports equivalence in the "religion and state" linkage nor that assuming a confrontation between these two concepts offers an accurate description of the reality they purportedly represent. Advocates of equivalence create a gap between ideology and life, and supporters of atomistic liberalism create a gap between practice and liberal ideology, which comes to the fore in their conception of identity.

To clarify this issue, let us ask: what is the conception of identity represented by atomistic liberalism, and in what sphere is this iden- tity realized? Many philosophers and theoreticians have noted that the conception of identity in atomistic liberalism continues the notion of identity dominant in classic rationalism and in the Enlightenment, whereby the identity of the self is not created in the historical-social-cul- tural domain. Rationalism and the Enlightenment assumed that a person's identity as a human creature is a universal matter, and that particular- istic aspects are insignificant, random, variable, and do not determine the individual's being as a person. Descartes' "thinking self" is not a specific "thinking self" living in a particular place and culture, but a universal one. The rational, autonomous self is every self who is a human creature rather than a specific human creature. The principle of individuality has always been an irrational principle, precisely because of the variable and random character of the self. The authentic self is merely the universal self, the rational human creature who can create and shape his or her life in intelligent ways.[29]

Atomistic liberalism added to the rationalist tradition elements from Romanticism, which is opposed to rationalism.[30] Romanticism exalted the private, special, authentic self. But what is this "self"? Romanticism answers this question in a language similar to that of rationalism: the true self is the hidden self below and beyond the person's historical-social-cultural concrete manifestations. Both Romanticism and the Enlightenment, then, assumed the existence of a true self that does not necessarily overlap its real historical-social-cultural manifestations.

Atomistic liberalism thus drew on these two great traditions and, inspired by them, developed a special conception of identity. Liberal tradition placed the autonomous self who shapes itself from itself as a supra-model of its spiritual world, thereby expressing its closeness to Romanticism. But the assumption that every person is an autonomous creature, meaning a creature able to shape its own life appropriately, drew on the rationalist tradition and on the Enlightenment, which approached rationality as an element common to all human beings as such.

Atomistic liberalism set up a conception of identity stating that human beings shape their worlds out of themselves and the role of the state is to enable this. This assumption led to the view that the public sphere, rather than a realm where human beings shape and realize their identity, is the realm where people with different self-identities meet, and the role of the state is to ensure it will be free and open to this diversity.

These perceptions of identity and of the public sphere, as noted, are not easily reconciled with the recognition of the historical-social-cultural character of human identity. According to this approach, which I will call the "constructionist conception" of identity, people's identity is not given, nor is it an "essential" basis found outside or beyond their experience as human beings. This experience has horizons: people's identities are shaped out of what they have absorbed and internalized from the culture and the tradition into which they were born. They do not create themselves *ex nihilo*; when they are born, they are part of a history and a culture and belong to an existent cultural-social-historical community. Yet, not only the horizon of the past makes individuals what they are, but also the horizon of the present—what they encounter and experience in the course of their lives. They experience an encounter with other communities, which present to them various forms of organization and meaning— some have a historical culture and some do not evolve from historical associations. Thus, for instance, we all have an association with contexts of meaning and organization such as a family, a workplace, and social and cultural communities such as a synagogue or political circles. A person's identity is shaped within these contexts as well.

Two basic patterns can be said to shape identity: one diachronic and one synchronic. The diachronic axis is all the events of the past playing a role in the creation of identity, and the synchronic axis is all the contexts of meaning in the present that play a role in the shaping of identity.

This view of identity is not free of problems. The basic question in the constructionist view of identity is whether people are merely the product of the meaning contexts that create their identity, or whether they have a core of identity that transcends these contexts, judges them, evaluates them, and mediates between them. I have discussed these questions elsewhere in greater detail.[31] Several conclusions following from this view of identity are significant in the current context. First, human identity is not woven outside the concrete cultural-social context, that is, human identity is not some essentialist element found outside and beyond these contexts. Second, human identity is not static, since it is shaped by a series of dynamic links between the synchronic and the diachronic axes. People change according to their past, to their present communities of association, and to the weight they ascribe to them in their lives. Third and most significant, the public sphere is not a neutral arena for an alienated and barren encounter of identities; people are not autonomous creatures who live as "monads without windows." The public sphere is where the diachronic and synchronic axes actually meet, and people become who they are through a discourse of identity that unfolds largely in the public field. The public realm is the scene of the deepest conflicts and confrontations, since human identity is shaped through the actual movement unfolding in the identity discourse.

Romantics and rationalists, not by chance, assigned little importance to the public sphere. They assumed that human identity does not depend on the concrete life contexts of human beings, and therefore concluded that the public realm is the realm of fraud and concealment where concrete human existence disappears. Liberals tried to overcome this obstacle by assigning another purpose to the public sphere and, more precisely, to the political field that is such a significant component of it. The first liberals held that people will only prosper in conditions that ensure human freedom, but this is the prosperity of human beings who are by nature individuals. Negative freedom, in the term coined by Berlin,[32] promised human beings non-interference with their world. Their ability to become whatever they wish is now guaranteed. The public-political sphere will henceforth provide optimal protection of these freedoms.

But how will the person's identity be realized outside the public sphere? Indeed, the greatest achievement of atomistic liberalism—and also its weakness—is the restriction of identity to the private sphere. Only a discourse of rights will take place in the public-political sphere, meant to ensure the identity developing outside it. Some of the critiques targeting this perception of identity were presented above, and particularly important for my concern here is the meaning of these critiques for the Jewish-Israeli discourse of identity. The choice of atomistic liberalism in Israel implies a failure to acknowledge not only the constructionist character of human identity in general, but also the constitutive element of Jewish-Israeli existence. This existence unfolded vis-à-vis Jewish history and tradition. The secularization of Jewish religion is what enabled in the past the recognition of religion's special role as the bearer of Jewish tradition and culture.

This identity, however, cannot be exclusively secular. Secularism is the distinctive sign of the rise of human sovereignty and of the acknowledgement of a domain amenable to human shaping. Secularism is the liberation of life from the yoke of the church and its laws; it is the condition for the shaping of open, dynamic, and variable identities—but it cannot be identical to them. The materials from which human beings shape their identity are the materials of the history and the culture given to them. For Jews, these materials are the legacy of Jewish culture and tradition.

The pathos that seeks to turn the State of Israel into a state that is only liberal empties this identity from any meaning since it formulates a stance that is fundamentally negative—"just not religion," and relinquishes the public-political field that is considered irrelevant from the perspective of identity.

This critique targets both the advocates of religion and state separation and the supporters of instituting a Torah regime, since, even though the latter admit the importance of the political-public realm, they do not acknowledge the dynamic character of identity. They do not recognize the decisive importance of the identity discourse that unfolds precisely in the public realm. This lack of recognition on their part expresses a gap between the practice of their lives and the ideology conveyed in the equivalence of the semantic compound "religion and state," since they too conduct their lives and shape their identity in diverse contexts of meaning. They too belong to various communities—workplaces, social frameworks and so forth, and they too read different texts and shape their concrete identity as an ongoing voyage between these identity contexts. The various contexts in their lives are reinterpreted according to the order of priorities they themselves determine. Even the most important contexts of meaning, such as the halakhic ones, are reinterpreted in light of their association with others. Thus, for instance, the religious-Zionist who believes in gender equality—a value absorbed in a non-halakhic context of meaning—reshapes the halakhic context of meaning according to this value.[33] This dynamism disappears or, more precisely, is silenced when the discourse hinges on the metaphoric-symbolic compound "religion and state." Unlike daily practice, the discourse on this metaphor shapes rigid dispositions unsuited to real life, as clearly evident in the words of R. Shlomo Goren.[34] Although he recognized the democratic-liberal framework, he formulated a dogmatic position concerning the discourse of identity:

> Although our country is fundamentally a democracy founded on the principle of individual freedom, and although its legal system and its regime of governance are determined through the free expression of the people's will, this principle cannot

apply to the holy laws of the Torah of Israel, which are the roots of the people's soul and the contents of its eternal uniqueness throughout the world . . . The mystery of the people's existence and the miracle of renewed redemption latent in the renaissance of the state should be credited to the sacred values of our Torah, which preserved the wholeness of the people and acted as a fence and a barrier to absorption and assimilation into the nations of the world . . . Ignoring them or formally putting them to the people's renewed vote . . . remove the strong basis of our right to exist as a people and a state and infringe on our eternal rights to the Land of Israel. Since time immemorial, the absolute identification between Judaism as expressing the uniqueness of the Jewish people and its Torah have been known and obvious to the Jewish people and to the entire world . . . So is the absolute identification and union between the national aspirations of the Jewish people and the national and spiritual goals and aims of the Torah of Israel.[35]

This programmatic passage provides a suitable prism for understanding the mechanism whereby supporters of the "religion and state" linkage shape their dispositions. R. Goren did not deny the liberal element but delimited it to the context of private life, to the realm of personal freedom. Even within this realm, however, the liberal element is limited by a rigid collectivistic-historical perception of identity. This approach is shaped as a myth that binds concrete history as well. The Zionist project, which culminates in the creation of the State of Israel, is merely a confirmation of this approach to identity. Actual events cannot negate this myth. Although the history of Zionism and of the establishment of the State of Israel is the history of the secularization of the Jewish people and the rise of identity conceptions alternative to the religious one, this matter is blurred through the symbolic power of collectivistic identity. Secularization is acknowledged only insofar as it touches on day-to-day activities, but goes entirely unrecognized in the realm of identity.

The conclusion emerging from this analysis is that the significant impact of the "religion and state" metaphor is related to its power to shape a semantic field of intensive confrontation between dispositions. These dispositions are not only a result of the metaphorical meaning of the "religion and state" linkage; they express contexts of meaning that preceded the discourse on religion and state relations. This discourse, however, which is a vehicle for the creation and channeling of the dispositions, increasingly becomes a movement of polarization and radicalization. Supporters of the "religion and state" antithesis are increasingly pushed into an atomistic liberalism removed from concrete life, describe the other through rigid negative features, and deny the discourse of identity. Advocates of an equivalence in the "religion and state" linkage are also pushed into rigid dispositions that suit neither what they purportedly represent—Halakhah—nor their own concrete world, while denying or at least marginalizing the liberal discourse of rights. Both sides portray one another in demonic terms, negating the full value of the other's world and identity.

PUBLIC DISCOURSE IN ISRAEL AS A NEGATING DISCOURSE

Why has the religion and state controversy unfolded as it has? Why is it a dichotomous negating discourse hinging on the semantic field of the "religion and state" linkage? Why does it not unfold at the level where it truly takes place—the problematic field of the relationship between a liberal world view on the one hand, and the recognition of the central role of the public-political dimension of identity on the other?

The Political Thesis

I will refer to the first solution to this riddle as "the political thesis." This thesis states that the special character of the discourse in the semantic field of religion and state relations results from the crucial role of politics in our lives. Jonathan Shapira described Israeli society as "a society held captive by politicians":

> Politics in Israel is modeled on what the professional literature calls absolute politics, wherein the political system dictates the rules of behavior and thought in all the important areas of

social action, as well as the society's moral norms. This politics is the reversal of liberal politics, where the civil society enjoys a measure of autonomy in the state and participates in the determination of its aims.[36]

The political thesis would seem to provide a key for the solution of this riddle. The political system, which controls public practice, shapes the discourse in Israel and has (or, more precisely, the politicians have) a strong interest in exacerbating conflicts in order to achieve political gains. Politicians are not thinkers and social critics. They work within a political field that has typical rules of conduct, and shaping a metaphorical field of opposition between black and white is an accepted mode of behavior, adopted because it expresses the absolute mastery of politics in the public discourse. Shapira argues that absolute politics is not liberal politics. But if this thesis is correct, a paradox emerges: absolute and non-liberal politics actually creates polarization between atomistic liberalism and national collectivism. Generally, absolute approaches tend to dismiss and deny the individual particular realm, whereas in Israeli politics, political absolutism leads to the creation of an atomistic liberal sphere.

For several reasons, however, this explanation is not sufficient to clarify the semantic field of the "religion and state" linkage. The first reason is related to the restricted scope of the "interest theory." Geertz points to two main approaches prevalent in the study of the social factors of ideology. He refers to them as the interest theory and the strain theory, and analyzes their mutual relationship.[37] According to the interest theory, "ideology is a mask and a weapon"; according to the strain theory, ideology is "a symptom and a remedy." "In the interest theory, ideological pronouncements are seen against the background of a universal struggle for advantage; in the strain theory, against the background of a chronic effort to correct sociopsychological disequilibrium."[38] According to this theory, people escape into ideology because of anxiety.

Geertz emphasizes that these two theories are not necessarily contradictory—since people can be moved to act by both interest and strain—yet he holds that the interest theory is simplistic and less efficient, and finds two fundamental flaws in it. One touches on its basic psychological and sociological assumptions, since the interest theory does not supply a suitable method for analyzing the motives of people operating in ideological contexts:

> Lacking a developed analysis of motivation, it has been constantly forced to oscillate between a narrow and superficial utilitarianism that sees men as impelled by rational calculation of their consciously recognized personal advantage and a broader, but no less superficial, historicism that speaks with a studied vagueness of men's ideas as somehow "reflecting," "expressing," "corresponding to," "emerging from," or "conditioned by" their social commitments.[39]

The second flaw lies in the fact that the interest theory sees in social practice a continued struggle for power and might. It describes social action in Machiavellian terms, and argues that ideology is no more than "a form of higher cunning."[40] This theory does not take into account the role of ideologies "in defining (or obscuring) social categories, stabilizing (or upsetting) social expectations, maintaining (or undermining) social norms, strengthening (or weakening) social consensus, relieving (or exacerbating) social tensions."[41] Since interest theory places the struggle for interest at the center, it does not take into account all the factors that confer meaning on ideology and on the semantic field it establishes.

If we accept these critiques, the political thesis does not appear to be a particularly successful explanation of the public discourse in the semantic field of "religion and state," since it reduces the semantic field of meaning to interest. Furthermore, this thesis does not properly distinguish the public field from the political field.

The second reason for rejecting the political thesis is that, in Israel, the tense dispositional contrast concerning the "religion and state" linkage is not limited to the political field (where politicians operate), but covers also the public sphere (where the actors are not necessarily politicians). Furthermore, the public field does not necessarily operate according to interests: it reflects and expresses the strains, desires, and hopes of those active in it. In the public field, individuals and societies meet one another. This encounter does not necessarily take place under a Machia-vellian cover of concealment and deceit, or under a regime of reduction to interest. The struggle over the "religion and state" linkage in the public sphere often reflects a true struggle for identity, culture, and practice, and not a cynical self-serving pursuit.

People operating in the public realm are often extremely suspicious of politicians. Even if we agree with the thesis that Israeli society is held captive by politicians, we must take into account that there are islands where free agents operate—academics, intellectuals, and media people, for whom suspicion of politicians is inherent in their consciousness and their action. This suspicion largely neutralizes the control of political interests. From a critical perspective, these islands often create forces that hold politicians captive through the press, public opinion, and particu-larly the legal system—they create forces that move the political field. This analysis raises doubts concerning the power of the political thesis to expli-cate the rivalry created in the semantic field of religion and state relations.

The Struggle for Hegemony Thesis

The thesis I wish to propose is closer to Geertz's strain theory. Geertz was critical of this theory too, but more moderately. In his view, the strain theory, like the interest theory, lacks "anything more than the most rudimentary conception of the processes of symbolic formula-tion. There is a good deal of talk about emotions 'finding a symbolic outlet' or 'becoming attached to appropriate symbols'—but very little idea of how the trick is really done."[42] As usual for him, Geertz refers us in his critique to the lack of correlation between the causal explanation and the autonomous meanings of ideological symbols. Nevertheless, he concedes concerning the strain theory: "Diagnostically it is convincing; functionally it is not."[43]

The thesis I will present relies on the strain theory but I will argue that, in the current context, the gap between causal analysis and the anal-ysis of the meaning context can easily be overcome, as clarified below. At this stage, I will point out that the validity of the strain theory in the Israeli context rests on the claim that the strain, which I describe below, is what shapes the unique structure of the Israeli discourse. The general structure of the discourse, then, does not transcend the strain that created it but actually preserves it.

The contrasting Israeli discourse about the "religion and state" semantic linkage mirrors the patterns of the Jewish identity discourse conducted for more than a century. Secularization offered an alternative to the traditional perception of Jewish identity by pointing out that Jews belong to two circles of identity: the ethnic circle, meaning the circle of their birth, and the religious circle, meaning the circle of norms and beliefs requiring them to live within a Jewish community.[44]

The prevailing approach in Jewish tradition was that even those whose deviant behavior had drawn them away from the religious circle of Jewish identity still belonged to the ethnic circle: "A Jew, even though he has sinned, is still a Jew." Paradoxically, the very labeling of deviants as deviant is what enabled others to still view them as members of the community.

In his well known book devoted to the study of the Indian caste system,[45] Louis Dumont points out that religious societies are organized through a hierarchic mechanism that determines the status of individuals and groups. The hierarchic structure ensures both the identity of the collective and the status of those who are marginalized. According to Dumont, the hierarchy of religious societies is "the principle by which the elements of a whole are ranked in relation to the whole, it being understood in the majority of societies it is religion which provides the view of the whole, and that the ranking will thus be religious in nature."[46]

Societies created by a hierarchical mechanism live in harmony precisely because they have a clear principle for determining the ranking of the groups within them. We, who are used to the principle of equality, find it hard to endorse a hierarchical conception that has become entirely alien to us. However, according to Dumont, this hierarchical mechanism actually ensures toleration and every group knows its place in the ranking. Dumont says about the castes in India:

> People have often noted what has been called the tolerance of Indians and Hindus. It is easy to see what this feature corresponds to in social life. Many castes, who may differ in their

customs and habits, live side by side, agreed on the code which ranks them and separates them. In the Hierarchical scheme a group's acknowledged differentness, whereby it is contrasted with other groups, becomes the very principle whereby it is integrated into society.[47]

Without entering into a sociological analysis of marginality within the hierarchical structure, I will note that marginality is a specific kind of hierarchical relationship whereby the marginalized group, whose practice is considerably different from the mainstream legacy of the group as a whole, is perceived as inferior.[48]

This complex picture of hierarchy and marginality relationships characterized the relationship between the Jewish collective and deviant individuals or groups as well. The expansion of alternative patterns of Jewish identity, however, including such variations as the Zionism of Ahad Ha-Am or the Reform and Conservative movements, disrupted this picture. These groups refused to be included in the hierarchical web and to consent to their place within it. They were unwilling to accept the marginal status allotted to them by the Jewish collective, and struggled for primacy. In their context, it was Jewish religion that was pushed to the sidelines and became one more version, less relevant than others, of the Jewish identity that was presented anew. The battle was now on for the center rather than the periphery. The hierarchical "whole" and the harmony it enabled—collapsed. This *Kulturkampf* had to accumulate negative power, since every one of the various positions could take up the top spot only by negating the status of the other. The Orthodox religious community could not accept a marginal status; given the threat posed by the alternatives, it had to negate them altogether. Similarly, the new alternatives could only break through from the margins by negating the traditional center. The discourse of identity thus became a discourse of increasing mutual negation.

The result of this negation is twofold: first, it leads to radicalism concerning the other. The other is described only in negative terms as demonic, as the opposite of the good represented by the self. But the negation of the other is not sufficient, since identity is also—and perhaps mainly—shaped by the self. When the negation of the other is radical, when the other threatens the core of the identity, a radical consciousness of self develops as well.

Thus, supporters of the classic Jewish identity pattern struggle more and more to preserve the very element that singles out their identity, and the Orthodox therefore struggle against civil marriage or for the most radical version of conversion, which places observance at the center. This struggle is not really meant to impose a halakhic regime but to preserve the "Orthodox" circle of identity as the exclusive form of Jewish identity. This is the source of the rigidity that characterizes the dispositions of supporters of the "religion and state" equivalence—a rigidity expressing the struggle for the preservation of a threatened identity.

Opponents of this approach have been, for more than a century, in a strange situation. They must shape their identity and their existence vis-à-vis a powerful historical alternative in the life of the Jewish people and explain why an existing identity should be denied. This approach leads to increasing emphasis on the negative rather than the positive and fruitful element embodied by the new Jewish identities. This negation begins with the ethos typical of the Second and Third *aliyah* pioneers, who tried to erase almost every Jewish remnant from their identity,[49] and ends in enclosure within a liberal approach that exempts itself from the need to answer difficult questions about the shaping of Jewish identity in the public-political sphere.

The discourse wherein the question of Jewish identity turns into the question of religion and state relations is a crucial element in a process marked by the absence of a classic identity discourse. The public sphere, rather than the venue for an open discourse according to set limits, becomes the scene of a life and death struggle. Identity symbols turn into war paints— these adorn themselves with a Halakhah they have neutralized from its concrete form, and these adorn themselves with an atomistic liberalism where the cultural element vital to the shaping of identity has been neutralized. Both sides have renounced the free discourse where Jewish identities talk to one another and determine the parameters of their exchange.

A prominent expression of this move is a recent process, informed by attempts to reach some kind of accord regulating relationships between religious and secular citizens and between religion and state. This move institutionalizes the renunciation of a Jewish identity discourse in favor of a "truce" meant to ensure public tranquility. The various accords are an almost desperate and certainly pathetic attempt to hold the stick from both ends: refrain from conducting an identity discourse and ensure that this explosive situation will calm the public. Besides formal questions, such as on whose authority the proponents might offer these suggestions, this is certainly another attempt to shape an area of discourse wherein fundamental problems of Jewish identity are silenced. This area remains a bleeding wound.

The Jewish identity discourse is an "abnormal discourse,"[50] lacking an agreed shared framework. Its pattern, whereby supporters of the "religion and state" linkage conduct a "quasi-identity" discourse whereas their opponents conduct only a "discourse of rights," emerged against a specific historical background. The threat to the religious conception of identity fostered a trend in the religious public toward the increasing totalization of this conception, a persistent effort to impose an "inflated" identity to counteract any alternative option. By contrast, the alternative Jewish identity, whose cultural and historical depth is by nature weaker, has gradually been pushed into atomistic liberalism as a defense mechanism that leaves broad room for the shaping of Jewish identities.

Neither of these parties has invented anything *ex nihilo* nor have they formulated a new approach that is simply a reaction to the opposing threat. Supporters of the "religion and state" linkage are backed by their religious world and its trove of meanings, and supporters of the opposition are backed by their Jewish-cultural world on the one hand, and their liberalism on the other. The dynamic of their "life-and-death" struggle and of their mutual negation, which took shape in the course of modern Jewish history, has pushed each one of the parties into an ideology that fixates and also radicalizes one component as exclusive and dominant. Supporters of the "religion and state" semantic compound as an equivalence have turned religion into a static, total element that allows no further meaning context beyond the "halakhic" one. In this approach, as noted, Halakhah is a concept that retreats further and further from concrete Halakhah.

Supporters of the "religion and state" compound as an antithesis have increasingly emphasized autonomy as the underlying value in the conception of Judaism as a culture. Autonomy reflects an acknowledgment of culture as the product of human action. This element appeared together with the secular conception of Jewish identity and is concretized in atomistic liberalism, which highlights autonomy more than all the other identity positions.

This polarized shaping of each one of the parties involved in the discourse about the meaning of the "religion and state" symbol does not fully convey their separate existence. Supporters of an equivalence in the "religion and state" compound do not conduct their lives along the polarized dispositions that create the equivalence discourse, and do recognize contexts of meaning free from the total and collective approach typical of these dispositions. Nor do supporters of an antithesis in the "religion and state" compound found their entire lives on an atomistic discourse of rights lacking any perception of identity—the practice of their lives expresses a conception of identity both in the private and public realms.

The polarized discourse conducted by atomistic liberalism and by the collectivistic approach emerges through the confrontation processes enabled and encouraged by the semantic field of the "religion and state" metaphor. Indeed, these confrontation processes do not fully express the practice, but suffice to provide an effective defense weapon to each side, given the strain and the threat posed by the other.

SUMMARY

The "religion and state" question is generally formulated as a political question, that is, a question bearing on the character and political sovereignty of the regime. The thesis I have attempted to present is that this formulation does not reflect the meaning of the semantic field created by the "religion and state" metaphor. In its standard formulation, this realm of discourse is the exposed tip of the iceberg in a Jewish identity discourse that is deeper and more primary, but has been left vague and blurred by the historical context of its development.

Many questions are related to the character of the identity discourse: what are its borders? What is the relationship between its distinctive political aspects and its cultural aspects? What is the status of the identity symbols? What is the status of the other—the Moslem, the Christian, the Druze—in the Jewish identity discourse and in the public sphere where it is conducted? Although these questions obviously require separate discussion, they cannot undermine the need for a new analysis of the area of discourse called "religion and state." In its political formulation, this area of discourse blurs the genuine realm that the political discourse pretends to represent—the problem of Jewish identity or Jewish identities.

NOTES

1   Clifford Geertz, *The Interpretation of Cultures: Selected Essays* (New York: Basic Books, 1973), 210–11.
2   Charles Taylor, "Atomism," in *Comunitarianism and Individualism*, ed. Shlomo Avinery and Avner de-Shalit (Oxford: Oxford University Press, 1992), 29–50.
3   Benjamin Neuberger, "Religion and State Arrangements in Europe" [Hebrew], in *The Conflict: Religion and State in Israel* (Tel Aviv: Yedi'ot Aharonot, 2002), 336–53.
4   Eliezer Goldman, *Expositions and Inquiries: Jewish Thought in Past and Present* [Hebrew], ed. Avi Sagi and Daniel Statman (Jerusalem: Magnes Press, 1996), 16–17.
5   Gershon Weiler, *Jewish Theocracy* (Leiden: Brill, 1988) ch. 1; Benedict de Spinoza, *Tractatus Theologico-Politicus*, trans R. H. M. Elwes (London and New York: George Routledge and Sons, 1905), ch. 18.
6   See Avi Sagi, "Judaism and Democracy: Indeed at Odds?" [Hebrew], *Democratic Culture* 2 (1999), 169–87.
7   Spinoza, *Tractatus Theologico-Politicus*, 220.
8   On this question see Avi Sagi, *Tradition vs. Traditionalism: Contemporary Perspectives in Jewish Thought*, trans. Batya Stein (Amsterdam-New York: Rodopi, 2008), ch. 3.
9   On Neriah's stance and on the surrounding controversy see Asher Cohen, *The Prayer Shawl and the Flag* [Hebrew] (Jerusalem: Ben Zvi Institute, 1998), ch. 7.
10 See, for instance, Moshe ben Maimon, *The Book of Divine Commandments* (*Sefer ha-Mitzvoth of Moses Maimonides*) trans. Charles B. Chavel (London: Soncino, 1940), positive commandment 176.
11 R. Shaul Israeli, *Sefer Amud ha-Yemini* [Hebrew] (Jerusalem: Eretz Hemdah, 1992), 101–2. See also Jacob Levinger, *From Routine to Renewal: Pointers in Contemporary Jewish Thought* [Hebrew] (Jerusalem: De'ot, 1973), ch. 9; Michael Zvi Nehorai, "Can a Religious Deed Be Coerced?" [Hebrew], in *Between Authority and Autonomy in Jewish Tradition*, ed. Zeev Safrai and Avi Sagi (Tel-Aviv: Hakibbutz Hameuchad, 1997); Avi Sagi, *Jewish Religion after Theology*, trans. Batya Stein (Boston: Academic Studies Press, 2009), ch. 1.

12   On this question, see Eliyakim G. Ellinson, *Non-Halakhic Marriage* [Hebrew] (Jerusalem: Dvir, 1975); Pinhas Schiffman, *Who Is Afraid of Civil Marriage?* [Hebrew] (Jerusalem: Jerusalem Institute for Israel Studies, 1995); idem, *Doubtful Marriage in Israel Law* [Hebrew] (Jerusalem: Hebrew University of Jerusalem, 1975).

13   *Mamzerut* is a halakhic category that defines persons born from forbidden relationships (a woman's adultery, incest) or to a parent defined as a *mamzer*.

14   Schiffman, *Doubtful Marriage*, 97; idem, *Who Is Afraid of Civil Marriage*, ch. 5. See also Levinger, *From Routine to Renewal*, ch. 10.

15   I owe a significant debt for this analysis to Schifmann's book, *Who Is Afraid of Civil Marriage*.

16   Maimonides, *The Code of Maimonides*, Laws on Forbidden Intercourse, 13:14.

17   Ibid., 14:15.

18   See R. Menachem Kirschbaum, *Responsa Menachem Meshiv* (Benei Berak, 1936), no. 42.

19   See Avi Sagi and Zvi Zohar, *Transforming Identity: The Ritual Transition from Gentile to Jew—Structure and Meaning* (London: Continuum, 2007), chs. 12–14.

20   On this issue, see Taylor, "Atomism."

21   On communitarian positions and their connection with liberalism, see mainly Yael Tamir, *Liberal Nationalism* (Princeton: Princeton University Press, 1993).

22   For a systematic and illuminating formulation of atomistic liberalism that is opposed to the collectivistic-Jewish identity conception, see, for instance, Yigal Elam, *The End of Judaism* [Hebrew] (Tel Aviv: Yedi'ot Aharonot, 2000).

23   Ibid., chs. 4–5.

24   See Menachem Mautner, *Law and the Culture of Israel* (Oxford: Oxford University Press, 2011), 127–42.

25   This was an expression greatly favored by *Haaretz* writers in the 1980s as a description of the religious parties.

26   Geertz, *The Interpretation of Cultures*, 201ff.

27   His reaction was published in *Iton Tel Aviv*, July 19, 2002.

28   Geertz, *The Interpretation of Cultures*, 207.

29   See also Alessandro Ferrara, *Reflective Authenticity: Rethinking the Project of Modernity* (London: Routledge, 1998).

30   On the interface between Romanticism and atomistic liberalism see Isaiah Berlin, *The Roots of Romanticism* (Princeton: Princeton University Press, 2001), ch. 6; Nancy L. Rosenblum, *Another Liberalism: Romanticism and the Reconstruction of Liberal Thought* (Cambridge, MA: Harvard University Press, 1987).

31   Avi Sagi, "Identity and Commitment in a Multicultural World," *Democratic Culture* 3 (2000): 167–186.

32   Isaiah Berlin, "Two Concepts of Liberty," in *Four Essays on Liberty* (Oxford: Oxford University Press, 1969), 118–172

33   This issue was analyzed at length in the works of Eliezer Goldman. For an analysis of this approach, see Sagi, *Tradition vs. Traditionalism*, chs. 4 and 8.

34   R. Shlomo Goren was a central rabbinic figure in Israel's public life. He was the first Chief Military Rabbi and established the Military Rabbinate. In 1972–1983, he was Chief Rabbi of the State of Israel.

35   R. Shlomo Goren, "On the Problem of Religion and State" [in Hebrew], in *Religion and the State*, ed. Matityahu Rotenberg (Tel Aviv: NRP, 1964), 79.

36 Jonathan Shapira, *A Society Held Captive by Politicians* [in Hebrew] (Tel Aviv: Sifriat Po'alim, 1996), 131.

37 Geertz, *The Interpretation of Cultures*, 201.

38 Ibid.

39 Ibid., 202

40 Ibid.

41 Ibid., 203

42 Ibid., 207.

43 Ibid.

44 For an analysis of this question, see Avi Sagi and Zvi Zohar, *Circles of Jewish Identity: A Study in Halakhic Literature* [in Hebrew] (Tel Aviv: Hakibbutz Hameuchad, 2000), chs. 10–12.

45 Louis Dumont, *Homo Hierarchicus: The Caste System and its Implications*, trans. Mark Sainsbury (London: Paladin, 1972).

46 Ibid., 66.

47 Ibid., 191.

48 For a seminal discussion of marginality and hierarchy in the relationships of Jews, Christians, and Moslems, see Mark R. Cohen, *Under Crescent and Cross: The Jews in the Middle Ages* (Princeton: Princeton University Press, 2008), ch. 6. An important part of the perspective I offer here is influenced by Cohen's theses.

49 See David Canaani, *The Second Aliyah and its Attitude toward Religion and Tradition* [in Hebrew] (Tel Aviv: Sifriat Hapoalim, 1976); Moti Ze'ira, Rural Collective Settlement and Jewish Culture in Eretz Israel during the 1920s [in Hebrew] (Jerusalem: Yad Yitzhak Ben-Zvi, 2002).

50 See Richard Rorty, *Contingency, Irony, and Solidarity* (Cambridge: Cambridge University Press, 1991), 320

The Right to the Land: From Moral Justifications to Religious Justifications and Back Again

11

DANIEL STATMAN

Questions concerning the right of the Jewish people to its land versus the rights of its non-Jewish inhabitants have troubled Zionist thinkers since the earliest days of Zionism. The realization that the implementation of this right, namely, the establishment of the State of Israel, involved the displacement of hundreds of thousands of Arabs from their homes only reinforced the resulting ethical dilemma.[1] The dilemma surfaced again after the Six-Day War as a result of the settlement project throughout what has become known as "Greater Israel." Perhaps I should make it clear from the outset that the object of these introductory words is not to say that the Jewish people do not have a right to the territories gained in 1948 and then in 1967, but only to suggest that the settlement that followed the conquest must have created a dilemma in the Zionist mind and—more importantly—that this dilemma could not have escaped the notice of religious thinkers. My aim in this chapter is to illustrate the way in which the latter group addresses this dilemma. I attempt to show that although "officially" the religious camp relies on religious considerations to solve the dilemma, at some point they shift gears and turn to the considerations and language of morality.

More precisely, I make two claims. The first is that the moral dilemma concerning the right of the Jewish people to the Land of Israel ("The Right to the Land") cannot be adequately resolved by religious considerations, but at some stage must be replaced by moral ones. The second is that the arguments put forward by religious writers fluctuate between religious and moral justifications, and indicate dissatisfaction with the religious claims. In other words, I demonstrate the failure of the attempt to bypass the relevant moral discourse by relying on religious discourse in its stead, and I show that this failure is implicitly recognized by religious writers. If I am right, then the problem of the Right to the Land, whether in the context of the Zionist project in general, or in the context of settlement throughout Judea and Samaria in particular, is far more vexing for religious thinkers than either religious or even non-religious thinkers tend to assume.

In the first part of the chapter, I present what seems to be the fundamental philosophical dilemma faced by attempts to offer a religious justification for the Right to the Land and for the Zionist settlement in the occupied territories. In the second part, I illustrate this dilemma through a critical analysis of the attempt to base the Right to the Land on a Talmudic principle, according to which conquest determines ownership.

THE RIGHT TO THE LAND AND THE *EUTHYPHRO* DILEMMA

As elaborated elsewhere,[2] the fundamental dilemma in any discussion of the relation between religion and morality was raised many years ago by Socrates in the dialogue called *Euthyphro*, hence "the *Euthyphro* dilemma." The heart of this dilemma is the claim that religious justification for moral claims is either invalid or begs the question of the validity of the claims themselves. Suppose one offers a religious justification for the claim that X is a moral obligation, namely a claim that is anchored on some proposition about God, typically that God issued a command to do X. The logic of this argument is simple.

1) God commanded that X be done.
2) Therefore, X is a moral obligation.

The obvious question that arises is the following: how can a commandment by God logically justify the conclusion that what God commands *is a moral obligation*? A possible answer is that the claim assumes what is known in the philosophical literature as a "divine command theory of morality," according to which morality depends on religion. This theory, however, encounters serious philosophical difficulties, of which the claim at hand is an excellent example. Without relying on other premises, the fact that some authority—human or indeed divine—commands its subordinates to perform X seems to fall short of justifying the conclusion that X is a moral obligation. Moreover, even if this view could be defended from a philosophical point of view, it has been almost completely rejected in Jewish tradition.[3]

In response to this difficulty, an alternative answer might be proposed. On this answer, we are entitled to move from the premise that God commanded X to the conclusion that X is a moral obligation on the basis of the assumption of God's moral perfection. Because God is all-righteous and all-just, if He commanded X, then X is necessarily morally required. However, this solution to the above dilemma comes at the cost of relinquishing, or significantly weakening, the religious basis for X. It implies that, in the final analysis, X is a moral obligation not because God commanded it, but because of substantive moral reasons that guide the actions of God, so to speak. The fact that God commanded X provides us with a strong reason to *believe* that X is correct, which is not the reason *why* it is correct. Therefore, if one wishes to understand why X is a moral obligation—to really grasp the *reasons* that support this assertion—then simply claiming that God issued a command that X be done does not offer even the beginning of an answer.

To be sure, we often trust the advice of professionals, such as doctors and computer technicians, and follow their instructions, even without fully understanding the basis for their advice. When the instructions of such professionals appear reasonable, it is indeed rational to follow them. When they appear unreasonable (such as "drink three cups of paraffin a day," or "immerse the computer in the bath to get rid of its virus") we ask for explanations and try to understand them. Similarly, the move from premise (1) to conclusion (2) in the argument above appears natural and smooth only insofar as the command is perceived as compatible with basic moral concepts. When, however, it is not, the assertion "X is God's commandment" is not very helpful in explaining how X might be a moral obligation, and one is forced to search for moral reasons that apply to the case at hand.

What is true about God's commands is true also of His deeds, namely, of whatever happens in the world (if one assumes some form of divine providence). Saying that a particular event is good merely because God brought it about does not provide any clue to understanding why this is so, especially if the event raises disturbing thoughts, such as in cases involving the deaths of innocent people. In such cases, the assertion that God is behind the act not only fails to solve the problem, but actually also aggravates it, leading to the following question: How can an all-just and all-benevolent God bring about, or even allow, such outcomes to occur?

In light of these considerations, it is not surprising that philosophers and commentators throughout history have attempted to provide "standard" moral explanations for apparently problematic commandments, as well as for apparently unjust acts and events. They do not attempt to resolve the theological-moral difficulty raised by the death (or the killing) of innocent people on the basis of statements such as "it was the will of God," but offer alternative explanations, such as that the innocent victim will be compensated in the world to come, that his death was necessary to prevent him from sinning and thus harming himself or society in the future, and so on. The working assumption of these commentators is that, first, God's commands and deeds are in keeping with the justice, goodness, and loving kindness that are always attributed to Him and, second, that human beings, despite their limited understanding, can explain the compatibility between divine actions or commandments and justice. As mentioned elsewhere, such explanations turn the concept of divine goodness from an abstract idea, the acknowledgment of which is an empty statement, to a concrete idea, which can be the source of inspiration and a model for imitation.[4]

With this brief introduction in mind, let us now turn to the question of the Right to the Land. According to a widespread view, this right, which is supposed to establish the legitimacy of the occupation and settlement after the wars of 1948 and 1967, is grounded in religious premises. R. Isaac said:

> It was not necessary to begin the Torah [whose main objective is to teach commandments, with this verse] but from "This month shall be for you" (Exodus 12:2), since this is the first commandment that Israel was commanded [to observe]. And what is the reason that it begins with Genesis? Because of [the verse] "The power of His works He hath declared to His people in giving them the heritage of the nations" (Psalms 111:6). For if the nations of the world should say to Israel: "You are robbers because you have seized by force the lands of the seven nations [of Canaan]," they [Israel] could say to them, "the entire world belongs to the Holy One, Blessed Be He. He created it and gave it to whomever it was right in his eyes. Of His own will He gave it to them and of His own will He took it from them and gave it to us."[5]

The claim that the land belongs to the People of Israel is based here on two assumptions: that the Land of Israel belongs to God, as does the entire world; that God took this land from the Seven Nations who dwelt there and gave it to the Jewish people. For many years, religious philosophers and educators have drawn on these words of Rashi as the standard justification for settling the land. The great Talmudic scholar, Ephraim Elimelech Urbach, noted the prevalence of this line of argument fifty years ago:

> The young religious person generally appears, at least outwardly, to have no problems. As far as he is concerned, all the questions have already been answered . . . One example will suffice, from a confused article in De'ot, 1963. The author writes: "The secular Jew has to find many contorted arguments to explain the return of his people to its land after thousands of years of wandering . . . It is even more difficult for nonbelievers to explain, if only to themselves, the evacuation and expropriation of the Arabs and the settlement on their land at the time of the War of

Independence, and self-accusation among them [the Jewish non-believers] is rife today. The religious person, however, conveys internal calm and confidence in the necessity and justifiability of this act. The explanation is familiar to anyone who has ever read a portion of the Bible with Rashi's commentary."[6]

It is interesting that the author to whom Urbach is referring takes for granted that the War of Independence involved "evacuation and expropriation [rather than voluntary departure or escape] of the Arabs and the settlement on their land" long before the revelations of the New Historians and the rise of post-Zionism. Moreover, he believes that such acts created a moral problem, one so serious that, viewed from a non-religious point of view, it cannot be resolved. Nevertheless, merely by virtue of his reading of Rashi, the young religious person conveys "internal calm and confidence in the necessity and *justifiability* of this act" (italics added). What was perceived as an act of unjust eviction prior to the reading of Rashi, is perceived as necessary and just after the reading.

The assumption that only believers have a good answer to the question of the Right to the Land is often used to show the apparent advantage of religious Zionism over secular Zionism, which is presented as resting on very shaky ground. A clear expression of this line of thinking in recent times can be found in an article by Emunah Elon, a predominantly religious writer, in a special edition of the magazine *Eretz Acheret*, which was devoted to the question of how internal decisions within religious Zionism might influence the future of Israeli society. According to Elon, the secular call for a withdrawal from Judea and Samaria ultimately undermines the right of Jews to reside in Tel Aviv or in Haifa, that is to say, it undermines the entire Zionist project:

If the Zionist movement is not founded on the "religious" basis of the divine promise to our ancestors, it has no raison d'etre in Judea and Samaria or within the boundaries of the Green Line, either. It is becoming increasingly clear, even if not everyone will admit it yet, that only the Torah can justify the ingathering of Jews of the past 150 years from all over the world to the heart of the Middle East, and the price—which all would agree has been heavy—that the Arab inhabitants of the land have been forced to pay."[7]

Elon does not deny that Zionism has demanded a heavy cost from the Arabs, and she apparently believes that the cost is so high that it cannot be justified by standard moral considerations. In her opinion, only the "Torah of Israel" can offer justification for such a high cost.

Can it really? Let us recap the moral question to be resolved. A nation dwells on some territory for many generations. Another nation arrives, evicts, and expropriates the first nation and settles on the land. Such acts are indisputably morally problematic. To justify them, the aggressive nation claims that the evacuation and dispossession of the land was performed on God's authorization; therefore, there is no room for moral concern. But the problem is not only unresolved, it is exacerbated. It is not resolved because this solution does not offer the smallest lead toward understanding why removing the first nation from its land was *right*. As explained above, the very fact that God commanded or authorized some act is insufficient in itself to explain the justice of it, especially when the act looks very problematic from a moral point of view. The problem is exacerbated because it points to a troubling difficulty regarding the nature of God: What kind of a god arbitrarily uproots a nation from its land and settles another nation in its place ("gives according to His will, and takes according to His will")?

We can, therefore, formulate the fundamental difficulty in the religious answer to the question of the Right to the Land as a version of the *Euthyphro* dilemma. The religious answer asserts that the Jewish people has the right to its land (and hence, presumably, is allowed to evict and expropriate the non-Jewish inhabitants) because God has commanded them to do so. Now God's authorization is either based or not based on moral considerations. If it is—then, ultimately, the Right to the Land is based neither on divine will, nor on divine power ("The power of His works He hath declared to His people in giving them the heritage of the nations"[8]), but on "regular" moral considerations. If that is the case, then to understand why the Jewish people has a moral right to its land, these considerations must be highlighted and defended. If, however, God's authorization is not based on moral considerations, but rather on His arbitrary will, then the proposed answer is completely unhelpful in regard to solving the *moral* problem.

A possible reaction to this dilemma would be to say that God always acts righteously and justly, therefore His prescribed distribution (that one nation will inherit one land, and another nation will inherit another) is morally sound. Nevertheless, our limited minds are unable to comprehend why this is the case, just as we cannot comprehend why some righteous people suffer or why *Mamzerim* (children of marriages forbidden by the Torah) should be punished for the sins of their parents. On this line of argument, relying on God's command does not assume that He acts arbitrarily, but neither does it make God's command superfluous in a way that would enable us to rely directly on the relevant moral considerations.

This is a reasonable reaction, but it means that believers fare no better than non-believers *vis-à-vis* the moral challenge posed by the occupation and settlement in the Holy Land, and it is unclear how they might acquire the internal calm and "confidence in the necessity and justifiability of this act" referred to by Urbach.[9] By claiming that their minds are too limited to comprehend how it might be morally sound to evict a nation from its land and settle another nation in its place, the believers admit *that they have no satisfactory answer to the question regarding the moral Right to the Land.* Their position in relation to the moral problem at hand is akin to that of those who generally trust their doctor, but who have received seemingly unreasonable instructions from him in specific circumstances. They might obey the doctor by virtue of their trust in him, but would do so with uncertainty and reluctance, and would not pretend to their doubting friends that they understand why it is right to follow the doctor's peculiar instructions.

A different response to the above dilemma is to distinguish between human and divine justice and to suggest that, although human justice fails to provide an explanation for the Right to the Land, divine justice *does* provide an answer, and that it is on this type of justice that the religious claim rests. However, the distinction between these two notions of justice is not entirely clear. If the concept of divine justice refers to how

God applies the principles of justice—those same general principles that are incumbent upon everyone—then this distinction seems to resemble a version of the previous response. It says something like the following: God indeed acts according to the tenets of justice, but as His intentions are hidden from us, we do not really understand His actions. If, however, what is meant by "divine justice" is that God acts in accordance with principles that are different from, and even opposed to, our familiar principles of justice, then this answer comes very close to the view that God acts according to His will rather than according to what is just.

Furthermore, study of the Bible shows clearly that the moral expectations from God, so to speak, are that He will act according to justice in its usual sense, not according to some other notion of justice. When Abraham complains that indiscriminate annihilation of the entire population of Sodom contradicts the divine values of righteousness and justice, God does not silence him by saying something like "my justice is of a different kind," but accepts as self-evident that the killing of a righteous person along with a wicked person is unjustified. In a similar way, Jeremiah takes for granted that justice demands reward for the righteous and retribution for the wicked, and therefore challenges God: "Right wouldest Thou be, O Lord, were I to contend with Thee, yet will I reason with Thee: Wherefore doth the way of the wicked prosper? Wherefore are all they secure that deal very treacherously?" (Jeremiah 12:1). The idea of divine justice, therefore, cannot rescue the believer from the aforementioned dilemma.

In sum, if believers admit that the Zionist enterprise is morally problematic because of its repercussions for the Arab inhabitants of the land, they cannot circumvent this problem by drawing on religious claims. If they recognize the existence of a moral problem, they have no choice but to dirty their hands, as it were, and delve into the relevant moral discussion to respond to the internal criticism, i.e., the voice of conscience, as well as the external criticism, i.e., the allegations of robbery voiced by Jews and non-Jews alike. It was to this conclusion that I was referring in the second part of the title to this chapter: "From moral justifications to religious justifications and back again." The Right to the Land raises a *moral* problem, and as such directs us to moral considerations. But such considerations seem intimidating to some religious people, who fear that taking them seriously might force them into positions that they would rather not take. Hence, they try to avoid such considerations and rely, instead, on religious ones, such as Rashi's commentary. Nevertheless, because of the deep connection between divine commands and morality, which was explained above through the *Euthyphro* dilemma, exploring the religious considerations ends up restoring, so to speak, the suppressed moral considerations.

Let me now return to Rashi's words (cited above), and examine whether they indeed support the claim that the Jewish people has an eternal, unconditional right to the land, a right that necessarily takes precedence over the rights of others. Rashi does not say that the land belongs to the Jewish people, or to any other nation, but that it belongs to *God*, who, at a certain point in time, gave it to the Seven Nations, and then, at another point in time, took it from them and gave it to the Jewish people. The expression "He gave it to them by fiat, and by fiat, He took it from them and gave it to us" indicates the fragility and instability of any human entitlement to the land, as such a right depends completely on God's will. In the same way that He willed to take it from the Seven Nations, He could change His mind and give it back to them.

Moreover, as evident from many places in the Bible, the land is taken from its inhabitants not through some arbitrary act, but as a result of their moral-religious level:

> Defile not ye yourselves in any of these things; for in all these the nations are defiled, which I cast out from before you. And the land was defiled, therefore I did visit the iniquity thereof upon it, and the land vomited out her inhabitants. Ye therefore shall keep My statutes and Mine ordinances, and shall not do any of these abominations; neither the home-born, nor the stranger that sojourneth among you—for all these abominations have the men of the land done, that were before you, and the land is defiled—that the land vomit not you out also, when ye defile it, as it vomited out the nation that was before you. (Leviticus 18:24–28)

According to these and many similar verses, the right to live in the Land of Israel is conditional on the moral and religious level of the nation wishing to dwell there. Any nation that does not meet the conditions set by God will be evicted, or "vomited out," to use the harsh words of the Torah. This principle applies to Jews and non-Jews alike: the Land of Israel vomited out the Canaanites because of their shameful deeds ("and the land will vomit out its inhabitants"), and if the Israelites imitate such deeds, they will be vomited out likewise. Even though God has promised to eventually return the Jewish people to its land (hence "the promised land"), the right to inhabit the land at any specific point in history is always conditional. Furthermore, if the nation that dwells in the land at a given point in time does *not* defile it through bad behavior, it cannot be evacuated from it even if this means a delay in the Jewish people's return to its land. This is clear from the Covenant made between God and Abraham: "And in the fourth generation they shall come back hither; [i.e., only the fourth generation, and not before] *for the iniquity of the Amorite is not yet full*" (Genesis 15:16).

What follows is that not only does the religious viewpoint fail to justify the internal calm and with it the unshakable confidence in the Right to the Land mentioned earlier, but it has quite the opposite effect: It leads to rather somber thoughts about the existence of this right in the current historical period. In the Israeli reality of corrupt leadership, increasing gaps between the rich and poor, public desecration of the Sabbath and many other sins that do not bear mentioning here, the warnings in the Torah about the repercussions of such behavior from the point of view of the Right to the Land should be taken (again, from a religious point of view) in all seriousness. In this iniquitous atmosphere, frequently lamented by rabbis, it is difficult to understand how believers can, nevertheless, proclaim that the Jews of today have an unequivocal right to the land, and state confidently, as did those at the time of Ezekiel: "The land is given us for inheritance" (Ezekiel 33:24).

Had Ezekiel lived today, he would surely have answered them as he answered our ancestors: "Wherefore say unto them: Thus saith the Lord God. Ye eat with the blood, and lift up your eyes unto your idols, and shed blood; and shall ye possess the land? Ye stand upon your sword, ye work abomination, and ye defile every one his neighbor's wife; and shall ye possess the land?" (Ezekiel:25–26).

Finally, the fact that inheriting the land depends on the behavior of the people does not contradict the recurring biblical promise that the Land of Canaan will be given to the Jewish people. This is because this promise means simply that at the end of days, after repeated cycles of sin-exile-repentance, the Jewish people will repent, gaining full entitlement to the land, and will then inhabit it forever (just as the other nations will inhabit their own lands at the end of days[10]).

THE RIGHT TO THE LAND AS BASED ON CONQUEST

Another example of how the religious discussion on the Right to the Land is logically compelled to rely on moral claims can be found in an article by R. Abraham Sherman, who refers to Israel's conquests in 1948 and 1967 to establish the right to the occupied land. This is how he develops his argument. In his introduction, Sherman declares unequivocally that "the legal basis for Jewish sovereignty over the Land of Israel is rooted in The Book of God's Law, the Bible."[11] Even the arguments against this right—raised by non-Jews—were based, at least in earlier times, on (distorted) interpretations of the Bible, as is apparent in the story of Alexander of Macedonia in the Babylonian Talmud (Tractate Sanhedrin 91a). This notwithstanding, says Sherman, the current arguments against the Jews' Right to the Land are not based on biblical exegesis, but on "the nature and the legality of Israel's wars with the Arab states and the Palestinians." Therefore, it is worthwhile to examine the halakhic view on this matter and to present "a halakhic clarification of the legal validity of Israel's wars for determining sovereignty within the nation, but, nonetheless, from the Torah point of view." However, as I attempt to show in this section, the discussion of "the Torah's point of view" eventually requires that moral considerations are addressed under what Sherman calls "the ethical (*yosher*) test."

Now let us take a detailed look at the way halakha is supposed to establish the "legal validity" of the Jewish people over the land between the Mediterranean Sea and the Jordan River, and at the way this validity relies—somewhat unexpectedly—on moral considerations. The argument is based on the Talmudic explanation of certain verses in the Bible that ostensibly teach us nothing, and therefore "ought to be burned." However, says the Talmud, these verses express a fundamental biblical principle:

> R. Shimon ben Lakish said: There are many verses which to all appearances ought to be burned but are really essential elements in the Torah, [e.g.,] "and the Avvim, that dwelt in villages as far as Gaza, [the Kaphtorim, that came forth out of Kaphtor, destroyed them, and dwelt in their stead]." (Deuteronomy 2:23) In what way does this concern us?? Inasmuch as Abimelech adjured Abraham, saying "that thou wilt not deal falsely with me, nor with my son, nor with my son's son" (Genesis 21:23), "the Holy One Blessed be He said Let the Kaphthorim come and take the land away from the Avvim, who are Philistines, and then Israel may come and take it away from the Kapthorim." Similarly, you must explain the verse "For Heshbon was the city of Sihon the king of the Amorites, who had fought against the former king of Moab, and [taken all his land out of his hand, even unto the Ammon]" (Numbers 21:26). In what way does this concern us? Inasmuch as the Holy One Blessed be He had commanded Israel, "Be not at enmity with Moab" (Deuteronomy 2:9). He therefore said: Let Sihon come and take away the land from Moab and then Israel may come and take it from Sihon. This, indeed, explains R. Papa's saying: "Ammon and Moab were rendered clean [unto Israel] through Sihon." (Tractate Hulin 60b)

According to Resh Lakish, the abstruse and apparently redundant historical information that the Kapthorim destroyed the Avvim [the Philistines] and inherited their land helps us resolve a disturbing difficulty in the Bible. Abraham makes a covenant with Abimelech, King of the Philistines, and promises him that neither he nor his descendants will take Abimelech's land. Yet when the land of Canaan was conquered by the Israelites, they did fight against the Philistines, apparently violating the covenant. How could they do this? The explanation offered by the Talmud in this paragraph is that since the Kaphthorim had conquered the

Philistines before the Israelites arrived and had taken possession of the entire territory, Israel's conquest over the Kapthorim did not constitute a breach of the covenant with Abimelech. Similarly, regarding Sihon, King of the Amorites, who had fought the King of Moab and conquered all his land: this conquest and the change in possession implied explains why Israel was permitted to conquer the land of Moab despite the command, "Be not at enmity with Moab." On conquering Moab, Sihon gained full ownership over this territory, thus invalidating the prohibition against conquering it: The biblical prohibition was against taking *Moabite* territory, but when the Israelites arrived in the region, it had already become *Amorite* territory. In R. Papa's words, "Ammon and Moab were rendered clean in Sihon."

The principle that the Talmud formulates here determines that the conquest of land in war transfers full ownership to the conqueror without any residue. Although the accepted rule in halakha is that land cannot be stolen, namely, that landowners never lose their claim to land stolen from them, the law regarding land taken in war is different. R. Shneur Zalman of Liadi (1745–1812) views this law as anchored in the authority of the king: "If a king—even a gentile king—conquers another state in war, he acquires it together with all the rivers and forests in it. (See Maimonides, *Laws of Kings*, end of Chapter 4, and how much more so regarding Israel). If he sells or gives a forest in it to one of his subjects, that person acquires full ownership over it . . . For this is one of the statues and laws of kingship, that the entire land with its rivers and forests belongs to the king, be it his native country or the lands that he conquers in war. And the statues of kingship are binding, just laws, like the laws of the Torah."[12]

The argument is simple. The laws of kingship are just as binding as the laws of the Torah; these laws grant the king (or any political ruler) ownership over the territory that he conquered in war. Therefore, the implications of such conquest in terms of ownership are binding not only from a political-legal point of view (according to the Laws of Kings), but also from a halakhic point of view. It is revealing that in the section quoted, R. Shneur Zalman connects the aforementioned law to Maimonides' statement in the *Laws of Kings*, which determines that territories gained in war by the King of Israel "belong to him. He may apportion them to his servants and soldiers as he desires and keep the remainder for himself. In all these matters, the judgment he makes is binding."[13]

According to R. Shneur Zalman, then, the law that enables the expansion of borders through conquest does not derive from the unique status of the king of Israel, or from the value of the land of Israel, but is a corollary of a general law that grants kings the power to extend the borders of their kingdoms through war.

What is the implication of applying this principle to Israel's conquest in the War of Independence? According to R. Frank, who is quoted by R. Sherman, the principle implies that all the conquered land and property are considered to be in Jewish possession. Contrary to this, according to R. Herzog, the conquest itself does not entitle transfer of the conquered territory to the conqueror's possession, unless he has a clear intention to settle the territory, and has received international approval for this: "Even though I have publicly stated that we gained ownership over the land through conquest in war, I now know that the government of Israel has not yet declared ownership through conquest. This has not yet been decided, and it depends on the decision of the nations in the peace agreement."[14]

In R. Sherman's opinion, R. Herzog is correct, because, as explained by R. Shneur Zalman from Liadi above, the validity of ownership through conquest is derived from the Law of Kings and from the principle that the Law of the King is the Law (*Dina Demalkhuta Dina*). Therefore, "when international law does not authorize ownership through conquest, and the local government has not yet fixed the boundaries, the conquest might not yet constitute ownership."[15] In any event, it is clear that, according to R. Herzog, conquest that does receive international approval does grant the conquerors ownership over the territory taken by war.

An argument on these lines was developed by R. Saul Yisraeli, identifying the British conquerors as the landowners, and basing his argument on the UN approval to transfer ownership of the land to the Jewish people: "The landowners are considered to be those who acquired ownership through conquest in war, and these were the British, who had conquered the land and continued to rule it as custodians on behalf of other nations to whom they had transferred the right of ownership (a right they had obtained through conquest in war) and from whom they received the mandate at that time. If so, the decision made by these nations, who were in possession of the land, is valid. And the Arab peoples have no right to the land . . . *because ownership through a war of conquest turns the conqueror into landowner* . . . and the state, in itself, is legal according to the Torah point of view."[16]

This is quite a surprising argument. According to R. Yisraeli, the relevant conquest for determining the Jewish people's Right to the Land was not the Jewish-Israeli conquest over the Arabs in 1948, but the British conquest over the Turks in 1917. The British became landlords through conquest, and gained legal power to transfer the decision about the fate of the land to the League of Nations (and afterwards to the United Nations), who decided to bequeath the land to the Jewish people to establish an independent state.[17]

The principle that conquest transfers ownership seems morally problematic. Granting ownership to the conqueror of any land or property is tantamount to awarding a prize for aggression and encourages further aggression. It goes without saying that the principle is diametrically opposed to existing international law, which unequivocally states that the occupying power is forbidden to annex territory conquered in war. It accords more with the rules of the jungle or of the Mafia than with the settling of international relations. This difficulty has not gone unnoticed by halakhists, and in response, they interpreted the principle under discussion as applicable only to *justifiable* conquest. In halakhic terms, it was suggested that one must distinguish between the Law of the King (*Dina Demalkhuta*), which is binding, and robbery by the king (*Hamsnuta Demalka*), which is not, and has no legal validity. R. Sherman concluded that when a state wages war for an unjust cause, the *Dina Demalkhuta* principle does not apply, and hence, ownership of the land taken in that war does not transfer to the conqueror. The outcome of this line of thought is that one cannot determine that any war transfers ownership without first determining that the war was just. As R. Sherman stated, it all depends on one question: "Was there a justifiable and legal reason for going to war?"[18]

This modification of the principle under discussion makes good sense, but it means that this principle cannot be drawn upon to establish the right to the territories conquered in 1948 and 1967 before first demonstrating that these wars were morally justified. Following the argument in the first part of the chapter, this means that the religious-halakhic basis for the Right to the Land cannot circumvent the moral discussion. To R. Sherman, the moral answer regarding these two wars is obvious: "Without a doubt, Israel's wars of 1948 and 1967 were defensive wars, to save her from her enemies. And if so, the outcomes of these wars (the occupations) should grant sovereignty to Israel [over the territories Israel occupied]."[19]

Nonetheless, the moral picture is far more complex and far less clear. First, some people believe that Israel's wars were not entirely defensive, and that, at least in 1967, the war was in Israel's interest and the nation was not simply forced into it.[20] Second, even if some country has a moral justification to wage war, it is not allowed to expand its borders thereafter, and doing so looks like a case of "robbery" in Sherman's terminology. This point is easy to understand when comparing the acquisition of ownership over enemy land and property. According to the principle that conquest transfers ownership, the conqueror takes possession of both the conquered territories and property. However, from a moral point of view, even in a just war, one is not allowed to help oneself unrestrainedly to the possessions of the aggressor state. The same is true for the land: usurpation of enemy land is difficult to justify even if the war is defensive.

In these brief comments, I do not intend to take a side in the debate about the justness of Israel's wars in general and of the 1948 and 1967 wars in particular. I merely point to the fact that this question is incredibly complex from a historical, legal and moral viewpoint. Hence, it calls for a cautious—and convincing—answer before one can hope to apply the halakhic principle under discussion ("Ammon and Moab were rendered clean [unto Israel] through Sihon"). If the answer is indeed convincing—namely, that the relevant war was just, and that this justness somehow legitimizes the taking of territory—it is doubtful whether the Talmudic principle is still required. The moral considerations would then seem to do all the necessary work in establishing the Right to the Land.

The need to refer to moral considerations also arises from R. Sherman's discussion about the implications of the UN decision regarding the State of

Israel's right to the territories it occupied, especially in 1967. I mentioned R. Sherman's argument that the conquest-transfers-ownership principle is based on the Talmudic principle that "the Law of the King is Law" (*Dina Demalkhuta Dina*). However, it seems that the "Law of the King" that applies between states today is international law. As this law determines that Israel has no right to the territories conquered in the Six-Day War, this Talmudic principle would delegitimize their annexation from a halakhic point of view. Sherman recognizes this difficulty and responds by saying that "the international law must pass the ethical (*yosher*) test that qualifies the Laws of Kingship in order to qualify as *Dina Demalkhuta.*"[21] As the United Nations failed this test in its systematic discrimination against Israel throughout the years, its decisions, therefore, do not qualify as *Dina Demalkhuta* and are not halakhically binding.

One can again see how the halakhic ruling relies on a prior moral decision. Only after applying the ethical test, which is based on morality rather than on the halakha, can we know whether a specific law is included within *Dina Demalkhuta,* and is therefore halakhically binding. R. Sherman believes that there are grounds to disqualify all UN decisions concerning Israel because of its general discriminatory policy. However, even if this view of the United Nations is accepted, an additional problem exists regarding the status of central international treaties and agreements that are signed by almost all the countries in the world. These treaties, which unequivocally forbid ownership through conquest, are a clear expression of "the accepted rules among [decent] nations,"[22] and, therefore, should be binding under the principle of *Dina Demalkhuta*. Hence, by virtue of this principle, Israel should have been made to withdraw from the territories conquered in 1967. However, whereas with the UN there is some basis for the complaint that its decisions are laced with prejudice against Israel, the same cannot be said about a document such as the Geneva Convention, which does not directly concern Israel and was not "tailored" to harm it or to deprive the nation of its rights.

In other words, once R. Sherman admits that international law gains halakhic validity if it passes the ethical test, he must accept that any parts of this law that do pass the test are halakhically binding. Since treaties such as the Geneva Convention successfully pass the test (and Sherman provides no indication to think otherwise), they must be binding. Sherman might respond by saying that the international law is one entity, so to speak, so that if one part is rejected, i.e., the UN decisions concerning Israel, it is rejected in its entirety, including the treaties mentioned above. This seems ad hoc and, if taken seriously, would lead to a complete revocation of the category of *Dina Demalkhuta*, understood by Sherman himself as the "the accepted rules among [decent] nations."[23]

In conclusion: For several rabbis, the idea of "Ammon and Moab were rendered clean in Sihon," which assumes that conquest transfers ownership, serves as the halakhic-legal basis for the Right to the Land, a basis seemingly independent of moral considerations. One version of the argument bases this right on the British conquest of 1917, while others base it on Israel's conquest in 1948. Either way, the aforementioned principle is supposed to assure the Jewish people's Right to the Land on which it established its state in 1948 and its right to the land occupied in 1967. I have tried to show that, contrary to how it seems at first, the application of this principle to real-life political cases cannot be detached from considerations of justice, because, according to an established interpretation of this principle, conquest transfers ownership only in a just war, and only when in keeping with the law of the nations (which also has to pass the ethical test). When the principle passes all these tests, it is unclear whether it plays any independent role in justifying the Jewish people's right to the land.

SUMMARY AND CONCLUSIONS

The majority of rabbis, certainly from the religious-Zionist stream, take for granted the Jewish people's eternal and unequivocal right to its land, a right that extends, in the current historical reality, from the Mediterranean Sea to the Jordan River. They interpret the vacillations and hesitations, which trouble some non-believing Jews regarding this right, as an expression of weakness. For the rabbis and their followers, the problem of the Right to the Land is either easily resolved, or does not arise in the first place. Rashi's famous commentary on the first verse in Genesis is perceived as providing a conclusive answer to any queries about this issue.

I have attempted to show that this line of thinking is superficial and misguided. If moral questions arise regarding the Right to the Land—and one can hardly deny that some tough questions *do* arise in this context—they cannot be circumvented by religious arguments, whether based on God's ownership of the world, or on talmudic principles, such as conquest transfers ownership. The reason for this inability to evade the moral discussion is common to all the aforementioned arguments, and this is because, in general, the commands of God do not determine moral obligations. Therefore, believers can profess to have resolved the troublesome moral questions regarding the Right to the Land only after using historical-legal-moral tools, the exact same tools that are at the disposal of their non-believing counterparts. If no satisfactory solution to the moral problem exists, then the religious Zionist and the secular Zionist are in the same deep trouble.

Finally, I should state that I take no stance in the hot political and ideological debate between Zionists and their opponents and between Right and Left. In particular, and to remove any shadow of a doubt, I did not assume here that the Jewish People does *not* have a moral right to its land (or to the territories occupied in 1967). My argument is that those who believe that such a right exists cannot hide behind religious arguments alone, but need to base their belief on moral considerations. No shortcuts are open to the believer on the way to establishing this right. I also attempted to show that, because of this, the religious discourse on the Right to the Land tends not to rely purely on religious arguments (although such arguments are "officially" declared to be sufficient) but tends to fall back on general moral and legal arguments. On the one hand, these arguments seem to strengthen and reinforce this right, but, on the other, they expose the contender to moral criticism. When you start to play the moral game, there's no way back.

NOTES

1   See Benny Morris, *The Birth of the Palestinian Refugee Problem Revisited* (Cambridge: Cambridge University Press, 2004).
2   Avi Sagi and Daniel Statman, *Religion and Morality* (Amsterdam: Rodopi, 1995), Part I.

3 Divine command theory of morality: see ibid., Parts I–II. Avi Sagi and myself addressed the issue of divine commands being a moral obligation in detail in our article "Divine Command Morality and the Jewish Tradition," *Journal of Religious Ethics* 23 (1995): 49–68.

4 Sagi and Statman, *Religion and Morality*, chap. 2.

5 *The Pentateuch and Rashi's Commentary*, ed. R. Abraham Ben Isaiah and R. Benjamin Sharfman (New York: S. S. & R. Publishing Company, 1976), 1.

6 E. E. Urbach, *On Judaism and Education: Collected Essays* (Jerusalem: School of Education of the Hebrew University, 1967) [Hebrew], 20–21. (*De'ot* ["opinions"] was a Hebrew journal, subtitled *A Journal for Religious Academics*.)

7 Emunah Elon, "Israel's Leadership Will Become Increasingly Religious," *Eretz Acheret*, October 1, 2009, at http://www.acheret.co.il/en/%20http:/?cmd=articles.278&act=read&id=1712 (accessed June 15, 2012).

8 *The Pentateuch*, ed. Isaiah and Sharfman, 1.

9 Urbach, *On Judaism and Education*, 20–21.

10 Ammon and Moab were given the land of Ar (Deuteronomy 2:9–19) and will return to their inheritance after they have been punished for their misdeeds: "Yet will I turn the captivity of Moab in the end of days, saith the Lord" (Jeremiah 48:47); " But it shall come to pass in the end of days, that I will bring back the captivity of Elam, saith the Lord" (Jeremiah 49:39).

11 Rabbi Abraham Sherman (born 1941) is an Israeli ultra-Orthodox rabbi and a member of the Supreme Rabbinical Court. Rabbi Abraham Sherman, "Wars of Israel: Halakhic Validity for Determining Sovereignty in the Land of Israel," [Hebrew] *Techumin* 15 (1995): 23–30; quotation, 23.

12 *Shulchan Aruch HaRav*, Hoshen Mishpat, Laws of Abandoned Property (*hefker*), section III.

13 An interesting implication of this statement (on political-legal and halakhic implications) can be found in the Radbaz's answer to the following question: Reuben was a pawnbroker and owned a store in a certain city. One day, he was expelled from the city along with the rest of the Jews. Later, the city was conquered by the Pope, and eventually, by a duke, who gave Simon pawnbroker rights in the very same store. Reuben claimed that he had precedence over the store, and sued to evict Simon. The Radbaz ruled that even though, in general, one never loses one's title to one's land, the situation is different when the land is lost as a result of war, which resets, as it were, all prior ownership. Drawing on the principle of Ammon and Moab being rendered clean in Sihon, the Radbaz determined that "even though at the time of the first king, all of Israel were prohibited from taking Reuben's store, once the kingdom had been lost to him and had become the property of another, any Jew could take the store, as it was part of the new kingdom" (Radbaz, *Responsa*, chap. 3, 1773). Quotation from *Laws of Kings*, Chapter 4, Halakha 10.

14 Rabbi Tzvi Pesach Frank (1873–1960), a renowned halakhic scholar and the Chief Rabbi of Jerusalem for several decades. Rabbi Yitzhak HaLevi Herzog (1888–1959) was the first Chief Rabbi of Ireland, from 1921 to 1936; from 1937 until his death in 1959, he was Ashkenazi Chief Rabbi of Palestine and of Israel after the establishment of the state in 1948. Quotation from Rabbi Herzog, *Psakim Vekatavim*, Part 3, Chapter 37, Section 4.

15 Sherman, "Wars of Israel," 27.

16 Rabbi Saul Yisraeli, *Eretz Hemda* (Jerusalem: Mosad Ha-Rav Kook, 1982) [Hebrew], 35–36. Rabbi Shaul Yisraeli (1909–1995) was one of the distinguished rabbis of religious Zionism.

17 For a similar argument regarding the legal outcomes of the British occupation of Palestine, see Reuben Gafni, *Our Historical and Legal Right to the Land of Israel* (Jerusalem: Sifriyat Torah VeAvodah, 1933), [Hebrew], 134–35.

18 Sherman, "Wars of Israel," 29.

19 Ibid.

20 See, for example, Motti Golani, *Wars Do Not Just Happen: On Memory, Power and Choice* (Tel Aviv: Modan, 2002) [Hebrew], especially 185–203. On his account of the events before the 1967 war, it was Egypt, much more than Israel, that was "drawn into it against her best interests."

21 See Sherman, "Wars of Israel," 30.

22 Ibid.

23 The precise content of the rule of the Law of the King is Law is "extremely vague," as remarked by Shmuel Shiloh at the beginning of his comprehensive book *Dina Demalkhuta Dina* (Jerusalem: Academic Press, 1975) [Hebrew]. For the purpose of the present argument, I rely on R. Sherman's own interpretation of this principle.

The Liberal/Multicultural Nature of the Religious Accommodations for the Palestinian-Arab Minority in Israel: A Curse or a Blessing?

12 MICHAEL M. KARAYANNI

INTRODUCTION

Multicultural theory has become a mainstay for legitimizing minority group rights. It is often used in order to justify the accommodations provided to ethnic, religious and national minorities in Western democracies. Group autonomy, group representation in governmental bodies, official recognition of minority languages and cultures, exemptions from legal obligations and more, are all forms that multicultural theory seeks to justify.[1] At the heart of the argument is the notion that such accommodations are essential for individual minority group members to live full cultural and social lives within their respective groups. Individuals need their group identity to exist and function as autonomous individuals, and are thus entitled to have such identity protected through group accommodations.[2] Otherwise, so the argument goes, minority members will run the risk of assimilation and of being dominated by the majority culture, thereby losing part of their identity. So, in essence, multiculturalism has a strong liberal justification for group-based accommodations.[3]

In spite of the theory's explanatory and persuasive power, the effect of multiculturalism on immigrant minorities in Western democracies has been limited. Although certain group rights are granted to indigenous minorities, immigrants are more expected to adjust to the hegemonic norms and culture of the host country. Questions have furthermore been raised about the possible implications and effects of minority group norms and practices, now preserved and protected by group accommodation, on individual group members. This is especially relevant to what has been termed 'illiberal' minority practices. For example, does the argument from multiculturalism legitimize the application of group norms that discriminate against women?[4] And to what extent does multiculturalism approve the authority of religious groups to determine the education of children?[5] In this chapter I would like to discuss the legal implications of branding certain group accommodations as liberal/multicultural, specifically regarding the jurisdiction granted to the Palestinian-Arab minority in Israel over matters of family law. These accommodations, unlike the jurisdictional authority granted to Jewish religious institutions in Israel, have traditionally been perceived as liberal and a form of a multicultural accommodation. After providing a brief overview of the accommodations granted to the Palestinian-Arab religious communities in Israel, I will make three major arguments: first, that these accommodations may not qualify as liberal/multicultural; second, that perceiving the accommodations as liberal/multicultural works to limit judicial review over the internal handling of the Palestinian-Arab religious communities, and the limited nature of judicial review works to strengthen the religious community as a group but at the same time to weaken the rights of individual group members that seek to contest intra-group norms and policies; and third, this same perception has the potential of promoting genuine reforms within Palestinian-Arab religious communities that would have been much harder to achieve were it not for the labeling of their jurisdiction as a form of a liberal/multicultural accommodation.

BACKGROUND

Israel is a highly diverse society. Nationally, there exists a Jewish majority that at the end of 2008 numbered 5,569,200 forming about 75.6 per cent of a total population of 7,374,000.[6] About 20 per cent of the population is Palestinian-Arab (1,487,600).[7] The remaining portion (317,100) are unidentified as Jews or Arabs but are mostly immigrants who acquired Israeli citizenship under a special provision in the Law of Return, 1950[8] (being the relative of a Jew) or have acquired permanent residence in Israel under special circumstances.[9] Another group is that of foreign workers, estimated at 222,000, who do not appear in the official census.[10]

In terms of religion, too, Israeli society comprises many groups. The Jewish majority is divided into secular, traditional and religious groups, with the latter including a well-established ultra-Orthodox community.[11] Within the Jewish traditional and religious communities other divisions exist, such as between Ashkenazi and Sephardi Jews, and between Orthodox, Conservative and Reform Judaism.[12] However, as far as Israeli law is concerned, none of these Jewish communities forms a separate religious community. In respect of the Palestinian-Arab community there are three main divisions: Muslims, numbering about 1,200,000 (16 per cent of the total population); Druze, numbering about 120,000 (1.6 per cent); and Christians, numbering about 150,000 (2 per cent).[13] The Palestinian-Arab Christian community is divided into ten recognized religious communities: (1) the Eastern (Orthodox) Community; (2) the Latin (Catholic) Community; (3) the Gregorian Armenian Community; (4) the Armenian (Catholic) Community; (5) the Syrian (Catholic) Community; (6) the Chaldean (Uniate) Community; (7) the Greek (Catholic) Melkite Community; (8) the Maronite Community; (9) the Syrian (Orthodox) Community; and (10) the Evangelical Episcopal Church in Israel.[14] In addition to these there is the Baha'i Community—a religious group recognized since 1971.[15]

These divisions have legal implications. Under the long-standing Ottoman *millet* system these religious communities have been empowered to establish their own religious courts and apply their own religious norms to their members in a number of personal status matters.[16] The religious courts of the recognized religious communities are accorded exclusive jurisdiction over the matters of marriage and divorce of their local members. In other matters of personal status, like those pertaining to alimony, child custody and inheritance, the religious courts have the judicial capacity to deal with such issues and apply their religious norms only if all of the concerned parties consent to such jurisdiction. Without such consent, the parties must resort to the regular civil courts (the Court for Family Affairs) which on certain issues, like alimony, will still apply the relevant religious law of the parties instead of the usual civil territorial norm. So in essence the religious identity of local Palestinian-Arab citizens of Israel serves in a number of spheres to connect the individual to a particular legal system. It can determine the governing law (*lex causae*) for a certain relationships, exactly as the law of the place where the tort was committed or that where the contract was concluded can determine the governing law in each of these disciplines.

This jurisdictional capacity is not accorded only to the Palestinian-Arab religious communities, for the Jewish rabbinical courts in Israel have almost the same jurisdictional capacity over the local Jewish population. Moreover, many other Jewish religious institutions are also recognized, such as the Chief Rabbinate, Local Religious Councils, Jewish religious schools and more. However, in previous work I have shown that there is an essential difference between the justifications for the religious accommodations of the Palestinian-Arab community and those behind the religious accommodations of the Jewish majority.[17] The accommodations granted to the Palestinian-Arab religious communities are taken to be a form of minority (group) accommodation that is multicultural and liberal in nature.[18] So if authority is granted to the Palestinian-Arab religious communities giving them power to adjudicate the matters of personal status of their members, it is done because of Israel's proclaimed democratic norms that seek to respect religious diversity among its non-Jewish religious communities. Thus, in terms of normative justification, the religious accommodations for the Palestinian-Arab minority in Israel are a continuation of the long-standing Ottoman *millet* system, by which minority religions were tolerated by granting prescriptive and judicial jurisdiction to community institutions over their members.[19] This perceived justification for the jurisdiction accorded to the Palestinian-Arab religious communities has also relegated these religious affairs to Israel's "private" sphere. The jurisdiction is the private matter of the religious minority rather than that of the state. These attributes are inherently different from those characterizing the jurisdiction accorded to Jewish religious institutions/norms. Given the Jewish nature of the State of Israel, the jurisdiction accorded to Jewish religious institutions/norms was perceived as yet another public feature, albeit controversial at times, of the State of Israel as a Jewish state. This is obviously the result of the inherent intertwining of religion and state within Judaism itself.[20] Still, it is Israel's definition as a Jewish state, and not its definition as a democratic state, that has justified the religious accommodations granted to Jewish religious institutions and Jewish religious norms. After the establishment of the State of Israel as a Jewish state it can no longer be said that the Jewish community in Israel is just another *millet*.[21] Rather, the matter of Jewish religious jurisdiction has essentially been "nationalized," thus becoming part of Israel's "public" sphere.[22] Consequently, the policies directing the Israeli establishment's actions when coming to recognize Jewish religious institutions/norms were particularly conscious of the need to preserve Jewish identity and Jewish unity, even when such recognition was anathema to the liberal ideals of considerable portions among the Jewish community.

One significant implication of this basic distinction is the ease with which the Israeli establishment was willing to recognize non-Jewish religious communities and grant them official status. This recognition was afforded and maintained notwithstanding the fact that some of these communities are relatively very small, numbering no more than a few thousand members. On the other hand, though Reform and Conservative Judaism are major streams among Jews world-wide and have a considerable representation in Israel, their quest for recognition by the Israeli establishment has always been an up-hill battle and largely unsuccessful. This recognition was always measured against the dictates of Jewish identity and unity in the State of Israel in which Orthodox Judaism was perceived as hegemonic; yet the recognition of non-Jewish religious communities was measured against the state's commitment to recognizing diversity.

The perception maintaining the religious accommodations of Palestinian-Arab religious communities as a form of a liberal/multicultural accommodation was enforced by three overlapping elements. The first was external in nature and had to do with the Israeli establishment's overall policy toward the Palestinian-Arab minority. From the inception of the State and to some extent to this very day, the Palestinian-Arab minority was conceived as a security threat, one which government agencies in Israel have sought to control.[23] One form of control was by segmentation: by fragmenting the Palestinian-Arab minority into different groups the government was better able to effectuate its control policy.[24] In this respect, the *millet* system that was used under the Ottoman Empire, according to which the local Palestinian-Arabs were divided into different religious groups, proved to be a boon to the State of Israel in that it facilitated fragmentation and control. More pertinent to our discussion, the fragmentation of this community into different religious groups can be better maintained when such matters are perceived as liberal/multicultural and relegated to the private rather than the public sphere, for it then becomes normatively easier to justify and preserve the existing *millet* conception.

The second element, also external in nature, was less concerned with the establishment's policy of control over a national minority, but was more related to the effort of strengthening yet further the Jewish character of the State of Israel and the quest to gain legitimacy. Maintaining the distinctness of the religious identity of the Palestinian-Arab minority and relegating it to Israel's private sphere helped guard Jewish identity from being diluted or blurred.[25] Maintaining separate identities, as the *millet* system obviously does, works to prevent the development of one all-embracing secular civic identity that could replace the existing ethnic-religious one. Moreover, as part of its effort to gain legitimacy, Israel committed itself to maintaining the religious freedom and organization of its non-Jewish population,[26] so as to show that despite being a Jewish nation state it did not discriminate against other religions.

The third force that worked to preserve the private nature of the Palestinian-Arab religious accommodations was internal in nature. Both the religious and the political leadership of the Palestinian-Arab minority supported the existing structure of religious jurisdiction; however, each worked in order to achieve its own goals. The religious leadership acquiesced to the existing state of religious jurisdiction because it allowed it to maintain its power base, although it has constantly called for more judicial and administrative authority.[27] The political leadership, on the other hand, traditionally sidestepped the question of the religious jurisdiction of the different Palestinian-Arab religious communities in an effort to avoid internal conflict that could inhibit the central agenda of attending to the status of the Palestinian-Arab community as a whole.[28] It is also safe to assume that the Palestinian-Arab minority itself is interested in religious endogamy, or at least has never spoken against it.[29]

This difference in the nature of the religious accommodations granted to the two communities, the Jewish and the Palestinian-Arab, is what I call the 'paradigm of separateness' in religion and state relations in Israel.[30] And this schism between the groups also explains why the debate over religion and state in Israel has generally excluded the Palestinian-Arab community. For this debate has been defined by the conflict between public recognition for religious institutions and norms on the one hand and liberal democratic norms on the other hand. As such, the debate found the jurisdiction of the Palestinian-Arab religious communities beyond its defining parameters—this jurisdictional authority was itself liberal (and multicultural) in nature rather than in conflict with such principles.

What grounds, then, are there for conceiving the religious accommodations given to the Palestinian-Arab community as a form of liberal/multicultural accommodation? Do they in fact qualify as such, given the normative threshold set by multiculturalism as a normative theory? This is the question that I now turn to.

THE RELIGIOUS ACCOMMODATIONS AND MULTICULTURAL QUALIFICATIONS

It is often assumed that recognition for minority religious institutions/norms comport with the will of the group, or at least with the will of the majority of the group. This assumption is so pervasive that there is no real discussion in the literature dealing with multiculturalism about how to guarantee that the accommodation actually suits the interests and will of the minority group. However, it is essential, in my opinion, that for the group accommodation to be regarded as multicultural/liberal it must accord with the predominant wishes of the group members. This requirement stems from a basic notion of justice that anyone who is required to follow the classification of norms 'must in principle have an effective voice in its consideration and to be able to agree to it without coercion.'[31] I also think that if the group, religious or otherwise, is accommodated by granting it powers of autonomy, such as the capacity to establish religious courts and apply religious norms over group members, that the relevant community members will be asked not only whether they are interested in such an accommodation in general but also whether the particular form of the accommodation is also accepted by the majority of the relevant group. It is exactly this standard pertaining to the will of the majority among the group which to my mind makes the essential difference between a group accommodation that is coercive in nature (accepted only by a minority within the minority) and one which is multicultural in nature (accepted by the majority of the group). I also believe that the more the group accommodation permits the imposition of group norms on group members, such as the power to apply religious norms on them, the more imperative it is to find a majority among the accommodated group that approves of the accommodations and of its different features. Additionally, for group accommodations to be truly multicultural, they must serve the individual members of the community. After all, multiculturalism is based on a liberal conception pertaining to the subjective well-being of the individual member.

If we accept this condition, then there is a serious doubt whether the accommodations granted to some of the Palestinian-Arab religious communities qualify as multicultural. One example is the Greek Orthodox community. This community is controlled by a group of a foreign clergy from Greece, who can barely speak Arabic, which is the language of the local Palestinian-Arab Greek Orthodox community. The judges of the Greek Orthodox ecclesiastical courts are appointed at the sole discretion of the Church's administration without any input or supervision from either state authorities or the community members. This situation used to be the norm also in other Middle-Eastern countries, such as Egypt, but it was changed through reform that abolished foreign control of local churches. However, calls for a similar change by the Palestinian-Arab Greek Orthodox community have not been answered, either before or after the establishment of the State of Israel.[32] It is thus questionable whether the existing accommodations granted to this community are really multicultural, given that the constituency it is meant to accommodate actually objects to its form and practice.

This is also true to some extent of the Muslim community. Although their community affairs were handled over the years by *qadis* and *imams* coming from the community itself, state authorities have applied different control policies over the handling of community affairs. This policy was evident in the appointment process of these religious figures to their posts, always conducted under the close supervision of government authorities. A request made by Muslim leaders to have a Muslim as head of Muslim affairs in what used to be the Ministry of Religious Affairs was denied, and the position was 'passed from one Jew to another.'[33] Another instance demonstrating how religious accommodations can stand against the wishes of the religious community is concerned not in what has been granted but more with what has been taken away. This was the case of the handling of Muslim religious endowments (*waqf* property) by state authorities. Through a series of legal enactments, these endowments were defined as absentee property, based on the fact that several members of the Supreme Muslim Council, the body that administered the property in Mandatory Palestine, had fled the country.[34] This allowed the State of Israel, through the authority of a governmental organ called the Custodian of Absentee Property, to take over this property. This again raises the question of whether the jurisdiction and authority granted to the Muslim community in Israel is really autonomous and whether it can be seen as multicultural. Is it conceivable that the Muslim community would agree to such measures?

Another major problem with classifying the religious accommodations of the Palestinian-Arab community in Israel as multicultural has to do with the nature of the norms applied by some of the religious communities to matters within their exclusive jurisdiction, i.e. matters of marriage and divorce. The literature dealing with multicultural theory has noted the predicament that arises from accommodations to groups. As groups are accommodated, especially by empowering them to apply their norms to their members, the individual rights of certain members, primarily women and children, can be severely undermined,[35] even if the majority within the group is willing to go along with the accommodation. In liberal discourse concerned with individual well-being, there have been suggestions to legitimize only certain forms of group accommodations, such as instruments designed to protect the specific group from the larger society (external protections) but not accommodations that allow the group to prescribe norms against its own members (internal restrictions).[36] One test that is applied is whether an internal restriction allows an individual belonging to the group to 'exit' from the group, thereby having some form of relief from the internal restrictions.[37]

The proposed solutions of the multicultural predicament are problematic in a number of ways.[38] Even when groups are accommodated by external protections, the accommodation often works to preserve existing social structures, such as patriarchal practices, thus indirectly legitimizing gender discrimination within the group. As to the question of exit, some individuals cannot leave their group; others might want to be free from one particular norm but not from others, and still want to be part of their group. Some systems lack a sphere that one can exit to, thus making the option of exit unrealistic.[39]

Taking these and other cases into account, one proposition of group rights theory stands out as uncontestable: the greater the external group accommodation granted by the territorial legal system, the less such a system will be able to provide internal guarantees of individual well-being. This refers particularly to hierarchically organized groups, such as religious communities,[40] but is less applicable to cultural groups that are accommodated in an effort to preserve aspects of their cultural identity that are not hierarchically organized, such as language.

In light of the foregoing reservations, it is unfortunately clear that the religious accommodations granted to the Palestinian-Arab religious communities cannot be regarded as multicultural. I would like to offer two reasons why the existing accommodation cannot qualify as multicultural. First, the religious jurisdiction accorded to the different Palestinian-Arab religious communities embodies several forms of internal restrictions, especially in respect to gender inequality. One example is the divorce norms applied by some of these communities. Under Islamic and Druze family law, the husband can unilaterally dissolve the marriage without stating any cause for his action, while the wife cannot.[41] Another example can be found in the Code of Family Law of the Greek Orthodox community, most of which was compiled in the fourteenth century in the Byzantine Empire.[42] The Code allows only a limited number of causes for divorce that are unequal in terms of gender. Thus, for example, under the Code the husband can petition the Greek Orthodox court for divorce if his wife slept outside of their house without his permission. This does not apply to the husband. Most intriguing are the causes under which divorce cannot be granted: a wife cannot petition for divorce if she was whipped by her husband or beaten by him with a stick. Yet these outmoded laws are maintained by accommodations granted to this community.

Second, in Israel there is no exit option mainly because there is no civil regulatory-scheme of marriage and divorce that can offer a sphere to which an individual can exit to. So even if Arab citizens, especially women, came to exit their group jurisdiction,[43] given the exclusive jurisdiction accorded to their community religious courts in matters of marriage and divorce, they have nowhere to go.

There are thus serious doubts as to whether the religious accommodations for the Palestinian-Arab community qualify as multicultural. In essence what they really represent is a group accommodation that is neither liberal nor multicultural in nature.

RELIGIOUS ACCOMMODATIONS AND INSTITUTIONAL JUDICIAL REVIEW

Characterizing the accommodations granted to the Palestinian-Arab religious communities as multicultural is not merely a matter of semantics, since this carries with it a major legal implication: a restricted form of judicial review on the part of state institutions relating to the actions of Palestinian-Arab religious communities.[44] From the point of view of the religious community, this reserved form of judicial review no doubt works to strengthen the community structure by giving the community institutions more leeway in conducting their internal affairs. However, from the point of view of members of the community with liberal agendas, this restricted form of judicial review weakens them when coming to contest their community's authority. In the literature dealing with multicultural accommodations, the United States Supreme Court case of *Santa Clara Pueblo v Martinez*[45] stands out as a powerful example.[46] According to the rules of the Native American Santa Clara Pueblo tribe, the offspring of a woman who marries outside the tribe are not considered tribe members, whereas the offspring of a man who marries outside the tribe are tribe members. These rules were contested in court as discriminatory, but the United States Supreme Court accepted the tribal rules as instrumental in the self-definition of the tribe, and denied judicial relief to the petitioners. Although the decision fosters the Native American tribe's autonomy, it simultaneously works to undermine the rights of individual female members of the tribe and their offspring, who were raised in the tribe yet were denied membership.[47]

A similar multicultural predicament exists in Palestinian-Arab religious communities, especially in the 10 Christian communities. On the one hand, these communities have the highest degree of autonomy in handling their internal affairs.[48] Not only are they free to apply the respective laws of marriage and divorce to their members, but unlike other religious communities, they are free to appoint the clergy to their religious courts without the involvement or supervision of any public official or agency. This state of affairs may not be in the best interest of individual members of these communities. While community identity is no doubt strengthened by such autonomy, the rights of individuals are severely undermined. This is evident for example in matters of divorce among Christians, for according to the Catholic and Orthodox codes divorce is either forbidden or severely restricted, and in many cases does not depend on the mutual consent of the couple.

The Israeli Supreme Court further strengthened the autonomy of the religious courts at the expense of individual members in the case of *Jadday v President of the Judgments Execution Office*.[49] After the Greek Catholic Melkite Ecclesiastical Court found a husband liable to pay alimony to his wife, the husband petitioned the Israel Supreme Court, arguing that the composition of the Greek Catholic Melkite Ecclesiastical Court of Appeals was illegal. This was, according to the husband, because the judges who reviewed his appeal were appointed by the Greek Catholic Melkite Patriarch, who resides in Lebanon, which is at war with Israel.

The court denied the husband remedy, claiming that the rules of war do not prevent Israel from recognizing the authority of the Greek Catholic Melkite Patriarch in Lebanon, and that Israel, by preserving the existing *millets*, had also accepted the existing hierarchical structure of the these churches.

The court's stance in *Jaday* is admirable in terms of granting a religious organization freedom in conducting its internal affairs. Few states would recognize the authority of a foreign institution that also happens to be operating from what is conceived to be an enemy state. However, this same configuration is extremely problematic from the point of view of the individual petitioner seeking judicial assistance to secure the proper administration of authority within his or her religious community. Even if the Greek Catholic Melkite Patriarch in Lebanon had misused his authority, an administrative review of his actions by the Israeli Supreme Court would be ineffective, given that the Patriarch resides in Lebanon. The recognition of the patriarch's authority strengthens the internal structure of the ecclesiastical court system, but diminishes the capacity of individual members to seek judicial review from state authorities.

Jewish religious institutions in Israel, on the other hand, are treated in a fundamentally different way. The wide statutory recognition these institutions have received makes them susceptible to a lively judicial and administrative review by the civil authorities, especially the Israeli Supreme Court.[50] The vibrant discussion of religion and state within the Jewish community has also generated strong feelings among Israeli decision-makers and their constituencies. Judges and other state officials who deal with controversies of concern to the Jewish community are influenced in the judgment process by their own personal ideals.[51] Many officials come from the secular Jewish community and they actively promote their secular ideals, resulting in the weakening of religious norms and the religious establishment within the Jewish community, and the concomitant strengthening of individual members.[52]

This was made evident in the case of *Shakdiel v The Minister of Religious Affairs*.[53] The case dealt with a petition filed by an observant Jewish woman, Lea Shakdiel, who sought membership in the Jewish religious council of the town of Yeruham. Ms. Shakdiel had been denied membership because she was a woman. In this respect it is important to note that Jewish religious councils are established under the Jewish Religious Services Law of 1972. Each of the established religious councils provides a wide range of religious services in the localities they serve, such as the 'performance of wedding ceremonies, maintenance and operation of ritual baths (*mikvaot*), support for synagogues and other religious institutions, and arranging cultural activities of a religious nature.'[54] The court accepted the petition and held the religious council's restriction on female membership to be illegal. The judgment itself is comprehensive in terms of providing Jewish law sources that back the petitioner's pursuit for equal treatment in such bodies as the religious councils. However, the main holding of the Court was that once the religious councils had gained statutory recognition it became necessary to judge their actions according to the norms of Israel's administrative law—a body of law that forbids discrimination on the basis of sex.[55]

However, because of the paradigm of separateness I mentioned earlier, the religious institutions of the Palestinian-Arab religious communities received only minimal statutory recognition.[56] Additionally, the Palestinian-Arab political agenda is principally nationalistic. Even with the rise of Islam as a political movement among this minority,[57] no real secular movement has emerged that actively and positively advocates a secular political agenda, let alone an anti-religious one. Interestingly, the Communist party, for a long time active in leading the national struggle of the Palestinian-Arab community in Israel,[58] has seldom if ever discussed religion and state issues concerning this community.[59] The lack of real debate within the Palestinian-Arab community is more remarkable given the vibrant nature of the debate over religion and state within the Jewish community. Indeed, scholarly work on religion and state in Israel has occasionally noted that the Palestinian-Arab community seems to be acquiescent in terms of the jurisdictional powers accorded to their religious institutions.[60]

A similar outcome is discernable when the Israeli Supreme Court deals with the judicial capacity of religious courts to deal with personal status matters. While the Court consistently limits the jurisdictional capacity of Jewish rabbinical courts, it expands the jurisdictional capacity of the Palestinian-Arab religious courts.[61]

The severe effect of the religious norms on the well-being of individual members was not lost on the Knesset (the Israeli parliament) and the Israeli Supreme Court. Over the years a number of measures were taken to safeguard individual well-being against the encroaching effect of group religious norms.[62] The Knesset has taken the following steps:

1) Criminalizing polygamy,[63] unilateral divorce[64] and the solemnization of marriage of minors (under the age of 17);[65]
2) Guaranteeing the equal inheritance rights of minors even when the inheritance proceeding is handled by a religious court;[66]
3) Recognizing common law marriages, thereby offering individuals who are unable to marry according to their relevant religious norms the possibility of instituting a form of partnership;
4) Restricting the exclusive jurisdiction of Muslim Shari'a Courts and Christian courts only to matters of marriage and divorce, where before these courts had exclusive jurisdiction to adjudicate alimony claims filed by Muslim and Christian wives against their husbands, to the detriment of the petitioners.

On part of the Israeli Supreme Court one can mention:

1) In 1970 the Court rejected a polygamous Muslim husband's claim that the Israeli court was jurisdictionally incompetent to try his indictment on the grounds that the second marriage was solemnized outside the sovereign borders of the State of Israel.[67]
2) In 1984, the Court recognized a cause of action in torts for the unilateral divorce of a Muslim wife in light of the fact that such an act constitutes a criminal act, even if valid under Shari'a.[68]
3) In 1995 and despite previous rulings, the Court was not willing to recognize the exclusive jurisdiction of Shari'a courts to adjudicate a paternity action brought by a married Muslim wife against a man who was not her husband.[69]
4) In 2004 and despite previous rulings, the Court dismissed the claim that the Druze religious courts had ancillary jurisdiction to deal

with an alimony claim when a divorce claim was already pending before it.[70]

Some doubts were cast as to whether these measures were effective. Very few are prosecuted for polygamy,[71] and the law on the marriage of minors has never been fully enforced.[72] I would also venture to say that this is the case with respect to prosecution for unilateral divorce. Serious doubts have been raised as to whether the establishment of a concurrent jurisdictional capacity is ultimately beneficial for women.[73] Moreover, some of these reforms took place not to improve legislation but in order to level the field among the religious communities.

The perceived multicultural/liberal nature of the jurisdiction accorded to the Palestinian-Arab religious community has presented itself as imaginary rather than real. When examined against the normative ideals of multiculturalism/liberalism, serious doubts arise as to whether the existing structure is indeed as it is perceived to be. The labeling, therefore, serves as a curse—it affords the existing structure legitimacy that it does not have.

THE POTENTIAL FOR REFORM

Even if the characterization of the jurisdiction accorded to the Palestinian-Arab religious communities as a multicultural/liberal accommodation is a normative myth, it can still have a number of significant implications on how the courts and the Israeli establishment deal with the existing jurisdictional capacity of these communities. In the preceding discussion I have demonstrated how this perception can adversely affect individual members who are disinterested in the internal restriction of their respective religious communities. But this curse can turn into a blessing. The same liberal/multicultural perception can serve as a powerful springboard for the advancement of important internal reforms if they happen to be liberal in nature. If the particular Palestinian-Arab religious community or the Palestinian-Arab community at large seeks to advance modern liberal norms to govern their family law—perception by which their jurisdiction in the sphere of family law is liberal/multicultural will assure the initiative a free sail forward. Moreover, given that this jurisdictional competency is conceived as separate and different from that of the Jewish community then they cannot be foiled on the pretext of jeopardizing Jewish unity or muddling Jewish identity.

One central example is the basic legal instrument regulating surrogacy agreements in Israel: the Surrogate Motherhood Agreement Law of 1996 (SMAL).[74] This legislation is partially influenced by Jewish law (*halakha*), especially in determining the preconditions necessary for making valid surrogacy agreements.[75] One such precondition is the requirement contained in SMAL, section 2(5), under which the carrying mother must be of the same religion as the intended mother.[76] However, since the dictates of Jewish *halakha* are irrelevant to the non-Jewish population, the same section allows surrogacy agreements to deviate from the religious matching requirement, 'where all parties to the agreement are non-Jews.' So when all parties to the surrogacy agreement happen to be Palestinian-Arabs, the provision for religious matching is relaxed. This scheme benefits Palestinian-Arabs, even though this may not have been the section's intention, for it increases their chances of finding a surrogate mother from among this religiously diverse national community.

The normative implication of allowing non-Jewish populations greater leeway in religious accommodations in surrogacy and in other cases can be a catalyst for intra-group reforms. Because of their separateness, the religious accommodations for the Palestinian-Arab religious communities can be rearranged without affecting the dictates of Jewish religious-secular agreements, or, for that matter, any other internal Jewish compromise. Indeed, a number of factors have so far conspired to make it difficult for institutions inside and outside the Palestinian-Arab religious communities to initiate reforms in intra-group practices. However, notwithstanding the effects of such factors, in some spheres Palestinian-Arab religious communities can push for intra-group reforms with very good chances of success. The internal organization of the Palestinian-Arab religious communities might be one such sphere. For example, the recognition that religious accommodations of Palestinian-Arab religious communities are justified on a group accommodation basis legitimizes the claim that the community should be free to pursue elections for all community institutions. Once religious officials become accountable to their constituencies, they will work harder to safeguard the interests of individual members, and thus lessen the intensity of the predicaments that arise between the group and the individual. In fact, certain events provide *prima facie* evidence that major religious Palestinian-Arab communities, such as the Muslim[77] and the Greek Orthodox[78] are indeed interested in increasing the control of their community members over religious institutions. If the political leadership of the Palestinian-Arab community takes up this cause, there are good chances for achieving major reforms in the internal organization of Palestinian-Arab religious communities.

The blessing in characterizing the jurisdiction of Palestinian-Arab religious communities over matters of family law as liberal/multicultural in nature can also be realized if and when one of these religious communities opts for adopting a more liberal regime of norms to regulate their families. This indeed was the case in regard to the Druze community. The Druze community gained full official recognition as an independent religious community in 1957.[79] Some four years later, the religious leadership of the community adopted the Druze family law in effect in Lebanon.[80] The Israeli establishment, represented by the Ministry of Religions, saw no need to intervene in the substantive norms pertaining to the Druze community, perceiving such a matter as "an internal matter of the community."[81] Yet it should be noted that this code of family law was known as a most advanced code of norms prescribing that the husband should treat his wife as an equal partner, complete restriction on polygamy, making the husband's adultery a cause for divorce, and entitling the wife with monetary compensation if unjustly divorced.[82]

I also venture in saying that such reforms, if initiated today in other Palestinian-Arab religious communities, would probably be backed by Jewish secular forces as well, mainly due to the effect this may have on relations between religious and secular Jews. If religious institutions within the Palestinian-Arab community can undergo such reforms that guarantee the accountability of the religious institutions to community members, then the Jewish community should also attempt to implement such reforms; although that would be a much wider reform that would affect the very definition of the state itself.

CONCLUSION

This chapter has sought to discuss the common perception of the religious accommodations for the Palestinian-Arab minority in Israel as a form a liberal/multicultural accommodation. I dealt with the essential question of whether these accommodations actually qualify as such and the meaning of the corollary to this, the reserved judicial review on intra-religious institutions and practices. Although in one sense the religious accommodations of the Palestinian-Arab minority are not liberal/multicultural and may therefore be seen as unjust, I stressed that the liberal/multicultural myth of the accommodations can be strategically used as a fulcrum to change the current situation. The answer to the question asked in the title of this paper, whether religious accommodations for the Palestinian-Arab minority are a blessing or a curse, would have to be that they are both: at present more a burden than a benefit, but one that, with proper management, may turn out to be a blessing in disguise.

NOTES

1   See Jacob T. Levy, "Classifying Cultural Rights," in *Ethnicity and Group Rights*, ed. Ian Shapiro and Will Kymlicka (New York: New York University Press, 1997), 22.

2   Individual and group identity: some perceive the religious community as possessing a right for religious liberty that is independent of the right of individuals for religious liberty. Under this perception, the religious community as such has a right to organize in order to maintain its separate group identity. See Julian Rivers, "Religious Liberty as a Collective Right," in *Law and Religion*, ed. Richard O'Dair and Andrew Lewis (New York: Oxford University Press, 2001), 227, 231.

3   Will Kymlicka, *Liberalism, Community and Culture* (New York: Oxford University Press, 1989); Joseph Raz, "Multiculturalism," *Ratio Juris* 11 (1998): 193; Joseph Raz, "Multiculturalism: A Liberal Perspective," *Dissent* 41 (1994): 67.

4   Susan Moller Okin, "Is Multiculturalism Bad for Women?" in *Is Multiculturalism Bad for Women? Susan Moller Okin with Respondents*, ed. Joshua Cohen, Matthew Howard, and Martha C. Nussbaum (Princeton: Princeton University Press, 1999), 7.

5   See *Wisconsin v Yoder*, 406 US 205 (1972).

6   CBS Statistical Abstract of Israel 2009, available online: http://www.cbs.gov.il/ shnaton60/shnaton60_all.pdf, Table 2.1 [CBS Statistical Abstract].

7   Ibid.

8   The relevant provision is that of a 1970 amendment: *Law of Return (Amendment no 2)* 5730-1970, 14 LSI 28 (1969/70), article 4A(a): "The rights of a Jew under this Law and the rights of an *oleh* under the Nationality Law, as well as the rights of an *oleh* under any other enactment, are also vested in a child and a grandchild of a Jew, the spouse of a Jew, the spouse of a child of a Jew and the spouse of a grandchild of a Jew, except for a person who has been a Jew and has voluntarily changed his religion." The amendment adds in article 4B: "For the purposes of this Law, 'Jew' means a person who is born of a Jewish mother or has become converted to Judaism and who is not a member of another religion." See generally, Menashe Shava, "Comments on the Law of Return (Amendment No. 2), 5730-1970 (Who is a Jew?)," *Tel-Aviv University Studies in Law* 3 (1977): 295..

9   CBS Statistical Abstract, supra note 6, at 79.

10   Ibid.

11   See Shlomit Levy et al., *A Portrait of Israeli Jewry: Beliefs, Observations, and Values Among Israeli Jews* (Jerusalem: The Israeli Democracy Institute, 2002), 5–6. "Division of Traditional and Religious Communities: Palestinian-Arab Community," CBS Statistical Abstract, Table 2.2.

12   See Ephraim Tabory, "The Israel Reform and Conservative Movements and the Market for Liberal Judaism," in *Jews in Israel: Contemporary Social and Cultural Patterns*, ed. Uzi Rebhun and Chaim I. Waxman (Lebanon, NH: University Press of New England, 2004), 285; Basheva E. Genut, "Note, Competing Visions of the Jewish State: Promoting and Protecting Freedom of Religion in Israel," *Fordham International Law Journal* 19 (1996): 2210, 2151; Izhak Englard, "Law and Religion in Israel," *American Journal of Comparative Law* 35 (1987): 185, 191.

13   CBS Statistical Abstract, supra note 6, at Table 2.2.

14   See R. Gottschalk, "Personal Status and Religious Law in Israel," *International Law Quarterly* 4 (1951): 454–55. The Evangelical Episcopal Church was recognized in 1970: see Order of Recognition of a Religious Community (Evangelical Episcopal Church in Israel), 1970, K.T. 2557, 1564. Bahai community: Order of Religious Community (The Bahai Faith), 1971, K.T. 2673, 628.

15   *Order of Religious Community (The Bahai Faith)*, 1971, KT 2673, at 628.

16   See Marc Galanter and Jayanth Krishnan, "Personal Law and Human Rights in India and Israel," *Israeli Law Review* 34 (2000): 101; Amnon Rubinstein, "Law and Religion in Israel," *Israeli Law Review* 2 (1967): 380, 384–88; Amnon Rubinstein, "State and Religion in Israel," *Journal of Contemporary History* 2 (1967): 107, 111–12. See also Asher Maoz, "Religious Human Rights in the State of Israel," in *Religious Human Rights in Global Perspective: Legal Perspectives*, ed. Johan D. van der Vyver and John Witte, Jr. (The Hague: M. Nijhoff Publishers, 1996), 349, 355; Asher Maoz, "Enforcement of Religious Courts' Judgments under Israeli Law," *Journal of Church and State* 33 (1991): 473.

17   See Michael M. Karayanni, "The Separate Nature of the Religious Accommodations for the Palestinian-Arab Minority in Israel," *Northwestern University Journal of International Human Rights* 5 (2006): 41; Michael M. Karayanni, "Living in a Group of One's Own: Normative Implications Related to the Private Nature of the Religious

Accommodations for the Palestinian-Arab Minority in Israel," *UCLA Journal of Islamic and Near Eastern Law* 6 (2007): 1.

18   See Ilan Saban, "Minority Rights in Deeply Divided Societies: A Framework for Analysis and the Case of the Arab-Palestinian Minority in Israel," *New York University Journal of International Law and Politics* 36 (2004): 885, 900, 942–48, 954–60, characterizing the religious accommodations granted to the Palestinian-Arab minority in Israel as a "group-differentiated right" and as a "modest form of self-government"; David Kretzmer, *The Legal Status of the Arabs in Israel* (Boulder, CO: Westview Press, 1990), 163–68, discussing the religious organization of the Palestinian-Arab religious communities under the heading of "group rights"; see also Itzhak Zamir, "Equality of Rights for Arabs in Israel," *Mishpat u-Mimshal* 9 (2005): 11, 26, 30 [Hebrew], regarding the jurisdiction of Palestinian-Arab religious communities to adjudicate matters of marriage and divorce as a group right; Amnon Rubinstein and Barak Medina, *The Constitutional Law of the State of Israel,* 6th ed. (Jerusalem: Schocken, 2005) 429–35 [Hebrew], referring to the religious organization of the Palestinian-Arab religious communities as a limited form of self-government.

19   See Edoardo Vitta, *The Conflict of Laws in Matters of Personal Status in Palestine* (Tel-Aviv: S. Bursi, 1947), 3–4.

20   See Asher Maoz, "State and Religion in Israel," in *International Perspectives on Church and State,* ed. Menachem Mor (Omaha, NB: Creighton University Press, 1993), 239, 243: "divest Jewish culture and heritage from religious elements and one is left rather empty handed." Therefore, scholars in Israel who seek to legitimize the Jewish character of the State of Israel go out of their way to stress how wrong it is to impose Jewish religious norms on members who do not opt for a religious life-style. See Alexander Yakobson and Amnon Rubinstein, *Israel and the Family of Nations: Jewish Nation-State and Human Rights* (Jerusalem: Schocken, 2003), 150–65 [Hebrew]; Asa Kasher, *Spirit of a Man: Four Gates* (Tel Aviv: Am Oved, 2000), 19 [Hebrew].

21   Rubinstein, "Law and Religion," 408, notes that while under Ottoman rule and the British Mandate, the religious accommodations granted to the Jewish community were motivated by the value of autonomy and the interest of not intervening in the internal affairs of the Jewish community, the reason today is the "reverse: the interest is that of preserving the unity of the Jewish People." Nationalization of Jewish religious accommodation:

22   I have previously doubted the normative utility of the public–private distinction, given the fact that many public interests can be translated into private ones and vice versa. See Michael M. Karayanni, "The Myth and Reality of a Controversy: 'Public Factors' and the *Forum Non Conveniens* Doctrine," *Wisconsin International Law Journal* 21 (2003): 327.

23   *See* Ian Lustick, *Arabs in the Jewish State: Israel's Control of a National Minority* (Austin: University of Texas Press, 1980).

24   Kais M. Firro, *The Druzes in the Jewish State: A Brief History* (Leiden: Brill: 1999), 102–4; Majid Al-Haj, *Education, Empowerment, and Control: The Case of the Arabs in Israel* (Albany: University of New York Press, 1995), 73, 121.

25   Sammy Smooha, "The Model of Ethnic Democracy: Israel as a Jewish and Democratic State," *Nations and Nationalism* 8 (2002): 475, 485, maintaining that religious endogamy as preserved by the religious communities is one of a number of measures used to preserve Jewish identity. See also Ruth Gavison, "Jewish and Democratic? A

Rejoinder to the 'Ethnic Democracy' Debate," *Israel Studies* 4 (1999): 44, 45, stating that "even the decision to grant the Arabs [in Israel] linguistic autonomy and not to assimilate them into Jewish culture was made by Jews, and primarily for Jewish interests."

26   See Partition Plan with Economic Union, annexed to Resolution Adopted on the Report of the Ad Hoc Committee on the Palestinian Question: Future Government of Palestine, G.A. Res. 181(II), U.N. Doc. A/RES/181(II) (Nov. 29, 1947), chapter 2(4): "The family law and personal status of the various minorities and their religious interests, including endowments, shall be respected."

27   David M. Neuhaus, "Between Quiescence and Arousal: The Political Functions of Religion, A Case Study of the Arab Minority in Israel: 1948–1990" (PhD diss., Hebrew University of Jerusalem, 1991), 16, states that traditional religious institutions within the Arab minority have sought to preserve traditional confessionalism "in their efforts to preserve the social structure from which their authority derives."

28   Manar Hasan, "The Politics of Honor: The Patriarchy, the State and the Murder of Women in the Name of Family Honor," in *Sex, Gender, Politics*, ed. Dafna N. Israeli et al. (Tel Aviv: Ha-Kibbutz ha-Me'uhad, 1999), 267, 297–301 [Hebrew]. See also Aida Touma-Sliman, "Culture, National Minority and the State: Working Against the 'Crime of Family Honour' within the Palestinian Community in Israel," in *"Honour": Crimes, Paradigms, and Violence against Women*, ed. Lynn Welchman and Sara Hossain (London: Zed Books, 2005), 181–82; Ran Hirschl and Ayelet Shachar, "Constitutional Transformation, Gender Equality, and Religious/National Conflict in Israel: Tentative Progress through the Obstacle Course," in *The Gender of Constitutional Jurisprudence*, ed. Beverley Baines and Ruth Rubio-Marin (Cambridge: Cambridge University Press, 2005), 205, 224–25.

29   Michael M. Karayanni, "In the Best Interests of the Group: Religious Matching under Israeli Adoption Law," *Berkeley Journal of Middle Eastern and Islamic Law* 3 (2010): 1, 36–61.

30   See Karayanni, "The Separate Nature of the Religious Accommodations"; Karayanni, "Living in a Group of One's Own."

31   Iris Marion Young, *Justice and the Politics of Difference* (Princeton: Princeton University Press, 1990), 34.

32   See Daphne Tsimhoni, "The Greek Orthodox Community in Jerusalem and the West Bank, 1948–1978: A Profile of a Religious Minority in a National State," *Orient* 23 (1982): 281. Indeed it is because of this distance between the local Greek Orthodox community and the Greek clergy that associations and clubs, governed by community members, developed among the Greek Orthodox community. See Daphne Tsimhoni, "Continuity and Change in Communal Autonomy: The Christian Communal Organizations in Jerusalem 1948–80," *Middle Eastern Studies* 22 (1986): 398.

33   Mark A. Tessler, "The Middle East: The Jews in Tunisia and Morocco and Arabs in Israel," in *Protection of Ethnic Minorities: Comparative Perspectives*, ed. Robert G. Wirsing (New York: Pergamon Press, 1981), 245, 265.

34   See Kretzmer, *The Legal Status of the Arabs*, 167–68. See also Alisa Rubin-Peled, *Debating Islam in the Jewish State: The Development of Policy toward Islamic Institutions in Israel* (Albany: State University of New York Press, 2001).

35   Avigail Eisenberg and Jeff Spinner-Halev, eds., *Minorities within Minorities: Equality, Rights and Diversity* (Cambridge: Cambridge University Press, 2005); Ayelet Shachar,

Multicultural Jurisdictions: Cultural Differences and Women's Rights (Cambridge: Cambridge University Press, 2001); Leslie Green, "Internal Minorities and Their Rights," in *The Rights of Minority Cultures*, ed. Will Kymlicka (New York: Oxford University Press, 1995), 257–58.

36   Will Kymlicka, *Multicultural Citizenship: A Liberal Theory of Minority Rights* (New York: Oxford University Press, 1995), 37, argues that "liberals can and should endorse certain external protections where they promote fairness between groups but should reject internal restrictions which limit the right of group members to question and revise traditional authorities and practices."

37   On the different roles of exit in multicultural theory see Oanagh Reitman, "On Exit," in *Minorities within Minorities*, ed. Eisenberg and Spinner-Halev, 189.

38   See Suzanne Last Stone, "The Intervention of American Law in Jewish Divorce: A Pluralist Analysis," *Israeli Law Review* 34 (2000): 170.

39   L. Green, "Internal Minorities and their Rights," in *The Rights of Minority Cultures* (Oxford: Oxford University Press, 1995), 256, 264–67.

40   See Frances Raday, "Culture, Religion and Gender," *International Journal of Constitutional Law* 1 (2003): 663.

41   See HCJ 2829/03 Plonit v. Druze Appellate Court in Acre [2006] IsrSC 60(4) 159.

42   See Frederic M. Goadby, *International and Inter-Religious Private Law in Palestine* (Jerusalem: Hamadpis Press, 1926), 134–35 .

43   Catherine A. MacKinnon, "Sex Equality under the Constitution of India: Problems, Prospects, and 'Personal Laws,'" *International Journal of Constitutional Law* 4 (2006): 181, 198–202.

44   Ori Stendel, *The Minorities in Israel: Trends in the Development of the Arab and Druze Communities 1948–1973* (Jerusalem: Israel Economist, 1973), 8: "from the establishment of the State, the government's policy has been not to interfere in the religious affairs of the various communities," and all communities "maintain a considerable measure of internal autonomy"; Martin Edelman, *Courts, Politics, and Culture in Israel* (Charlottesville, VA: University Press of Virginia, 1994), 88, 98–99, argues that reforming the personal law of the non-Jewish population in Israel has not been a government priority and that the government refrained from intervening in such issues so as not to aggravate minority religions by insisting that they conform to the majority's norms.

45   *Martinez*, 436 US 49 (1978).

46   See Shachar, *Multicultural Jurisdictions*, 18–20.

47   In *Martinez*, 436 US 49, denial of membership for children meant also denial of emergency medical treatment by the Indian Health Service, for which one of the children was in dire need.

48   See State of Israel, Implementation of the International Covenant on Civil and Political Rights (ICCPR): Combined Initial and First Periodic Report of the State of Israel (1998), 227: "compared to the other religious communities in Israel, the Christian communities maintain the highest degree of independence in managing their affairs."

49   HCJ 101/54, [1955] IsrSC 9, 135.

50   See Izhak Englard, "The Conflict between State and Religion in Israel: Its Ideological Background," in *International Perspectives*, ed. Mor, 219, 231.

51 Gidon Sapir, "Law or Politics: Israeli Constitutional Adjudication as a Case Study," *UCLA Journal of International Law and Foreign Affairs* 6 (2001): 169, argues that Israeli constitutional adjudication in religion and state matters is to a large extent a matter of politics rather than law, especially because Supreme Court Justices tended to reach legal conclusions that better suited their ideological background.

52 See Asher Cohen and Bernard Susser, *Israel and the Politics of Jewish Identity: The Secular-Religious Impasse* (Baltimore, MD: Johns Hopkins University Press 2000), 97–106. See also Gideon Sapir, "Religion and State in Israel: The Case for Reevaluation and Constitutional Entrenchment," *Hastings International and Comparative Law Review* 22 (1999): 617.

53 HCJ 153/87, [1988] IsrSC 42(2) 221 [*Shakdiel*].

54 Israel ICCPR Report, supra note 47, at 244.

55 Shakdiel, supra note 52, at 234, 236, 238 and 241 (per Justice Elon); at 273, 274 and 275, 278 (per Justice Barak).

56 Karayanni, "Living in a Group of One's Own," at 8–15.

57 See Joel S. Migdal and Baruch Kimmerling, "The Odd Man Out: Arabs in Israel," in Joel S. Migdal, *Through the Lens of Israel: Explorations in State and Society* (Albany, NY: State University of New York Press, 2001), 173, 191.

58 See Elie Rekhess, *The Arab Minority in Israel: Between Communism and Arab Nationalism 1965–1991* (Tel-Aviv: Ha-Kibbutz ha-Me'uhad, 1993) [in Hebrew].

59 See Danny Rubinstein, "The Religious-Secular Rift Among Israeli Arabs," *State and Religion Yearbook 5755-5754* (Tel Aviv: Ha-Kibbutz ha-Me'uhad, 1994), 89 [Hebrew].

60 See Ruth Lapidoth and Michael Corinaldi, "Freedom of Religion in Israel," *Israeli Reports to the XIV International Congress of Comparative Law,* ed. Mordechai Rabello (Jerusalem: Harry Sacher Institute for Legislative Research and Comparative Law, 1994), 273, 289: "although the jurisdiction of the Rabbinical Courts is no broader than that of some of the other communities, it has given rise to special problems and considerable opposition from many Jews, while it seems that no such resentment with regard to tribunals of other religious communities has been recorded." See also Steven V. Mazie, *Israel's Higher Law: Religion and Liberal Democracy in the Jewish State* (Lanham, MD: Lexington Books, 2006), 213.

61 Pinhas Shifman, *Family Law in Israel*, 2nd ed. (1995), 364–65 [in Hebrew]; Pinhas Shifman, "Jurisdiction of Rabbinical Courts over Marriage and Divorce Effected Abroad," *Mishpatim* 6 (1975): 372 [in Hebrew]; Yizhak Kahan, "Rabbinic and Secular Jurisdiction in Israel," *Diné Israel* 7 (1976): 205, 208 [in Hebrew].

62 For a general survey of the improvements civil norms have brought to Muslim women in Israel, see Aharon Layish, *Women and Islamic Law in a Non-Muslim State: A Study Based on Decisions of the Shari'a Courts in Israel* (New Brunswick, NJ: Transaction Publishers, 2006).

63 *Penal Law*, 5737-1977, section 176, LSI Special Volume: Penal Law (1977).

64 *Penal Law*, section 181.

65 *Marriage Age Law*, 5710-1950, 4 LSI 158 (1949–50).

66 *Succession Law*, 5725-1965, section 155(c), 19 LSI 58 (1964–65).

67 *State of Israel v Azaizeh* CrimA 135/70, [1970] IsrSC 24(1) 417.

68 *Sultan v Sultan* CA 245/81, [1984] IsrSC 38(3) 169.

69 *Plonit v Ploni* CA 3077/90, [1995] IsrSC 49(2) 578.

70 *Bader (Mari'ee) v Mari'ee* HCJ 9611/00, [2004] 58(4) IsrSC 256.

71 Polygamy prosecutions: see Anat Lapidot-Firilla and Ronny Elhadad, *Forbidden yet Practiced: Polygamy and the Cyclical Making of Israeli Policy*, Center for Strategic and Policy Studies Papers, No. 1 (Jerusalem: Hebrew University of Jerusalem, School of Public Policy, 2006), at http://public-policy.huji.ac.il/pub.asp?cat=242, (accessed June 26, 2012).

72 See Andrew Trietel, "Conflicting Traditions: Muslim Shari'a Courts and Marriage Age Regulation in Israel," *Columbia Human Rights Law Review* 26 (1995): 403.

73 See Menashe Shava, "The Proposed Family Court Act (Amendment No. 4) (Comparing Jurisdiction), 1998—Is It Truly a Blessing for Muslim and Christian Women?" *Ha-Praklit* 44 (1999): 358 [Hebrew].

74 *Surrogate Motherhood Agreement Law (Approval of the Agreement and Status of the Child)*, 5756-1996, SH 176.

75 See Carmel Shalev, "Halakha and Patriarchal Motherhood—An Anatomy of the New Israeli Surrogacy Law," *Israeli Law Review* 32 (1998): 51.

76 Ibid, at 66–67.

77 See *Al Sorouji v Minister of Religious Affairs* HCJ 282/61, [1963] IsrSC 17 188.

78 See Robert Brenton Betts, *Christians in the Arab East: A Political Study* (Atlanta, GA: John Knox Press, 1978), 44.

79 See Nissim Dana and Salman Fallah, "The Status of Druze and their Community Organization," in *The Druze* (Ramat-Gan: Bar-Ilan University Press, 1998), 159, 166 [Hebrew].

80 Ibid. at 169.

81 Ibid. at 168–69.

82 See Aharon Layish and Salman H. Fallah, "Communal Organization of the Druzes," in *The Arabs in Israel: Continuity and Change*, ed. Aharon Layish (Jerusalem: Magnes Press, 1981), 123, 134–35 [Hebrew]

PART V

SOCIETY, CULTURE, AND DEMOGRAPHY

Is Israeli Society Disintegrating? Doomsday Prophecies and Facts on the Ground

13

ALEXANDER YAKOBSON

It is well known that Israeli society is polarized, fragmented, and on the verge of disintegration. We have lost our common ground—or perhaps there never was real common ground, and it was all an illusion and a manipulation? The melting pot failed, but it has not been replaced with a properly multicultural society. The "community campfire" has disappeared—the various groups are gradually withdrawing into hostile, alienated ghettos. This is how Israeli society is described regularly: in the media, in the arts, and in academia. The description has largely come to be taken for granted. These are the basic assumptions underlying many analyses of the reality in Israel and of the future we are to expect. Many present this picture with regret and concern, while others do so with a strange sort of *schadenfreude*. There is, however, a broad consensus that this is indeed the general picture—and, in any case, that these are the prevailing trends: even if the pessimists are exaggerating in their descriptions, they are correct in identifying the general direction.[1]

In what follows, I intend to argue that the general picture is wrong, and even more importantly, that the main trend is the opposite of the one described above. The answer to the question: "are we still one people?"

is that today we are one people more than we ever were in the past. Of course, "one people" does not mean a uniform people, devoid of internal contradictions and exempt from disagreements. No such "one people" exists in the free world. In fact, this is obviously even more correct regarding the non-free world; political freedom means, first and foremost, the freedom to express and emphasize disagreements. Some of the complaints and criticisms that are voiced regarding the state of Israeli society are justified, some are exaggerated, while others are unfounded. All of this is normal in an open, free society, and one should not become over-excited, even about exaggerated criticism. Nevertheless, it is worthwhile to note, from time to time, the magnitude of the gap that has opened between reality and the fashionable way to present it. If it is true that criticism benefits the criticized, this rule should presumably apply to criticism of the criticism as well.

ONE PEOPLE—NOT TO BE TAKEN FOR GRANTED

The most fateful question relating to our "being one people"—not on the plane of ideological definitions, but as regards our basic ability to live and function in one state—is, of course, what in Israel is called "the communal question" ("communities" signifying the Jewish immigrants' different countries of origin). At the outset, it was not obvious that people from "seventy Diasporas"—according to the well-known Israeli cliché, which happens to be fairly accurate—about half of whom originated in Europe and half in the Islamic Middle East (while each half is comprised of sub-groups among which significant differences exist as well), could connect with each other to comprise a modern, functioning democratic nation. This accomplishment is today taken for granted, but, every so often, it is worth noting that it is unparalleled even in the history of countries that experienced mass immigration. No country has ever absorbed immigration on such a scale and under such conditions within such a short period. Within the first decade of the state, the 650,000 Jews in the country absorbed well over a million immigrants. Had France, for instance, absorbed more than 100 million immigrants within a decade, and immediately granted them French citizenship—what would have become of France? For a realistic comparison, we must have in mind not the wealthy, strong France of today, but post–World War II France.

The bloody riots that erupted on several occasions in East Timor can provide us with a certain comparative perspective. In the case in question, a small Christian people had conducted a prolonged struggle against the (Muslim) Indonesian rule that had been forced upon it, had sacrificed a large part of its population during the struggle, and had finally achieved independence. For the purpose of their courageous struggle against foreign rule, the residents of East Timor were indeed one people. However, when, after achieving their independence, the time for nation-building came, it became clear that tensions between the different ethnic and local groups comprising its population are threatening to tear the country apart (though recent years have seen a marked improvement).[2] The cultural differences between the various communities that comprise Jewish-Israeli society were in many ways no less significant than the differences and tensions that caused bloodshed in East Timor (something wholly unheard-of in the relations between various Jewish Israeli communities), though many of that small country's inhabitants probably still feel an external danger threatening its independence.

During Israel's first decades, it was very popular within the Arab world to prophecy Israel's internal disintegration due to the differences between its various ethnic groups, which were devoid of real national common ground (so they claimed) and were brought to Palestine by the Zionists from all around the world in order to establish their artificial state. The differences between the Ashkenazim and those who had immigrated to Israel from Arab countries received a pivotal role in this scenario. Today, these claims are voiced less frequently, but they are still heard from time to time. In this vein, Sheikh Nasrallah declared the following in one of his public addresses: "This [Zionist] entity, which has many strengths . . . has weaknesses as well. One of its most important weaknesses is the fact that it is an extraneous entity. It is not deeply rooted. Another of its weaknesses is the fact that its society is not homogeneous. Some Falasha Ethiopians, some from Russia, and some from I don't know where . . . They are bound together by a baseless and unfounded myth. Another weakness of this entity is that its people came because they were promised security, peace, and a life in the land of milk and honey. But if they encounter something else, they will leave this land."[3]

It is interesting that Nasrallah chooses to mention the Ethiopians and Russians. Has he despaired of the Ashkenazim and Sephardim disintegrating Israel from the inside (after the latter discover their true nature as "Jewish Arabs")? In any case, it is not superfluous to point out, from time to time, that the project of integrating immigrants from the "seventy Diasporas" to form one Hebrew-speaking nation in Israel—functioning, economically developed, and democratically governed—this project, whether "artificial" or not, whether "unfounded" or not, has been a remarkable success.

INTER-COMMUNAL TENSIONS—NOT WHAT THEY ONCE WERE

This tremendous accomplishment was naturally accompanied by tremendous difficulties. At the outset of the 1980s, it almost seemed at times that the entire edifice might collapse under the weight of tensions and pressures stemming from these difficulties. The 1981 election campaign is a case in point. These were the elections when Dudu Topaz derided the "riffraff" (using a Hebrew term with strong anti-oriental connotations) at a Labor mass meeting in Tel Aviv, a campaign riddled with petty violence, ugliness, and hatred. The two political camps stood opposite each other— half a people versus half a people—with a mixture of political enmity and a deep sense of emotional and cultural alienation, while the ethnic backdrop of the rift was obvious to all. They could have seemed at the time like two hostile tribes, rather than rival political camps. When either side said "us" or "them," this was frequently accompanied by an obvious ethnic overtone.

Today, we are a far cry from this situation. Of course, the ethnic ("communal") issue is still an important topic in Israeli reality. The economic gaps have not been reduced but have widened since the 1980s, and it is well known that a link exists between economic status and communal origin. However, the communal rift as such has greatly weakened. The "communal genie," as it is called, still affects Israeli politics, but it is obvious that its power has very much decreased since 1981. Today, it cannot be used to recruit such energies of enmity and bitterness, enthusiasm and identification. Throughout the 1990s and 2000s, parallel to the rise of the discourse about the disintegration of Israeli society, an opposite process took place in the field: the ethno-cultural rifts, including their manifestations in the political realm, were softened and became more moderate. Now, one cannot imagine an election campaign like the one in 1981, in which the rift between the two major sections of the people, according to ethnic and cultural criteria, played such a pivotal role.

Shimon Peres's changing public standing can serve as a symbol of the long way we have come since then. In 1981, the man was detested by a large part of the public. The hate toward Peres symbolized a much broader hatred—the hatred and bitterness of many of the "other Israel"—Sephardic, traditional and right-wing—toward "the first Israel"—Ashkenazi, secular and connected with the establishment and with the Labor party. The hatred toward Peres ebbed away long ago. Throughout the years, the public apology to him, while showering him and his contribution to the state with praise, has become a fashion trend of sorts among those who cursed and threw tomatoes at him in 1981. Even the bitter struggles of the first years of the Oslo process did not change this trend in the long run. The attacks directed at Labor party leaders during the Oslo years were very clearly political, free of an undertone of ethnic bitterness. For a good number of years now, Shimon Peres has been a politician at the heart of national consensus. This has not happened because his views have become more moderate—the opposite is the case. His political opinions are significantly more to the left than his stance in 1981, when he firmly rejected a Palestinian state and negotiations with the PLO, but was still accused of being a leftist and a hater of Israel. Obviously, Peres has not since then become less Ashkenazi, less secular, or less identified with the establishment; even his accent has not changed. Rather, all of these things stopped playing against him. Today, he is an admired president; before that, he served in the government and in Kadima alongside those who had been his bitter enemies from the Likud and had derived every possible political benefit from the wide-spread popular revulsion with Peres. The political opinions of these people are also a lot more left wing (on the Palestinian issue) than those of Peres himself in 1981. The leaders of Kadima had made every effort to attract Peres to their party, since polls clearly showed that his joining Kadima would contribute significantly to its public support (even though the polls, as usual, were overly optimistic about him). The years in which the softening of the ethnic tensions took place, and, later on, the attenuation of political tensions, are also the years when the disintegration, fragmentation, and never-ending radicalization discourse flourished and blossomed here.

THE DISINTEGRATION DISCOURSE VERSUS THE FACTS

The phrase "the Ashkenazi establishment" itself, which was still very relevant in the early 1980s, has today lost much of its significance in most areas. This has occurred first and foremost in the political realm, where numbers talk and votes are counted. The past two decades have seen foreign, defense and finance ministers of Sephardic origin. What is perhaps even more significant is that during this period, Sephardim have reached some of the highest positions among the powerful "mandarins" of the finance ministry. It is well known that David Ben-Gurion dreamt of a Yemenite chief of staff. Who even cares, today, about the ethnic origin of the chief of staff? The military and security establishment is no doubt one of the most open in this respect. The legal establishment is more conservative; however, even the fact that a person of Tunisian origin served for many years as the Attorney-General—one of the most powerful positions in the state—is taken for granted today. Ironically, it is precisely those parts of the establishment, including the academic establishment, who view themselves as being in charge of social criticism (including the issue of discriminating against the Sephardim) that are the place where the phrase "Ashkenazi establishment" is still more relevant than in most of the other areas.

Moreover, the widespread phenomena, over time, of marriages between the different ethnic groups means that today, one cannot divide the Jewish population in Israel into "Ashkenazim" and "Sephardim." As opposed to the situation in the past, most of the Israeli youth do not have a clearly defined ethnic identity; their leisure culture, mode of dress, and the Hebrew they speak do not make ethnic identification possible. All of these facts are well known, and are not novelties. However, knowing each fact separately does not add up to an accepted, coherent picture; therefore, the disintegration discourse continues to dominate, although it negates facts that are known to all. It is therefore well worth pointing out that in the crucial, decisive field, the one on which the entire Israeli enterprise of nation-building has hinged—the phrase "we are one people" is true today more than it has ever been in the past.[4]

It is true that assessing the magnitude of this accomplishment versus the flaws and failures that the realization of any great national or social project entails depends to a great extent on one's ideological departure point. However, the direction of dependence is the opposite of what is commonly assumed: the further one moves away from the Zionist departure point, the more one should logically be expected to appreciate these accomplishments. From a Zionist perspective, it might be argued, what has happened gives no particular occasion to wonder at: the immigrants who came to Israel from all over the world, East and West, were not immigrants in the ordinary sense; that is, people of different national identities who came to a foreign country and had to be integrated, with all the attending difficulties. Rather, both they and the Israeli Jews who received them belonged, according to this outlook, to the same people—the Jewish people. The Jews throughout the world, in the different and diverse Jewish communities, had always, according to this view, regarded themselves as belonging to one people, and had dreamt of the day when they would return to their ancestral homeland land from all the corners of the earth and re-establish their state. From this perspective, it is no wonder that once this dream was realized and Jews from all over the world found themselves in the same country, they basically managed to get along with each other— rather, it should be asked why they have not been able get along better.

On the other hand, the further one moves away from the Zionist departure point and begins to question the concept of one Jewish people comprising all of the world's Jews, the more one emphasizes the cultural differences between the Jewish communities in different countries (and the similarity of each community to each country's non-Jewish population), the more one sees the arrival of the Jews in Israel as "immigration" in a more or less usual sense as opposed to *aliyah*—in general, the more one adopts a discourse which is considered more "critical" in the sense of undermining the Zionist ideological assumptions—there is, in fact (at any rate, on this topic) less room for criticism and more occasion for wonder. As an enterprise of *aliyah*, Zionism is an impressive accomplishment; as an enterprise of immigration, of such a scope and make-up, the accomplishment is no less than phenomenal. If it were truly immigrants who came here from all around the world—not Jews from Poland and Yemen who came to what they regarded as their national homeland, but Poles and Yemenites who happened to be of the same religious persuasion (though many of them were in fact secular) and immigrated to a foreign country— then it is little short of a miracle that a state that is half "Polish" and half "Yemenite" can even exist, function, and develop, sustain a democratic government, and avoid violent ethnic strife.

"JEWISH ARABS"—CRITICISM?

Obviously, even on the assumption that the immigrants from various countries viewed themselves at the outset as belonging to the same people—meaning, that they belonged to the same people—this is still a very impressive accomplishment. "The Jewish people" as one people comprised of communities all around the world was an idea, a belief, a feeling, a cultural ideal—not a social reality. This people's different components—and they were very different—were not required to live alongside one another and maintain a society and a state together. At the outset, it was not obvious that this ideal would withstand the test of actualization any more than many other ideals of the modern era. The further the distance from the Zionist assumptions and the more emphasis that is given to the undoubtedly substantial differences between the various Jewish communities, as opposed to their common denominator, the more remarkable is the accomplishment.

This applies, *a fortiori*, to the fashion trend of calling those who originate from the Arab countries "Arab Jews."[5] This term is fairly banal if used in the same sense as the Jews of Russia being called "Russian Jews." Just as those who came from Russia have been influenced, to a greater or lesser extent as the case may be, by Russian culture, so have those who came from the Arab countries been influenced, in varying degrees, by Arab culture in its different local versions. However, the term "Arab Jews" is not usually meant to convey this banal message, but to signify a rejection of the Zionist concept that regards the Jews of the West and East as belonging to the same people. Arab Jews, in this sense, are persons to whom, at the time of their *aliyah*, Judaism was a religion only, and not a national identity that they shared with Ashkenazi Jews. Their national identity, with its various cultural characteristics (first and foremost, the language) was, according to this view, Arab. The "Ashkenazi establishment," to whom all this is directed with the clear intention of irritating it, is today much less Ashkenazi than in the past, and has no reason for any particular irritation, since on the list of the State of Israel's worries, the question of the Sephardic Jews' loyalty to the Jewish state and to the idea of Jewish peoplehood occupies the very last slot. Still, it is worth noting that those who insist on defining the immigrants from Arab countries, at least at the point of their coming here, as Arabs of Mosaic persuasion, attribute—however little they realize it—an unparalleled degree of enlightenment, inclusiveness, and liberalism to the Zionist state. Obviously, no Western country (and the people in question naturally view the Zionist state as intrinsically Western) ever dreamt of allowing Arab immigration on such a vast scale into its territory, to the extent that these "Arabs" would eventually become a majority within it, while immediately granting citizenship to the immigrants and integrating them—eventually, all the way to the highest positions of government—as has happened in Israel.

From a Zionist viewpoint, it can and should be maintained that this integration is still far from perfect, but it is obvious that no other Western country can claim to have come close to such a level of accepting and integrating "Arab" immigrants. It is worth mentioning that Arab states, too, are not accustomed to integrating Arab immigrants from other Arab countries to this extent, although they are considered as belonging to the same Arab nation (following the terminology widely accepted in the Arab world) and, overwhelmingly, to the same religion.[6] In fact, the Arab oil countries treat Arab work immigrants with far less benevolence than many European countries.

The Zionist state itself, of course, did not view things in that way and did not attribute such glory to itself. It viewed itself not as a recipient of Arab immigration but as a builder of a national home for the Jewish people. Some will argue that the true motive was in fact demographic, rather than the officially proclaimed desire to bring Jewish brethren to the land of Israel. But, of course, the demographic consideration itself (of strengthening the Jewish majority in the country) hinged entirely on the assumption that those arriving belong to the Jewish people rather than to the Arab nation. Whoever denies this assumption is, perforce, reduced to admiring the success of the integration of these "Arab immigrants," and should in all fairness be in favor of awarding Israel the Nobel Prize for openness and inclusiveness as the country most open and welcoming to Arab immigration in all of history.

That being so, it is better to return to the traditional Zionist terminology: that of Jewish *aliyah* and its "absorption." The Zionist terminology is preferable not because it reflects the full complexity of the situation and of the identities involved—of course it doesn't. We know that identity is a complex issue, not easily susceptible to unequivocal definitions. The Zionist terminology is preferable because it reflects the cultural and social reality in Israel better—a lot better—than any other general definition, and also because it provides the sole reasonable basis for criticism of all the shortcomings, flaws, failures, and injustices that have accompanied Israeli nation-building. If one wants to live up to the ideal of the in-gathering of the exiles, there is still plenty of room for improvement.

THE RUSSIANS ARE COMING—A SUCCESS STORY

In the 1990s, the ability of Israeli society to absorb and integrate immigrants withstood another difficult test—the mass *aliyah* from the former Soviet Union. Today, there is no novelty in saying that the absorption of the "Russians" has, all in all, and despite innumerable difficulties and problems, been a great success story. Surveys show that well over eighty percent of this population (including the non-Jews among them, to be discussed below) is satisfied with the decision to come to Israel; they view Israel as their home.[7] At the outset, it was not obvious that this would be the case. At the beginning of the 1990s, quite a few viewed this *aliyah* more as a flood than bountiful rain. There were concerns that a Russian ghetto would emerge, undermining the hegemony of the Hebrew language in Israel, and, in general, creating a segregated society lacking a "common language" with other Israelis. Today, it is clear that these worries were unfounded: the children of these newcomers are speakers of Sabra Israeli Hebrew (for better and for worse).

Certainly, the million newcomers who came to Israel were not completely absorbed in the country in a manner that would render them an unrecognizable presence. The melting pot of the 1950s is irrelevant to the conditions in Israel today, and to the far more liberal and pluralistic norms that have taken root here since that period.[8] "Melting" is a problematic metaphor, and one is reluctant to use it today—although any sort of integration is, to some extent, melting. However, there is no doubt that the overwhelming majority of newcomers, and even more so, their children, belong to Jewish-Israeli society. No Russian "national minority" will be created here.

Today, noting the great contribution of this wave of *aliyah* to Israeli society in various fields has become a cliché. There is a strange coexistence between this cliché and another that became popular in the 1990s, one that concerned the disintegration and fragmentation of Israeli society and its utter failure to integrate immigrants. Clearly, both cannot possibly be correct.

We are talking about one million people who came to Israel within a few years. This is a less impressive accomplishment than the absorption of the mass *aliyah* of the 1950s, which occurred under far more difficult circumstances and by a much smaller absorbing society, but, by any comparative international standard, this is a highly impressive accomplishment. This is also true with regard to the large population of newcomers who were "non-Jewish"—with and without quotation marks.[9] Indeed, in many cases this refers to people with a Jewish father and a non-Jewish mother, who are not Jewish according to Jewish religious law (halakha). However, they may well have possessed, when they came to Israel, a significant Jewish awareness (plus a Jewish family name, and memories of antisemitism). These are "non-Jews" only in the eyes of the Orthodox establishment. Many other cases concern spouses of Jews, or those with more distant familial ties to Jews—in any case, people who lacked significant Jewish consciousness when they came to Israel. Integrating this large population into Israeli society is not a simple challenge. However, for all the difficulties, and despite some negative phenomena that have attracted public attention, the general picture is positive. The greater majority of this population strives to fully integrate into Hebrew-speaking Jewish-Israeli society. In practice, it does not need conversion for this integration to succeed (though conversion could, in many cases, alleviate the process, were the rabbis to demonstrate the necessary flexibility). This is precisely how joining a sovereign nation is supposed to occur, as opposed to a community in the Diaspora, according to the "civic nationalism" model: immigration and naturalization, adoption of the country's language and culture, full integration into the country and identification with it. The Orthodox establishment is doing all it can to impede this process, but luckily, its actual power is limited.

JOINING THE JEWISH PEOPLE—WITH OR WITHOUT CONVERSION

The Law of Return, which is often disparagingly referred to as an "ethno-religious" law, has in fact—through granting citizenship to a wide range of non-Jews with family ties to Jews—transformed the Jewish national identity in Israel into one less ethnic (in the narrow sense of ethnic descent) and less religious, more civic, and more cultural. Some view this as a paradox—an unintended consequence of the operation of the Law of Return.[10] In fact, however, this is a perfectly logical natural result of realizing the idea of a modern Jewish nation state—even if many of its supporters had not thought of it. This idea cannot be realized without bringing a large number of non-Jews to Israel, due to the wide scale of intermarriage that characterizes many Jewish communities. The only way to avoid this result would have been to give up the idea of mass Jewish immigration from countries with high rates of intermarriage. From the moment these people arrive in Israel, it is a clear national interest that they become an inseparable part of the "one people" this chapter is dealing with—the Hebrew-speaking Jewish majority in Israel—and not remain outside it, culturally or socially. This is also what most commonly occurs. The Law of Return (together with the Citizenship Law related to it) assists greatly in this regard, since these people receive Israeli citizenship immediately upon arrival. The Orthodox establishment and its policies influence this process in the opposite direction. However, what determines the situation more than anything else is, of course, the desire of these people to be absorbed and to integrate, and the willingness of Israeli society to absorb and integrate them. In general, there is great readiness for this on both sides.

Conversion, which is the traditional way of joining the Jewish people, means adopting the Jewish culture—in its traditional version. Today, this is not the sole version of Jewish culture that exists. The importance of the revolution brought about by modernity, the *haskala* (Jewish enlightenment), Zionism, and the State of Israel, which have created secular cultural alternatives to the world of Jewish religion and tradition, should not be underestimated. However, this religion and tradition still represent an important version of Jewish culture shared by a substantial part of the public. Among those who do not fully share it, many are significantly influenced by it and value its importance; in any case, no one denies that it is a legitimate version of Jewish culture. Therefore, there is nothing wrong with the fact that conversion continues to be an accepted method of joining the Jewish people; that is to say, in Israeli terms, joining Jewish-Israeli society. But the social and cultural reality in Israel, along with the Law of Return, also creates the possibility of *de facto* integration into this society, unrelated to halakhic definitions. It is natural and appropriate for a modern state that includes a large secular population and well-developed secular culture to offer such an option. The religious establishment can still bring individuals into the national collective through the conversion process, but it cannot prevent the entrance of those who enter, *de facto*, through a different door.

This situation does not fulfill the expectations of the devotees of the Orthodox religious monopoly of Jewish identity in Israel. From their perspective, it is essential to insist that halakha should determine the outer limits of the national collective, even though it is obvious that it does not determine what goes on within them—the actual way of life of most Israelis. Neither can this situation satisfy the desires of those radical secularists who favor a full separation not only between the institutions of religion and state but also between the Jewish peoplehood and the Jewish religion—as, for example, suggested by A. B. Yehoshua. This important Israeli writer is in favor of cultivating a Jewish national identity in Israel separate from religion (rendering it open for members of other religions to join), and advises the Jewish religion to disconnect from its attachment to the Jewish people (thereby becoming attractive to potential converts who are uninterested in adopting a new national identity).[11]

DEFINING THE LIMITS OF NATIONAL IDENTITY—WHAT ABOUT "MEMBERS OF ANOTHER RELIGION"?

It is highly doubtful that the creation of a collective identity that is completely detached from Jewish religious heritage is congruent with historical consciousness and the real cultural character (in all its versions) of the people under discussion. This is the case regardless of how one wishes to define this identity: the Jewish people in Israel, the Jewish-Israeli people, the Hebrew people (the term once strongly favored by the Zionist movement), or simply the Israeli people (bearing in mind that the Arab citizens clearly constitute a national minority with a distinct identity of their own)—as some prefer. All of these labels and combinations of labels relate, after all, to the history and culture of the same people; the difference between them is a matter of nuances, and all the arguments about them are of somewhat less than fateful importance. However, even if it were possible, with a sufficiently stubborn effort, to create a Jewish-(Israeli) peoplehood whose culture would be completely detached from the Jewish religion and tradition, there is no way to force the Jewish religion, on its part, to detach itself from the Jewish peoplehood. Anyone with any knowledge of this religion's contents should be aware that such a disconnection would signify the creation of a different religion (as has occurred once before). As long as a religion exists which views itself, and is perceived by many Jews, as the distinct traditional culture of the Jewish people, the result will be that adopting this religion means adopting an important version of Jewish culture—in other words, joining the Jewish people.

One should not discount the possibility that Israeli reality will create, over time, an option of fully joining Jewish-Israeli society and its culture, not only for those who are of non-Jewish origin (without conversion) as already happens *de facto* today, but also for members of other religions, while they continue to adhere to their religion as an important aspect of their cultural identity. Such a result would contradict the definition of the limits of the Jewish peoplehood ("not a member of another religion"), which was adopted by the Supreme Court (rejecting, by a majority decision, a petition of a person of Jewish origin who had become a Christian monk to be recognized as a Jew for the purpose of receiving citizenship under the Law of Return[12]) and, following this precedent, by the Knesset. This definition has deep historical, cultural and emotional roots. However, this result—creating the option of "members of other religions" within the national collective—is congruent, after all, with the logic of a modern nation-state. In my opinion, this matter should be left for the future to deal with through social and cultural development, without taking an ideological stance on it. However, even if this is the general direction, the option of joining the Jewish people through conversion to Judaism will continue to exist and be accepted by the non-religious public as well.

The phenomenon of joining the Jewish people by adopting its religion, which is accepted by the secular public as well, is one of the expressions of the continuous influence of religious tradition on Jewish-Israeli culture. In any imaginable future, the secular Jewish public in Israel will include many more of those who are significantly influenced by Jewish religious tradition than of those who cannot be considered part of the Jewish people under the Orthodox halakhic definition. Therefore, although there are irreconcilable ideological differences between the religious position and the secular one in this matter, even this sensitive issue cannot tangibly threaten our being "one people."

The full congruence between Jewish peoplehood and the Jewish religion, which is the ideal from the perspective of halakhic Judaism, has not existed since the rise of Jewish enlightenment and secularization, and certainly cannot exist today, with secular Hebrew culture flourishing in

Israel. However, there are many intermediate situations between a full congruence and full detachment, and it is reasonable to assume that the complex relationship between religion, state, and Jewish peoplehood will unfold in the foreseeable future within this middle ground. The true distance between the positions of most of the religious and most of the secular in Israel is shorter than the impression one might receive from the sharpness of the polemic on matters of religion and state, and from the way in which the opposing ideological positions are formulated. Most of the observant population does not truly aspire to transform Israel into an undemocratic halakhic state, and most of the secular people do not wish to utterly disconnect from Jewish tradition—whether on the personal plane or with regard to the character of public life in Israel.

INTEGRATION OF THE "KNITTED KIPPOT" IN THE MAINSTREAM

The above should be taken into account when relating to the religious–secular rift in Israeli society. This rift plays a significant role in the disintegration discourse. However, in this area as well, it seems that the main direction of development—although not the only direction—is the opposite.[13] Despite worrying manifestations of radicalization and separatism, the main development throughout the 1990s and 2000s has been the integration of the national-religious public into the Israeli mainstream in various fields, the most obvious and well-known being military service and commanding positions therein. This process occurred during the period when the character of public life in Israel, in many areas, became more secular—primarily with regard to the issue of Sabbath and *kashrut* (dietary laws) observance (or, to be more precise, their non-observance). In this area, the status quo was gnawed at significantly in favor of the secular public. In the late 1970s and the early 1980s, at the start of a prolonged period of government coalitions dominated by right-wing and religious parties in Israel, it was difficult to imagine that one day Orthodox politicians would offer the secular public a "package deal" whereby the malls would be closed on the Sabbath, and in exchange, they would accept the principle that cultural and entertainment establishments are allowed to operate on that day. It could hardly have been imagined that the answer from the secular side would be that the deal was not worthwhile to the secular people, since the opening of cultural and entertainment establishments was a *fait accompli*, and that the malls that already opened on Shabbat should be considered "liberated territory that will not be returned." Today, it is difficult to believe that at the end of the 1960s, the High Court of Justice had to overrule the Labor government in order to allow television broadcasting on the Sabbath.

The increasing integration of the "knitted kippot" into the Israeli mainstream is therefore genuine integration and not an exercise in gaining control. This is an integration into a society that is, for the most part, a modern, liberal society that has gone through a process of additional modernization and liberalization during the last couple of decades due to various social and economical factors. This integration—not a simple process, from the perspective of the national-religious public itself—did not entail increasing coercion of halakhic behavioral norms on secular society (beyond the traditional status quo, mainly in the field of personal status). Neither did it entail a victory of the political outlook upheld by most of the observant public—the idea of Israeli rule over the entire historical land of Israel: the Israeli state has repeatedly acted against this principle since early 1990s. Some have expressed concern that the massive entrance of members of the knitted kippot community into the commanding roles in the army would lead to increasing the religiosity of the IDF, and doubted the readiness of the observant soldiers and officers to follow orders that contradict the directives of the rabbis whose religious authority they accept. But what has actually happened—at least up to now (one cannot be fully sure about the future)—has been, in the main, "IDF-ication" of the Orthodox rather than "Orthodoxisation" of the IDF. In Israeli reality, "IDF-ication of the Orthodox" means a process of moderation and acceptance of the burden of democratic national authority. During the disengagement from Gaza in 2006, in which, to one extent or another, thousands of observant soldiers and officers took part, these people refuted, in a highly impressive manner, the concerns with regard to their willingness to follow lawful orders rather than rabbinic directives on political matters, in case of a contradiction.

The vast majority of uniformed Orthodox must have opposed the disengagement politically, and many of them clearly viewed it as contrary to their world view and to their cherished values. However, despite grave and irresponsible halakhic rulings issued by revered rabbis urging soldiers to disobey, the phenomenon of refusing to carry out orders was not even marginal—it was wholly negligible. The uniformed Orthodox withstood this difficult test of practical loyalty—beyond all rhetoric—to the state, the rule of law, and Israeli democracy. It was lucky for Israel that they did not heed the rabbis' rulings; nor were they influenced by any of the fashionable theories regarding "conscientious objection" in political matters, which had been fostered for years in certain circles within the Israeli left. The practical, destructive significance of these theories is an invitation to each political camp and sub-camp in Israel to declare that their stance on the country's main political controversy is a "matter of conscience," which is supposed to provide an exemption from the duty to obey lawful orders stemming from democratically adopted political decisions.

THE STATE VERSUS POLITICAL HALAKHIC RULINGS

It may be said that through the uniformed Orthodox, the entire national-religious public has withstood the test of loyalty to democracy. Obviously one should not underestimate the danger posed by extreme, anti-democratic elements in this community. However, it is clear today that these elements do not speak for its majority. In the 1980s and early 1990s, when the wave of extreme religious nationalism was at its peak, it was impossible to know that this would be the result during trying times. Of course, one has to bear in mind that in the future we may have to face even more difficult trials.

The issue of the state's ability to implement a political decision that would be considered illegitimate by extremist rabbis, allegedly on religious grounds was for years the most grave question mark hovering above the ability of the Israeli democracy to function. All the other flaws of the Israeli system of government and political culture relate to the quality of public life, while this issue goes to the very roots of the basic question: who rules the state and who makes critical decisions in it? In this sense, this issue also gave rise to the question "are we still one people"?—a people as a sovereign political community that has an agreed-upon decision-making mechanism. During the peak years of the bitter struggle against the Oslo accords, there were moments—the most prominent and tragic being the assassination of Yitzhak Rabin—when one could not help wondering about the answer to this question. It is of great importance that the disengagement from Gaza provided us with proof that there is, in this country, no halakhic veto—or rather, no political-ideological veto disguised as halakhic—over democratic decisions on vital political issues.

This fact testifies, in contrast to pessimistic assessments that have been heard repeatedly, to the resilience of the Israeli democracy and to its legitimacy in the eyes of most of the public. It can be argued that this legitimacy applies to democracy chiefly in its minimalist, procedural sense—respecting the principle of democratic majority rule as an agreed-upon system of decision-making—and is far from being unequivocal with regard to the values and principles of liberal democracy. However, any clear-cut distinction between the values of democracy and its institutions is largely artificial. The character of the institutions reflects the values on which they are based, the foremost one being the principle of equality, which is manifested in the universal and equal suffrage. Moreover, the functioning of these institutions is subject to political and legal constraints that are closely bound up with these values. Therefore, it is natural that those fundamentalist elements that deny the values of democracy also deny the authority of its institutions. As it turns out, their real influence is limited.

It is impossible to do justice to the complex issue of the Haredi (ultra-orthodox) public and its relationship with Israeli society and the state—a topic that I do not pretend to be sufficiently familiar with—within the framework of this short paragraph. However, it can be said that, as opposed to earlier times when a trend of radicalization and separatism was prevalent in this community, there have been, in recent years, significant signs of rapprochement—at least with regard to specific issues and by some parts of the community—to the mainstream of Israeli society. This is not an ideological revolution, but mainly a result of pragmatic concerns. This trend is encouraged (not always openly) by some of the leaders of this community, who seek to improve its economic situation and understand that the present model of the "learning society" that, *de facto*, encompasses the entire Haredi community (and is unprecedented in Jewish history) cannot be sustained. There are also some significant displays of cultural and social "Israelization" among Haredim, and of the adoption (selectively, to be sure) of certain aspects of modernity in their midst. In this context one can point out the clear prevalence of the standard Israeli Hebrew among them, the massive introduction of computers and internet into their society (despite rabbinic efforts to forbid it), the prominent presence of Haredim at sites of national importance from Yad Vashem to Masada, and the emergence of a more positive attitude toward the days of national remembrance. It seems that the terrorist attacks of the 2000s—which struck the Haredi population as well—strengthened trends of identification with general society and its distress, and with the security forces. The activities of ZAKA display a willingness to give actual expression, involving a high level of personal dedication, to this identification. There are even initial signs (admittedly, rather modest) of gnawing at the Haredi taboo against military service. It is difficult to assess the power of these trends at this stage, but there is, at the very least, a possibility that they will continue to gain strength.[14]

POLITICAL POLARIZATION—NOT WHAT IT ONCE WAS

And finally, to the political rift. Beyond all political vicissitudes, it seems that the strategic trend that characterizes Israeli politics in recent years is the strengthening of the political center, and a significant decrease of the ideological gaps between the major segments of the population. This trend has been prominent ever since the outset of the confrontation with the Palestinians in the year 2000. Ariel Sharon's change of direction toward the center, which was manifested dramatically in the "disengagement" and its political ramifications, turned this trend into the most prominent hallmark of Israeli politics in the 2000s. However, this change of direction began even earlier. The first Netanyahu government was the one to cross the Rubicon of relinquishment, in the name of the Israeli right wing, of the principle of the "undivided Land of Israel." It accepted the principle of territorial concessions within the framework of a political agreement and actually evacuated certain territories in Judea and Samaria. Today it is clear that the principle of territorial compromise and partition, as such, is no longer controversial among the main political forces in Israel. Of course, one should not belittle the significance, and the practical implications, of remaining disagreements on important questions regarding Israel's relations with the Palestinians, but, ideologically at least, a controversy that had split the Israeli public and the Zionist movement for decades has been, in the main, settled. Even evacuation of settlements is no longer taboo. At the time of the evacuation of the Gaza settlements, the major argument of most of the opponents was that concessions were being made unilaterally, with Israel gaining nothing in exchange. There is a vast difference between the traditional ideology of the Israeli right and the Benjamin Netanyahu's declared acceptance of the idea of the Palestinian state.

Simultaneously, the positions of most Israelis who had belonged to the large camp that had supported the Oslo agreements in the early 1990s have undergone a change too. Most of those who had been affiliated with the "half nation" (more than half, at the outset of the process) who supported Oslo today understand very well that there was not a little amount of truth in the warnings of the Oslo opponents with regard to the security risks involved, and regarding their assessment of Yasser Arafat as a peace partner. The assumption that peace depends solely upon Israel's willingness for concession, and that the occupation that started in 1967 is the only issue from the perspective of our neighbors (aside from marginal extremist elements), is an assumption no longer accepted by most of this public. Of course, this does not prevent dogmatic and "ultra-orthodox" elements on the Israeli left to cling to this assumption, which has long become for them a tenet of faith not requiring rational proof; but these comprise only a small minority among the voters of the left-wing parties in the 1999 elections. It is obvious that the controversy over these political issues continues and will continue yet. However, the ideological gaps, on these issues, between the mainstream right and the mainstream left have narrowed considerably.

CULTURAL PLURALISM AND COMMON GROUND

Israeli society is a complex, culturally pluralistic society. This pluralism is given a significantly greater measure of legitimization—and rightfully so—than in the classic "melting pot" era that characterized the 1950s. This validation of pluralism in society, along with all of its public manifestations, is a natural result of a lengthy process of modernization and liberalization that brings the best and worst of the modern capitalist developed world to Israel. It is this process that ensures better protection of individual's legal rights; that has allowed stronger expression than ever of the voices of protest and grievances within society; that makes it difficult for the state and the establishment to impose cultural norms of any kind; and that has deepened economic gaps. Anyone who is looking for signs of weakness and even disintegration in a free, pluralistic society will find them easily. This, however, is a highly misleading picture—not because the weaknesses are not real, but because the sources of such a society's strength will usually greatly surpass its weaknesses.

This chapter has dealt with Jewish-Israeli society. One must bear in mind that a large Arab population, a considerable part of the citizen body, exists in this country. This national minority is not part of "the people" in the sense of a national-cultural collective that we have dealt with here (since both groups have always considered themselves as belonging to two distinct peoples in this sense), but it is certainly part of the "people" in the sense of a civic community, and the question of its status in the country is an important aspect of the general picture of Israeli society. The complex issue of the relationship between the Jewish majority and this minority, including its problematic link to the Arab-Israeli and Israeli-Palestinian national conflict, is beyond the scope of this chapter. In any case, it is clear that the aim should be to endow, as much as possible, the Israeli citizenship and civic community with a significant content, beyond formal legal aspects, for all citizens of the state.[15] At the same time it is clear that under Israeli conditions, two distinct national identities will continue to exist within the citizen body of the state—as is the case in any country with a substantial national minority who insist on their right to preserve their distinct identity. The traditional model of civic nationalism, French-style, under which all the country's citizens are regarded as sharing the same national identity, is inapplicable in Israel, since it contradicts the culture, the self-definition, and the political will of the majority and the minority alike.

The increasing legitimacy of cultural pluralism and intellectual fashions that specialize in "deconstruction" and slaughtering holy cows, and excessive concerns and exaggerated sensitivities on the part of some of the "guardians" of the traditional Zionist narrative have all joined forces to present this pluralism as a sign of the disintegration of the society and national collective. This is completely unfounded. Even if one wishes to describe the Jewish-Israeli identity as a "federation of tribes" (an exaggerated description in itself, considering the blurred borders between the "tribes," the mutual influences between them, and the number of people who do not fully belong to any "tribe"), it must still be remembered that the subcomponents (or sub-tribes) of this society have a strong common ground. In recent years, the dominant trend—though it is not the only one, as is the way of social trends—is that of strengthening this common ground rather than weakening it. The response to the question "are we still one people" is that today, we are one people more than ever in the past.

Author's note: This is an English version of a paper originally published in Hebrew in 2008. There is an important point on which I find myself less optimistic today: it appears that the hard-line ideological right is stronger politically, and the extremist and violent groups among the national-religious right are more determined and dangerous than they seemed in the aftermath of their resounding defeat during the 2006 disengagement in Gaza. These groups are certainly only a minority within this camp, but the dangers they present, both physically and politically, are greater than I thought then.

NOTES

1   See e.g. Baruch Kimmerling, *Immigrants, Settlers, Natives: Israel Between Plurality of Cultures and Cultural Wars* (Tel Aviv: Am Oved, 2004) [Hebrew]. For a relatively mild version of the public discourse on this topic, see for example Yossi Sarid, "The Myth of Israeli Solidarity," *Haaretz*, October 21, 2011, written after the release of

Gilad Shalit and the attendant celebrations: "Israeli society was and remains torn . . . And every camp is divided internally, and anyone who is not with us is against us," "Israeli solidarity [is] a lovely fairy tale . . . 'Paying such a high, painful price for his release reflects the deepest feelings of the Jewish heart.' The exact reverse is also a possibility, that the release reflects a dread of the loss and disintegration of solidarity."

2   See on this J. Scambary, "Anatomy of a Conflict: The 2006–2007 Communal Violence in East Timor," *Conflict, Security and Development* 9, no. 2 (2009): 265–88.

3   Al Manar Television, May 2, 2006, translated by MEMRI.

4   See on this, for example, E. Ya'ar, "Continuity and Change in Israeli Society: The Test of the Melting Pot," *Israel Studies* 10, no. 2 (2005): 91–128.

5   See, for example, Y. Shenhav, *The Arab Jews: A Postcolonial Reading of Nationalism, Religion and Ethnicity* (Stanford: Stanford University Press, 2006).

6   See S. S. Russel, "Migration and Political Integration in the Arab World," in *The Arab State*, ed. G. Luciani (Berkeley: University of California Press, 1990), 377–82. Jordan is the most generous Arab state in this respect, whereas the Gulf states are the most restrictive.

7   On being a success story: see, for example, Moshe Lissak and Eliezer Leshem, *From Russia to Israel: Identity and Culture in Transition* (Tel Aviv: Hakibbutz Hameuchad, 2001) [Hebrew]; Moshe Kenigshtein, *'Russkoye' lizo Israilya: cherty sozialnogo portreta* (Moscow: Mosty Kultury, 2007) [Russian]. Both the inevitable difficulties that attend the integration of such a huge wave of immigration and the fact that this is, overall, a success story are reflected in the findings of Majid Al-Haj, a professor of sociology at Haifa University. He puts great emphasis on ethnic tensions and frictions within the Jewish-Israeli society in general, and, in particular, the ethno-cultural distinctiveness of the "Russians." He nevertheless concludes that in "the younger generation [of immigrants] . . . the Israeli component [of their identity] seems to be gaining the upper hand;" and as far as mainly the older generation is concerned, "support for the existence of Russian-ethnic institutions is not the outcome of the immigrants' despair with and alienation from Israeli society," but rather fits well into, and strengthens, the currently prevailing pattern of what he defines as "ethnocratic [i.e., Jewish-dominated] multiculturalism" in the country—Majid Al-Haj, *Immigration and Ethnic Formation in a Deeply Divided Society: The Case of the 1990s Immigrants from the Former Soviet Union in Israel* (Leiden: Brill, 2004), 105, 108, 216. Surveys: see on this A. Yakobson, "Joining the Jewish People: Non-Jewish Immigrants from the Former USSR, Israeli Identity and Jewish Peoplehood," *Israel Law Review* 43, no. 1 (2010): 6–9.

8   Cultural pluralism within the Jewish-Israeli society is sometimes defined as multiculturalism—employing this term in a non-radical sense that assumes, alongside diversity, strong common ground between the different groups (including the centrality of Hebrew). See, for example, M. Mautner, A. Sagi, and R. Shamir, eds., *Multiculturalism in a Democratic and Jewish State* (Tel Aviv: Ramot—Tel Aviv University, 1998) [Hebrew]. According to Shafir and Peled, the incorporation of the Russian-speaking immigrants, accompanied by an acceptance of a considerable degree of cultural distinctiveness on their part, points (among other factors) "in the direction of greater pluralism, even multiculturalism" in Israel—G. Shafir and Y. Peled, *Being Israeli: The Dynamics of Multiple Citizenship* (Cambridge: Cambridge University Press, 2002), 309. Kimmerling argues that a Jewish state is essentially incompatible

with genuine multiculturalism, chiefly as regards the status of the Arab minority (but also because of the ties between Jewish religion and state—B. Kimmerling, "The New Israelis: Multiple Cultures without Multiculturalism," *Alpayim* 16 (1998): 263–308 [Hebrew]. However, the cultural and language rights of the Arab minority in Israel are in fact very considerable—see, for example, S. Smoooha, "The Regime of the State of Israel: Civil Democracy, Non-Democracy or Ethnic Democracy," *Soziologia Israelit* 2, no. 2 (2000): 593–94 [Hebrew]; A. Yakobson and A. Rubinstein, *Israel and the Family of Nations: The Jewish Nation-State and Human Rights* (Cambridge: Cambridge University Press, 2009), 118–21. Full civic integration, rather than the right to preserve the minority's cultural distinctiveness, is clearly the main problem.

9   See A. Cohen, *Non-Jewish Jews in Israel* (Ramat Gan and Jerusalem: Faculty of Law, Bar Ilan University, Shalom Hartmann Institute and Keter Publishing House, 2006) [Hebrew]; Yakobson, "Joining the Jewish People."

10   See Y. Weiss, "The Golem and its Creator, or How the Law of Return turned Israel into a Multi-Ethnic State," *Teoria u-vikoret* 19 (2001): 45–69 [Hebrew].

11   A. B. Yehoshua, *Homeland Grasp* (Tel Aviv: Hakibbutz Hameuchad, 2008): 13–80 [Hebrew].

12   HCJ 72/62 Rufaizen v. The Minister of Interior [1962] IsrSC 16 2428; see on this A. Rubinstein and B. Medina, *The Constitutional Law of the State of Israel*, 6th ed. (Jerusalem: Schocken, 2005), 398–99 [Hebrew].

13   See, for example, Y. Sheleg, *The New Religious Jews—Recent Developments among Observant Jews in Israel* (Jerusalem: Keter, 2000) [Hebrew].

14   See, for example, E. Sivan and K. Caplan, eds., *Israeli Haredim: Integration without Assimilation?* (Jerusalem: Van Leer Institute, 2003) [Hebrew]; K. Caplan, *The Internal Popular Discourse in Israeli Haredi* Society (Jerusalem: Merkaz Zalman Shazar le-Toldot Israel, 2007) [Hebrew].

15   As opposed to the rhetoric of most of the political leaders and of the intellectual elite of the Arab community, the polls conducted among the Arab public at large indicate that this is indeed the case to a significant—though of course far from sufficient—extent. The consistent trend that emerges (naturally, with ups and downs) is that the numbers of Israeli Arabs giving positive answers to questions on Israeli patriotism, while much lower than in the case of the Jewish majority, are nevertheless substantial. In a 2009 survey (conducted shortly after the military campaign in Gaza), forty-five percent of Arab citizens agreed with the sentence "I am proud to be an Israeli;" the 2008 the figure was fifty-three percent—Mano Geva and Eppie Ya'ar, "Patriotism Survey 2009," PowerPoint presentation, Herzliya Conference (2009), http://www.herzliyaconference.org/_Uploads/2997ManoGeva.ppt, (accessed June 22, 2012). In Tamar Hermann et al., *Israeli Democracy Index 2011*, trans. Karen Gold and Zvi Ofer (Jerusalem: IDI Press, 2011), 52.8 percent of Arab citizens (and 87.9 percent of the Jewish ones) said that they were proud of being Israeli; 20.6 percent were "very proud" and 32.2 percent were "quite proud" (among the Jews, 64.7 percent were "very proud" and 23.2 percent were "quite proud"), 131–33.

The Palestinian Israelis' Attempt to Challenge the Jewish State in Education: A Citizenship Act or a Radical Shift?

14

AYMAN K. AGBARIA

INTRODUCTION

The education field has been a central arena for religious, ethnic, and national minorities' struggles for cultural recognition and group-based rights worldwide, especially in divided societies. On the one hand, the state enlists various aspects of the education system in the nation-building identity process to produce and disseminate its "philosophy of integration." In other words, the state perpetuates through the education system its "official knowledge" of its story of peoplehood. In doing so, the state highlights certain narratives, while dimming and even denying others, especially in school subjects such as history, civics, geography, and literature. On the other hand, minorities often resist the state's attempts to impose an official narrative that does not recognize and accommodate their historical memory. As the state attempts to naturalize the hierarchical relations between the different groups in it and to indoctrinate students through the education system with the concept that these relations are morally justified and ultimately beneficial to all groups' members, despite the domination and discrimination they entail, minorities, especially indigenous ones, react with defiance. They take actions and present challenges that seek to transform the existing majority–minority relations to be more just, equitable, and cognizant of their collective memory and identity, especially in the education field, which is often perceived as a main site for contention and as a main domain to fulfill collective rights of language and self-rule for these minorities.[1]

Focusing on recent developments in the field of education, this chapter grapples with the educational activism of Arab civil society in Israel. Specifically, it presents a case study of a recent initiative to establish an independent Arab Pedagogical Council (APC). (For the purposes of full disclosure, I note here that I have been involved in advancing this initiative in its early stages.)

I argue that the APC initiative, although controversial and challenging to the very definition of Israel as both a Jewish nation-state and a democracy, should be considered an "act of citizenship" and a civic "contentious performance," rather than a sign of radicalization and separatism. As such, the APC initiative, established and administered by the Follow-Up Committee on Arab Education (FUCAE), represents the quintessence of the Palestinian ethno-national politics in Israel that renounce Jewish exclusivity and hegemony and advocate for differential group rights for the Palestinian minority in Israel. The FUCAE, and other similar organizations,[2] draws on both the indignity of the Palestinian minority and the Israeli citizenship as the political platforms upon which they predicate their demands to redefine and redistribute the material and symbolic state resources using strategies of advocacy, lobbying, applied research, and media campaigns. In doing so, they seek to change the dominant discourse from within: to stand against it with the democratic tools that this discourse provides and the structure of opportunity it affords.

For Engin Isin and Greg Nielsen, citizens are constituted as political actors through their "acts of citizenship," which are defined as "acts that transform forms (orientations, strategies, technologies) and modes (citizens, strangers, outsiders, aliens) of being political by bringing into being new actors as activist citizens (claimants of rights and responsibilities) through creating new sites and scales of struggle." These citizenship acts, when undertaken as collective action by social movements, could be perceived as "contentious performances." For Charles Tilly, social movements are performers of contentious politics, as they lead sustained public efforts to raise collective demands that target authorities by creating specialized associations and coalitions. Tilly defines the politics of contention as "interactions in which actors make claims bearing on someone else's interest, in which governments appear either as targets, initiators of claims, or third parties." Through contentious politics, social movements do two things. First, they create new connections among individuals, organizations, networks, and coalitions. Second, they activate, deactivate, and redraw boundaries separating one actor from another, creating collective stories about the two sides.[3]

That said, my overarching argument in this chapter is as follows. The initiative to establish the APC is a political and ethical act, through which Arab civil society organizations and activists in Israel constitute themselves as independent political actors, citizens, and claimants of rights, entitlements, and responsibilities for the quality of life and future of the Palestinians in Israel. Similar to many other activities, including programs to produce and disseminate alternative and complementary curricular materials in history and civics, this initiative of Palestinian educational activism in Israel is, more than anything else, an act of "interruptive democracy in education" that enlarges the boundaries of democratic dissent in Israel. Based on the idea that, among other things, democracy is about the possibility for opposition and change, Lynn Davies describes interruptive democracy as "the process by which people are enabled to break into practices which continue injustice. It is an 'in-your-face' democracy—not just taking part, but the disposition to challenge . . . It is by definition non-linear, finding spaces for dissent, resilience and action."[4]

This chapter consists of four sections. The first and second sections provide, in broad sketches, background information on the political backdrop of the APC initiative and on the Arab education system in Israel. The third section presents the goals and rationale for the establishment of the APC. In describing this initiative, I draw heavily on my personal acquaintance with its leading figures and founding documents, as detailed later. The chapter ends with concluding thoughts on the initiative.

PALESTINIANS IN ISRAEL: A POLITICAL BACKGROUND

The state's ideologies, policies, and practices constitute different categories of citizens, which in turn produce diverse political identities and models of membership for the citizen in his or her polity. In this regard, Gershon Shafir and Yoav Peled argue that Israeli citizenship is differential, hierarchical, and in service of the political interests of the Jewish majority. This majority is constituted as a gated ethno-national polity that excludes Arab citizens, who are treated as an aggregate of individuals entitled to selective individual liberal rights. Put differently, Israel is an excellent illustrative case in which, drawing on Rogers Brubaker's conceptualization, the "nation" is imagined as an ethnocultural community distinct from the citizenry of the state. When "nation" is imagined in this way, nationalism can be internally as well as externally exclusive, for it can define some fellow residents, even fellow citizens, as outsiders to, perhaps even enemies of, the nation.[5]

The Palestinian minority is also an example of what Will Kymlicka distinguishes as national minorities who have acquired their minority status involuntarily and often unwillingly, due to historical circumstances of colonization, territorial expansion, and similar factors. These minorities, according to Kymlicka, are entitled to collective group-differentiated rights, including rights of self-government. The Palestinian minority in Israel is such an involuntary minority. After the *Nakba* (catastrophe) of 1948, the Palestinians who remained within the boundaries of the newly created State of Israel became a national minority, "ruled by a powerful, sophisticated majority against whom they fought to retain their country and land." In 2010, this minority constituted about seventeen percent (approximately 1.2 million people) of the total population of Israel.[6]

Notwithstanding other important turning points in the history of the Palestinian minority *vis-à-vis* the State of Israel, the signing of the Oslo Accords in 1993 between the Palestinian Liberation Organization (PLO) and the State of Israel signaled a moment of reflexivity. The Accords made it clear to the Palestinians in Israel that they did not share any feasible political future with the rest of the Palestinian people. Marginalized once by the Jewish majority in Israel and once again by the majority of Palestinians who are not Israelis, the Palestinians in Israel came to realize that their status as a "trapped minority" was not temporary, and that the establishment of a Palestinian state would not necessarily guarantee an improvement in their political status in the Jewish state. Therefore, since the mid-1990s, the attempts to seek a solution for the crisis of the Palestinians in Israel have become more palpable and more critical of the exclusive nature of Israel as an ethnically based state.[7]

Significantly, the tragic events of October 2000, in which thirteen Palestinian citizens of Israel were killed by Israeli police forces after police forces ignored their right of protest,[8] reminded the Palestinians in Israel that despite peace talks, it was clear that citizenship for Palestinians in Israel would always remain partial, incomplete, and under harsh control. Most importantly, these events and their aftermath intensified the lack of trust in the effectiveness of Israeli parliamentary politics as a promoter of collective action, as a vehicle for social mobility, and as a shield against the state's restrictions and violence. The perceived ineffectiveness of Palestinian political leadership generated more room for collective action by the leadership of Palestinian civil society.

Since 2000, the political role of this leadership in the campaign for Palestinian civil and national equality in Israel has undoubtedly become increasingly more significant, varied, independent, and proactive.[9] Convinced that political recognition and allocation of resources are inherently interdependent, Palestinian civil society in Israel has begun to focus on renouncing the exclusive definition of Israel as a Jewish state and placing more emphasis on the indigenous status of the Palestinian minority in Israel to justify demands for collective rights in a variety of domains, such as culture, religion, and education.

However, in this new political discourse, predominantly led by civil society organizations, citizenship is still viewed as the main instrument for socio-economic mobilization, development, and democratization and as the major maneuvering space for negotiation, resistance, and contention for the Palestinians in Israel. This political discourse has culminated in the publication of four documents, entitled the *Future Vision* documents,[10] in which diverse Palestinian intellectuals and activists proposed new political arrangements to concede more power-sharing, recognition, and equality to the Palestinian minority in Israel.

These documents present a double challenge: the continuity of Palestinian nationalism and the inclusion of Israeli citizenship. They do so by embracing, indeed centering, the liminality[11] of the Palestinians in Israel as a political platform upon which to articulate and realize possibilities for reforming Israeli citizenship, and to introduce and open venues to explore the extent and depth of difference between the Palestinians in Israel the rest of the Palestinian people.

More than anything else, these documents present an authentic search for a new self-definition, a new identity for the Palestinians in Israel. In the words of the introduction to the *Future Vision* document: "the goal of this work is to respond to the crucial question: 'Who are we and what do we want for the good of our society?'" The document's answer to this question is that the Palestinian minority in Israel should exercise the right of self-determination in Israel in the form of a cultural autonomy through which they could enjoy collective rights, including self-government rights in language, religion, and education. For the Palestinians in Israel, the fulfillment of these rights is not territorial, but rather cultural and linguistic. It is worth noting that these documents raise demands not only *vis-à-vis* the state, but also the Arab local government and civil society organizations, calling on them to assume more responsibility for addressing issues such as poverty, development, and the status of women.[12]

Clearly, the deteriorating conditions and failing achievements of the Arab educational system are a main concern in these documents. For example, the *Future Vision* document has an entire chapter on education, which recommends various policies to be adopted by the state and a variety of measures to be taken by the Arab local government municipalities and the Arab civil society organizations. Among these, there is an explicit call for the Palestinians in Israel to "aspire to attain institutional self-rule in the field of education, culture and religion that is in fact part of fulfilling their rights as citizens and as part of the Israeli state . . . The State should recognize the Palestinian Arabs in Israel as an indigenous national group (and as a minority within the international conventions) that has the right within their citizenship to choose its representatives directly and be responsible for their religious, educational and cultural affairs." Elsewhere in the same document, the state is explicitly directed to provide a "guarantee of self-rule of the Palestinian Arabs in the fields of education, religion, culture and media and recognizing their right to self determination with respect to their collective life complementing their partnership within the state." The chapter that proposes a strategic vision for Arab education also discusses "the right of the Palestinian Arabs in Israel (as indigenous people in their homeland) to self-administration of the educational system and to self determination of its policy." In another document, *The Haifa Declaration*, there is an avowal that the state should guarantee the Palestinians' "right to cultural autonomy, which includes the rights to develop policies for and to administer their own cultural and educational affairs."[13]

Such demands gave a boost to the establishment of an independent APC, which is seen as a concrete step towards advancing self-steering capacities of cultural autonomy in education, as I will explain in the following sections. The connection between the APC initiative and the *Future Vision* documents, as an embodiment of the new political discourse described earlier, was officially recognized in the Follow-Up Committee on Arab Education board's decision to adopt the recommendation in the education section of *The Future Vision* in 2007.

ARAB EDUCATION IN ISRAEL

The state education system in Israel is divided into different sectors, which cater to the various social groups in Israeli society. Jewish and Arab schoolchildren, as well as secular and religious Jews, attend different schools. In this regard, the state differentiates between different sects and levels of religiosity, providing state-funded learning environments for a variety of Jewish groups. The State Education Law (1953) recognizes the existence of separate and independent educational systems for secular and religious state schools. However, the law, which defines the structural components and goals of state education, does not officially recognize the existence of an Arab education system, which in reality functions as a separate and marginalized body within the state education system. The single instance of legislative acknowledgement of "non-Jewish" education appears in Article 4 of the State Education Law, which states that "in non-Jewish educational institutions, the curriculum shall be adapted to the special conditions thereof." Specifically, the law provides for the Minister of Education to promulgate regulations for the adaptation of the provisions of the law to the needs of those students.[14]

After decades of this law ignoring the existence of Arabs, it was amended in the year 2000. Article 2(11) of the amended law decreed that among the objectives of education was the learning of "the language, culture, history, heritage, and unique tradition of the Arab population and of other population groups in Israel, and recognition of the equal rights of all citizens of Israel." However, this positive development was perceived as too little too late, as the amendment did not grant any level of autonomy to the Arab education system or provide for the amendment's objective to be implemented in the curricula.

The issue of the depth and scope of the autonomy of the Arab education system and its capability for self-administration, similar, for example, to the state religious education system, has been a long-standing controversy. For example, in 1996, Professor Amnon Rubinstein, then Minister of Education, appointed an Arab Advisory Council, with Arab and Jewish members, in accordance with new special regulations that he had sanctioned for this purpose. The regulations stipulated that the goal of the council was to examine the situation of Arab education and to propose to the minister programs and actions that would advance Arab education and integrate it within the state education system. The regulations delegated power to the council to assist the minister in crystallizing educational and pedagogical policies that would ensure the equal status of the Arab citizens, taking into consideration their heritage and their linguistic and cultural distinctiveness. However, the regulations did not oblige the minister to advise the council, as is the case with the pedagogical council of the state religious education system, let alone to accept its recommendations. Furthermore, the regulations did not provide any resources or specify any mechanisms for its implementation. The council, after a series of discussions, submitted a report to the minister regarding how to improve Arab education and change its structure. Among other things, the council recommended establishing an independent Arab pedagogical council within the Ministry of Education. To cut a long story short, Rubinstein rejected the recommendations of the council's report and, consequently, the majority of the members resigned. Despite the fact that the regulations are still in place, the council never formed again and its work never resumed.[15]

The chronicle of the Arab Advisory Council exemplifies how the disregard for national and cultural uniqueness goes hand in hand with the marginal, almost incidental, participation of Arab academics and educationalists in education policy and decision-making. In 2008, there were only 129 Arab employees in the headquarters and regional offices of the Ministry of Education, comprising 6.4 percent of the entire ministry staff. The literature on the Arab education system on the whole confirms Sami Mari's earlier observation that the State of Israel uses Arab education to control the Arab minority in Israel. Mari contended that Arab education was designed by the state's policies "to instill feelings of self-disparagement and inferiority in Arab youth; to de-nationalize them, and particularly to de-Palestinize them; and to teach them to glorify the history, culture, and achievements of the Jewish majority." In line with this argument, Majid Al-Haj also alleged that Arab education in Israel is in constant tension between the desire of the Arab minority to use it as a tool for socioeconomic mobility and the use of education by the state as a means of controlling the Arab minority. This control is exerted, among other means, through voiding the curriculum of any national-ethnic content, co-opting Arab academics and turning them into technocrats and their teaching apolitical.[16]

Regrettably, these observations seem to still be valid. In August 2009, the new minister of education, Gideon Saar, presented his educational policy to the Israeli government in a document entitled, "The Government of Israel Believes in Education."[17] This policy statement included comprehensive steps for achieving the goals of strengthening values education and improving academic achievement within the Israeli education system. However, it barely addressed the distinctive educational and cultural needs of Arab education. While noting the deteriorating performance of Arab-Palestinian students in national and international tests, it did not propose special programs to bolster achievement levels. Minister Saar's plan also aimed to strengthen education in the area of Zionist, democratic, and civic values, including reinforcing students' connection to Jewish heritage through academic studies, visits to historical sites, promoting enlistment in the Israeli army, and bolstering the overall connection between society and the education system. At the same time, the plan neglected Arab-Palestinian heritage and historical sites and made no attempt to propose any notion of values education for the Arab education system or any possibility for a shared civic culture in Israel.

This plan is representative of unrelenting attempts in recent years to marginalize expressions of a collective Palestinian identity within the Israeli public. Such attempts have been widespread and particularly strident since 2009. They reflect the current far-right influences within Prime Minister Benjamin Netanyahu's government. The right's renewed rise to power has brought with it a number of bills that propose a wide range of infringements on Arab-Palestinian civil rights. These bills take aim at everything from citizenship status to the right of recognition of Palestinians' historical experience and collective memory. For example, just recently, the "*Nakba* Law," which prohibits state funds from being used to commemorate the *Nakba* (literally "catastrophe"—the Palestinian term for Israel's establishment) and the bill allowing small communities to set up admission committees were passed. *Haaretz*'s editorial comment on both laws was as follows: "The two laws are the latest in a growing list of disgraceful legislation whose entire purpose is to discriminate against Israel's Arab citizens, intimidate them and deny them their rights . . . These laws . . . are dangerously chipping away at Israeli democracy."[18]

This denial of the collective Palestinian memory is intensely reflected in recent pedagogical decisions made through the Ministry of Education. For example, in 2009, Ministry of Education regulations removed the term *Nakba* from the curricula and textbooks used in Arab schools and took the unusual step of collecting all copies of an eleventh- and twelfth-grade history textbook, *Nationalism: Building a State in the Middle East*, which presented the Palestinian claim that there had been ethnic cleansing in 1948. In 2010, the Ministry of Education banned a textbook entitled *Learning the Historical Narrative of the Other*, which presented both the

Israeli and the Palestinian narratives. In the same year, Dr. Zvi Zameret, chairman of the Pedagogical Secretariat of the Ministry of Education, mandated the revising, indeed rewriting, of the widely used civics text-book, *To Be a Citizen in Israel*. He objected to the text as "too critical of the state"; he was particularly disturbed by a sentence that read: "Since its establishment, the State of Israel has engaged in a policy of discrim-ination against its Arab citizens." These examples are indicative of the recent ultra-nationalistic mania that has been spreading and taking hold of Israeli politics and education.[19]

At the same time, Arab educational performance continues to fall short, behind that of the Jewish education system. For example, in the last international assessment of the TIMSS (the Trends in International Mathematics and Science Study), in a list ranking a total of forty-nine countries, Israel was rated twenty-fourth in mathematics. However, Israeli Jewish students separately would have ranked nineteenth, while Israeli Arabs would have come in thirty-fourth. Meanwhile, students in neigh-boring Arab countries—for example, Lebanon, Jordan, and Syria—scored higher than Israel's Arabs in math. Similar gaps also exist in science. The 2009 results from PISA (the Program for International Student Assess-ment) are also instructive. For example, in a list of approximately sixty-four participating countries, while Israeli Jewish students alone would have ranked seventeenth in language literacy, Israeli Arabs would have come in fifty-seventh.[20]

To understand how these gaps originate, we can look at two indica-tors, both of which illustrate the disgraceful and ignominious working conditions of the Arab education system. First, a joint report produced by the Ministry of Education and the Follow-Up Committee on Arab Education indicates that by the end of 2012, the Arab education system will be short some 9,236 classrooms. Yet when the Ministry of Education and the Ministry of Finance allocated funding in 2009 for approximately 1,600 classrooms per year, only 600 were for Arab education. The second indictor involves the quality of curricula, based on a recently released research report published by the Arab Cultural Association. According to this report, there were more than 16,000 language and syntax mistakes in the textbooks of all subjects studied in the third through ninth grades in the

Arab education system. In math books for eight- to fifteen-year-olds, there were at least 7,532 mistakes; in three geography and history books, there were 3,939 mistakes. Hundreds of mistakes were also found in textbooks for the study of the Arabic language.[21]

That said, admittedly, the government did implement several programs, such as the "Five Years Program" (*Tochnit Ha'humesh*), in order to narrow the gap in resources allocation and achievement between Arab and Jewish schools in Israel. However, none of these policy plans created long-term sustainable change. Moreover, the governmental committees formed and official reports drafted[22] to improve Arab education in Israel failed to realize that issues related to Arab education are not merely and solely pedagogical or budgetary, but also political and structural. Above all, they failed to recognize that the Arab education system in Israel should serve a distinct national and indigenous minority. More specifically, these committees and reports did not address structural issues of governance and budgeting and did not consider alternative structures that would grant more autonomous and self-administration capacities. Instead, they provided short-sighted, partial, additive, incremental, and sporadic solutions that are still centralized and that exclude, to a large extent, the Arab leadership in local government, the academy, and Arab civil society. These were often solutions for managing the gaps between Arab and Jewish education, rather than for closing them.

THE ARAB PEDAGOGIC COUNCIL

In September 2008, the FUCAE held a press conference in Nazareth to announce the launch of a new public campaign to found an Arab Pedagogical Council (APC) for the Arab education system in Israel, under the title "The Arab Pedagogic Council: collective right and educational need."[23] Based in Nazareth, the FUCAE was founded in 1984 as a public non-profit organization, under the auspices of the National Committee for Arab Mayors and the Supreme Follow-Up Committee for the Palestinian Arabs in Israel. It represents the Arab public in its struggles to fulfill the right to education, including advancing equality between Arab and Jewish education and advocating for new legislation and structural reforms for the Arab education system that would enable Arab pupils to develop their cultural and national identity and would achieve self-steering capacities for the system.

According to the FUCAE's official website, its primary objective is to "advance Arab education on all levels in the belief that each and every child has the fundamental right to education, self-fulfillment, and equal opportunity to realize his or her abilities and talents." To achieve this, the committee identifies four main goals: equal education for Arabs and Jews in all aspects, including the physical surroundings and infrastructures of the educational institutions, their budgets and resources, standards and achievements; amendment of the existing framework and objectives of Arab education, and initiation of educational and cultural policy in order to increase the Arab public's involvement in deciding on educational and cultural policy; development of Arab students' national-cultural identity; increased Arab and Israeli public awareness regarding the condition of Arab education.[24]

The goals and areas of activity of the FUCAE indicate that the state and state institutions are the focus of its activity. FUCAE seeks to realize the right of Arab students for equal education, both as individual entitled citizens, and as a national minority, with regard to material resources and the recognition that enables the formation of a national and cultural identity.

To return to the APC initiative: according to Majid Al-Haj, the call to establish a special pedagogical secretary for Arab education, whose head and members would be Arab and which would be responsible for curricular issues, was first raised and officially approved at the second annual convention of Arab local authority heads and mayors in May 1984. This demand was raised again in 1989, at the third annual convention. Later, in 2006, as discussed earlier, this demand appeared forcefully in the *Future Vision* documents.[25]

The early demands were raised based on a functional, rational, consumerist ideal, according to which an independent Arab council was instrumentally viewed as a vehicle to improve Arab education and to facilitate more Arab participation. The demands raised later, especially in the *Future Vision* documents, were part of the new political discourse described earlier in this chapter. This political discourse emphasized collective rights, the politicization of the indigenousness of the Palestinians in Israel to demand self-determination group-based rights, and a continuous challenge to the Jewish characteristics of the state. However, there has been considerable confusion as how to practically attain institutional self-rule in the field of education. Specifically, there have been two overlapping voices with regard to the APC. The first voice speaks in favor of an independent, autonomous Arab education system (stream) within the Ministry of Education that would have its own pedagogical council, similar to the one that the state religious education stream has. The second voice speaks in favor of an independent APC that, while recognized by the Ministry of Education, would operate from the outside as a watchdog organization to guard the strategic interests of Arab education, as part of the Arab civil society. It would continue to exist regardless of the institutions the Ministry of Education might develop within it, even if an Arab pedagogical council or secretary were established within the ministry. Although this would be a welcome development, it would not be a reason to dissolve the APC, which would continue to work from the outside as an authentic representative body of the Arab public.

The campaign for establishing the APC quickly received widespread public support. A 2011 poll showed that the vast majority of individuals in the Arab sector, more than 90 percent, supported statements that called for regulating the status of Arab education in a special new law, having more Arab influence on and participation in the making of curricular policies, reflecting the Arab culture and heritage in the curricula, and establishing an Arab pedagogical council similar to the state religious education. These findings were not surprising, as they were in line with the results of the survey conducted by Khalid Abu-Asbah in 2007, in which he found a wide consensus among Arab educators and principals, as well as Arab leadership, on the need to establish a self-steered Arab education system.[26]

On the other hand, the findings in the Jewish sector were slightly surprising, as they revealed some support as well. The poll indicated that one-third of the Jewish public supported passing a special law that would regulate and recognize the cultural distinctiveness of the Arab education system in Israel. One-third also supported establishing a self-steering

Arab education stream within the Ministry of Education, similar to the state religious education stream. Moreover, fifty-five percent of the Jewish public supported, in various levels, the curriculum in Arab education reflecting the culture and history of the Arab society in Israel. Fifty-one percent agreed that Arab educational leaders should be allowed to exercise more influence on the curricula and textbook content.[27]

A variety of concerns were raised with regard to the APC initiative and voiced at roundtables and conferences, including a July 2008 conference jointly organized by the Legal Clinics of the Faculty of Law at Tel Aviv University and Dirasat, the Arab Center for Law and Policy. At this conference, in which I took a leading part, several concerns were raised in regard to the prospect and trajectory of the APC initiative.[28] These included the following:

- The initiative might lead to national separatism and segregation, and to widening the tense rift between Arabs and Jews.
- At times of privatization, the initiative might encourage the state to direct fewer resources to and decrease its responsibility for Arab education, under the guise of encouraging cultural recognition, decentralization, and the devolution of authority in education—namely, the state could advance recognition at the expense of equality.
- In the absence of Arab political power in the parliament and government, Arab education, if autonomous and separate, would receive fewer resources and attention from the government, as there is no political power to serve its interests, as, for example, Jewish religious groups do for Jewish education.
- The Arab community does not yet have the professional capabilities and the required political and social readiness for this move, as there is no consensus on either Arab education goals and values, or the scope and depth of the autonomy required for Arab education.
- Without consensual exit rights for the minorities within the Palestinian minority, one self-steering Arab education might jeopardize the internal diversity and multiculturalism of the Palestinian minority, which is composed of different cultural and religious groups.

- An autonomous Arab education might lead to indoctrination, disregard of personal autonomy and parental choice, and eventually enabling increased influence of fundamental religious and extreme political groups.
- The initiative would provide only a partial solution that emphasized politics of recognition at the expense of politics of equality in the distribution of the state's resources, and it would be better to position the establishment of the Arab education system within a wider political rearrangement of the majority–minority power relations in Israel.

To address these concerns, the campaign emphasized that the overarching objective of this initiative was to empower Arab education through the realization of the Arab minority of Israel's basic right to education. More specifically, the FUCAE clarified that it sought to establish a professional body that would take a more proactive role in guiding and supervising the quality of curricular policies and practices in Arab schools in Israel, including curricula guidelines and textbooks, especially in key identity-building subjects, such as language, history, civics, geography, and social studies. The role of the council would be to steer Arab education to gain a wider consensus on the goals and core curricula content, better engagement with the Palestinian history and culture, and an improved encounter with the social problems facing Arab society, such as violence, poverty, and unemployment.

To start with, the campaign, before the actual establishment of the council, aimed at raising awareness and starting a public deliberation with regard to three central problems in Arab education:

- The lack of updated goals to direct the pedagogic work in Arab schools and assist in prioritizing its missions and in guiding Arab educators regarding their moral and professional dilemmas.
- The lack of formal legal status for Arab education, protected by law and including the basic human rights of the Arab minority to education.
- The lack of a special professional, representative, and autonomous administrative structure within the Ministry of Education, empowered

to comprehensively, systematically, and efficiently address the pedagogic needs of the Arab education system and to propose curricular policies that would be in line with the requirements of international law with regard to the right to education in the context of an indigenous minority.

The campaign emphasized that the FUCAE aspired to gain the recognition and cooperation of the Ministry of Education. The campaign's founding document asserts: "Our demand for a separate Arab educational system is not an expression of a (separatist) desire to break away from the State of Israel. On the contrary, it is a demand for recognition and for support to practice our unique culture, just like the Israeli religious educational system." Despite explicit calls for coordination, the Ministry of Education renounced the idea and refrained from cooperation.[29]

Nevertheless, in July 2010, a council was established as a voluntary group of thirty leading Arab academics and professionals. Professor Muhamad Amara, a prominent sociolinguist and a leading civil society activist, was elected to chair the council. The group started a process of strategic planning for its activities, managed to receive funding from the New Israel Fund and the European Union, commissioned a series of position papers, initiated a public debate to draft specific goals for the Arab education system in Israel, and launched a series of study tours, conferences, and roundtables.

CONCLUDING THOUGHTS

The initiative was launched under the motto, "the Arab pedagogic council is a collective right and an educational need." This slogan vividly captures the dual nature of this initiative. On the one hand, it entails a practical, even consumerist, pragmatic approach that seeks to propose solutions for the actual problems of the Arab education system. Here, the emphasis is on educational needs with regard to a variety of issues, including reforming teacher education, improving achievement in national and international tests, enhancing parental involvement, advancing more decentralization, and adapting the curricula to accommodate the cultural needs of the Arab students. On the other hand, the initiative reflects a strong approach of politics of identity and belonging, drawing on international law to support the strategic interests of Arab education in quality education, power sharing, and having a seat at the table of policy-making, recognition of the Palestinian narrative and the distinct social problems that the Palestinian minority faces in Israel, and equality in the allocation of the material and symbolic resources of the state.

Of course, the two approaches overlap and reflect the recent transformations in Arab politics in Israel, addressed earlier. Yet, what has become more clear is the interaction of compromise and competition between two types of identity politics—one substantially liberal, the other substantially communal. On the one hand, the APC initiative reflects a partial withdrawal from and disappointment with liberal politics based on relationships with the state and the rights derived from it. These "state-centered politics" strive to greatly influence government policy and change the structure, distribution, and representation of power in Israel. These politics place their trust in the possibility of changing government priorities through advocacy, lobbying, research, litigation, and involving governmental ministries and agencies in projects designed to improve the quality of life among the Arabs and advance their political participation within the citizenship framework.

On the other hand, the APC initiative is also indicative of a strengthening of "community-centered politics," which focus on culture and community. The community-centered politics discourse sanctifies the values of belonging and service to the political-civil community; its core is the concept of responsibility, which receives the emphasis placed on rights in liberal discourse. These politics strive to influence the community's priorities, self-definition, and character, in addition to the nature of the social and political organizations working in its midst. Community-centered politics places its trust in changing the community's priorities, achieving internal consensus, and constructing independent political institutions and processes.

Both of these approaches are reflected in the APC initiative's objectives and activities. The first approach, which is state-centered and oriented toward integration, is visible in arguments for the APC made during the deliberations on the initiative—the desire to propose corrections and changes to the Ministry of Education's curricula and to produce complementary and alternative curricular materials, to have a legal and administrative status similar to the religious state education, to propose new specific legislation for the Arab education system, and to have a collective voice in the debate on the core curriculum in Israel—and in the debate on the recent proposal for a "Public Education Law," promoted by Hakol Hinuch, the Movement for the Advancement of Education in Israel.[30] The second approach, which is community-centered and oriented toward community empowerment, is seen in objectives such as having consensual goals for Arab education through public deliberation; having a professional body that is capable of steering Arab schools; claiming responsibility over the deteriorating working conditions and achievement of the Arab education system; advancing the establishment of a self-steering democratic Arab education that would be a fulfillment of the minority's collective right to education; and nourishing the national and cultural identity of the Palestinians in Israel, and protecting their cultural liberty.

Yet, as the APC initiative is heavily engaged with both Israeli citizenship and Palestinian nationalism, it seeks to transform both. It does so by making two pivotal demands: to transform Israel into a state of all its citizens; and to recognize the Palestinians in Israel as a national minority. In the education field, the first would in effect terminate the exclusive Jewish hegemony over public state education as a public sphere in which, for the most part, only the narratives and interests of the Jewish majority are cultivated and protected. The second actually means exercising collective rights in the framework of self-administration and cultural autonomy for the Palestinians in Israel. The assumption is that the first satisfies the civic aspirations of the Palestinians in Israel, while the second fulfills their national aspirations.

Nonetheless, the two aspirations are not separate or disconnected. On the contrary, one reframes and constitutes the other. To clarify, this initiative challenges the separation between Palestinian nationalism and Israeli citizenship by presenting two overlapping types of demands. The demand to transform Israel into a state of all its citizens primarily challenges the imbalance of power *vis-à-vis* the majority society and questions the willingness of the Palestinians to accept the implications of a positive and inclusive Israeli response to this demand. The second demand primarily challenges the wholeness and the political continuity of the Palestinian people. It further questions the relationships between the indigenous Palestinian citizens in Israel and other parts of the Palestinian people in the Palestinian-occupied territories and the Diaspora, suggesting that the Palestinians in Israel are an independent political actor within the Palestinian people, searching for its own common good and right for self-determination as an indigenous minority in Israel. Therefore, claims are raised not only *vis-à-vis* the state, but also Arab local government and civil society organizations to assume more responsibilities. In this regard, Israeli citizenship is taken as a maneuvering space for resistance, as a structure of opportunity, and as a resource for political mobilization.[31]

The various demands raised through the APC initiative embody a strong commitment to the ideal of a "deliberative democracy," in which deliberation is seen as a tool for increasing political participation and the quality of democratic decision-making. Again, the deliberation is not restricted to interaction with the state, but also involves Arab politics. More specifically, bearing in mind that deliberation, among other things, is also about reflectivity and creativity, the APC initiative has also created a tense space of contention and disagreements between itself and the FUCAE, the incubating organization of the initiative. In this space, the leaders of the initiative have often been critical of some of the FUCAE activities, and these leaders have been consistent in their attempt to differentiate the initiative as politically more inclusive, more creative, and focusing more on strategic interests rather than on practical needs. With this initiative, participants become claim-making subjects who challenge aspects of extent (rules and norms of exclusion and inclusion), content (rights and responsibilities), and depth (of belonging) of citizenship in the field of Israeli education.[32]

Most importantly, participants become claimants of three types of rights—political, economic, and social: the right to participate in the political process of curricular policy-making; the right to enjoy a fair distribution of recognition and identity-building resources; and the right to be free from oppression and domination. More specifically, they become claimants of the right to education. This type of right is indeed a universal, inalienable, and non-discriminatory human right, which was recognized in the Universal Declaration of Human Rights in 1948, and has since been enshrined in various international conventions. This right is predicated upon the idea that for education to be a meaningful right, it must be available, accessible, acceptable, and adaptable.[33]

In the context of the APC intiative, notwithstanding the principle of the best interests of the child, availability means that public state education in Israel should provide educational opportunities, especially schooling, that are required to respect parental freedom and the cultural liberty of the minority to choose the form and content of education that is suitable for their children. In the same context, accessibility means that public state education in Israel must be non-discriminatory and that the system must activate certain mechanisms to ensure that the marginalized Arab minority in Israel has access to and influence on decisions and policy-making in education. However, the most important principles in this initiative are acceptability and adaptability. Acceptability means that the content of the Arab education is relevant, non-discriminatory, and culturally appropriate; whereas adaptability requires that Arab education be adapted locally to suit specific contexts of the Palestinian minority. The demands of the APC are not specific only to Arab education, as they would also require education in Israel to be more pluralistic, culturally appropriate, and more open and tolerant, especially in the curricula, towards diversity, multiple narratives, and specifically the cultural and linguistic needs of the Arab pupils.

To conclude, the APC is a citizenship act geared to constitute the Palestinian minority as a claimant of the right to education. It has great potential for peace and reconciliation, as it demands accommodation and recognition—rights that ultimately would mitigate the conflicts and tensions in minority–majority relations in Israel—and it generates pride and belonging. It is another contentious performance in the search for equality in the political status of the Arab citizens and for a public sphere, especially in education, in which different and competing perceptions of the good can coexist.

NOTES

1   Education as arena for minorities' struggles: Tony Gallagher, *Education in Divided Societies* (New York: Palgrave Macmillan, 2004). Education as part of nation-building process: Lawrence J. Saha, Holger Daun, and Joseph Zajda, *Nation-Building, Identity, and Citizenship Education: Cross-cultural Perspectives* (Dordrecht: Springer, 2009). Philosophy of integration: Adrian Favell, *Philosophies of Integration: Immigration and the Idea of Citizenship in France and Britain* (Houndsmill, UK: Palgrave in association with the Centre for Research in Ethnic Relations, University of Warwick), 2001. Perpetuation of official knowledge: Michael W. Apple, *Official Knowledge: Democratic Education in a Conservative Age* (New York: Routledge, 2000). Story of peoplehood: Rogers M. Smith, *Stories of Peoplehood: The Politics and Morals of Political Membership* (Cambridge, Cambridge University Press, 2003). Site of contention for minorities: Will Kymlicka, *Multicultural Citizenship: A Liberal Theory of Minority Rights* (Oxford: Clarendon Press, 1995).

2   On acts of citizenship and on contentious performance, see Engin F. Isin and Greg M. Nielsen, eds., *Acts of Citizenship* (London: Zed Books, 2008); Charles Tilly, *Contentious Performance* (Cambridge: Cambridge University Press, 2008). Similar organizations to the FUCAE include, among others, the Masuau Institute for Arab Civil Rights, the Adallah Legal Institute for Arab Minority Rights, and the Arab Center for Alternative Planning.

3   Isin and Nielsen, *Acts of Citizenship*, 39. Charles Tilly, *Social Movements, 1768–2004* (Boulder, CO: Paradigm, 2004). Tilly quotation from Tilly, *Contentious Performance*, 5. On the politics of contention, see also Charles Tilly and Sidney Tarrow, *Contentious Politics* (Boulder, CO: Paradigm, 2007).

4   Production and dissemination of other curricular materials: see, for example, the initiative of Ibn Khaldun—The Arab Association for Research and Development and the Center to Combat Racism—to produce and distribute an alternative list of terms under the title, "Identity and Belonging," to introduce Arab pupils to cultural icons, symbols, and institutions of the Palestinian people. This initiative was developed in response to the Ministry of Education's core curriculum program of 2005—"100 Concepts in Heritage, Zionist and Democracy Program" (The 100 Concepts Program)—that was designed for middle-school pupils (grades seven to nine) in both the Hebrew and Arabic school systems. See more in A. Ghanem, "'Identity and Belonging': A Pioneering Project Which Must Be the Starting Point for an Alternative, Comprehensive Educational Plan," *Adalah's Newsletter* 27 (July–August 2006), http://www.adalah.org/newsletter/eng/jul-aug06/ar2.pdf (accessed June 26, 2012). On this matter, also see Y. Peled, "The 100 Terms Program: A Rawlsian Critique," *Adalah's Newsletter* 27 (July–August 2006), http://www.adalah.org/newsletter/eng/jul-aug06/ar1.pdf, (accessed June 26, 2012). Davies, "Interruptive Democracy," final quotation, 19.

5   Gershon Shafir and Yoav Peled, *Being Israeli: The Dynamics of Multiple Citizenship* (Cambridge: Cambridge University Press, 2002). Majority as against Arab citizens:

Oren Yiftachel, *Ethnocracy: Land and Identity Politics in Israel/Palestine* (Philadelphia: University of Pennsylvania Press, 2006). R. Brubaker, "In the Name of the Nation: Reflections on Nationalism and Patriotism," *Citizenship Studies* 8 (2004): 115–28.

6   Kymlicka, *Multicultural Citizenship*. Quotation from Sami Khalil Mari, *Arab Education in Israel* (Syracuse, NY: Syracuse University Press, 1978), 18. Statistics: Khamaisi, *Arab Society in Israel*.

7   Marginalization of Palestinians in Israel: Al-Haj, "Identity and Orientation." Trapped minority: D Rabinowitz, "The Palestinian Citizens of Israel, the Concept of Trapped Minority and the Discourse of Transnationalism in Anthropology," *Ethnic and Racial Studies* 24 (2001): 64–85. A. Ghanem, "The Palestinians in Israel: Political Orientation and Aspirations," *International Journal of Intercultural Relations* 26, no. 2 (2002): 135–52.

8   Y. Peled, "Citizenship Betrayed: Israel's Emerging Immigration and Citizenship Regime," *Theoretical Inquiries in Law* 8, no. 2 (2007): 603–28.

9   See more on Palestinian civil society in Shany Payes, *Palestinian NGOs in Israel: The Politics of Civil Society* (London: Tauris Academic Studies, 2005); A. Jamal, "Strategies of Minority Struggle for Equality in Ethnic States: Arab Politics in Israel," *Citizenship Studies* 11, no. 3 (2007): 263–82, and "The Counter-Hegemonic Role of Civil Society: Palestinian-Arab NGOs in Israel," *Citizenship Studies* 12, no. 3 (2008): 283–306.

10   See more on the politics of contention in the context of the Palestinian minority in Israel in Amal Jamal, *The Palestinian National Movement: Politics of Contention, 1967–2005* (Bloomington, IN: Indiana University Press, 2005). The *Future Vision* documents include *Future Vision*; *Equal Constitution for All*; *Democratic Constitution*; and *Haifa Declaration*. See more on these documents in Agbaria and Mustafa, "Challenging the Boundaries"; Jamal, *Palestinian National Movement*; and Jamal, "Political Ethos."

11   See more on the meaning of the status of liminality of the Palestinians in Israel in Ghanem, "Natives and Citizens."

12   Quotation from *Future Vision*, 6. Demands on other Arab organizations: Totary, "Future Vision Documents."

13   Quotations from *Future Vision*, 10–11, 15, 18, and Haifa Declaration, 16.

14   State Education Law, 5713-1953, 7 LSI 113 (1952–53) (Isr.). There were several amendments to the statute. A Hebrew consolidated version, accessed June 27, 2012, is available at http://cms.education.gov.il/EducationCMS/Units/Zchuyot/Chukim/Veamanot/Chukim/ChokChinuchMamlachti1953.htm. See more on the legal status of Arab education in Israel in Y. T. Jabareen, I. Abu-Saad, and D. Champagne, "Law and Education: Critical Perspectives on Arab Palestinian Education in Israel," *American Behavioral Scientist* 49, no. 8 (2006): 1052–74.

15   K. Abu-Asbah, *Arab Education in Israel: Dilemmas of a National Minority* (Jerusalem: Florscheim Institute, 2007) [Hebrew].

16   Employee numbers: Parliamentary Inquiry Committee, *Minutes No. 7*. See more on the history and current conditions of the Arab education system in Abu-Asbah, *Arab Education in Israel*; Abu-Saad, "Palestinian Education in Israel"; Majid Al-Haj, *Education, Empowerment and Control: The Case of the Arabs in Israel* (Albany: State University of New York Press, 1995); Jabareen and Agbaria, "Education on Hold";

I. Makkawi, "Role Conflict and the Dilemma of Palestinian Teachers in Israel," *Comparative Education* 38 (2002): 39–52; Mari, *Arab Education in Israel*; and A. E. Mazawi, "Teachers' Role Patterns and the Mediation of Sociopolitical Change: The Case of Palestinian Arab School Teachers," *British Journal of Sociology of Education* 15, no. 4 (1994): 497. Mari's observation: Mari, *Arab Education in Israel*, quotation, 37. Al-Haj, *Education, Empowerment and Control*.

17   Ministry of Education, "Israeli Government Believes in Education."

18   "Silence over Nakba Law Encourages Racism" (editorial), *Haaretz*, March 25, 2011, http://www.haaretz.com/print-edition/opinion/silence-over-nakba-law-encourages-racism-1.351694 (accessed June 20, 2012).

19   "Israel Bans Use of Palestinian Term 'Nakba' in Textbooks," *Haaretz*, July 22, 2009, http://www.haaretz.com/news/israel-bans-use-of-palestinian-term-nakba-in-textbooks-1.280515 (accessed June 20, 2012). Or Kashti, "Israel Pulls Textbook with Chapter on Nakba," *Haaretz*, October 19, 2009, http://www.haaretz.com/print-edition/features/israel-pulls-textbook-with-chapter-on-nakba-1.5858 (accessed June 20, 2012). Or Kashti, "Education Ministry Bans Textbook That Offers Palestinian Narrative," *Haaretz*, September 27, 2010, http://www.haaretz.com/print-edition/news/education-ministry-bans-textbook-that-offers-palestinian-narrative-1.315838, (accessed June 20, 2012). Or Kashti, "Education Ministry Revising Textbook for Being Too Critical of Israel," *Haaretz*, August 29, 2010, http://www.haaretz.com/print-edition/news/education-ministry-revising-textbook-for-being-too-critical-of-israel-1.310751 (accessed June 20, 2012)—more recently, in 2011, the education minister, relieved of his role as the ministry's chairman of its professional advisory committee on civics, along with another panel member, Professor Suzie Navot, expressed opposition to changes in the civics curriculum being pushed by the ministry's pedagogical secretariat: Or Kashti, "Battle over Civics Ends in Ouster of Two Critics," *Haaretz*, May 26, 2011, http://www.haaretz.com/print-edition/news/battle-over-civics-ends-in-ouster-of-two-critics-1.364081 (accessed June 20, 2012).

20   See more details on the results of the Arab education system in national and international tests on the website of the National Authority for Measurement and Evaluation in Education—RAMA, http://cms.education.gov.il/educationcms/units/rama/ [in Hebrew] (accessed June 20, 2012).

21   Shortage of Arab classrooms: Kashti, "The Plan." Funds provided for Arab classrooms: Committee on Education, Minutes No. 27. Mistakes in Arab textbooks: Jack Khoury, "Israel's Textbooks in Arabic Are Full of Mistakes, Study Finds," *Haaretz*, May 9, 2011, http://www.haaretz.com/print-edition/news/israel-s-textbooks-in-arabic-are-full-of-mistakes-study-finds-1.360617 (accessed June 20, 2012).

22   See an evaluation report of the impact of the "Five Years Program to Advance the Arab and Druze Education System" on the matriculation exams on the website of the National Authority for Measurement and Evaluation in Education–RAMA at http://cms.education.gov.il/NR/rdonlyres/356E62A2-3F98-4925-B4D4-DFF69ABA5768/8085/h1.pdf [Hebrew]. The committees and reports included the Yadlin Committee (1972), the Peled Committee (1975), the Harari Committee (1986), the Ben Peretz Committee (1999), the Goldstein Committee (1999), the Katz Committee (1999), the Lapid Committee (2003), and the Dovrat Committee (2003). For further details on

the subject of state-appointed committees, see Abu-Asbah, *Arab Education System*; and Abu-Asbah, *Arab Education in Israel*.

23 This section draws on my personal experience, formal and informal discussions with the leading figures in the FUCAE and the APC, and the founding position papers that I have authored for both bodies. These documents include Agbaria, "Towards Crystallizing a Framework"; Agbaria, "FUCAE Position"; and Agbaria, "Guidelines for the Public Campaign." See more on the establishing of the APC in Jabareen and Agbaria, "Education on Hold," 52–68.

24 Follow-Up Committee on Arab Education, http://arab-education.org [Arabic, with English translation available] (accessed June 27, 2012).

25 Al-Haj, *Education, Empowerment and Control*. See more on the history of the demand to establish an autonomous administration for the Arab educational system in Israel, including the establishment of an Arab pedagogical council in Abu-Asbah, *Arab Education System*; and Abu-Asbah, "Establishment of an Independent and Autonomous Administration."

26 Abu-Asbah, An Alternative Structure.

27 Or Kashti, "Survey: One Third of the Jews Support Regulating the Status of the Arab Education System," January 21, 2011, http://www.haaretz.co.il/hasite/spages/1210916.html [Hebrew] (accessed June 20, 2012).

28 See more on these discussions in Jabareen and Agbaria, "Education on Hold."

29 Yousef T. Jabareen and Ayman Agbaria, "Education on Hold: Israeli Government Policy and Civil Society Initiatives to Improve Arab Education in Israel," http://dirasat-aclp.org/arabic/files/Education-on-Hold_Dirasat_2010.pdf [Hebrew] (accessed June 27, 2012).

30 See more on the debate on the core curriculum in Israel in Markman and Yonah, "Nationalism, Multiculturalism and Core Curriculum." See more on the Public Education Law at the website of Hakol Hinuch, http://www.hakoled.org.il [Hebrew] (accessed June 20, 2012).

31 The double challenge to both Israeli citizenship and Palestinian nationalism is further explored in Agbaria and Mustafa, "Challenging the Boundaries of Israeli Citizenship." Israeli citizenship as maneuvering space: O. Haklai, "Palestinian NGOs in Israel: A Campaign for Civic Equality or 'Ethnic Civil Society'?" *Israel Studies* 9 (2004): 157–68; Jamal, "Strategies of Minority Struggle" and "The Counter-Hegemonic Role."

32 Deliberative democracy: Amy Gutmann and Dennis Thompson, *Democracy and Disagreement* (Cambridge, MA: Belknap Press, 1996). Extent, content, and depth of citizenship: Isin and Nielsen, *Acts of Citizenship*.

33 On the right to education: Joel Spring, *The Universal Right to Education: Justification, Definition, and Guidelines* (Mahwah, NJ: Lawrence Erlbaum, 2000). Requirements for education to be meaningful right: Katarina Tomasevski, *Manual on Rights-Based Education: Global Human Rights Requirements Made Simple* (Bangkok, Thailand: Unesco—Asia and Pacific Regional Bureau for Education, 2004).

15 The Future of Nationhood in Israel

DAVID PASSIG

The last century proved that very few[1] succeeded in forecasting the future of Israel. Even the few whose forecasts turned out to be correct employed a process that could, at best, be called hitting the target while shooting in the dark. There was no use made of a reliable methodology—one that would be open to evaluation.

Serious methodological problems are continuously evident in the forecasts we constantly hear about Israel, because they can be considered—at least from the point of view of Futures Thinking—as the ruminations of a novelist, personal inclinations, subjective values and assumptions; some based on fact, and others not. Few of the forecasts were made on the basis of any research methods, and very few of them can be said to be based on valid and reliable methods of forecasting. At the very best, they lean on statistical methods that are linear extrapolations of processes that took place in the past. Unfortunately, few know, for example, that the reliability of forecasting based on linear extrapolation is no greater, on average, than thirty percent.

Futures' research of the last seven decades has proved that in the immediate and short range (two to five years) prediction reliability of linear extrapolation can reach up to 30 percent. If we are trying to predict trends beyond two to five years, the reliability of the forecast descends to 20 percent, especially when the systems we study are more complex and unbalanced. Thus, failure to formulate reliable predictions, which are the result of rational, valid, and transparent methodologies, could be fatal to anyone seeking to understand the trends.

Therefore, herein I would like to suggest a different methodology, with which I would like to evaluate trends in the nationhood of the State of Israel in the long range—by mid twenty-first century.

This methodology could provide an alternative explanation for the forces that are driving delegitimization of Israel as a national entity. This methodology can help us identify Israel's future social trends. Its reliability in forecasting trends has been established to be more than sixty percent.

Universal Force Theory

Future research methodologies may be divided into two categories. The first category includes methodologies that are employed in the analysis of trends that already exist. The great majority of the trends that the public is familiar with belong to this category.

The second category includes methodologies that are employed in studying trends that have yet to be born or develop. The seeds of trends of this sort must of necessity already exist, but have yet to sprout. Futurists, aided by these methods, try to identify trends, which at the time the analysis is being made, are considered dead-ends by most of the experts in their field. At the time of their formulation, they are usually seen by the public and by the experts as illogical or very unreasonable. However, it seems that their predictive reliability is no less than the average range of the first category (sixty percent).

One of the Futures' research methodologies, with the help of which futurists attempt to study trends that have yet to develop, is called "Universal Force Theory." This theory hypothesizes, in simple language, that if we want to identify trends that have yet to develop, we must not try to identify changes that are taking place in the present, as they are trends that already exist. Instead, we must identify the force behind those changes, its underlying dynamics, or the hidden, subsurface assumptions that shape those changes. If we are successful in identifying the force that drives those changes, if we are successful in formulating it in clear way, then, with the help of the resulting diagnosis, we will be able to set forth trends with which most of the experts will not agree at the time they are presented.

Supposed Driving Forces of Israel

Public discourse in Israel, from the days of the first Zionist Congress of more than one hundred years ago up to today, has revolved around the issue of the source of the dispute between the People dwelling in Zion and the Arabs of the region. It sometimes seems that the Israeli community, reflecting notions in world Jewry at large, has yet to finish debating the question of the driving forces behind this blood-drenched conflict. It would appear that there has yet to be a methodical approach to the understanding of the conflict.

This does not mean that there have not been renewed efforts to deal with this issue, and it does not mean that there are not people who have reached conclusions regarding the driving forces behind this conflict. However, to the best of my knowledge, there has yet to be performed a study of this issue using a Futures' methodology. Those who concern themselves with the driving forces of the conflict, and who have done so in the past, have reached their conclusions as the result of evaluations whose sources and reliability are difficult to measure. Beyond that, people with the same sources and evaluations arrive at different, and sometimes opposing, conclusions. Many of those who have dealt with the conflict and who do so today base their conclusions on beliefs that are hard to evaluate, or that are based on wishful thinking (with which it is hard to argue), or that are hard to verify.

A number of conclusions regarding this issue can be found, both in the past and in the present, in Israeli and international public discourse. There are different variations of those conclusions. In essence, they are as follows:

- The driving force behind the conflict is *economic*: In other words, control over the land and other natural resources is what motivates the parties to clash.

- *Cultural*: Middle Eastern cultures (Druze, Bedouin, Circassian, Muslim, Christian, and others) are not ready to accept a Western entity into their midst; one that has a rhythm of life, values, and aspirations that are opposed to what is acceptable in this region.
- *National*: two new national entities are struggling to define their identities. Unfortunately, these definitions careen into one another at many junctures—economic, cultural, and religious.
- *Humanitarian*: one side's right to self-definition is so aggressive, as a result of thousands of years of suffering and repression, that it leaves no humanitarian space for the right to self-definition of the neighboring entity.
- *Ethnic*: two ethnic groups are struggling over the ownership of a particular piece of territory. The Jews claim that the land was promised to them 3200 years ago, in a transcendental promise, while the peoples of the region—without relating to the question of whether this is historically true or not—claim that they are the descendants of the Philistines and Canaanites who lived in this territory well before anyone promised anything, without asking their opinion on the matter.
- *Religious*: Islam and Judaism have been struggling for the authenticity of their religious narratives for centuries—beginning with the issue of who was bound up as a sacrifice by Abraham, and ending with the past, present, and future religious significance of the Temple Mount.

I do not intend to maintain here that one of the above is more authentic than any of the others, or that it is the most basic driving force behind the dispute. It is clear that everyone who believes in one driving force or another has a number of sources on which that belief is based. On the contrary, I want to suggest an alternative version, which will attempt to answer the question why many have failed, for more than one hundred years, to agree on a prime diagnosis of the driving force that has been keeping this blood-drenched conflict going. I would like to suggest here that it is possible to overcome this lack of agreement in order to identify another driving force that lies in the deepest stratum of this dispute, and holds us back from bringing it to a discussion sufficiently thorough to lead to a solution. Without solving the dilemma that dwells at that deep stratum, it will be difficult to solve the disagreement regarding the diagnosis, and to begin to work toward its solution.

Meta-Analysis of the Driving Forces

From the perspective of the Universal Force Theory method, it seems that the parties who believe in each one of these forces haven't noticed that they have been trying to explain the hidden assumptions of the conflict through their behavioral expressions. Practically speaking, it could be that their discourse has erred in defining those reasons as the driving forces behind the conflict. It could be that they identify only a deeper aspect of already existent trends that are expressed as a political, social, cultural, economic, religious, or ethnic dispute.

It could be that the above are not the driving forces behind the dispute, but related phenomena and byproducts of another invisible force that we still need to identify. If we are able to identify that force, we will be more easily able to reach an agreement as to how it affects and shapes the future of our region. I hope that we will then be able to derive from it a more effective policy approach that will benefit the Israelis and the other peoples in the region. The fact that there is no agreement regarding the driving forces we have described above is an indication that we are occupying ourselves only with the explanations of phenomena that have existed for a long time, and that express themselves in security, economic, and other manifestations. We are dealing solely with the examination of the situation. It appears that we are not dealing with the roots and dynamics that are the driving force behind it.

When we take a serious look at the Universal Force Theory method, we see that the deeper one looks beneath the surface, and tries to map out the center of the seismic pressure that expresses itself in some point above the surface, only then do we have a chance (and still, humbly, with only a 60 percent degree of probability) of succeeding to identify its nature, degree of power, direction, and the time at which the earth will quake.

After thorough examination of the above-mentioned list, I am forced, in all humility, to entertain the doubt that it is nothing but a list of temblors and above-surface phenomena that are almost certainly not the driving force itself.

If this hypothesis is correct, we will evidently witness other eruptions in various places, and the list of causes mentioned above will grow longer. The new wave of antisemitism can serve as an example: for instance, the delegitimization of the State of Israel's rights to self-defense, and to the management of its internal politics without external interference.

A Matrix of Interactions

One of the techniques that may assist us identifying the original driving force is to arrange the phenomena that are visible above the surface in a matrix, and to attempt to identify the interactions between the different parts of the matrix. As seismologists try to identify the center of a seismic activity, analysis of interactions, by drawing lines between phenomena charted on the matrix, can lead us to the center of what is going on. The point at which these lines cross could be the source of the above-surface phenomena.

Meta-analysis of the development directions of the interaction lines leads the vector to a point that is very deep indeed, beneath the surface of the dispute, at the height of which we find ourselves today.[2]

A Possible Driving Force

The more above-surface points we have available, and the more we are able to draw certain lines of interaction between them, creating a more reliable matrix. As strange as it may sound, we have yet to locate sufficient above-surface points to enable us to identify the driving source with a high degree of reliability. Above all, it is difficult for us to connect clear lines of interaction between points so that we can reliably say that, at this stage, we are able to identify the deepest source with a high degree of certainty. Having said that, the list of reasons or phenomena available to us today can provide sufficient indication for us to begin to identify the area from which a more primal driving force of the Arab–Israeli dispute radiates.

The goal of Table 1 is to provide the reader with a sample of the phenomena as they find expression on the surface, and are driven by

Table 1. A three-dimensional rendering of the matrix. It is possible to extend the matrix further into the third dimension, and to add breaking points and points of tension that indicate a deeper driving force.

Ethnic	Cultural	National	Economic	Humanitarian	Religious
Bring the Falashmoura to Israel	Renounce sovereignty over the Temple Mount	Jerusalem forever united	Laws of Shmita and modern economics	Disengagement or transfer of populations	Judaism as the official state religion

	Economic	Religious	Ethnic	Humanitarian	National	Cultural
Cultural	Shabbat as a regular business day	Definition of "Who is a Jew?"	Knesset debates in Arabic as well as Hebrew	The right of non-Jews to purchase homes in Jewish towns or on lands of the Jewish National Fund	National service for those who don't serve in the IDF	The performing of Wagner's music at public cultural events
National	Privatization of defense industries	The Law of Return	A state for all its citizens	The Separation Fence	National Service for minority members	Permission for minority members to sing an alternative national anthem
Humanitarian	Increased support for one-parent families	Increased old-age pensions	Citizenship for the children of foreign workers	Social security benefits for the families of those involved in terror	"Focused assassination of terrorists" is execution without trial	Mixed communities (Jews and Muslims)

	Economic	Religious	Ethnic	Humanitarian	National	Cultural
Ethnic	Equal opportunity for members of minorities	Citizenship for non-Jewish soldiers	The status and rights of olim from Ethiopia	The use of unnecessary force in demonstrations by minority groups	A differential core educational program for members of minority groups, the ultra-Orthodox, and others	Strengthening minority women's rights for those who work outside the home
Religious	Daylight saving time until after the Fall holidays	Certificates of kashrut from the State Rabbinate or from the ultra-Orthodox	Ashkenazi versus Sephardic Jews	Citizenship for the non-Jewish parents of IDF soldiers	Equal status in providing religious services for Reform rabbis	Equal rights for social benefits for homosexuals
Economic	A capitalistic or social-democratic state	A Shmita year in a modern economy	Equal rights for those who don't serve in the IDF	Increased children's allowances for large families	Equal opportunities	Equal opportunities for working women

the clash between elements of the Israeli nationhood of today (as if they were the driving forces). The table suggests that there must be a deeper driving force that propels these above-surface phenomena.

Jewish-Israeli Identity as a Driving Force

It looks as if the lines in our matrix lead to an interesting point beneath the surface. It seems that the lines lead in the direction of the Jewish identity of the Israeli people. To be more precise, in the direction of the area of the future images of Israel as a Jewish state. It regards the issue of how the Jews in general, and the Jews residing in the Land of Israel in particular, individually and collectively, see the significance of the State of Israel, past and present, and especially how they perceive the *raison d'être* of its existence as a modern nation in the future.

There is no denying that the State of Israel is an illogical national phenomenon. To the best of my knowledge, there is no example in modern history of a new national entity that penetrated a distant land, and defined its national identity on the "religious characteristics" of individuals who came from every corner of the globe—without a common spoken language, without a common national culture, without a common religious tradition (only about ten percent of world Jewry in the last century defined themselves as Orthodox, and forty percent as Conservative, Reform, Reconstructionist, Neolog, and others. The remaining fifty percent defined themselves as traditional, secular, and even atheists), with no common ethnicity (there are, thank God, black, white, and yellow Jews, as well as from every other color of humanity). In brief, even if they did not have a clear, common religious identity, they gathered and committed to the establishment of a new national state; something that they had heretofore never had.

The only force that united this group of people was its bitter fate and common religious narrative, which was and is still a matter of great controversy. Over the years, this controversy gave birth to another religion, and to serious side effects—such as messianic movements, which changed their faith, or various movements that betrayed individuals to the regime in power.

Three Strata

It appears that there are three strata to this driving force. Of late, the Jews have carried out a satisfactory clarification of only one of them. Until the Jewish people in the Diaspora, and the Jewish people resident in the Land of Israel will clarify for themselves all three strata of their Jewish national identity, it will be exceedingly difficult to make an authentic beginning of a solution to the conflict between them and their surroundings. The three strata, which make up the driving force of the conflict, are three paradigms of the *raison d'être* for an Israeli nationhood: *a land of refuge*, *a land of choice*, and *a land of mission*.

A Land of Refuge

The first stratum is the definition of a covenant of fate, which unites the Jews who reside in Israel. At the outset of the twentieth century, most of the Jews in the world maintained that there was nothing sufficiently real to their covenant of fate to unite the various Jews of all corners of the world, so that a historic adventure, such as the establishment of a national state, would succeed. Despite many efforts during the first half of the twentieth century, a tiny minority of world's Jews responded to the call to "make Aliya to Palestine." Only the cataclysmic Holocaust convinced some of the remnants of the Jewish people, and the nations of the world, to support the establishment of a state for the Jews (the majority of the Jews moved to other places on the globe). The mission of the state, or so they imagined, would be to gather those spared from the conflagration, and other persecuted communities, in order to build something like a wildlife reserve in which an endangered species of persecuted humans might be preserved. Support of this idea was meant, of course, to salve the conscience of the enlightened nations, whose moral bankruptcy had been exposed for all to see.

There are still those who refer to the national entity that arose based on this stratum "the land of our affliction."[3] Very few believed that the covenant of fate would be able to attract enough people to establish a new national state for part of the Jewish people.

Defining this covenant of fate has taken about sixty years since the establishment of the state of Israel. By the end of the first decade of the twenty-first century, the State of Israel reached that important point. For the first time in the history of the Jewish people, since the biblical conquest of the land, the world's largest Jewish community was resident in Zion. According to all the estimates, the largest Jewish community in the world since World War II—the Jewish community in the United States—declined in size to less than 5.2 million people, while the Jewish community in Israel rose to 5.8 million. If we add to that number approximately 290,000 immigrants whose Jewish identity is in doubt, then Israel in 2011 has more than 6 million Jews. The size of the world's Jewish population is estimated at the beginning of the second decade of the twenty-first century at around 13 million people. By way of comparison, at the beginning of the eighteenth century, there were only about 3 million Jews worldwide.[4] Before World War II, the Jews numbered approximately 18 million. After the war, there remained only 12 million. It is sad to say, but were it not for the Holocaust, European Jewry would number about 30 million people at the beginning of the twenty-first century, and perhaps more. Most important of all is that, without the State of Israel, it is possible that there would be only from 7 million to 9 million Jews in the world.

This stratum has been highlighted and made clear enough so that 45 percent of the Jews of the world adhere to it. We may sum it up in the phrase "a land of refuge." Most of those forty-five percent came to the young State of Israel because they had no place on earth where they could build a better life for themselves. Most of those who had alternatives, and who took the chance, did not choose to join the small gathering of Jews in Zion. At the beginning of the twenty-first century, not many Jews outside Israel remain, for whom this stratum is their driving force. If, however, there should occur a disaster in some part of the globe, this disaster could become the fount of more human resources motivated by their status as refugees. An eventuality of this sort cannot be ruled out, as it is possible that we are not making a proper reading of the earthquakes on the surface of events.

A Land of Choice

The second stratum of Israeli national identity is only beginning to become clear at the outset of the twenty-first century. There are two reference points, which reflect this stratum, that are expected to be realized in the near and far future. The first is expected in 2015, or 2020 at the latest. In those years, we expect that more than fifty-one percent of the Jews of the world will live in Israel (taking into account the fertility and immigration rates that have characterized the State of Israel in the first fifty years of its existence, minus the attitude of the Jews who remained in countries defined as "states of refuge"). The second reference point is expected between 2030 and 2035, or 2040 at the latest. In the fourth decade of the twenty-first century, we estimate that seventy percent of the Jewish population of the world will live in the land of Israel.

There is a seventy percent likelihood that those trends will take place, for two main reasons. First, only two Jewish communities are on an upward growth trend at the start of the twenty-first century. All the other Jewish communities in the world are in the process of numerical decline. The Jewish community resident in Israel at the beginning of the twenty-first century is the Jewish community with the greatest fertility rate and natural growth in the world. The other Jewish community with an upward population trend is that resident in Germany, as a result of immigration from the formerly Soviet countries and Israel. The average fertility rate of communities in the Diaspora is around 1.2 to 1.4 children per woman, while the fertility rate in the Jewish community of Israel has been stable, at 2.8 children per couple, for some time, with a constant tendency to increase in times of war. Thus, since the outbreak of suicide bombing in the years 2000–2004, the average number of births increased each year. In 2000 it was 2.5 and by 2010 it was 2.9.

The second reason is the issue of assimilation in the Diaspora. The average rate of intermarriage in the Diaspora has run at about 55 percent in the last decade, and the trend seems to be growing at a constant rate.

The significance of these two reference points is that, on one hand, the number of Jews in the Diaspora is decreasing steadily. On the other hand, the number of Jews resident in Israel is steadily increasing (because of natural growth, and as a result of *aliyah*—although the latter will dwindle in proportion to the rate to which we were accustomed in the first fifty years since the establishment of the State of Israel).

In a situation in which the force of refuge works itself out, it remains to be seen if the stratum underneath it will begin to bring about above-the-surface changes. This stratum, so it seems, will be defined in terms such as "*the land of choice.*" Since most of the residents in Israel define their presence in Israel as being the result of having no alternative, it is hard for all of us to see how that mindset could change.

One may therefore assume that the driving force of Jewish identity will make itself felt politically, economically, socially, and culturally during the next thirty years. The behavioral terms of this stratum of driving force will express themselves in interesting and surprising ways in the Israeli public forum. It appears that one of those expressions might be, for example, the nullification of the Law of Return within the next twenty years. Public discourse will be occupied with the fact that a law that permits any Jew arriving on Israeli soil to be accepted as a refugee will no longer be necessary. Moreover, it will become germane to examine the individual applicant's seriousness of choice, and his or her ability to contribute to the Jewish community in Israel.

A more sensitive calibration of this approach will enable the analyst to distinguish between the Jew and the non-Jew's seriousness of choice and ability to contribute to the Jewish community. A non-Jew may also join those who are dwelling in Zion, although with a status that the Israeli legislator will have to formulate and define very carefully indeed.

A Land of Mission

The third level that evidently will drive the changes and shape the surface phenomena of the future is the deepest driving force of the conflict between the nationality of Israel and the nationality of its neighbors. We can label this stratum "covenantal mission."

In order for a people to exist, it needs a covenantal mission under which all its energy and *raison d'être* can be rallied. A people without a covenantal mission leaves no mark on history. Eventually that people slips away into the creases of time. Peoples who shaped the fate of humanity over time had clear missions. They survived the trials of history for hundreds and thousands of years. A mission needs a clear, succinct formulation for it to be an authentic, powerful driving force. It should be able to be expressed in a very short phrase—two or three words. Two examples support this statement.

The American people have a short, clear covenantal mission. That is part of what evidently turned the United States into the most active world power of our generation. That mission is sealed in two words: "individual freedom." The Constitution and the laws of the United States derive from that covenant. It is the driving force of the institutions they have established, the force behind their foreign policy, and is that which supports the wars they wage.

Most people do not understand how a president could stand up before the world and declare that he would see to the liberation of the Iraqi or the Egyptian citizen from the yoke of tyranny. Especially puzzling is that he was prepared to spend a huge amount of the American taxpayers' money to build free institutions for the failed countries, even if the price of all this included the lives of hundreds of American soldiers. There are those, for example, who think that the driving force of the war on Iraq is oil. That is plainly not the case. It is true that there are interests of that kind, but they are not the driving force.

The second example is the covenantal mission of the European Community. In its emergence, this community understood that it needed a covenantal mission. It needed something that would unite its different parts, and contain the strength that drives its institutions in a way that would place its stamp on the future of humankind. The European Community understood that in order to write a constitution, to conduct a foreign policy, to sign trade agreements, and to wage wars, it had to formulate a covenantal mission that could be expressed in two words, as short and simple as is possible. In fact, late in 2004, they succeeded in formulating a phrase that will evidently be the central axis of the future of the European Community. The Europeans have proposed the following as their covenantal mission: "unity in diversity." There will be those who claim that such a covenant is too ambitious for a continent that, over the last two thousand years, has known so many clashes over precisely the issue of difference. Nevertheless, we shall see.

After the Israeli people clarifies sufficiently for itself all the strata of its covenantal mission—"land of refuge" and "land of choice"—it will reach the crucial point in shaping the deepest stratum of its driving force. It will need, if it wants to survive, to formulate its covenantal mission.

The State of Israel was established to base its existence on a partial covenant of fate. Systems Theory teaches us that there is no reasonable likelihood that this will be sufficient for continuing as a people in a modern state. Beyond that, it teaches us that a covenant of fate is like time-limited glue. It can hold many individuals together as a people for a while—one or two generations at best. Glue of this sort dries up and ceases to hold, eventually. When its power to hold ceases to exist, what remain are scattered shards. Based on those fragments, the people must formulate a covenant of mission, as the new European Community has done.

We have also learned that a minority of a people cannot take on the weighty task of formulating a covenant of mission. A majority of a people must be present in the country at the time of the covenant's formulation in order for it to be drafted and accepted. It is likely that most of the Jewish people, according to the rhythm of present population trends, will be resident in Israel within the next forty years. Only then, in my estimation, will the Jewish people be able to undertake the task of formulating the Covenantal Mission for the State of Israel, most of whose citizens will be Jews. Until that time, we will be witness to the further weakening of the covenant of fate.

No challenge such as this one has been presented to the Jews in their long history, so we cannot provide the next generation with an allegory from the past to which they can refer in their deliberations. The challenge is of the order of magnitude characterized by the rebirth of a people. The people bases itself on its past, but breaks new paths to the future. It draws sustenance from the collective memories and traditions of the past, but ignores them in order to undergo its renaissance. The challenge of preparing a generation for its time in history is a weightily responsible assignment. We must not take this challenge lightly. Many of us today do not understand our task. There are those who ask only to preserve the past, and others who ask only to ignore it. Today's educators have to define their task in light of the challenge that will be placed before our children in the future.

THE COVENANTAL MISSION FOR ISRAEL AS A NATION-STATE OF THE JEWISH PEOPLE

Today, probably no one in Israel or in the Diaspora could imagine a relevant covenantal mission for Israel as a nation-state of the Jewish people, and how it will finally be formulated in another fifty years. It is immensely difficult to imagine what could be a covenantal mission of a Jewish, Middle Eastern, democratic, and modern state, with a twenty-five percent non-Jewish minority. There never has been an entity such as this one in 3200 years of Jewish history. There are many who even believe that an entity of this sort cannot exist and function.

The Jews' consciousness, as it developed over thousands of years in the Diaspora, is communal at most, but decidedly not national. Communal considerations alone were etched into the Jewish way of thinking. The Jewish people resident in Israel will need an approach to thinking different from that which exists today, in order to formulate a covenantal mission valid and authentic enough to carry the nation far into the third millennium. The organizational, social, religious, and cultural considerations must become national ones.

The Jewish people lost this mindset in the course of a hundred generations of living in the Diaspora; it is entirely possible that such a mindset never existed. It is conceivable that the Jewish people had a monarchical mind-set in the days of the kings, or a tribal one. There was, however, no national mind-set, because the Jewish people never had an organizational framework in the form of a national, democratic state. I believe that only a majority of the Jewish people concentrated in the land of Israel will have the power to invent the national mind-set with which the Jews will be able to begin to formulate their covenantal mission.

This way of thinking could radiate new insights to the whole people in Israel and to those remaining in the Diaspora. It is my hope that these insights will assist the coming generation to formulate an accepted mission-related task for a modern, democratic Jewish state in the Middle East that includes a large minority population.

Unfortunately, I find it difficult at this particular point in time to imagine a covenantal mission that draws its rationale from other contexts. Like the rest of this generation, we have difficulty in escaping the mind-set and contexts imprinted on us over thousands of years.

HINTS OF A NATIONAL, CIVIL COVENANTAL MISSION

If one makes the effort, it is possible to identify the distant edges of a national, civil covenantal mission. It is important to stress that we might err here. On one side, the lower edge can be a mission similar to that of the Maccabi Tel Aviv sports club, and the spirit it symbolizes when it wins championships. On the other side, on the upper edge, there could be a mission like that of "Light unto the nations," with all that would entail—social, economic, scientific, ethical, religious, and legal (in the sense of religious law) aspects.

For curiosity's sake, and not because I think that this will be what develops, I will explore one possible mission that provides us with a hint of a new thought context. The next mission could be formulated as follows: "a synergy of cultures."

The mission of Israel could be the building of a junction of cultural nodes that would make cultural, cognitive, and political integration possible for cultures of the West and of the East. A behavioral expression of a mission of this sort could occur on different scientific and social levels; for example, developing new scientific theories based on Systems Theory, which would be compatible with the modern, technological, global, complex, and multifaceted world.

By dint of painstaking work over thousands of years, the Jews developed a systemic tradition of complex integration between the concepts of the individual and society. Interesting insights were developed regarding holistic systems and the tasks of their component parts. The people also took on the task of establishing organizational, economic, community, and legal systems, which were managed with considerable efficiency and which proved their worth over a period of millennia.

It is possible that young Israel's subcultures—those that came from Western and Eastern communities—are the epistemological foundations of a mission of this sort. If the Jews in Israel succeed in taking the bull by the horns, and jumping onto his back, they will be able to gallop forward in creative directions, to new levels of achievement, with the cultural mission of a nation in renaissance. A mission of this sort could take an important place among those of modern, advancing nations, and could provide us with a respite from our dispute with them.

My intention is not in the direction of a religious mission for the Jewish people. I am talking about a national mission. The Jewish religion had, and remains with, a clear religious mission. It can be summed up in two words: "worshiping God." At the same time, Judaism as a religion, so far as I am familiar with it, needs to add another facet to its identity: a national covenantal mission for a modern state.

THE DRIVING FORCE BEHIND THE ARAB–ISRAELI DISPUTE

How is everything detailed above connected with the bloody conflict between the State of Israel and the peoples of the Middle East? Beyond that, how is this dispute tied to the phenomena such as the new antisemitism, and to the feeling that "the whole world is against us" that accompanies it?

It appears that the driving force behind the dispute between Israel and the peoples of the region is possibly nothing more than an *identity crisis*. It is a drama that has been going on for about 3,700 years—from the time of Abraham—and has reached its climax with the establishment of the Jewish state in 1948. In order for the conflict between Israel and the other peoples of the region to be settled, a new aspect of Jewish identity must emerge—a distinct and viable national mission. This national mission must draw from past traditions, present insights, and future ideas.

The Jewish nation of the Jewish people will have its right to exist recognized by the community of nations only when it has clarified its future mission for itself. Only when the Jews resident in Israel have a clear, razor-sharp mission will the peoples of the region be ready to genuinely start the process of accepting the Jews as one of them. It will be possible to begin to negotiate its right to exist as a nation in the region, not merely as a religion, only when most of the Israelis have a clear idea of what is unique to them as a nation. This is not to say that it will be easy, only that it will be clear to all just what the nation of Israel is, and what its historic mission for the future will be. The surrounding nations as well as many other world nations will continue to argue with Israel and challenge its legitimacy to exist, but the arguments will be on an equal footing.

TRENDS

In the meantime, underneath the surface, the Earth will continue to rumble, because the Jews in Israel have yet to begin the process of clarifying the matter of their mission-related identity as a modern and democratic nation. Many forces will continue to pull this identity in different, conflicting directions. There will be those who will want to see the mission of the State of Israel as a state for all its citizens, as every other modern state defines itself. There will be those who will want to see its mission as a religious entity, as per the dream of thousands of years. There will be those who will wish to see Israel's mission as that of a megalopolis, and as a technology hub, as per the dream of many business leaders, and according to the spirit of globalization that pervades the very air they breathe. There will be yet others whose desire will be to pull the mission in directions that will only emerge in the years to come.

It is difficult to tell, from the point in time that these words are being written, what will finally take shape. One thing, however, is clear to this writer: the result must be unique to the Jews, their past, and to the degree to which they understand the future of the human race. Any other compromise will not last, and will not provide a fitting response to the pressures of the peoples of the region, or to those of the peoples of the world.

Those pressures will mainly find expression in a demand for the geographical definition of the Jewish-Israeli people. So long as these people are not clear regarding the matter of their identity and mission, they will not be able to stand up to the pressures for geographical definition, and will always have to provide a logical response not available to them, on the subject of their needs, and of their rights to this, or some other territory.

So long as those pressures exist, there will be no peace in the land. This will not be because the Jews resident in Israel do not want peace, or because they have not made efforts to achieve peace, but because the Jews will not have the right to live in peace because they have not yet institutionalized their rights by making a clear definition of their mission. There is a bumpy road ahead. As sad as it is to say the following, civil war remains, as it happened in many other nations that went through similar processes, one of the eventualities that could slow the process considerably, and send the nation into years of panic, terrible loss of life and of national direction.

Despite this, in the final analysis, the Jews have arrived in the twenty-first century at a historical landmark dreamed of by generations and generations of the downtrodden and rejected. They have arrived at this point with immeasurable resources of experience and history, and of collective wisdom acquired with much trial and labor. The Jews arrive here with the wet-behind-the-ears *chutzpah* of a young, dynamic, and optimistic young man, together with the thick skin of an old man, rich in experience and in troubles overcome.

The Jews have never been better prepared for the task set before them. After 3,200 years since Joshua's conquest of ups and downs, of challenges and obstacles, they have reached a situation better than they have ever known. With the exception of short periods in their history, the Jews have never been so well organized. They have never had political institutions—local and international—in such a vital and robust condition. Never before have the majority of the Jews in the world possessed so many rights and freedoms in their places of residence, in the Diaspora or in Israel. It has been thousands of years since the Jews were able to bear arms and defend themselves. It is the first time in thousands of years that the Jews have an international strategic status; a status that has been growing and becoming stronger with the years. It is true that there are many threats to their existence, of the most frightening sort, but it is also true that Israel's ally is the most important superpower of the age.[5]

By any criteria, the Jewish people dwelling in Zion, and the Jewish people residing in the Diaspora are currently experiencing the most important golden age in the history of the Jews. The spiritual and scientific creation, the physical building, and the social, geopolitical, and geo-economic involvement are of the highest quality the Jews have known in hundreds of years.

To the best of my understanding, there has yet to be a generation so well prepared to take on the task of formulating the Jews' covenantal mission as is this generation. What is lacking is the mandate that requires the consensus of the majority of the Jews. The broad consensual support, which only a majority of the Jews can provide, will grant ethical sanction to the covenantal mission. Such sanction is necessary if the mission is to be of binding significance for the generations to come. It is necessary in order to provide the spiritual power needed to redefine Judaism and the components of its identity in a different national platform, as well as Judaism's cognitive ability, and the imagination needed to stand up to the task. It is an honorable task dreamed of from the Jews' days as the nomadic followers of Abraham in Haran, of ancient Babylon.

It looks as if all the signs point to a situation in which the Jews are ready for the last stage before their final renaissance. Afterwards, their lives will begin to become normal; with reasonable difficulties, such as passions, disappointments, struggles, and many successes, just like all the nations of the world.

EPILOGUE

It is true that futurists attempt to study various ways in which different trends can lead, in order to better conceptualize the future. However, in all sincerity, futurists do not believe that there actually exists a "place" known as "the future." All theories—beginning with Einstein's Theory of Relativity, and continuing to the most recently formulated ideas, such as the physicist Gell Mann's theory of Information Gathering and Utilizing Systems (IGUS), and the work of robotics theoretician James Harrie—maintain that the feeling of "time passing" is only a cognitive fiction. Past, present, and future are nothing but an individual's and a group's processing of information. The way in which they process a bit of information is what dictates their relationship to their environment, which acts or reacts to the frameworks they have created.

From this point of view, the superficialities mentioned in this chapter are merely an attempt to construct a framework with the help of which we could build an environment that would meet the nationhood needs of the Jewish people in Israel. In other words, we are merely trying to point in the direction of the solution to our dispute with ourselves and with other frameworks of the peoples around us, in the Middle East and beyond.

NOTES

1   At the time of the Biluim—the 1880s—there were 34,000 Jews and 330,000 Arabs in the land of Israel. The Jews made up ten percent of the population. The great historian Dubnow was negatively impressed by the flow of immigrants of the first *aliyah*, and predicted that by the year 2000 there would be only 500,000 Jews in the land. In not many years' time it looked as if he had been right. At the end of World War I, the population included 55,000 Jews and 500,000 Arabs. The 1:10 ratio was maintained. On the day Independence was declared, May 15, 1948, there were 600,000 Jews and 980,000 Arabs; approximately forty percent were Jews living west of the Jordan River. The chief statistician at the time, Roberto Bacchi, recommended postponing the declaration of the state, out of fear that the demographic problem would end the state's existence. To our great good fortune, Ben-Gurion ignored him. About twenty years later, Levi Eshkol chose to ignore the later-to-be-debunked warning after the Six-Day War that by 1987 there would be an Arab majority west of the Jordan.

2   This analysis, we must confess, is only one of several possibilities. The nature of matters of this kind of analysis is that they are affected by a great degree of subjectivity, the source of which it is difficult to get. As a result, it affects the analyst's point of view. Below, I will try to relate to the source of my subjectivity.

3   A. B. Yehoshua generally refers thus to the connection of the Jews to his country.

4   Jewish community in Israel: press announcement by the Israeli Central Bureau of Statistics, December 30, 2010. Eighteenth-century figures.
T. Bisk and M. Dror, *Futurizing the Jews: Alternative Futures for Meaningful Jewish Existence in the 21st Century* (Westport, CT: Praeger Publishers, 2003).

5   There are those who will maintain, on one hand, that this promises nothing for Israel in the future, and on the other, that this alliance works against Israel's best interests. In any case, the alliance is widely considered the most important strategic asset that the State of Israel has had to date.

Index

Page numbers with "*n*" indicate notes.

www.ingramcontent.com/pod-product-compliance
Lightning Source LLC
Chambersburg PA
CBHW050330270326
41926CB00016B/3395

9 781618 113924